Decision Support Models and Expert Systems

David L. Olson

Texas A & M University

James F. Courtney, Jr.

Texas A & M University

Macmillan Publishing Company
New York

Maxwell Macmillan Canada
Toronto

Maxwell Macmillan International
New York   Oxford   Singapore   Sydney

To our children,
whose education made this project necessary.

Editor: Vernon R. Anthony
Production Editor: Constantina Geldis
Cover Designer: Robert Vega
Production Buyer: Patricia A. Tonneman

This book was set in Times Roman and was printed and bound by Book Press. The cover was printed by Phoenix Color Corp.

Macmillan Publishing Company
866 Third Avenue
New York, New York 10022

Macmillan Publishing Company is part of the
Maxwell Communication Group of Companies.

Maxwell Macmillan Canada, Inc.
1200 Eglington Avenue East, Suite 200
Don Mills, Ontario M3C 3N1

Library of Congress Cataloging-in-Publication Data

Olson, David Louis.
    Decision support models and expert systems / David L. Olson, James
  F. Courtney, Jr.
      p. cm.
    Includes index.
    ISBN 0-02-389340-0
    1. Decision support systems. 2. Expert systems (Computer science)
I. Courtney, James F. (James Forrest), 1944–   . II. Title.
T57.95.O47 1992
658.4'03–dc20   91-21482
                                     CIP

Printing: 1 2 3 4 5 6 7 8 9   Year: 2 3 4 5

Preface

This book focuses on the application of computer systems to aid business decision making. Included are a variety of systems that have been developed over the past three decades, spanning a wide range of decision types. Computer systems have been the most exciting development in business in recent times, revolutionizing the way business is conducted. Computers provide the means to give managers far more information than could have been imagined a few decades ago. Systems are available that go beyond providing information, adding the potential to conduct more thorough analyses of business problems. Other systems extend support to emulating experts. The concept of computers running manufacturing operations has been a reality for a number of years. The potential to apply expert systems to develop knowledge about business operations is a developing application.

Computer systems have limits. They are not going to replace all human functions of management. But the competitive advantage due to computerization is going to make it mandatory to understand the things computers can do for business. It is an uncomfortable subject, because the subject matter is constantly changing. People think of new and better things to do with computers each day. New and exciting software products are developed each year. This environment is further complicated because new hardware systems are developed (and become popular) every few years.

Computer support to business decision making is presented. This is done by first focusing on an overview of computer support to business decision making (Chapter 1). Chapters 2 and 3 discuss decision making in general, with Chapter 2 discussing individual decision making and Chapter 3 discussing organizational factors.

Five chapters are devoted to decision support systems. Chapter 4 presents an overview of the DSS concept. The value of data and means to collect it are discussed in Chapter 5. The focus of Chapter 6 is on how to organize data and access it electronically. Chapter 7 discusses how to analyze data and draw conclusions. Two of the most valuable general computer tools are discussed in Chapters 6 (databases) and 7 (spreadsheets). Chapter 8 presents concrete examples of decision support systems. Models are not necessary for a DSS, but they can provide powerful tools to aid decision maker learning. Three supplemental chapters at the end of the text provide exposure to the analytic tools available for DSSs. Supplemental Chapter 1 discusses forecasting models, Supplemental Chapter 2 explains linear programming, and Supplemental Chapter 3 presents simulation. Note that the rest of the book can be used without coverage of these three modeling chapters.

A major change in the way business is conducted is the trend toward more participative decision making. Computers have provided a means to communicate much more rapidly, along with a variety of tools that can make groups better understand the complexities of decisions, as well as the positions of other people. Current group decision support systems are reviewed in Chapter 9, along with actual applications and problem areas that have yet to be resolved. We feel that this chapter provides a view of a highly important topic, given that we expect a much higher degree of group decision making in future business operations.

Executive information systems are a relatively new class of computer support focusing upon giving decision makers important information in real time, tapping the potential of computer capabilities much more than has been traditional in the past. Chapter 10 discusses some of the benefits and capabilities currently available. It concludes with the idea that although such systems currently are very expensive (and therefore tend to be found at top levels of the organization), the ideas and developments in pursuing the goal of providing decision-making information as quickly as possible will soon find its way throughout the organization.

Probably no topic involving computer systems is more popular than that of expert systems. Chapter 11 presents a general discussion of expert systems, followed by a chapter focusing on the use of an expert systems shell, with example applications. The topic of knowledge acquisition is dealt with more thoroughly in Chapter 13, and knowledge representation is discussed in Chapter 14.

Finally, Chapter 15 reviews two areas where computer systems have been applied in a manner which has changed the way business is conducted. The most spectacular application involves program trading in the securities market. We do not know the total impact of program trading on business. It does represent in a highly visible manner the potential for computers to influence business. The other application discusses decision support available to support the real estate industry. Business related developments in neural networks, a radically different application of artificial intelligence, are discussed. Other fundamental changes possible in the near future are discussed, focusing on system impact on organizational communication and the potential for automatic development of business knowledge.

Examples and Assignments

Each chapter presenting a technique includes some example material. There are also optional project assignments in most chapters. The intent of the book is to provide a broad overview of what is available and to see the value of such approaches in decision support systems. Using the project approach, there is more material than one semester of classes can cover. The content can be used flexibly, and those topics not covered in class could be used as independent project alternatives.

Our philosophy is that knowledge is gained through observation. We have sought to emphasize applications, with the text intended to provide a framework presenting the most important concepts involved in a topic. Applications are presented in short form, focusing on the content of the chapter, seeking to demonstrate important concepts related to computer support to business decision making.

The book is organized with the intention of providing a framework for a variety of pedagogical approaches. A large number of references are provided for courses focusing upon readings. The book includes a large dose of applications from the literature, along with our interpretation of these articles in light of recent material. Student reading of the articles themselves is encouraged, providing them deeper understanding of the applications, as well as other factors discussed in greater detail by the original authors. Furthermore, reports of more current applications could be reviewed, and thought given to the implications of what is found in these new applications.

Another approach is to involve students in hands-on activities. Knowledge is reinforced by doing. Project suggestions are available in many of the chapters, but we would emphasize that a number of other options are available. Material for exploration of human decision making is given at the end of the second chapter. AHP application is easily accomplished given the material in Chapter 2. Data collection is an activity that can be pursued through a variety of assignments. Spreadsheets are widely available, with many productive student activities. Supplemental Chapters 1 through 3 involve management science material, with many assignment possibilities available from many sources. (Management science material could be omitted.) Expert system applications would probably involve the need for some shell. Chapter 12 presents some ideas.

Computer Support Required

Our experience is that use of computer systems is a highly effective means of reinforcing concept understanding. There are many useful computer packages available that can provide needed support. Decision support systems can consist of a wide variety of configurations. This is especially true for model support. Generally available software could support specific chapters. Regression analysis is supported by many packages, both mainframe and microcomputer. There are many spreadsheet packages available. IFPS is a little different from most, as is discussed in the chapter. AHP is supported by Expert Choice, as well as any FORTRAN code that solves for eigenvectors. Linear programming packages are widely available. LINDO has been found useful by the authors, although many new microcomputer packages look even better. There are many shells available to support expert system development. VP-EXPERT will be used to demonstrate examples.

We have included short "quick and dirty" guides intended to get students started using some specific packages. Spreadsheets are the basis for many effective decision support systems. At the end of Chapter 7, a guide for IFPS use is included. Statistical analysis is common in DSS, even when other models such as linear programming or simulation are used. At the end of Supplemental Chapter 1, guides for SAS, Minitab, and IDA are provided. LINDO is a widely used linear programming package. At the end of Supplemental Chapter 2, a guide for LINDO's use is included. Simulation analysis is less structured. Our experience is that BASIC is the easiest approach, with FORTRAN suitable for larger simulations requiring more efficient computer times. The last computer support considered is for expert systems. There are many useful shells currently on the market for rule-based systems. One of these, VP-EXPERT, is the focus of Chapter 12. A one-page guide for using VP-EXPERT and a one-page schematic of VP-EXPERT commands are provided at the end of that chapter. In addition, a copy of the limited student edition of VP-EXPERT is available from the publisher.

Discussion of computer systems inevitably involves strange phrases, and discussion of modeling techniques involves additional jargon. Therefore, a glossary of terms is provided at the end of the book.

We wish to express our appreciation for the comments made by the following reviewers: Greg Taylor, Wake Forest University; Richard O. Mason; David Russell, Western New England College; Mohammed Dadashzadeh, The Wichita State University; J.P. Shim, Mississippi State University; G. Lawrence Sanders, State University of New York; Warren Briggs, Suffolk University; David Van Over, University of Georgia; and David Yen, Miami University.

Contents

CHAPTER 1

Introduction

This book is designed to support a course in computer systems for decision support. A variety of systems are discussed, including decision support systems, group decision support systems, executive information systems, and expert systems. The focus of the book is the various roles these systems could play in aiding decision making.

The book also discusses the overall **decision process** and how **management information system** elements contribute toward that process. The intent is that the scientific method be used in applying the quantitative and computer models. The philosophy is that quantitative models, through DSS and expert systems, can *support* judgment and should not replace it. Hopefully, after a course using this book, students can recognize problem types, or even better, see opportunities to apply techniques in innovative ways.

The role of data is also important in aiding decision making. How to access raw data, including the many commercial sources of business data currently available, is addressed. How to organize data and access it electronically and how to analyze data to draw conclusions through analytic models are also discussed.

Computer systems can support business decision making in a variety of ways. The use of computers to support business has become the major growth area in the U.S. economy. Compared to the rest of the world, the United States has the greatest relative advantage in its technological expertise. Many useful applications for computers have been developed, and more complex and ambitious applications continue to be developed. Other fields also contribute to business analysis. Management science provides a framework for analysis of many business problems, as well as a variety of analytic techniques. Statistical analysis provides a means of measuring business performance, tools to aid in identification of problems and/or opportunities, and a means of projecting past performance to predict future operations. Regardless of the functional area of business, improved decision making should result from the collection of more accurate and complete data, stored efficiently for effective retrieval, applied in a scientific manner.

The intent of this chapter is to provide an overall framework for the use of computers to aid decision making. The decision-making environment and the role of a variety of computer systems in the decision-making process are addressed.

DECISION MAKING

Decision making is generally viewed as the most attractive part of management. Life, being fickle, does not always reward rational decision making. Businesses operate in a cyclical economy that is difficult to predict. Because business is competitive, eccentric decisions often work when they catch the competition off guard. However, the laws of probability and statistics and the theory of economics tell us that, in the long run, rational decision making will win out.

Because of the size of many U.S. organizations, systems for making decisions have been developed which seem to work (at least sometimes). Organizational structure includes a variety of levels of decision making, including operational, managerial, and strategic levels.

Operational Level

The hierarchy necessary to coordinate large numbers of employees leads to different approaches to decision making (Figure 1.1). At the lower levels of an organization, not much decision making is left. However, the owner cannot be everywhere. One way an owner can maintain tight control is through the use of standard operating procedures. Books of rules have been published describing actions to take in standard situations. For standard operating procedures to work, it is necessary for every possible situation to be anticipated. When this is possible, the environment is called highly structured. In reality, the person who

Figure 1.1 ▬▬▬▬▬▬▬▬▬▬▬▬▬▬▬▬▬▬▬▬▬▬

Operational	Activity Scheduling
	Inventory Control
Managerial	Personnel Actions
	Advertising Specifics
Strategic	New Market Entry
	Expansion or Contraction
	of production
	of sales

▬▬▬▬▬▬▬▬▬▬▬▬▬▬▬▬▬▬▬▬▬▬

follows such standard operating procedures is not making a decision at all, other than to obey or disobey. Such highly structured (well-defined) environments are precisely what a computer needs to operate. Because computers always obey, they can sometimes be used for operational-level decision making. However, computers are totally inflexible in responding to unexpected situations.

Expert systems are very often developed for complex business problems of a repetitive nature. Some unstructured problems where humans have developed effective rules of thumb can be dealt with through expert systems. Other less structured decisions involving high degrees of complexity can also be aided by expert systems.

Managerial Level

The position of manager exists because the owner cannot be everywhere. Managers are hired (usually) for their judgment. Judgment allows humans to make decisions even though they do not have all of the information they might want. Their ability to make decisions allows them to cope with unexpected problems or opportunities, enabling the organization to continue to operate. Generally, however, managers are given extensive guidelines (constraints) over the limits to their decisions. Although there is some structure in this environment (the guidelines), there is not enough structure to replace managers with computers. The intent of decision support systems is not to replace human judgment, but rather to provide a means to support it through more thorough analyses and access to more information in a timely manner.

Strategic Level

Somebody (or some group) within an organization has to make decisions about overall organizational policy (the guidelines). Strategic decisions and policies help define the constraints for lower-level activities. There are far fewer constraints upon strategic decisions. Strategic decisions generally involve a far longer time frame as well. These conditions yield an almost unstructured decision-making environment. However, the humans who do cope with such problems (or opportunities) can be expected to improve their decision making through the learning involved in rational analyses. Exploratory analytical models were highly limited in the past, because of the time and effort that were required. Computers can crunch such analyses in short order, however. Now that inexpensive, dedicated computers are available, the opportunity exists to explore more data and run more models.

DECISION MAKING IN BUSINESS

Decision making is a major element in operating a business. Most decisions are made under the pressure of time, without the opportunity to go into a research mode to analyze the problem thoroughly. Therefore, decisions are often made in an ad hoc manner, relying upon quick wits. Frankly, luck helps a great deal. But quick wits in business are developed through experience. Luck seems to be correlated with experience and judgment. Rational observation of a business, implicitly developing theories of cause and effect, and learning by mistakes, collectively, develop judgment.

Business has always involved the interactions of many people. People make assumptions, which are a human way of coping with the complexity of life. But many times assumptions are based on false speculation, which results in incorrect explanations and conclusions. Cautious decision makers tend to check assumptions. Computer systems (management information systems, especially databases) provide a much more powerful means of checking facts than that which existed decades ago. Making assumptions is a necessary part of theory building, as well as everyday life. Using past data, as well as observations of current operations, should result in assumptions closer to reality.

Some decision makers enjoy the helter-skelter environment that exists in many business settings. Some decision styles have been labeled "management by crisis." Critics of this style have been known to say that this type of decision maker would create a crisis if one did not exist. It would seem that thorough preparation would be a more suitable approach. Crises seem to occur with much less frequency if decision makers are well prepared. A scientific body of knowledge can be built for a business. But building such a body of knowledge is not as easy as it is for physics. It is not as easy because the business environment deals with people and social systems that are not as well behaved as physical systems. Furthermore, decisions usually must be made before theories are completely developed. But the same general principles can be applied. The primary requirement is the ability to learn, to refine a theory of what causes what, and to observe. Principles of scientific experimental procedure can also be applied. Mathematical models provide a means of doing this. A variety of computer system types expand the ability of decision makers to develop more effective decision-making capability.

COMPUTER SUPPORT TO BUSINESS

The development of computer support to business has undergone a rapid rate of growth (Figure 1.2). The original computers were very large, slow by today's standards, and much less capable of flexible application than those currently available. In addition, computers were enormously expensive. It is quite logical that the first applications of computers in business were to precisely defined problems with significant economic benefit to firms.

Clerical applications were among the first business computer applications. The amount of analysis conducted in a business is dramatically expanded by these applications. Time is critical in business. The first applications of com-

Clerical   Payroll, accounting

Database   Storage of facts, raw information

Management Information Systems   Repetitive reports
   support entire organization

End–User Computing   Personal systems

Decision Support Systems   Database, model base, interface
   tools to aid judgment for broad problems

Executive Information Systems
   Individual access to immediate status reports
   tools to find answers to questions quickly

Expert Systems   In depth analysis for narrow problems

Figure 1.2

puters were to perform well-defined operations in a timely way. Computers have been used for over 30 years for such applications as payroll, inventory records, cost report development, and so on. These clerical applications allow more detailed work to be done more accurately at a greater speed. Sometimes payroll is saved and costs reduced. Far more likely is a tremendous increase in the amount of work accomplished.

   Database management involves storing and retrieving data. The storing of a company's information is crucial not only for day-to-day operations, but also for providing a base of data upon which problems can be identified, projections of future operations can be made, and theories can be tested. This activity was done on a very small scale prior to computers, because of the need to collect large amounts of data and organize this data in the desired format. Initial computer technology in the 1940s and 1950s was applied to jobs with large payoff at minimum cost, and database activity was not always feasible. The development of greater computer capability may lead one to conclude that companies now know everything there is to know about how their operation works. Businesses must have a reason to collect and store data. Decisions often arise because of unexpected problems or opportunities, and more often than not, the desired data is not available in the desired form.

   Because tomorrow's questions are not predictable, there is a major policy decision to be made concerning what data to keep and what data to discard.

Storage costs money, and computer systems have finite capacities (although they are rapidly increasing). Furthermore, the more data that is stored, the more difficult it is to retrieve. Organizational power can be obtained from knowledge about where to find and how to retrieve data quickly. Computers have obvious potential in this area. Database packages in conjunction with networked microcomputers provide a great deal of flexibility for individual managers to keep track of whatever data is crucial to them, whereas extremely sophisticated technology to keep corporate-wide databases has been developed.

Management Information Systems

"If only we knew what was going on"

Management information systems (MIS) are valuable for collecting, organizing, and retrieving data, via computer systems. Data becomes information when some human learns something or modifies his or her theory based on that data. But there is a lot of information available, and when complex tradeoffs exist, simply having data may be insufficient.

Advances in computer technology in the 1960s led to the application of computer assets to provide managers a means to monitor the performance of the organization. Management information systems (MIS, centralized computer systems, information systems, data processing, etc.) exist to store and retrieve data in an efficient manner, as well as to provide management at all levels with information, through reports or databases, to answer queries. Efficiency is important because extensive hardware systems are required, as well as an extensive staff to operate the system, develop new applications, maintain the system, and administer it. MIS supports the entire organization, primarily through repetitive reports of key performance indicators. Because of the need to operate efficiently while supporting the entire organization, changes to the system require a great deal of coordination. Furthermore, there is no way that any computer system can keep up with all of the requests for new applications, so not all requests can be granted. Those requests that are not yet satisfied are referred to as the **applications backlog.**

With the advent of relatively inexpensive and easy-to-use microcomputers, it is now possible for many non-MIS personnel to use computers themselves **(end-user computing).** There is no end to the possibilities for effective use of computer resources by individuals. Secretaries (and even managers) can use word processing for letters and documentation. Those responsible for inventories can use database packages to keep track of local inventories. Spreadsheets provide a means for people to keep track of their workloads. Graphics packages make it possible for managers to develop stronger presentations. There is an unending number of things for which business people can use personal computers. This has resulted in an explosion of computer literacy in the 1980s. The impact on business is very difficult to measure. One would expect that people are more effective at doing their jobs when they use computers, although it is very difficult to measure this improvement in effectiveness.

The impact of end-user computing on the MIS is potentially good, as well as potentially bad. It may be good in that action is taken on much of the applications backlog. However, like knowledge, any gain results in the realization that there is much more to do. Furthermore, end users often find it convenient to tap centralized computer systems through available networking technology. This creates additional burdens for the administration of the centralized system. In addition, it is very difficult for management to control the amount of money spent on personal computer systems.

"If only we knew the future"

Analytic models provide business a means to study decision problems quantitatively. Some of the most useful types of analytic models involve forecasting. Many, if not all, business decisions would be easy if future events were known. Hindsight is always more accurate than assumptions made in the heat of the moment. But we cannot go back in time. **Forecasting** is a very crucial element in business decision making. It is an interesting exercise because decisions must be made with incomplete knowledge, often involving competitive players who are also making decisions.

"If only we knew the implications"

Management science (operations research) provides a series of analytic tools. Using these tools, models of business decision environments can be built. These models allow decision makers to experiment, with the intent of learning more about their environments. In order to learn, it is necessary for these decision makers to understand the critical assumptions and limitations of those models.

Management science can be described as the application of mathematical analysis to organizational problems. This field has developed a variety of powerful techniques that can be used to aid decision making, primarily by identifying what would be expected to happen given certain assumptions. These techniques almost always are impractical without a computer to perform the calculations. We will present examples of these modeling techniques in later chapters.

Decision Support Systems

The latest revolution in computer business applications has been the explosion in microcomputer use. In the past, the high cost of computers and special character flaws required to communicate with them led to centralized systems, scheduled as tightly as possible. Tremendously expensive systems need to be tightly scheduled in order for them to be cost effective. This constraint has led to high degrees of control over their use, resulting in years of red tape before new applications could be planned, approved, programmed, debugged, and implemented. One-time analyses by individual decision makers were impractical. All that has changed with the advent of cheap (for businesses) microcomputers. Now, if someone has a bright idea, it can be analyzed in a much more thorough fashion and—just as important—quickly. New software, such as electronic spreadsheets, allow more thorough analysis of the impact of a proposal on cash flow than is possible in a rigidly controlled system.

The term **decision support system** (DSS) has been used in a variety of ways. The distinguishing characteristics of a DSS include interactive access to data and models that deal with a specific decision that cannot be solved by the computer alone, but that requires human intervention.

The ability of businesspeople to use decision support systems is vastly enhanced by the application of **fourth-generation languages** (4GLs). Computers used to be relatively slow. It used to be very important to write very efficient code in order to utilize efficiently the limited available resource of computer time. However, in the last decade, computer capacity has exploded. Supercomputers exist to crunch numbers and fly through whatever else they are asked to do at tremendous speeds. More important to the average businessperson, microcomputers at the other end of the spectrum are also much more capable than they were in the past. With added computing power, it has been possible for instructions to be written in a less computer-efficient manner, which allows people to spend much less time studying the nuances and idiosyncrasies of computer languages. Fourth-generation languages make it very easy for people to use computers. This is a very important factor, not only for the use of decision support systems, but also for the use of expert systems, executive information systems, and MIS in general.

Many exciting developments in computer technology are on the drawing boards. The search for artificial intelligence has led to the development of expert systems, to release humans from some decisions or to greatly assist them by providing analysis of problems in other decisions. Fourth-generation languages lessen the requirement to communicate in the computer's terms, allowing broader use of computer systems by humans. Graphics capabilities are more impressive every year, releasing the constraints upon humans to express themselves and communicate.

The concept of decision support can utilize many of these developments. Decision support systems were proposed in the early 1970s. Keen and Scott Morton (1978) considered decision support systems to represent a point of view on the role of computers in the decision-making process. Assistance to managers in semistructured tasks was implied, with the intent of supporting rather than replacing managerial judgment. The emphasis would be on improving the effectiveness of decision making rather than on the efficiency of the system. Sprague and Carlson (1982) described decision support systems as shown in Figure 1.3.

Figure 1.3
(Based on Sprague and
Carlson [1982])

INTERACTIVE computer–based systems to
HELP decision makers use
DATA and **MODELS** to solve
UNSTRUCTURED problems.

Although all management information systems exist to support decisions, the capitalized letters identified by Sprague and Carlson are not inherent in most computerized business systems. Decision support systems are intended to assist specific decision makers, individually or in groups, rather than the entire organization. This allows custom design of a system. Often dedicated hardware and software access are available. Inexpensive microcomputer systems allow interactive use and are much more responsive to time requirements. Although large, centralized systems have much faster computational times, this advantage in computational speed does no good if the required job spends days or weeks in queue waiting to be run and hours in queue waiting to be printed.

Decision makers can use decision support systems interactively to build, and more importantly, to change analytic models of the decision problem. Interactive use allows immediate changes in assumed parameters, with rapid feedback, encouraging a learning process that is impossible when the decision maker has to wait extended periods of time for output. Decision support systems should ideally be linked to the primary database of the company for some types of data, but should not be limited to those items of data that have been declared useful for the organization as a whole. The decision support system should have a means of building and storing special data files, reflecting items important to the decision at hand. Access to analytic models that the decision maker considers useful should also be available. This is usually most efficiently accomplished through libraries of software, shared with other decision makers. But transportable disks containing useful software are very convenient and quite inexpensive. All of these features, in addition to the custom-designed feature of allowing individual output formats, provide a means of dealing with unstructured classes of problems.

With personal computers, decision makers (or their staffs) can utilize a wider variety of analytic techniques, tapping the central database or the DSS special database for specific information in a timely manner, displaying results in whatever format is desired (tables, graphics, color, etc.). You have the opportunity to go to work at a time when computer systems developed over the past 30 years will undergo radical change, primarily because of the development of less expensive equipment, allowing widespread use. People who become expert in how to design and set up decision support systems, including their relationship to central systems, access to central databases, and input and output devices on the computer system side, and the availability of analytic techniques, their required assumptions, and sensitivity to changes on the model side, will be valuable assets to organizations.

Group Decision Support Systems

Decision support systems were proposed with individual decision makers in mind. The idea was to custom-design computer systems to fit the decision-making style of one person. However, most decisions in contemporary society are made by groups. Decision support systems can be useful in this environment, not only by giving individual decision makers the means of learning more about decision problems, but also in communicating ideas to others.

A special set of computer systems has been developed to aid group decision making. **Group decision support systems** focus on expediting the exchange of ideas within a group. Although adding analytic models to these systems is possible, to date, most proposed systems have focused on encouraging the generation of ideas among participants (brainstorming), stimulating quieter group members to participate, and organizing collective thoughts into a workable consensus. These systems typically include the means of assessing group consensus, through identification of average opinions and through voting.

Executive Information Systems

Executive information systems provide new ways to apply computer technology. Through state-of-the-art systems, key information can be placed at the fingertips of top executives. This would mean developing systems that provide rapid access to corporate databases and daily reports, allowing the executive to obtain explanatory information quickly through "drill-down" systems. The intent is to give executives immediate access to status reports, as well as the ability to seek answers to questions, many of which are triggered by these status reports. Executive information systems are meant to provide top executives with an environment that would aid them in monitoring company operations in as timely a manner as possible. The focus is on evaluating organization performance rather than focusing on a specific decision. Therefore, although analytic tools are often useful, the emphasis is on query systems, custom-designed reports, and communication tools.

Expert Systems

Expert systems try to emulate the decisions of an expert in some particular problem domain and include ways to automate decisions in repetitive environments. These are appropriate when rare expertise exists or when complex operations would be improved by precise actions. Rare expertise can be preserved and multiplied. The effort involved is fairly intense, requiring thorough thought for complex decisions. This makes it necessary for a repetitive decision in order to make the effort worthwhile. However, with many expert system shells now available, the number of applications of expert systems has grown dramatically.

The study of artificial intelligence, seeking to get computers to accomplish whatever it is the human brain does, has led to the development of expert systems. There are many types of expert systems, some very effective. Basic demonstration expert systems are usually rule-based systems that classify objects in a complex environment. A series of questions is asked, with each question often depending on the answer to prior questions. Objects such as animals can be classified. This seems a trivial application, but there are useful real applications, such as classifying loan applicants by the amount of risk involved, determining legal courses of action in complex situations, or hiring new employees. Expert systems can go beyond rule-based questions, to incorporate data analysis. Real applications include systems that are fed the results of oil drilling samples to predict whether continued drilling is worthwhile, medical diagnosis of specific diseases (MYCIN), and computer system design.

Often the motivation for an expert system is the computerization of rare expertise. In concept, an individual who is very good at a specific type of analysis (such as scheduling a factory) can be used as the basis for developing an expert system to replace the expert. This obviously runs something of a risk for the expert. In practice, however, nobody claims to replace the expert, but rather to use the computer system to transport the expert throughout the world and record the expertise for posterity.

Expert systems have also been applied to perform mundane tasks thoroughly. An example is a large accounting firm, which developed an expert system for the initial interview with a prospective tax client. The traditional approach is to send trainees to gather the initial information. Obviously, there would be some expected variance in the quality of information gathered. The expert system guides the trainee to ensure all required information is obtained.

A feature of expert systems is that they generally require a very focused application area, and they require detailed development of expertise, as well as significant amounts of time to program and test. So far, this has meant years to develop a system to perform a very specific task. However, the application of expert systems is a real growth area, and one would expect future technology to improve to the point where many more applications can be developed in much less time.

Note the difference between an expert system and a decision support system. Expert systems are used for repetitive tasks, or they would not be worth developing. Decision support systems are used to cope with an unstructured environment involving specific decisions. Therefore, decision support systems need to be flexible in order to respond to changing environments. Expert systems, in concept, could replace human judgment (for a well-defined, specific application). Decision support systems are meant to support rather than replace human judgment, by providing computerized tools to aid human learning.

THE RELATIONSHIP OF SYSTEMS TO LEVELS OF DECISION MAKING

Computer support to business currently has a variety of forms. The early applications, as indicated before, were primarily clerical. Creation of payroll checks can be viewed as a production process, highly structured, totally capable of being turned over to the computer (operational-level decision making). This class of application has been labeled electronic data processing (EDP). The characteristics general to EDP are high degrees of structure, with little human interference required other than to build the system and maintain it.

Management information systems (MIS) are a step beyond EDP. Systems have been built that provide consistent, more accurate information to all elements of the business. This function is usually integrated with accounting. The purpose of management information systems is to provide everyone in the business with the information he or she needs. This function can be performed most efficiently on a centralized basis. Although management information systems aid strategic and operational levels, the primary support is at the managerial level.

Decision support systems also exist to provide information. But they seek to do more, by providing a tool for learning and exploration. The characteristic of this system is flexibility, because different decision makers operate best with different information. The operation of a DSS calls for custom-designed systems, along with the ability to communicate with the central system. Decision support systems can aid decision making at both the managerial and strategic levels.

Executive information systems provide a means to monitor organizational activity in a more effective manner. These systems are not focused on specific decisions, but are very effective in identifying operational problems, as well as providing background information that executives can use to better understand managerial and strategic situations.

Expert systems are a different approach to decision making. These systems require a repetitive environment and thoroughly defined problems. To date, this has meant applications primarily at the operational level. If artificial intelligence can be harnessed to develop problem structure in more complex environments, some day it may be possible to apply expert systems to managerial and strategic problems.

SCIENTIFIC APPROACHES TO BUSINESS

The scientific method infers a desire to explore what causes things to happen and the development of a framework (or theory) of relationships that can explain what has been observed. This requires a skeptical approach and involves a slow, systematic process of observing the system under study, developing hypotheses, conducting experiments, and building a more comprehensive body of knowledge. This process has worked very well in the physical sciences, resulting in trips to the moon, and so forth. Systematic studies of the social sciences, such as economics, are more elusive. Business decision makers have often had to make decisions under time pressure and traditionally have relied more upon intuition and faster forms of judgment. Economics is an important area of study, and there have long been attempts to apply specific scientific principles to this field. However, the nature of economic systems is far more complex than physics or chemistry. The relationships of business systems are not as well defined as the hard sciences and may even change over rather short periods of time.

However, the same general principles of the scientific approach can be applied to businesses. There are many questions crucial to the well-being of any firm. Demand for its products, efficiency of production, management of finances and personnel, and many other questions require decision making. A scientific approach to decision making should, in the long run, result in improved organizational performance. Management information systems in general provide a means of more systematically collecting and retrieving data, allowing more thorough explorations of cause and effect. Decision support systems can provide a vehicle by which decision makers can learn more about their businesses.

The Systems Approach

The systems approach views organizations as systems (a set of interrelated elements) and assumes learning through the collection of information on an ongoing basis. Large organizations often have people designated to become familiar with a phase of an organization's operations, such as personnel, marketing, and so on. These specialists can then provide the decision maker more thorough and accurate assessments of the impacts of new problems or opportunities, as well as assessments of potential decision impacts.

The systems approach to decision making can be viewed as a seven-stage process.

1. Problem Identification

Somehow a problem (or more optimistically an opportunity) must be identified. This is easy when things get out of hand. It is better, however, to act before things get out of control. This can be accomplished by thoroughly planning operations, to include standard production rates and activity budgets. Repetitive reports (from the central MIS for shared information, from the DSS for special requests) can aid in rapidly identifying problems and/or opportunities. This would usually be done by comparing actual and expected performance, looking for discrepancies. Executive information systems are specifically designed to aid executives in monitoring organization operations in as timely a manner as possible.

2. Data Collection

Once a problem and/or opportunity calling for a decision has been identified, the next step is to review the impact. If staff specialists are used, this amounts to a status report by each staff member. Generally, new situations bring up new questions, which can be investigated at this point. If time is tight, the degree of this data collection can be very limited. Decision support systems, with the capability of storing special data and with models for data analysis, can aid in data collection. The primary data collection devices, however, are humans with thorough knowledge of the information available and how to get it. They can do a much better job with computer help. Executive information systems give the executive powerful access to key information—either concerning internal operations or the external environment.

3. Alternative Generation

Some analytic models can actually be used to generate alternatives. In general, however, problems require human creativity for generation of alternative solutions. Group decision support systems provide for electronic brainstorming, a technique designed specifically to generate ideas about how to solve a problem.

4. Alternative Evaluation

This stage involves checking how alternative solutions are expected to impact the existing system. There will generally be tradeoffs in alternatives. Those alternatives involving the greatest expected payoff may well involve high degrees of risk. Analytic models have the potential for the greatest contribution in this stage of the process. The use of computer spreadsheets allows more detailed identification of expected cash flow, with repetitive analyses for alternative sets of assumptions. Mathematical programming provides a means of identifying optimal solutions to models of business problems. Statistical packages allow forecasting, as well as systematic analysis of collected data. Queuing models allow examination of how some systems can be expected to behave. Simulation allows modeling of more complex models. All of these models can provide a basis for analysis of alternatives.

5. Decision

Because computers are only capable of making projections subject to rather rigid assumptions, it should not be expected that computers will replace human judgment in unstructured decision making. Life is far more complex than can be entirely modeled with any technique we will examine. Computers and analytic models can contribute by expanding what decision makers consider and by providing a means for more thorough analysis. But the final decision responsibility remains with humans.

6. Implementation

Once a decision is made, it must be communicated to the organization. Those within the organization must also be convinced that they should do whatever the decision implies. Computers can help by transmitting instructions rapidly. This can be through the central system or through electronic mail to those with other decision support terminals. Communication can also be two way, allowing quicker identification of unconsidered factors. In this way, mistakes can sometimes be caught before damage is done by decisions based on incomplete information.

Beyond the initial communication of a decision, computer support provides a means of more quickly monitoring the results, or impact, of decisions. This can provide an incentive for compliance for sound decisions. It allows quicker identification of problems for unsound decisions. General organizational performance can be monitored as before through the central MIS. Decision support systems can be used for collection of newly designed, user-specific reports.

7. Monitoring

The decision-making process is not necessarily a one-time, clean operation. Decisions may be rational as judged by our understanding today. Tomorrow, conditions may change, or we may learn new information, either of which can make the decision we made inappropriate. Rather than a strict by-the-numbers process, decision making often involves retreats to prior stages. In fact, sticking with an old decision can be a dilemma in itself. Computers can continue to assist this process by the same monitoring operations used in stage 1 or by the continued analysis of alternatives in light of new information as discussed in stage 4. This seven-stage process is summarized in Table 1.1.

Table 1.1

	MIS	DSS	EIS
Problem Identi-fication	Primary support	Supplemental monitoring	A primary purpose
Data Collection	Database function	Supplemental databases	A primary purpose
Alternative Generation	—	Minor capability	? possibly
Alternative Evaluation	—	Primary support	? possibly
Decision	—	—	—
Implementation	Company-wide communications	Electronic mail	Electronic communications
Monitor	Watch reports for improvement	Collect special data	Watch reports for improvement

The following example demonstrates the application of a scientific approach to a real decision problem. A problem was identified, information gathered, a potential solution was developed, and an analytic technique was used to evaluate the impact of adopting this potential solution on the company's future position.

HUDON AND DEAUDELIN (IGA)
Calantone, Droge, Litvack, and de Benedetto (1989)

Hudon and Deaudelin entered the food chain business in the mid-1970s. Operating in Quebec, Hudon and Deaudelin owned the IGA brand name of supermarket. They faced a number of competitors. A major competitor, Steinberg, Inc., was noted for its aggressive pricing tactics. Steinberg, Inc., was a unionized chain, which faced some cultural difficulties in that it was viewed as an English store in a strongly French province. Furthermore, legal restrictions intended to create a climate encouraging small, locally owned stores placed pressure on Steinberg's operations.

Problem Identification

In 1983, there were four major competitors in the Quebec grocery retailing market. Because of pressures on its operations, Steinberg was expected to adopt a vigorous policy of major price cuts backed by heavy promotion. Steinberg had substantial financial resources, and it also had a history of adopting price wars. The president of Hudon and Deaudelin (IGA) was concerned about this prospect. Hudon and Deaudelin, the fourth-largest firm in the Quebec grocery market, expected that it would suffer more than the three larger firms if a price war developed. Hudon and Deaudelin's president sought a more creative, less expensive strategy to cope with Steinberg's expected move.

Data Gathering

In order to obtain sounder knowledge of options, Hudon and Deaudelin sponsored a study to examine the response of specific grocery product sales to price changes. In general, grocery sales are expected to vary inversely with price (as price goes down, sales should go up). However, not all grocery products have the same price elasticity (sales response to price). Some grocery products can be easily stored for long periods of time (such as flour, sugar, and other products). Other items, however, require replacement in relatively short periods of time (such as fruits). Past studies had reported that the frequency of purchases relative to promotions (advertising, price cuts, or other incentive programs) varied widely across product categories. Canned vegetables, some soaps, and canned fruit juice sales were found to be very responsive to promotion, whereas breakfast cereals, frozen pie shells, and rice were much less responsive.

Alternative Generation

The study involved a controlled experiment to identify those products whose sales would remain relatively stable even though prices were not dropped. The idea was that the Hudon and Deaudelin stores would respond to a price war through selective price decreases on products whose sales were sensitive to price, thus continuing to attract customers, but maintaining current prices on less sensitive products in order to minimize the expected losses due to the anticipated price war. A six-week experiment was designed, beginning with a two-week control period where prices were stabilized at their current levels. This was followed by a two-week period where 72 grocery products were randomly assigned to one of three groups (group 1—prices were increased 20 percent, group 2—prices were left unchanged, group 3—prices were decreased 20 percent). In the third two-week period, all 72 of these product prices were returned to the prices of the first two-week period. Prices on these products were not advertised over the test period, and only high-volume products with fairly stable weekly sales were used in order to increase the validity of the experiment. Further control was obtained by amassing more than sufficient inventory of these items. The purpose of the experiment was not revealed to employees. Total grocery sales were also measured to adjust for market variation.

Alternative Evaluation

This experiment yielded a basis for identifying a pricing strategy intended to keep IGA competitive during the expected price war with minimum impact on profits. There was a risk element as well. The president's utility function, trading off expected profit against implied risk, was used to evaluate alternative policies. The study confirmed that customers were highly sensitive to price changes in items that could be stocked up and less sensitive to price changes in items that were less storable.

In March 1983, Steinberg, Inc., announced a promotion offering coupons worth 5 percent of purchases that could be used for future purchases, as well as a program of weekly specials. Steinberg added staff to improve customer service. These policies reduced Steinberg's marginal profit from 20 percent to below 15 percent. To make up for this lost revenue, Steinberg required a 23 percent increase in sales volume. It expected competitors would require at least three weeks to react and evidently anticipated at least this much increase in sales volume from their promotion.

Implementation

However, the response of competition was very swift. The other two major grocers adopted similar price cuts within two hours of the Steinberg announcement. However, both suffered losses in profit of about 5 percent. Hudon and Deaudelin (IGA) adopted a policy based on the findings of the experiment. The store was closed for three days while staff reduced prices on selected items. This was accompanied by an advertising program. IGA experienced a small decline in overall margin, dropping from 20 to 18.8 percent. The price war lasted 14 weeks. Steinberg, Inc., found that it had actually lost market share (from 20 to 19 percent). Hudon and Deaudelin (IGA) increased market share, from 8.5 percent before the price war to 9.5 percent at its end, while sacrificing only 1.2 percent of its profit margin.

This case demonstrates the use of a scientific approach in dealing with a business problem. Based on sound understanding of specific customer response, a sensible policy was identified and adopted which enabled much more efficient response to a business problem than that of the competition. Because IGA was the smallest of the four major grocers in Quebec, this efficient response was important for company survival.

This case was an application of management science to a decision problem. Although the distinction is often nebulous, we would view a DSS as consisting of greater support to the decision maker in terms of data access, providing the decision maker a means of learning about the expected impact of adopting a decision. Certainly the approach used by Hudon and Deaudelin yielded a result very close to that which a DSS would have yielded. Data was used to analyze the problem, and an experiment was conducted which enabled identification of product sales response to price changes. This made generation of an effective solution quite easy. Specific product price changes were evaluated in terms of analysis of decision maker utility. But a full DSS could aid all of the process, monitoring key variables to identify situations calling for a decision, readily accessing data important to the decision (including a database to store new information), as well as the model analysis used in the case. Decision support systems are developed to cope with a decision of sufficient importance to merit system development.

Group decision support systems seek to aid decisions where decision-making authority is shared. This creates a much greater need for consensus building, in agreeing upon what the problem is and what objectives are to be attained, as well as the effectiveness of alternative solutions. Because of these added degrees of complication, most GDSSs that have been presented have focused on using computers to enhance communication between group members, seeking better understanding of member positions. Another feature of group decision support systems is computer support to enhance generation of ideas, through electronic brainstorming. Furthermore, these systems often provide electronic means of gathering member votes and opinions of alternative solutions. Although models could be incorporated in GDSSs, not much evidence of models in these systems has been reported.

Executive information systems utilize computers to maximize the amount of information available to an executive. Most of these systems focus on providing immediate status reports of key variables, along with the ability to provide greater detail upon request. Often, information external to the organization is incorporated through linkages to commercial databases. Models could be included, but are not present in all such systems. As we will discuss in Chapter 12, implementation of executive information systems often leads to widespread use throughout the organization. The general intent is to provide continuous access to key information relating to the organization.

Expert systems are a fourth type of computer system capable of supporting business decision making. Expert systems have quite a different focus than the other systems, however. Expert systems require development of a program of logic that is capable of dealing with a variety of situations. As with each of the other three systems, there is a fairly substantial development cost. This implies a fairly repetitive kind of decision problem. The quality of the expert system is directly related to the quality of expertise that is selected. Human participation in decision making is not required with expert systems (although human monitoring with the capability of vetoing obviously erroneous decisions would be a good idea).

All four of these systems involve applying computers to aid business decision making. They serve different roles, however. Executive information systems focus on providing information about business operations in real time. Group decision support systems generally focus on aiding mutual understanding among group members. Decision support systems focus on aiding human learning about the expected impact of adopting alternative solutions. Expert systems take accepted knowledge about a problem and apply it automatically.

SUMMARY

Computers have contributed a great deal in improving the operations of business firms. The potential is for vastly increased computer support. People can always ask computers to do more than is available with existing systems. The field requires familiarity with limitations as well as opportunities. Most limitations are a matter of currently available hardware, software, or data. The concept of decision support systems is an attempt to harness computer power, not with the intent of having computers make decisions, but with the intent of providing a tool with which decision makers can learn more about the expected impact of decisions. This involves solid technical understanding, familiarity with the operations of the business, and imagination. The purpose of decision support systems is quite different from the purpose of many other elements of the MIS. Operation of a DSS requires understanding of the specific requirements of the decision maker using the system. There are many ways to combine hardware, software, and data, a variety of analytic techniques available, and a variety of ways of presenting output. Decision support systems, to effectively support decisions, require custom design. Executive information systems require sophisticated development of data access. Expert systems require in-depth analysis, both to glean knowledge, as well as to encode it in a usable system. Someone expert in building such systems needs to be familiar with the framework of decision making, as well as the potential, limitations, and assumptions required of alternative analytic techniques.

REFERENCES

Calantone, R. J., C. Droge, D. S. Litvack, and C. A. de Benedetto. 1989. Flanking in a price war. *Interfaces* 19:1–12.

Keen, P. G. W. and M. S. Scott Morton. 1978. *Decision support systems: An organizational perspective.* Reading, MA: Addison-Wesley.

Sprague, R. H., Jr. and E. D. Carlson. 1982. *Building effective decision support systems.* Englewood Cliffs, NJ: Prentice-Hall.

CHAPTER 2

Individual Decision Making

The focus of this book is decision making. Many people consider decision making to be the most interesting part of business. Decision making is one of the important elements in business success, and it is what executives are hired to do.

This chapter will present a number of views of decision making, beginning with theoretical views, followed by observations of actual decision making. The consideration of multiple objectives and other complications in business decision making will be reviewed. The analytic hierarchy process will be presented as a means to support decision making when multiple objectives are present. This chapter will provide you:

- □ The theoretical **normative** view of business decision making
- □ Descriptions of actual decision-making environments
- □ The results of a study of actual executive decision making
- □ Consideration of multiple objectives in decision making
- □ The analytic hierarchy process as a means of supporting decision making
- □ A view of how computer systems can support the decision-making process

Decision making is one of the most studied activities of human behavior. Yet there is very little universally accepted knowledge about what makes decision making better. There is not even any metric that is universally accepted for measuring the quality of decision making. One common measure of decision making is financial success. However, no thoughtful consideration of decision making would settle for success as the ultimate measure of decision quality. The richest person in the world (whoever that is) is considered by many people to be more fortunate than wise. Being in the right place at the right time, being born wealthy, or being just plain lucky would probably all be given more weight than sound decision making in explaining success. The same is true for companies. Although employees of Standard Oil or IBM may voice great admiration for the wisdom of John Rockefeller or Thomas Watson, many others would blame other circumstances for the success of those companies. The truth probably includes a lot of sound decision making along with a lot of good fortune.

Because the topic of decision making is not well known, it should come as no surprise that there is no easy path to better decisions. A number of elements have been identified as important. The problem is complicated, because there is no direct relationship between good decision making and success. Good decisions are expected to lead to the best results more often than other choices available. But investors in the stock market know that the best decision will not always result in the greatest payoff.

Decision making is greatly complicated by the **imperfect knowledge** that inevitably exists when decisions need to be made. Decisions can always be postponed, but continuous delay is rarely the best option. **Time** is often a factor in decision making. There is also the complication of **competition.** In a chess match or in a football game, if you always make the same decision, you will soon run into an opponent who will clobber you. Most decisions are made in an environment where the outcome is not only a function of one decision maker's choices, but the choices of a multitude of decision makers.

There are diverse styles and approaches to decision making in business (Figure 2.1). Styles include participative and dictatorial. In the military, the dictatorial style prevails. If there are dirty jobs to be done, it works better if there is central control, with little questioning of commands. An extreme form of participative management is often found on some university faculties. If everyone is an "expert," participative styles allow each participant to contribute to the decision. Business decision making often involves forms of both extremes, depending on the individual styles of whoever is in authority, as well as organizational culture. There are alternative approaches to decision making

Figure 2.1
Alternative decision-making approaches.

RATIONAL
  Normative – How decisions should be made
  Descriptive – How decisions are made

NEGOTIATION
  Bargaining models

LEGAL
  Multiple advocate system
  View all sides of the issue

as well. Three broad categories of decision-making approaches are **rational,** **negotiating,** and **legal.** All three approaches have positive and negative features. Most theoretical discussion of decision making is based on the rational approach. We will discuss the negotiating and legal approaches later, based primarily on Murray (1986).

RATIONAL DECISION MODELS

The concept of rationality is the basis of most formal models of decision making. The idea is that models can be developed that will show the decision maker how decisions should be made in order to be successful. This approach is termed *normative,* as opposed to *descriptive,* because the model is suggesting how decisions should normally be made. In order for this philosophy to have meaning, its assumptions should be met. These assumptions are:

1. A set of relevant alternatives with corresponding outcomes is known.
2. The possible states of the world are known.
3. An established rule or set of relations producing a preference ordering on the alternatives can be developed.
4. There is a known function expressing what it is that the decision maker wishes to accomplish. This implies some objective function to be optimized or some means a decision maker uses to reflect value.

The fourth assumption reflects the concept of **utility.** There are many things most people want to accomplish in most decisions. In a business, profit is important. But profit at the expense of market share, labor relations, compliance with government regulations as well as societal norms is often difficult to reconcile. Utility was developed as a means to generate a function representing how humans measure value reflecting all objectives of importance to them.

The assumptions of the normative model are often difficult to accept in real situations. First, there are usually an infinite number of possible decisions. Second, preference ordering has proven more elusive than one might expect. Third, human decision makers often exhibit complex utilities. There are those who dispute the existence of utility functions. For those who accept that utility does exist, it must be admitted that an individual's utility function is highly complex and very difficult to capture.

UTILITY

Risk

We all recognize that risk is an important element in life. We spent 45 years worrying about the threat of World War III. The risks of nuclear radiation are heavy on many people's minds, not to mention global warming and the depletion of the ozone layer. On a personal basis, many of us have concerns about finances, social acceptability, and future status. A demonstration of personal concern about life's risks is the practice of purchasing insurance. Insurance companies (which have been very profitable) do not sell insurance at a loss, so it would appear the most cost-effective approach would be not to insure. But most of us have insurance for health, life, automobiles, and personal goods, because of the **risk.**

Risk is of paramount concern in business as well. Almost any investment involves a degree of risk. The tradeoff between expected return and risk is one of the most common types of decisions made in business. If we are to suggest systems that support business decision making, a review of risk would seem mandatory.

Risk comes in many forms. The components of risk include the magnitude of loss, the chance of loss, and exposure to loss. **Magnitude of loss** involves how much we might lose. This can be viewed on the negative side by how much our current status might decline (how much we might lose). It can also be viewed as opportunity cost, or regret. If we had made different choices in the past, we might recognize that we would have been better off. **Chance of loss** refers to probabilities. In a fair roulette game, we can precisely calculate the probabilities of outcomes. In horse races, probabilities are much more subjective. In business, chances of loss require estimation in a much more complex environment than a roulette wheel or even a horse race. **Exposure to loss** has to do with how much we can afford to lose. In a personal setting, this would include financial, health, social, and career dimensions. In business, profit of course is an important dimension, but other dimensions are important as well, such as market share, cash flow, employee relations, and other factors.

Humans take a variety of approaches to risk. Risk-neutral decision makers are considered the most objective, viewing outcomes in terms of expected value, to be discussed in the next section. Some humans like to take chances. This can be viewed as rational, if the magnitude of the payoff is valued very high relative to the status quo. Risk-seeking individuals strive for the best state, placing little weight on what is likely to happen or the worst that can happen. Examples might include sky divers or entrepreneurs. Most humans seem to be risk averse. Avoiding loss is more important to this class of individual than the most likely outcome. The profitability of insurance companies is a demonstration of this approach.

Of course, people are complicated enough to avoid universal classification. Most of us behave in a risk-averse manner in some situations (things for which we buy insurance), risk neutral in others (most of us buy groceries on the basis of price), and risk seeking in other situations. You might try to identify situations where you behave each of these three ways.

Modeling Decision-Making Risk

Expected value is a means of evaluating the worth of a certainty equivalent to an uncertain outcome. For uncertain outcomes, if all n possible outcomes x_i were known, along with their probability of occurrence $\Pr[x_i]$, the expected value $E[x]$ is

$$E[x] = \sum_{i=1}^{n} x_i \Pr[x_i]$$

Expected value serves as a useful means to identify the objective value of an uncertain event. Given accurate outcomes and probabilities of their occurrence, the expected value provides the mean long-run outcome. In gambling situations, each of six sides of a die have one-sixth probability of occurring. Dice have sides numbered from one to six. The expected outcome would be as shown in Table 2.1. Here the expected outcome is 3.5. Note that 3.5 is *not* a possible outcome, but represents the 50 percent point of the cumulative weighted distribution of outcomes.

Risk-neutral decision makers are expected to select the option with the greatest expected outcome, if they are **rational.** However, Bernoulli examined the **St. Petersburg paradox,** which gave players the opportunity to play the game where they would receive a payoff equal to 2^n, where n was the number of times an equiprobable two-outcome event (like a fair coin toss) repeated. The expected outcome of this game would be

$$EV = 2(.5) + 4(.5^2) + 8(.5^3) + 16(.5^4) + \cdots = \infty$$

What would you be willing to pay to play this game? Although the expected value is infinite, your authors would not pay that much to play, nor should you. People have been found to pay between \$15 and \$30. This is an extreme demonstration that rational decision makers can be risk averse.

Utility functions reflect the rational behavior of risk-averse people who do not act as if they made choices on the basis of expected value of outcomes. Utility is viewed as the transformed value scale of human decision makers. This utility function is rarely expressed, but viewed as internally operative.

Table 2.1

Outcome	Probability	Product
1	1/6	1/6
2	1/6	2/6
3	1/6	3/6
4	1/6	4/6
5	1/6	5/6
6	1/6	6/6
		21/6 = 3.5 = **expected outcome**

Another way humans approach decisions is through **regret.** If a particular decision is not selected, regret would be the amount of benefit missed if a favorable outcome had occurred. There are significant differences in human response to regrets. Human understanding of very low or very high probabilities is very poor. People purchase lottery tickets, despite infinitesimal chances of winning. People have been shown to give too much weight to extreme outcomes [see Kahneman and Tversky (1979)].

The difference between the expected value of a lottery and its certainty equivalent has been defined as the risk premium. Rational decision makers are expected to be willing to forgo this amount to avoid the risk involved in an uncertain choice. An insurance premium is an example of this concept. This factor adds an additional complication to the identification of a utility function. Not only must utility reflect the tradeoff between return and risk, but individual perception of probability as well. Utility is expected to vary by the specific decision choices available, as well as the circumstances under which these choices are being considered. Utility is generally identified by a series of lottery choices presented to the decision maker [see Keeney and Raiffa (1976), Bunn (1984), and Taylor (1991)]. This process can be unnatural to the decision maker and may be quite involved.

INDIVIDUAL DECISION-MAKING STYLES

In order to use a model, the model must fit the manager's style of thinking. McKenney and Keen (1974) viewed problem solving and decision making in terms of the processes by which individuals organized the information they perceived, bringing to bear habits and strategies of thinking. Consistent modes of thought develop through training and experience. Two major dimensions of these modes of thought are information gathering and information evaluation styles.

Information gathering relates to perceptual processes by which the mind organizes the various stimuli it encounters. When these stimuli are organized into information, it is the result of complex coding heavily dependent on the individual's mental set, memory capacity, and strategies. This mental activity is often unconscious. Information gathering involves rejecting some data that is encountered and summarizing and categorizing the rest. Two extreme types of information-gathering styles are **preceptive** and **receptive.**

Preceptive individuals use concepts to filter data. They focus on relationships between items and look for deviations from or conformities with their expectations. Precepts act as cues for both gathering and cataloging data.

Receptive thinkers are more sensitive to stimuli. They focus on detail rather than relationships and try to derive attributes from direct examination of the information they receive, instead of trying to fit new data to their precepts.

Each style has advantages and disadvantages in specific situations. Preceptive individuals tend to ignore important details, whereas receptive individuals may fail to shape details into a coherent whole. The preceptive style tends to lead to success in many marketing or planning roles. The receptive style favors auditing and other detail-oriented jobs.

Information evaluation refers to problem-solving processes. **Systematic** individuals tend to approach a problem by structuring it in terms of some method likely to lead to a solution. **Intuitive** thinkers usually avoid such commitment, but tend to try multiple solutions and trial-and-error techniques. Intuitive thinkers often discard information and are usually sensitive to cues that they cannot identify.

There are advantages and disadvantages for each style. Systematic thinkers tend to do well in production management. Intuitive thinkers tend to reinvent the wheel, but are better able to deal with ill-structured problems involving high volumes of data, nebulous criteria, or problems where there are no obvious solutions.

Problem Finding

Most modern theories of the decision-making process stress rationality. Decision making is treated as problem solving in this approach. The primary argument of McKenney and Keen is that decision making is situational and includes problem finding. The manager scans the environment and organizes perceptions. As much effort is given to clarifying values and intents as to dealing with predefined problems.

A manager's activities are bounded by formal job constraints, as well as informal traditions and expectations. Decision-making activity is therefore strongly influenced by the manager's perception of position. Decisions are cued by assessing mismatches between the expected and actual environments. Problems must be found, recognized, and defined.

When managers are flooded with information, they need to be able to filter this information and to be alert to trends and discrepancies. Receptive individuals are particularly suited to such tasks. Preceptive individuals are more suited to tasks where a concept of the environment is necessary rather than tasks where detail is more important. Intuitive individuals may better fit the global view, but may encounter difficulty when methodical analysis is required.

Individual styles develop out of experience. They reflect a propensity rather than a capacity. People tend to seek out tasks where they have perceived relative advantages, and they approach tasks and problems using the most comfortable mode of thinking.

Systematic thinkers tend to look for a method and make a plan to solve a problem (Figure 2.2). Solution quality tends to be justified by the method leading to it. This style would discard alternatives quickly and move through a process of increasingly refined analysis. Ordered searches would be more common.

Intuitive thinkers prefer to keep the overall problem in mind and redefine specific problems as they proceed. They rely more on hunches and defend solutions in terms of fit rather than method. They tend to consider a wider

	SYSTEMATIC	INTUITIVE
PRECEPTIVE	Production manager	Marketing manager
	Logistics manager	Psychologist
	Statistician	Historian
	Financial analyst	
RECEPTIVE	Auditor	Architect
	Clinical diagnosis	Bond sales

Figure 2.2
Typical tasks suitable for styles. (Modified and reprinted by permission of *Harvard Business Review*. An exhibit from "How Managers' Minds Work" by James L. McKenney and Peter W. Keen (May-June 1974). Copyright © 1974 by the President and Fellows of Harvard College; all rights reserved.)

variety of alternatives and continue to search for additional solutions. Alternatives tend to be explored and abandoned very quickly.

Receptive thinkers tend to suspend judgment and avoid preconceptions. They are more attentive to detail and precise interpretation of the data and insist on complete examination of the data. Preceptive thinkers tend to look for cues in the data set and focus on relationships. They tend to build sets of explanatory precepts.

There is no best way of thinking. A major problem in applying management science, however, is that because managers got where they are by a particular style, they tend to view the world from that perspective. Management scientists, through training, often have a fundamentally different style. A first step in successful implementation of management science is to recognize the different ways of viewing problems.

The management science view would be to identify a problem or opportunity, gather important data, build a model, experiment with this model, analyze results, and made a sound conclusion. This view, as McKenney and Keen emphasized, is developed through training and practice in an academic setting. Managers often develop a different approach, because in business operations, decisions often have to be made quickly, with available (rather than desirable) information. The intuitive, preceptive style is not the only style used in business, but it occurs frequently, because it matches the environment.

The idea behind decision support systems is to focus on the manager's view of the world. An ideal DSS would make use of models much easier, through model building systems and more automated solution procedures. McKenney and Keen had their own model of the world, focusing on their technical expertise in harnessing computer systems. They emphasized the role of databases and user interface as opposed to model systems.

In real life, **negotiation** is often used in decision making. The preferences of one decision maker have to be reconciled with those of other people. A **legal** style of decision making is based on the legal system of the United States (and elsewhere). The concept is that if each side of the issue is represented by a qualified advocate, the truth is more likely to be identified. We would agree that the multiple views obtained through this approach provide a broader basis for information. Furthermore, drastic mistakes due to failure to consider other views are more likely to be avoided. Both of these styles require consideration of group preference. We note here that there are things computer systems can do to aid decision making in group environments.

The debate about the proper way to view the world is not settled. People with experience in business are comfortable with their approach, because they have become good at it. They can cope with that system. Management scientists are more normative, seeking to provide decision support that proposes to lead to better decisions than the current system. At the beginning of this chapter, we saw that the normative view of modeling is not as appropriate as we might have expected. People's utilities have been found to involve more complexity than the normative model can capture. In addition, although many management science models have proven to be very effective in structured situations (situations where all of the important elements can be included in the model), there are many cases where management science models have *not* proven acceptable.

MULTIPLE OBJECTIVES

Profit has long been viewed as the determining objective of a business. However, as society becomes more complex and as the competitive environment develops, businesses are finding that they need to consider multiple objectives. Although short-run profit remains important, long-run factors, such as market maintenance, product quality, and the development of productive capability, often conflict with measurable short-run profit.

Conflicts

Conflicts are inherent in most interesting decisions. **Profit** has become a valuable concentration point for many decision makers because it has the apparent advantage of providing a measure of worth (Figure 2.3). One of the functions of money, after all, is to provide a scalar value of worth, determined theoretically by the market place. However, profit itself can have multiple aspects. The time value of money is crucial in business. Net present value is a useful concept, because it allows one to convert a stream of cash flow, over a prolonged period, into that stream's net worth today. Given alternative investments, the theory is that people will invest in such a way as to maximize net present value. But we observe that not all people invest in the same things. There is a lack of perfect information in reality. There are also varying levels of risk associated with alternatives. People have different views (and the same person's views change with time and circumstance) relative to risk. **Risk** becomes a second dimension

Figure 2.3
Business objectives.

Profit   Short run cash flow
                    Short run after-tax profit
                    Long run

Risk

Market Development

Capital Replenishment

Labor Relations

Other

for decision making. Furthermore, there are cash flow needs that become important in some circumstances. Historically, insufficient cash reserves have been a major cause for the closing of U.S. businesses. The net present value of an operation may be very attractive, but if there is insufficient cash to reach the payoff 10 years from now, the investment does little good. Furthermore, U.S. income tax laws have played a major role in business decision making, especially when tax law is used as a means to motivate actions desired by the government. Analysis based on after-tax profit may lead to different decisions than analysis based on pretax calculations. So profit itself has a number of dimensions.

There are other factors decision makers need to consider as well. Businesses need **developed markets** to survive. A naive approach would be to spend all of your efforts on developing a super product and wait for the market to come to you. The advertising industry in the United States is enormous. The reason for its existence is that it pays to advertise. There are so many products available that people are not going to expend effort to compare the value of all products on the market. The impact of advertising expenditure is often very difficult to forecast. Yet decision makers must consider the impact of advertising. This often forces decision makers to supplement the objective of profit and consider market development, even if there appears to be a temporary sacrifice to profit. Japanese decision makers seemingly place a higher emphasis on market share. Recent history indicates that this can have a very positive impact on long-range profit.

Capital replenishment is another decision factor that requires consideration of tradeoffs. The greatest short-run profit will normally be obtained by delaying reinvestment in capital equipment. Many U.S. companies have been known to cut back capital investment in order to appear reasonably profitable to investors. If there were perfect knowledge of the risk involved in retaining equipment which is wearing out, or in the productive improvements available from acquiring new technology, profit (in net present terms) would serve as a very good scale of value. But precise measures of such factors are not available. Judgment is required. Replenishment of capital can be viewed as an objective in itself.

Labor policies can also have an impact on long-range profit. In the short run, profit will generally be improved by holding the line on wage rates and risking a high labor turnover. In fact, in some industries, temporary employment is viewed as the norm. There are costs that are not obvious, however, in such a policy. First, there is the training expense involved with a high-turnover environment. The experience of the members of an organization can be one of its most valuable assets. Second, it is difficult for employees to maintain a positive attitude when their experience is that short-run profit is always placed ahead of employee welfare. In addition, innovative ideas are probably best found from those people who are involved with the grass roots of an organization—the work force.

There are a number of objectives that are important to a business. Decision makers need to consider multiple, often conflicting, objectives in many decisions. We will include multiple-objective considerations in some of the modeling chapters of the book, including the analytic hierarchy process presented later in this chapter, and means of multiple-objective analysis presented in Supplemental Chapter 2. Keeney and Raiffa (1976) and Zeleny (1982) provide useful introductions to multiobjective analysis.

STUDIES OF REAL DECISION MAKING

Utility Functions

The measurement and mathematical definition of a utility function is difficult. Grayson (1960) studied the response of an oil wildcatter to a number of different profit values and plotted the values on a graph. The resultant curve was later fit with a mathematical equation, yielding the formula:

$$U(\text{dollars}) = -263.31 + 22.093 \ln(\text{dollars} + 150{,}000)$$

That individual had a risk-averse utility curve (despite the general perception of wildcatters preferring risk). Other studies have confirmed that most people are generally risk averse, but no general utility form has been identified. It has also been found that individuals behave differently for marginal increases in current wealth as opposed to marginal decreases. This would lead to behavior that is inconsistent. The magnitude of value at stake seems to adjust people's behaviors, and sometimes people make intransitive choices. The question is: Are these people irrational or is there more to decision making than current theory recognizes? *Normative* approaches seek to improve the theory. The aim of the normative approach is to develop models that would suggest decisions superior to those of humans. *Descriptive* approaches seek to develop means that reflect how decision makers make choices. The aim of descriptive approaches is not to replace human decision making, but to improve the conditions under which decisions are made, by providing added information.

Management science approaches were developed with the normative idea of providing better solutions to complex problems. Decision support and expert system analyses were developed on a more descriptive idea. The concept of DSS is that models are useful for semistructured problem analysis, but it is recognized that the models are incomplete. Therefore, although decision maker judgment can be aided by computer support, the judgment of the decision maker is still the focus for decision making. Expert systems are artificial intelligence based. Artificial intelligence began as an attempt to capture how humans made decisions, a descriptive approach. For narrow, focused problems, expert systems can harness observed human decision-making behavior.

One of the most complete and current studies of decision making under conditions of risk was conducted by MacCrimmon and Wehrung in the early 1980s.

RISK TREATMENT
MacCrimmon and Wehrung (1986)

MacCrimmon and Wehrung studied the behavior of 509 executives in Canada and the United States relative to their responses to risk. A battery of tests were applied to measure individual and collective behavior. These tests were (1) a series of in-basket situations under time pressure, (2) a series of investment gamble decisions, (3) a series of risk–return tradeoff evaluations, and (4) a series of real money wager opportunities.

The **in-basket** tests involved placing the executives in a situation where they began a new job, reporting to the new position 35 minutes before leaving town. They were given letters involving a threat of a customer lawsuit and an opportunity to form a joint venture with competitor in a new market. Both situations required immediate action.

The responses of the executives were very interesting. First, executives were found to be unwilling to settle for the options given them, and they sought to develop new alternatives. Furthermore, they took steps to adjust the risk of available options. If the risk was based on the actions of other people, they commonly attempted to arrange negotiations. A frequent approach was to gain additional information, as well as time to obtain this information. If a key individual was available, executives often delegated the decision, along with a recommended action.

A wide variety of approaches to risk were identified. The executives tended to be relatively more risk taking when faced with the threat of a lawsuit, and more risk averse in the situation involving the opportunity to form a joint venture with a competitor. They were relatively more risk taking for decisions involving only losses, and relatively more risk averse when the choices involved different degrees of gain. Those managers who were more risk averse demonstrated more actions to modify risks, by gathering additional information, bargaining, delaying, or delegating.

The **investment gamble** test asked the executives what return would be necessary for investment in a personal situation, as well as a business situation. The tradeoff was between the executive's (or company's) current situation versus a gamble with a .5 probability of one-half of current wealth and a .5 probability of some amount of gain specified by the executive.

The executives were found to be strongly risk averse (over 98 percent), both for personal and business investments, where major losses were possible. Some executives refused to invest no matter what the possible gain. Executives who were willing to accept investment gambles were more risk taking for threats than for opportunities. There was more risk aversion in personal gambles than in business gambles.

Two dimensions of risk assessment were identified. There is variance in risk response between personal and business situations, as well as by chance of loss. High chances of loss result in greater risk aversion.

Executives were given a series of **risk–return** choices. This test measured preferences for combinations of rates of return and the probability of success. A risky opportunity was compared one by one with eight other options of varying return and risk. After these pairwise comparisons, executives were asked to rank their preferences for all nine options.

It was found that risk taking was more prevalent than risk aversion in this test. Managers who preferred the riskiest venture showed consistent risk-seeking behavior by rating the safest venture last, and vice versa.

Although executives usually considered more than two attributes, they tended to focus on a single investment attribute, usually the expected return. A number of other executives focused on major gains, but few focused on major losses, and virtually none focused on the payoff variation. A common approach was to eliminate alternatives with too low a chance for significant gain and then to order the remaining options based on the expected return.

A common theoretical approach in financial analysis is the **efficient frontier,** where investment alternatives are measured by the expected return and variance. The efficient frontier is considered to represent rational choices, with the lowest variance for equal return and the highest return for equal variance. A majority of the executives in this study did *not* make tradeoffs between the expected return and variance (80 percent). Of those who did consider both return and variance, many preferred *higher* variation to lower (seeking greater opportunity for spectacular gain).

A great deal of variance between individuals was noted. A preemptive model, where all alternatives without particular characteristics were discarded and more detailed analyses were conducted on the remaining alternatives, was very common.

The last experiment involved **real money wager** tests. Executives were asked to rank their preferences for five options over three different tests. Set A involved a common loss, with varying gains. Set B had a common best outcome, with varying losses (up to $274). Set C had a common probability of the worst outcome (.38).

For set A, the first option involved a $10 gain with certainty. The other options depended on the outcome of five randomly selected stocks, which were evaluated on a particular future day. The options had increasing payoffs contingent upon increasing numbers of favorable stock outcomes. Payoffs for these gambles ranged from $13.20 (requiring only one favorable stock outcome) to $414 (requiring four favorable outcomes). If the required number of favorable outcomes was not realized, the executive had to pay $20.

These gambles involved the risk of real money. A subset of the executives was to be randomly selected to actually pay their wagers. All of the wagers were designed to have an expected payoff of $10.

Executives were found to be highly risk averse in ranking wagers with a common chance of loss. They were generally risk averse when the options had a common loss amount, although some executives were risk taking. When faced with a common gain, they were again risk averse.

Fewer than 50 percent of the executives preferred lower variation in payoffs. This preference for higher variation was most noticeable when the loss amount was constant. Lower variation was preferred when the chance of loss was fixed.

Ten percent of the executives reversed their preference ranking between the sure alternative and a risky alternative when options were presented in different contexts. In all but one case, if the chance of loss was fixed, the sure alternative was preferred, whereas when the gain amount was fixed, the risky alternative was preferred.

These tests indicate a number of useful concepts in describing executive decision making. First, executives are not willing to accept options given to them, but seek to develop new alternatives. They use a variety of means to cope with hard decisions, including collecting more information, gaining control over events, delaying, and delegating responsibility.

Furthermore, individuals demonstrated very different approaches to risk in different situations. They tended to be much more risk averse with their own money than with the organization's money. These executives tended to be more willing to take risks once they were in a risky situation than when they had the option to avoid the situation. This behavior is *not* consistent with the rational model of decision making.

These findings enlighten our concept of how humans make decisions, as well as what computer systems can do to aid this process. We tend to focus on decision, assuming that it is a one-time event, where we can crisply and cleanly apply the decision-making process in a logical and systematic manner. However, real decisions often involve long periods of time. Although a decision can be made, new evidence in the future may change decision maker perception of what the correct decision should be. The decision-making process still holds, but there is often a great deal of backtracking and revision.

Often, real decisions involve the complication of a variety of objectives. Besides seeking increased profit, businesses need to develop markets, maintain cash flow, satisfy and develop the labor force, maintain a positive public relations environment, and a myriad of other objectives. Optimization models provide the best solution to any one objective. However, models can be used to optimize one objective and provide measures of attainment on the others. A variety of techniques are available to aid in reconciling multiple objectives. One means to evaluate solutions when considering multiple objectives is utility (or value function). The following section presents a technique that can aid decision makers in adding more structure to the evaluation step of the decision-making process.

ANALYTIC HIERARCHY PROCESS

We previously discussed the concept of utility as a means of combining a number of attributes. The analytic hierarchy process (Saaty 1980, 1982) has proven to be very useful in assisting decision maker selection. It has been used as a means of aiding multiobjective choice (Zahedi 1986; Shim 1989, for surveys). AHP has also been used in developing a weighted, combined objective function reflecting a number of objectives in mathematical programming applications (Mitchell and Bingham 1986; Bard 1986; Olson, Venkataramanan, and Mote 1986). This approach can convert subjective assessments of relative importance into a linear set of weights, which can then be used to rank alternatives or to serve as an objective function in other techniques.

Description of AHP

AHP has been widely used to convert qualitative factors to quantitative scales, both in analyses involving one decision maker, as well as in group settings. The AHP process consists of a series of stages. The first stage is to develop the hierarchy of the problem. Once the hierarchy is developed, the relative importance is identified through pairwise comparisons of ratio importances. Third, measures are obtained for the relative performance of each available alternative on each element of the hierarchy. AHP provides a means of converting these ratings to an overall performance measure.

In problems involving multiple objectives, AHP can be used either to rank a limited number of alternatives, or to develop an overall linear estimate of utility (a combined objective function). All factors (objectives) of importance can be considered. However, this may result in a large number of factors. Because of psychological theories concerning the limitation of the mind to consider more than some number of factors at one time, a hierarchy of these factors is recommended. The theory is that no more than seven factors can be considered at one time. To deal with problems involving more than seven factors, levels are considered. Factors in a common area of consideration are grouped.

For instance, assume a student is in the job market. A number of objectives are important to the student. Each individual would be expected to have a different set of factors considered important. A list might include:

PAY	Pay per year
PRO	Promotion potential
LOC	Location
TYP	Job type (type of work)
RIS	Risk of job loss
PRE	Job prestige
HOU	Hours per week
VAC	Weeks of work per year
DIS	Distance from home

AHP could be used to rate the relative performance of each specific job on each of these factors or to obtain a formula that could be applied to current and future job offers. If a linear approximation of utility is sought, these factors could be grouped in a hierarchy including reimbursement elements, work-type factors, and personal preferences, as shown in Figure 2.4.

Hierarchy

The next phase in the AHP is to obtain the relative importance of factors within each hierarchical level for each factor (Figure 2.5). This is accomplished through a pairwise comparison based on the ratio of importance of factors.

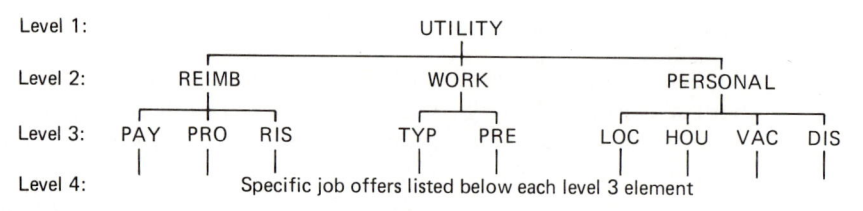

Figure 2.4

1 – Base factor **roughly equivalent** in importance to other factor

3 – Base factor **moderately** more important than other factor

5 – Base factor **essentially** more important than other factor

7 – Base factor relative importance **very strong**

9 – Base factor **overwhelmingly** more important than other factor

Figure 2.5
AHP subjective scale for pairwise comparisons.

Pairwise comparisons are conducted between all elements in that section of the hierarchy. Then a pairwise comparison would be required for overall utility, comparing reimbursement, type of work, and personal factors. Assuming they are ranked in order of greatest preference first, the upper right triangular portion of the matrix presented in Table 2.2 would be completed with the strength of preference given according to the scale exhibited. Even (or fractional) numbers can be used for ratings between the other ratings. In this example, there are three pairwise comparisons at level 1. REIMB is considered essentially more important than WORK, and overwhelmingly more important than PERSONAL. WORK is considered moderately more important than PERSONAL.

This pairwise comparison procedure is carried out for each hierarchical branch. Without considering available job offers, there is one pairwise comparison of three elements at level 1 and three pairwise comparisons of varying numbers of elements at level 2. AHP could be applied at level 4, or a formula measuring each decision alternative's performance on the lowest-level elements (those without subelements) could be applied. This last approach would be equivalent to a linearized utility function.

In order to obtain an accurate relative score for each pairwise comparison table, the square matrix is completed by entering the reciprocal of ratings at the corresponding symmetric locations. For the UTILITY pairwise comparison,

Table 2.2

Level 1:		UTILITY		
		REIMB	WORK	PERSONAL
	REIMB	1	5	9
	WORK		1	3
	PERSONAL			1

see Table 2.3. The relative scale of importance can be obtained by normalizing any column. Of course, because this is subjective, some inconsistency is often encountered.

For each column, the implied relative importance weights can be obtained by dividing each column element by the column total. A number of means exists to obtain the overall weights. Saaty proposes the eigenvector of this matrix. A matrix of pairwise comparisons consists of a series of ratios. A set of ratios for pairwise comparisons involving three elements is shown in Table 2.4. A more robust solution than the average weights can be obtained through the eigenvector. This is a more complex means of solution, demonstrated in Appendix. Normally, a computer performs this calculation.

This approach also provides a measure of consistency, which can be used to validate whether the differences in the ratios obtained were greater than expected at random. The consistency index is a function of (λ_{max}) and the number of elements (n) in the pairwise comparison:

$$CI = \frac{\lambda_{max} - n}{n - 1}$$

Here, ($\lambda_{max} - n$)/($n - 1$) = (3.02906 - 3)(3 - 1) = .01453. Saaty has proposed a cutoff limit of 10 percent of the mean inconsistency for random samples (Figure 2.6). If the consistency index for a pairwise comparison matrix is above this limit (which is a function of the number of factors compared), the pairwise comparisons should be redone with the intent of being more consistent.

The eigenvector for the set of pairwise comparisons given previously is

.75140 REIMB + .17818 WORK + .07042 PERSONAL

with a consistency index of .014 (λ_{max} = 3.029). This implies that REIMB factors have a utility weight of .75140 relative to WORK's .17818 and PER-

Table 2.3

Level 1:		UTILITY		
		REIMB	WORK	PERSONAL
	REIMB	1	5	9
	WORK	.2	1	3
	PERSONAL	.111	.333	1

Table 2.4

Column 1:	.763 REIMB + .153 WORK + .085 PERSONAL
Column 2:	.789 REIMB + .158 WORK + .053 PERSONAL
Column 3:	.692 REIMB + .231 WORK + .077 PERSONAL

Figure 2.6
AHP consistency limits.

MATRIX SIZE	MEAN RANDOM INCONSISTENCY	LIMIT
2	.00	.00
3	.58	.06
4	.90	.09
5	1.12	.11
6	1.24	.12
7	1.32	.13

SONAL's .07042. Of course, this implies no scaling problems in measuring reimbursement, work, and personal factors. The same procedure is used to determine the relative weights of the subelements of the hierarchy. For instance, PAY, PRO, and RIS are compared to determine the relative importance of the subelements of reimbursement. The resulting relative weights are then multiplied by .75140, the relative importance of REIMB, to obtain the weights for the level 3 elements.

As an example of combining levels, assume the pairwise comparison of elements under reimbursement (REIMB) were compared as shown in Table 2.5. The eigenvector for this matrix is

$$.64833 \text{ PAY} + .22965 \text{ PRO} + .12202 \text{ RIS}$$

with a consistency index of .00185 (well below .1). The final utility function implied by the analysis would be

$$a \text{ PAY} + b \text{ PRO} + c \text{ RIS} + d \text{ TYP} + e \text{ PRE} + f \text{ LOC} + g \text{ HOU} + h \text{ VAC} + i \text{ DIS}$$

Given that REIMB reflects .75140 of overall UTILITY and PAY represents .64833 of the contribution to REIMB, the implication is that the relative weights of *a, b,* and *c* would be

Table 2.5

	REIMB		
	PAY	PRO	RIS
PAY	1	3	5
PRO		1	2
RIS			1

$$a = .75140*.64833 = .48716 \qquad b = .17256 \qquad c = .09169$$

The rest of the coefficients would be developed similarly. The total analysis to obtain the formula would involve four pairwise comparison matrixes.

Again, note that in order to be appropriate, measures of each of these nine elements must be on a common scale. This can be accomplished by scoring each alternative (job offer) characteristic on a zero–one scale, with one being the ideal characteristic.

Alternative AHP Calculation

In order to obtain the eigenvector of weights for each pairwise comparison, some computer support is required. This is available on most mainframe computer systems. Furthermore, microcomputer packages exist. Generally, each pairwise comparison would need to be developed, and the resulting matrix entered into whatever format the package being used required. The hierarchy could easily be developed and maintained manually. Expert Choice (Forman) is a package that guides the decision maker through the entire process, to include identifying factors of importance, building the hierarchy, conducting the pairwise comparisons, and calculating the eigenvectors with consistency indexes.

Returning to the first pairwise comparison presented previously (combining REIMB, WORK, and PERSONAL factors into the top level of UTILITY), simple averages could be calculated as well. These would not be as robust as the estimates obtained from eigenvectors, but they would provide workable estimates. The procedure would take the pairwise comparison information, which would fill the upper triangular portion of the matrix, normalize each column, and average the weights across each row (Table 2.6). The full matrix can be normalized by dividing each column element by the column total (Table 2.7). These estimates of the relative weights differ slightly from those obtained from the eigenvector:

Eigenvector weights: .7514 REIMB + .1782 WORK
    + .0704 PERSONAL

Averaged weights: .7482 REIMB + .1804 WORK
    + .0714 PERSONAL

Table 2.6

	Original Information			Full Matrix		
	REIMB	WORK	PERSONAL	REIMB	WORK	PERSONAL
REIMB	1	5	9	1	5	9
WORK		1	3	1/5	1	3
PERSONAL			1	1/9	1/3	1

Table 2.7

when do we want very robust solns?

	Full Matrix			Normalized Matrix			Average of Row
	REIMB	WORK	PERSONAL	REIMB	WORK	PERSONAL	
REIMB	1	5	9	.7627	.7895	.6923	.7482
WORK	.2	1	3	.1525	.1579	.2308	.1804
PERSONAL	.1111	.3333	1	.0847	.0526	.0769	.0714
Total	1.3111	6.3333	13				

Although the eigenvector weights are more robust, the averaged weights are reasonably close and have the advantage that they can be obtained without a special computer code.

Hierarchy Completion

The rest of the hierarchy will be completed (using the eigenvector method), so that the final formula can be seen. Assume the WORK and PERSONAL pairwise comparisons are as shown in Table 2.8. To obtain the final formula weights for TYP and PRE, we recognize from the hierarchy that these elements are subsets of WORK, which was .17818 of total UTILITY. Therefore, the coefficients for TYP and PRE need to be multiplied by .17818. This yields .11879 for TYP and .05939 for PRE. Similar operations are applied to the PERSONAL elements. The final weights for level 3 elements become a formula:

$$
\begin{aligned}
\text{UTILITY} \quad = \quad & .48716 \text{ PAY} \quad && \text{(pay per year)} \\
+ \quad & .17256 \text{ PRO} \quad && \text{(promotion potential)} \\
+ \quad & .09169 \text{ RIS} \quad && \text{(risk of job loss)} \\
+ \quad & .11879 \text{ TYP} \quad && \text{(type of work)} \\
+ \quad & .05939 \text{ PRE} \quad && \text{(job prestige)}
\end{aligned}
$$

Table 2.8

	WORK			PERSONAL			
	TYP	PRE		LOC	HOU	VAC	DIS
TYP	1	2	LOC	1	3	5	2
PRE	.5	1	HOU	.333	1	2	.333
			VAC	.2	.5	1	.2
			DIS	.5	3	5	1
	(one paired comparison)			(six paired comparisons)			
	.66667 TYP + .33333 PRE						
	CI = 0 (perfect)			CI = .021			
			.46495 LOC + .13419 HOU + .07359 VAC + .32727 DIS				

+	.03274 LOC	(location)
+	.00945 HOU	(hours per week)
+	.00518 VAC	(weeks of work per year)
+	.02305 DIS	(distance from home)

This formula yields the relative importance of subjective elements and does not consider scale at all. Therefore, relative pay must be converted to a scale ranging from 0 to 1, as must every other element of the formula, if it is used in this fashion. Furthermore, note that the sign of RIS needs to be considered. If used as a formula, the riskiest job should receive a score close to (if not exactly) 0 in order to work. This formula could be applied to an individual's opportunities. Note that this formula becomes a linear approximation of the decision maker's utility function.

Another way to apply the system would be to utilize a fourth level and apply a pairwise comparison of each job opportunity on each of the nine elements at level 3. This would not require scaling. This approach requires considerably more pairwise comparisons, but is theoretically more appropriate.

There is a third way to apply AHP to the decision. That would be to have just one level, comparing the job opportunities with each other directly. This approach would probably be better, in that a utility function would not need to be developed at all. The analysis would be based on the overall preference of one job to another. However, the hierarchy (developing all the levels) does have benefits in that it forces consideration of those elements that matter. Furthermore, the resulting formula can be applied to offers not yet known.

Each individual would be expected to have an entirely different formula and, in fact, would most likely include a different set of factors considered important. The value of AHP is the ability to custom-design those factors considered important in the decision.

An example using AHP in a group decision context follows. The users of this application cited a number of positive features of this type of model. The model allows combination of quantitative and subjective evaluations of objectives. In addition, a valuable feature in this application was that it made it possible to explain what factors were considered, with a clear description of the relative importances assigned each factor. In this sense, an AHP model can improve organizational communication.

U.S. AIR FORCE ACQUISITION
Cook (1989)

In 1984, the U.S. Congress passed the Competition in Contracting Act, requiring competitive sources for acquisition of government systems. For those cases where it is economically infeasible to develop multiple sources, subsystem and component items are to be competitively obtained by the primary contractor. If the government feels that a prime contractor has not sufficiently developed competitive sources, the government can buy the subsystem or component separately and provide it to the prime contractor. This procedure is referred to as "breaking out."

Systems procurement decision making in the U.S. Air Force is typically the responsibility of the program director, assisted by staff functional experts. Because of the complexity of decisions facing the director, decision making is frequently delegated to middle managers, with final approval authority remaining with the director. Middle managers are expected to follow a rational, optimizing approach in recommending a course of action.

Problem Background

The program director for the F-15 fighter aircraft system is responsible for development, production, deployment, and initial operational support of F-15 aircraft (Figure 2.7). The subcontractor supplying a major radar system had a history of late deliveries, contributing to late deliveries of the aircraft from the prime contractor to the Air Force.

A common method of motivating suppliers is to solicit or develop alternative supply sources (break out the component). The decision alternatives included breaking out the radar system, finding other means of motivating improved performance, or readjusting the expected delivery times. The decision involved many criteria and alternatives. Some of these involved quantitative data, but others required qualitative judgments by functional experts. The decision group included engineers, a contracting officer, logisticians, manufacturing engineers, cost analysts, and a project manager.

The problem was to identify the decision criteria and to synthesize the quantitative and qualitative inputs from group members into an overall recommended course of action. Time was of the essence.

Analysis

The analytic hierarchy process was selected to support this decision after explanation of the technique to key group members. The package Expert Choice was used. The hierarchy developed was that shown in Figure 2.8. Once the hierarchy was constructed, the group developed weights for each of the criteria and subcriteria. The Expert Choice package provides verbal, numerical, and graphical means of developing these weights. The verbal mode (using the adjectives given in the chapter) was preferred by the group over direct numerical scales.

The next step was to compare the alternatives with respect to each of the subcriteria. The same verbal comparison routine was used. The package generates a ranking of alternatives with a numerical score based on the pairwise comparisons provided by the decision-making group. In this case,

COST
  PROC procurement
  OVHD overhead
  MCST management cost
  PENA penalty
MVIS   Management Visibility – ability of
  management to get necessary feedback
  CONF configuration
  SHIF shift
  MCON management control
INTE   Integration problems due to break out
  ACON add configuration
  TSHI technical shift
  INDF interdef
  SOFT software
MEFF   Impact on management effort
  CTRT contracts
  ENGR engineering
  MFGR manufacturing
  LOGT logistics
  PRMG project management
SCHE   Impact on delivery schedule
  LEAD lead time
  OFP
  MONY money impact

Figure 2.7
USAF decision criteria.

the recommended alternative was not to break out (.576 to .424) the radar system from the prime F-15 contract. An overall inconsistency index of .04 was obtained.

Evaluation by Users

The users felt that this system was useful, because an unstructured decision was transformed to one with more structure. This DSS increased group and management confidence in the decision-making process, and therefore the recommendation was adopted with greater confidence. The AHP provides precise definition of factors considered in a manner understood by all participants. Cook felt that this was valuable in building consensus. In the group's opinion, the process took less time than would have been required with an alternative methodology.

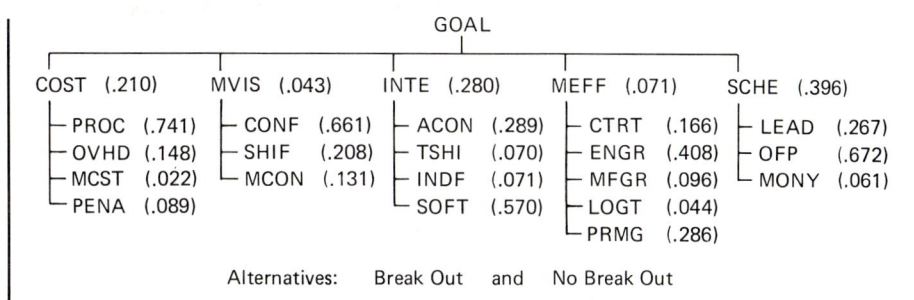

Figure 2.8
USAF decision hierarchy. (From Cook [1989])

In order to present the group's case to higher bureaucratic elements, a word processor (part of the software) was used to explain the rationale at each node of the hierarchy. The final decision of not breaking out the radar system was approved.

This example included a group decision, applying AHP across two levels. Those with decision authority provided the subjective information for the relative weights given to various policy elements, whereas technicians provided assessments of alternative performance on each of these policies. In this group decision environment, many of the policy opinions were shared, a necessary condition for this approach to work.

COMPUTER SYSTEM SUPPORT TO DECISION MAKING

This chapter has primarily dealt with analytic models of decision making. Computer systems can support this process in a variety of ways. Management information systems aid decision making by providing repetitive reports of organizational status, as well as serving as a database for questions. This function can be enhanced through executive information systems, which provide the opportunity to obtain key information on call and the ability to query databases interactively. In either case, many decisions are very easy once the key information relating to the decision is known.

Decision support systems are more directly focused on decision making. Note that in Chapters 4 and 8 we will point out that there are many forms of decision support systems, and models are not a necessary component of a DSS. However, models have proven very valuable in aiding decision maker learning about semistructured problems (and models can even be used to increase problem structure for unstructured situations). The primary intent of decision support systems is to aid decision maker learning about the decision environment and to try to predict the implications of alternative decisions.

Group decision support systems perform a different function, providing a means to find out what the rest of the decision-making group is thinking. Group decision support systems also provide a means to generate better ideas through brainstorming sessions. Consideration of negotiation and legal decision styles are obviously important in group DSS. Group decision making will be discussed in Chapter 3, and GDSS will be discussed in Chapter 9.

Expert systems operate on a different level of problem structure. In Chapter 11 we will see that expert systems can be used to apply standard rules through production rules. This application of expert systems involves taking approved knowledge about a type of problem and automating decisions, given information about specific features of a problem. Expert systems can also be viewed as having the capability of generating new knowledge in complex situations (artificial learning). Most business applications of expert systems involve the first type of application, where key features of a problem can be classified and conclusions programmed based on specific situations. Limiting our comments to production rule expert systems, we can comment on the relative roles of DSSs and expert systems. Whereas DSSs seek to enhance decision maker learning, expert systems provide a means to systematically apply what has been learned. Expert systems are knowledge-based systems, meaning that knowledge is stored (or is capable of being developed) by the system.

An important question is when to switch from one system to the other. For a summary of the potential contributions of MIS, DSS, and EIS to the decision-making process, see Table 1.1 MIS and EIS can provide primary support in identifying problems and gathering initial data (determining a decision needs to be made and finding out facts). DSS support usually is focused on alternative evaluation (learning). When decision makers become convinced that they know how to cope with a problem, expert systems can be harnessed to implement this expertise.

SUMMARY

This chapter addresses business decision making. We began with a discussion of theoretical normative decision models based on utility. We then examined studies of real decision making. We found that there are a number of factors involved in real decision making that place the normative approach in question.

A number of decision-making approaches are available. One of the most popular alternatives to the rational normative model is reliance upon decision maker judgment. This style of decision making has been in existence since business first began. Humans are given the burden of responsibility. They are also free to choose whatever they want (as long as they do not report to anyone), or whatever their superiors will allow them to do. If they report to superiors or if the cooperation of others is required, the ability to convince others of the soundness of their decisions becomes important.

Another approach is to rely upon negotiating. Here, there is a need to convince others who have a stake in the decision, as well as the ability to influence how the decision is made. Again, the ability to convince others is important. In this case, however, the situation is more complex, because there may be a number of other parties. Communicating arguments is important when others are involved in decisions. Analysis from a DSS can also support this approach, either by identifying differences in analysis due to different assumptions or as a means to better communicate ideas.

Computer systems should improve business decision making in a number of ways. Management information systems provide a source for official data collected on a regular basis. These can aid the decision-making process both in identifying decisions needing to be made, as well as in monitoring their results. Databases collecting crucial information can be maintained, within an MIS or on personal systems. Decision support systems provide supplemental information storage, as well as quick access to specific information and models for the evaluation of alternatives. Expert systems can be applied to more structured problem areas, implementing decisions on a broad scale.

Advancements in computer technology should expand the ability of decision makers to cope with decision making. They should be able to identify crises, problems, and opportunities quicker, although human imagination will still be required. Computers dramatically enhance the availability of and speed access to key information. Dramatic improvement in the ability to analyze alternatives, as well as communicate ideas, is now available. Electronic communication provides speed. Computer graphics, displays, and access to data tables improve the ability to present the basis for a decision, making it easier to convince others of the soundness (or easier to identify unsoundness) of decisions.

REFERENCES

Bunn, D. W. 1984. *Applied decision analysis.* New York: McGraw-Hill.

Grayson, C. J. 1960. *Decision under uncertainty: Drilling decisions by oil and gas operators.* Boston: Harvard Business School.

Kahneman, D., and A. Tversky. 1979. Prospect theory: An analysis of decision under risk. *Econometrica* 47:263–91.

Keeney, R.L., and H. Raiffa. 1976. *Decisions with multiple objectives: Preferences and value tradeoffs.* New York: John Wiley & Sons.

MacCrimmon, K. R., and D. A. Wehrung. 1986. *Taking risks: The management of uncertainty.* New York: Free Press.

McKenney, J. L., and P. G. W. Keen. 1974. How managers' minds work. *Harvard Business Rev.* 52 (3):79–90.

Murray, M. 1986. *Decisions: A comparative critique.* Marshfield, MA: Pitman.

Taylor, A. 1991. *Applied decision analysis.* Boston: PWS-Kent.

Zeleny, M. 1982. *Multiple criteria decision making.* New York: McGraw-Hill.

AHP

Bard, J. F. 1986. A multiobjective methodology for selecting subsystem automation options. *Management Sci.* 32:1628–41.

Cook, C. R. 1989. Decision support for the U.S. Air Force: Component breakout—a case history. In *DSS-89: Transactions of the Ninth International Conference on Decision Support Systems,* ed. G.R. Widmeyer, 259–64. Providence, RI: Institute of Management Sciences.

Forman, E. EXPERT CHOICE. McLean, VA: Decision Support Software, Inc.

Mitchell, K. H., and G. Bingham. 1986. Maximizing the benefits of Canadian Forces equipment overhaul programs using multi-objective optimization. *INFOR* 24:251–64.

Olson, D. L., M. Venkataramanan, and J. Mote. 1986. A technique using analytical hierarchy process in multiobjective planning models. *Socio-Economic Planning Sci.* 20:361–68.

Saaty, T. L. 1980. *The analytic hierarchy process.* New York: McGraw-Hill.

Saaty, T. L. 1982. *Decision making for leaders.* Belmont, CA: Van Nostrand–Reinhold.

Shim, J. P. 1989. Bibliographic research on the analytic hierarchy process (AHP). *Socio-Economic Planning Sci.* 23:161–67.

Zahedi, F. 1986. The analytic hierarchy process—a survey of the method and its applications. *Interfaces* 16 (4):96–108.

PROJECT IDEAS

Describe your mental model of the education process at your school. What decisions do you as a student have relative to obtaining your degree? What is your expected outcome of making different choices?

Describe your mental model of the job market. What decisions do you face in seeking employment opportunities? Describe the expected outcomes associated with each choice.

What is your view of a prospective employer's model of the job market? Organizations consist of many people. What kinds of mental models do interviewers seem to have? Do you expect these to coincide with the rest of the organization?

Students can seek to develop their own utility functions by identifying their indifference curves between return and risk. By plotting these indifference points, they can determine if they are consistent, as well as risk averse, risk neutral, or risk seeking.

The same indifference points can be developed for the tradeoff between any two objectives of importance.

Place yourself in the position of being in the job market. Identify factors and subfactors you feel are important in your personal opinion. Real stuff. The only requirement is that you list factors in more than one level. Assume you have the following opportunities. You are welcome to ask for further details regarding characteristics.

A. Database technician—major petroleum company—Houston, TX
    $29,000 per year, high promotion potential
    high risk of job loss
    8–5 5 days per week 50 weeks per year

B. Computer consultant—on campus—local community
    $18,000 per year, slow promotion potential
    low risk of job loss
    8–5 5 days per week 48 weeks per year

C. Management trainee—EDS—Flint, MI
    $26,000 per year, fast promotion potential
    high risk of job loss
    7–6 5 days per week 50 weeks per year

D. Beginning information systems analyst—major firm—Dallas, TX
    $30,000 per year, moderate promotion potential
    moderate risk of job loss
    8–5 5 days per week 50 weeks per year, no overtime

E. Information systems analyst—small firm—St. Louis, MO
    $29,000 per year, moderate promotion potential
    moderate risk of job loss
    7–6 5 days per week 50 weeks per year, lots of unpaid overtime

F. Software development—small firm—Phoenix, AZ
    $31,000 per year, moderate promotion potential
    moderate risk of job loss
    9–6 5 days per week 50 weeks per year, some unpaid overtime

G. Maintenance programming—oil company—Houston, TX
    $27,000 per year, slow promotion potential
    moderate risk of job loss
    8–5 5 days per week 50 weeks per year, all overtime paid

H. Independent (self-employed) computer consultant—Houston, TX
    Unknown pay, but pay *may* average $100/hour
    Should average 70 hours/month, 10 months/year
    Might only be 40 hours/month, could be 120 hours/month

This exercise is to develop a formula with AHP. You do not need to turn it in at this time (wait until you get the test batch of jobs).

Develop your AHP formula.

You have developed your formula for job selection. Please test your formula on the following jobs:

A. Data processing specialist—bank in College Station
   $18,000 per year, slow promotion potential
   medium risk of job loss
   8–5 5 days per week 50 weeks per year

B. Computer consultant—on campus—local community
   $20,000 per year, slow promotion potential
   low risk of job loss
   8–5 5 days per week 48 weeks per year

C. Freelance computer consultant—Brazos County, TX
   Unknown pay—but business *may* average $100/hour
   50 hours/month—probably 11 months/year
   could be 10 hours/month, could be 100 hours/month

D. Beginning information systems analyst—Big 8 firm—Dallas, TX
   $30,000 per year, moderate promotion potential
   high risk of job loss
   7–6 5 days per week 50 weeks per year, lots of paid overtime

E. Software sales—small international firm—Houston, TX
   $28,000 per year, high promotion potential
   moderate risk of job loss
   7–6 5 days per week 50 weeks per year, lots of unpaid overtime

F. Beginning information systems analyst—major firm—Fresno, CA
   $35,000 per year, moderate promotion potential
   moderate risk of job loss
   9–6 5 days per week 50 weeks per year, all overtime paid

G. Maintenance programming—oil company—New Orleans, LA
   $28,000 per year, slow promotion potential
   moderate risk of job loss
   8–5 5 days per week 50 weeks per year, all overtime paid

1. Score these jobs according to the scale you developed for the assignment and apply the formula developed in the assignment to these jobs.

2. *Using your judgment,* list your preference for these seven jobs.

Eigenvalue Calculation

e·ÿr (cC), },}, ÿρου=TΛυε)

The solution for this matrix associated with the maximum eigenvalue can be obtained by subtracting λ times the identity matrix from the pairwise comparison matrix, setting this equal to 0, and solving for λ. There will be n λ values that would satisfy this restriction (where n is the number of elements in the matrix). The maximum λ value is sought and is referred to as $λ_{max}$.

EIGENVALUE DEVELOPMENT

Given a matrix of pairwise comparison ratios **A**:

$$\mathbf{A} = \begin{bmatrix} w_1/w_1 & w_1/w_2 & w_1/w_3 \\ w_2/w_1 & w_2/w_2 & w_2/w_3 \\ w_3/w_1 & w_3/w_2 & w_3/w_3 \end{bmatrix} = \begin{bmatrix} 1 & 5 & 9 \\ .2 & 1 & 3 \\ 1/9 & 1/3 & 1 \end{bmatrix}$$

Solve $\mathbf{A} - λ\mathbf{I} = 0$ for λ:

$$\begin{bmatrix} 1 & 5 & 9 \\ .2 & 1 & 3 \\ 1/9 & 1/3 & 1 \end{bmatrix} + \begin{bmatrix} -λ & 0 & 0 \\ 0 & -λ & 0 \\ 0 & 0 & -λ \end{bmatrix} = \begin{bmatrix} 1-λ & 5 & 9 \\ .2 & 1-λ & 3 \\ 1/9 & 1/3 & 1-λ \end{bmatrix} = 0$$

The equations are

$$-2.02906w_1 + 5w_2 + 9w_3 = 0$$
$$.2w_1 - 2.02906w_2 + 3w_3 = 0$$
$$w_1 + w_2 + w_3 = 0$$

The solution is

$$w_1 = .751405$$
$$w_2 = .178178$$
$$w_3 = .070417$$

In this case, solution of the matrix yields

$$(1 - \lambda)^3 + 5/3 + .6 - 3(1 - \lambda) = 0$$

which simplifies to $3\lambda^2 - \lambda^3 = -.26667$. By computer search, the solution of this equation results in

$$\lambda_{max} = 3.02906$$

$$\lambda = -.014532 + .29635 \sqrt{-1}$$

$$\lambda = -.014532 - .29635 \sqrt{-1}$$

To obtain the eigenvector associated with λ_{max}, solve the equations implied in the table of consistency limits, along with the restriction that the sum of the weights adds to 1.

CHAPTER THREE

Organizational Decision Making

The previous chapter described various views of how individual people make decisions. This chapter discusses views of how decisions are made in organizations and how mathematical models can be developed to support the decision-making process.

This chapter will provide:

- A view of decision making in business organizations
- Different kinds of management science models
- How models can aid in problem identification (solution development)
- How models can aid evaluation of alternative solutions (solution selection)
- A brief description of cognitive maps

The organizational factors involved in decision making are gaining in importance. Today, it is not enough to make up one's own mind. The rest of the organization, superiors and subordinates, are almost invariably involved in major business decisions. This presents the opportunity for obtaining multiple views of decision factors, which should have a positive impact on decision quality. It also presents the requirement for additional time and analysis to make decisions.

This chapter begins with a discussion of the findings of Mintzberg, Raisinghani, and Theoret, who studied how organizations actually made critical strategic decisions in 26 different cases. Management science modeling to aid decision making is discussed. Next, a study by Pounds is presented to show how important mental models are in the decision-making process. Finally, cognitive mapping is presented as a technique to represent mental models in a form that makes them computerizable.

ORGANIZATIONAL DECISION-MAKING PROCESSES
Mintzberg, Raisinghani, and Theoret (1976)

This group conducted a field study of 25 strategic decision-making processes. They examined these processes over time, seeking to identify the specific steps involved in each decision. The decisions varied, including selection of new jet aircraft by an airline and the dismissal of a star announcer by a radio station. The aim of the study was to identify the structure of strategic decision making. The steps identified were synthesized to provide a framework of the strategic decision-making process.

There were six manufacturing firms, nine service firms, five quasi-governmental institutions, and five government agencies studied. The life of the decision-making process varied from less than one year to over four years.

The study found that strategic decision making involves novelty, complexity, and openendedness. Organizations were found to begin the process with little understanding of the decision situation and only vague ideas of appropriate solutions. The process was recursive, as new information was identified.

Types of Decision Stimuli

Decisions were found to have been triggered by a variety of stimuli. Some decisions were triggered by **opportunity.** Opportunity decisions were initiated on a voluntary basis, to improve an already satisfactory situation. **Problem** decisions involved some pressure due to an unsatisfactory situation, but not severe pressure. **Crisis** decisions were made in response to intense pressure. It was found that a particular decision-making process could shift from one category to another with time. Ignored opportunities could later emerge as problems, or even crises. A crisis could be converted to a problem through a temporary solution. Furthermore, crises and problems could be used as opportunities to develop innovative solutions.

Types of Solutions

Solutions were identified in a variety of ways. Some solutions were **given,** fully developed, at the start of the process. Other solutions were found **ready made,** fully developed, during the process. An example of this type of solution would be the purchase of a commercial product. **Custom-made** solutions were developed specifically for the decision. An example would be design of a new headquarters building. Ready-made and custom-made features were found combined in **modified** solutions, such as adapting equipment for a specific decision.

Elements of the Strategic Decision-Making Process

Based on the results of these studies, the decision-making process was categorized to include the routines and subroutines given in Figure 3.1.

IDENTIFICATION PHASE
    Decision Recognition Routine
    Diagnosis Routine

DEVELOPMENT PHASE
    Search Routine
    Design Routine

SELECTION PHASE
    Screen Routine
    Evaluation–Choice Routine
    Authorization Routine

SUPPORTING ROUTINES
    Decision Control Routines
    Decision Communication Routines
    Political Routines

DYNAMIC FACTORS
    Interrupts
    Scheduling Delays
    Feedback Delays
    Timing Delays and Speedups
    Comprehension Cycles
    Failure Recycles

Figure 3.1
Strategic decision process. (Based on Mintzberg, Raisinghani, and Theoret [1976]). Published in *Administrative Science Quarterly* Vol. 21, No. 2 by permission of *Administrative Science Quarterly,* © 1976.)

Identification Phase
The problem identification stage in the decision-making process discussed in Chapter 1 is the same as the decision recognition routine, and the data collection stage presented in Chapter 1 is the same as the diagnosis routine.

Decision Recognition Routine
Problems and opportunities must be identified among streams of data, usually ambiguous, mostly verbal, that decision makers receive. A common means of identification of a problem is to notice the differences between expected states and actual (or perceived) states. Common sources for this information include trends, standards, expectations of people, and theoretical models.

At least 18 of these studies involved multiple stimuli, from both inside and outside of the organization. This can involve a long period of development. In one case it took 25 years before a stronger signal triggered action. Sometimes a problem or opportunity can be recognized by one individual, but he or she may not be in a position to do anything about it until a significant amount of time passes. This case was found six times in the study. Crises, on the other hand, are clearly identifiable. Problems generally require multiple stimuli before action is triggered. One reason for this is that decision makers may be reluctant to act until a viable solution to the problem is identified.

Diagnosis Routine

Once a problem or opportunity has been recognized, the next step is to diagnose what is causing the problem or crisis, or the best means to take advantage of an opportunity. A common step (18 of the cases studied) was to tap existing information channels, as well as to seek additional information, in order to define issues. A formal approach to diagnosis is to create an investigating committee or task force or to hire consultants to analyze an issue. This occurred in 14 of the 25 cases. Diagnosis can also be more informal. Opportunities may require less investigation, whereas crises involve more time pressure.

The Development Phase

The two routines in this phase are very similar to the alternative generation and alternative evaluation stages of the decision-making process presented in Chapter 1. There is not, however, a precise match. Mintzberg, Raisinghani, and Theoret found that the greatest amount of decision-making resources were consumed during this phase. In only three cases did organizations begin with a fully developed solution, and in one of those it was necessary to redesign an alternative in order to gain organizational acceptance.

Search Routine

Search routines are efforts to find ready-made solutions. A variety of sources for these solutions were identified. **Memory** search scans human or documented organizational memory for solutions. This approach would seek similar situations and remember what was done before. **Passive** search waits for unsolicited alternatives to appear. **Trap** search involves seeking out solutions, such as requesting proposals from suppliers. **Active** search directly attempts to develop new solutions.

There seemed to be a standard approach, first trying to tap memory and passive search, and if that was not successful, to proceed to convenient forms of trap search. If these more familiar and less strenuous means do not provide solutions, custom design of solutions is often attempted.

Design Routine

Twenty of the twenty-five cases involved designed solutions. Some of these were custom made, and others were modifications of alternative solutions identified through the search routine. Custom-made solutions are usually complex and iterative. A common approach was to begin with some vague idea of an ideal solution, followed by more focused efforts to define the solution and its impact more completely. There was a great deal of recycling involved.

In the 20 cases using the design routine, 63 instances of design activities were identified. Those organizations that underwent this involved procedure tended *not* to make a selection from alternatives, but rather to adopt the custom-made solution. On the other hand, those organizations relying upon ready-made solutions typically selected an alternative from among a number of alternatives or modified solutions.

Mintzberg, Raisinghani, and Theoret noted the high cost of generating custom-made solutions and the relatively inexpensive cost of obtaining solutions identified through search. The development of computer resources through decision support systems may make the cost of custom-designed solutions much less and therefore lead to an increased use of design routines, as well as comparison of more alternatives.

Selection Phase

This phase includes the evaluation and decision steps in the decision-making process presented previously. We generally think of a clear-cut moment in time when a decision is made, once and for all. However, it was found that decisions were often factored into subdecisions, each requiring at least one selection step. This resulted in blending the selection phase with the development phase.

Normative literature views the selection phase in terms of sequentially determining criteria for choice, evaluating consequences of alternatives on each criterion, and making a decision. Mintzberg, Raisinghani, and Theoret found little clear-cut delineation of these routines. Therefore, three routines were described.

Screen Routine

If the search routine generates more alternatives than can be thoroughly evaluated, the screen routine is often invoked. This routine eliminates infeasible or inappropriate solution alternatives. This operation matches the behavior MacCrimmon and Wehrung found among many executives.

Little evidence of screening was found in the 25 cases. Mintzberg, Raisinghani, and Theoret attributed this to screening being an implicit part of searching. Many ready-made alternatives in the development phase were probably discarded because of screening.

Evaluation–Choice Routine

Evaluation and choice use judgment, bargaining, and analysis. Judgment involves the decision maker making a choice that is not, and possibly cannot be, explained. Bargaining involves group decision makers with conflicting objectives, each exercising his or her own judgment. Analysis involves objective evaluation, usually by technocrats, followed by managerial choice by judgment or bargaining.

Judgment was found to be the most common method, probably because it is fast, convenient, and less stressful than the others. Bargaining appeared in over one-half of the cases, typically when outside control or participation existed and when there were higher degrees of disagreement. Normative literature emphasizes the analytic mode. Little use of the analytic mode was found, and when it was used, it tended to be in larger organizations or where there were technical aspects to the decision.

Mintzberg, Raisinghani, and Theoret noted that the literature tends to focus on the evaluation–choice routine in decision making. They did *not* find nearly as much effort applied to this routine in the cases studied. When custom-made solutions were developed, evaluation seemed to be more of an official ratification of the solution, which was really determined during the design and diagnosis phases.

These findings amplify our previous discussion of the importance of alternative methods of evaluation to the normative theoretical approach. Strategic decisions often involve complex factors, which cannot totally be captured with analytic models. Furthermore, when analytic models are applied, decision makers should not be expected to adopt their suggestions unless the assumptions of the models, as well as how the models work, is understood. Current computer technology provides added power for decision makers to apply analytic techniques. But they still should not blindly adopt results from such models.

Authorization Routine

Decisions require authorization when the individual making the choice does not have the authority to commit the organization to action. Authorization was required in 14 of the 25 cases. Typically, authorization was a yes/no answer. If a level of the hierarchy authorizes a decision, further authorization is often required. On the other hand, authorization refusal led either to abandonment or revision of the decision. In a few cases, conditional authorization was obtained, leading to recycling to the development phase.

The need for clear communications is emphasized when authorization is required. Decision support systems can be used to clearly communicate the need for a decision, alternatives considered, and the basis for the alternative selected. Expert systems also have the ability to explain the logical path leading to a specific decision.

Supporting Routines

Mintzberg, Raisinghani, and Theoret identified three additional routines. Decision control routines guide the decision-making process. Communication routines provide means of exchanging information. Political routines enable decisions to be implemented. Although Mintzberg, Raisinghani, and

Theoret did not consider the implementation and monitoring phases, these routines serve much of the same purposes. The authorization, communication, and political routines address much the same activity as the implementation stage of the decision-making process. The backtracking common to all 25 cases emphasizes the need to monitor the results of implementing any decision.

Decision Control Routines

When operating within organizations, it is necessary to guide the decision-making process. **Decision planning** refers to actions involving scheduling the progress to solution, identifying development strategy, and estimating the resources a decision maker is willing to commit to obtain the desired solution. Constraints to the decision may be imposed, and an image of the ideal solution can be developed. **Switching** refers to the attention the decision maker gives to the next step in the process, to include choosing appropriate routines, such as diagnosis or search. These control routines are generally informal and flexible. Monitoring results is included in this class of activity.

Decision Communication Routines

Communication is pervasive in organizational decision making. The **exploration** routine involves scanning for information and passive review of unsolicited alternatives. The **investigation** routine involves focused search and research for special-purpose information. This routine was found most active during the development and diagnosis phases. **Dissemination** involves informing other members of the organization of the various phases of the decision-making process. It was found that dissemination was stronger for larger organizations and in later stages of the strategic decision-making process.

Political Routines

In order to implement most decisions, it is necessary to obtain the cooperation of others. The **bargaining** routine occurs among those who have some control over choices. This can involve convincing others that a decision is called for. Bargaining often resulted in longer decision-making processes. Sometimes organizations tried to preempt political resistance by disseminating information or by inviting participation in solution development.

Dynamic Factors

There were a number of factors identified which influenced the strategic decision-making process, by delaying, stopping, or restarting. **Interrupts** were found in 15 of the 25 cases. Unexpected constraints were encountered, forcing return to earlier phases. An example of this was the expropriation of a newly purchased plant. Sixteen of the cases involved political encounters. In one case, civic groups used legal action to block an airport runway. In six cases, unexpected new options became available. Interrupts were often found to lead to further interrupts.

Scheduling delays were often encountered. As evidence of this, only eight of the cases had a reported duration of less than one year. **Feedback delays** involve decision makers waiting for the results of previous actions, again leading to longer decision-making processes. **Timing delays and speedups** often result when managers take advantage of special circumstances or delay to await stronger support or better conditions for decision implementation.

Comprehension cycles describe the circular, rather than linear, progress of most strategic decisions. Some of the cycling between routines was due to added comprehension on the part of the decision maker. The most complex and novel strategic decisions seemed to involve the most cycling. Evidence of cycling was found in all cases, most often in the selection phase. **Failure recycles** occurred when no acceptable solution was identified. A variety of responses to this failure were found, which included delaying, lowering requirements, or appealing to a higher authority. The most common response, however, was to recycle back to the development phase.

This study highlighted the dynamic nature of real decision making. The salient feature seems to be that decisions involved a great deal of forward progress, along with backtracking in light of new circumstances. It seems mistaken to believe that once a decision is made, the problem has been solved.

The study also verified to at least some degree the decision-making process presented in Chapter 1. However, that process should be viewed as flexible. In these 25 cases, there was no common path from identification of a problem to decision and implementation. Furthermore, the decision-making process we presented in Chapter 1 focuses more on the use of decision support systems in evaluation of alternatives. Computer developments along with enhanced computer usability make it possible to do more than was reasonable when the Mintzberg study was conducted.

THE MANAGEMENT SCIENCE APPROACH

Modeling is creating an abstract view of reality. There are two distinct types of modeling important in aiding decisions with computers. Each decision maker has a **mental model** of his or her business environment. This mental model is the decision maker's theory of what makes the business function better or worse. This parallels a scientist's theory to make sense of his or her field. There are also many standard **management science models** that have proven to be effective in mathematically describing some business situations. When there is a very good fit between a mathematical model and the real problem, the problem is said to be highly **structured.** These mathematical models provide a means of experimenting with abstract solutions before plunging ahead and adopting the solution untested. Examples of these models include regression (identification of empirical relationships), simulation or spreadsheets (providing a mathematical means of experimenting on problems with a variety of difficult assumptions), and optimization models (providing a means to generate a very good alternative solution when more rigorous assumptions can be met).

The management science approach to organizational decision making seeks to develop explicit mathematical models of organizational problems so that they can be scientifically analyzed, at least insofar as possible. Certainly not all organizational problems can be formulated mathematically, but when a formal model can be developed, the analysis is usually more rigorous and exacting than would otherwise be the case. This approach began as an interdisciplinary effort, combining expertise in a variety of fields to deal with operational problems. Out of those efforts, a number of useful, model-based, techniques were developed.

Initial applications focused on operational problems. An example was the problem of waiting times when using telephone systems. Theories of mathematical relationships of telephone waiting lines were published prior to 1910. In the 1930s, the problem of locating radar stations to detect incoming German aircraft led to systematic study of location analysis. Assigning transportation vehicles to deliver goods from a variety of sources to a variety of destinations was an early problem leading to linear programming modeling. Although initial focus was on problems, as highly useful techniques were developed, the focus often shifted to refining these techniques and seeking additional applications.

Sometimes the fit between a model and reality is less than perfect. The idea of decision support system models is to combine a mathematical model where some of the assumptions are not exactly correct, or where some of the model assumptions are not precisely appropriate, with human decision maker judgment. The purpose of decision support systems and executive information systems is to give decision makers computerized tools to aid in the development and improvement of the decision maker's mental models of cause and effect. This can be done by providing a variety of data quickly and accurately, as well as by applying mathematical models. Expert systems usually incorporate complex mental models of some procedure that is not well understood, but whose results are well respected. Part of the expert system process is to investigate these mental models thoroughly, allowing them to be structured.

A number of these mathematical model types have been found to be very useful in aiding decision making in business. If a model can be built including all the truly important factors bearing on a problem and if accurate data is used in this model, the view is that a more scientific approach will lead to better long-run results.

Types of Management Science Models Available

The management science approach seeks to be systematic. One approach to problems is to tap experience. If a modeling approach worked in the past, there is a natural tendency for a systematic individual to apply similar approaches to new problems. This clearly has advantages over reinventing the wheel, or starting each analysis from scratch. A catalog (or tool chest) of available modeling types has been developed.

Figure 3.2 provides a listing of broad categories of management science techniques, along with some of the problem applications where these techniques have been found to be successful. The management science approach is to become technically skilled in the techniques available and then apply the appropriate technique when a problem is encountered. There is an obvious bias when a management scientist is very good at a particular technique. The first inclination is to view every problem as suitably analyzed by that technique.

Although mathematical models have proven highly useful, a general rule is that the more powerful the technique, the more rigid the assumptions of the technique. Whereas in well-structured problems, the appropriateness of assumptions can often be accepted, in less structured environments, model results have to be interpreted more as possibilities than as likelihoods. In highly unstructured environments, human mental theories (or conceptual models) are the only means of coping.

OPTIMIZATION
    Linear Programming   Resource allocation
                                      Distribution systems
    Dynamic Programming   Routing
    Integer, nonlinear, multiobjective, network flow

    Economic Order Quantity   Inventory
    Critical Path Method   Project scheduling

PROBABILISTIC
    Forecasting
    Simulation   Production flow
    Queuing Analysis   Waiting lines
    Markov Analysis   State flows
    Decision Analysis   Alternative evaluation

OTHER
    Game Theory   Competitive decisions

Figure 3.2
Management science model types.

MODELS APPLIED TO AID DECISION MAKING

The first impression of a model is a specific formulation appropriate to a particular technique, such as a linear programming model. McKenney and Keen (see Chapter 2) expanded that view to include any mental view of business operations important to a specific decision maker. Both types of models can be used to enable the decision maker to more effectively use the decision-making process.

Model Aid in the Problem Identification Phase

Failures to recognize problems are often easy to identify. These failures sometimes make headlines, such as passenger airplane engine or wing defects, bank and savings and loan foreclosures, and loss of market to foreign automobile manufacturers.

However, problem recognition is not nearly as simple as after-the-fact analyses might indicate. Nuclear power plants were started because, at the time, they seemed like low-cost, low-pollution alternatives. A decade later, many of these decisions do not look as good, because of cost overruns, heightened concern about radiation, and lower-cost alternatives.

After the fact, many opportunities can be seen to have been missed. If your great grandfather had had a better mental model of the future and had obtained the land in what now is the middle of Los Angeles, you would probably have a better life-style today. We all can think of things we did in the past that we could have done better. All decisions can be criticized. Perfect decision making does not exist and never will. However, we can seek ways to improve our decision making. This improvement will not lead to the best decision every time, but hopefully we could all improve our averages.

Bonge (1972) viewed failure to attain goals or to realize opportunities as leading to a state of organizational disequilibrium. Perception of this disequilibrium is necessary before a decision-making and problem-solving process can begin. Symptoms of this disequilibrium include low profits, backlogs of orders, employee turnover, and other indicators of performance worse than desired. Accurate diagnosis, however, requires that decision makers be able to filter out cases where no real problem exists from those where a fundamental problem looms. Just because profits this month are less than expected does not mean a manager should apply for a new job. Diagnosing the cause is required before a decision is made. Possibly the problem is due to a change in accounting methods. Possibly a special situation arose, and the organization may actually be doing quite well. If you buy stocks, you will rarely find your purchases to increase in value every day. If your stock drops in value, it could be because the entire stock market declined that day. It could be because of random variation, with no long-run implications at all. On the other hand, maybe the company is going bankrupt or losing its market. Maybe the entire stock market will collapse. The point is, identification of a problem is a very challenging and ongoing process. Few veterans of the stock market spend their gains the day they obtain them. There is a lot of variation expected.

Mental models play an important role in how we perceive the need to make decisions. We all have views of the world based on our experience and education. Mental models of this type are important in business, because they represent how decision makers identify the performance of the organization. When the need to make improvements is perceived, the need for a decision is triggered. Pounds (1969) presented a view of the role of models in problem identification.

PROBLEM INDENTIFICATION
Pounds (1969)

Contemporary management involves greater volume of decisions, as well as greater complexity. Analysis usually focuses on structuring and solving problems that arise. Sometimes the sources of problems are not recognized. Managers are responsible for identifying potential problems. Tradeoffs must constantly be made relative to the cost of further analyses with the potential return of these analyses.

The critical part of management is to identify problems, assign problem priorities, and allocate scarce resources to problems. These tasks often must be performed without benefit of a well-defined body of theory.

Pounds interviewed, observed, and interrogated 52 executives in a decentralized operating division of a large, technically based corporation. In the initial phase, executives were asked to describe the problems they faced and the processes by which they became aware of these problems. The second phase was observation of meetings, during which problems were identified, discussed, and sometimes solved. The third phase consisted of investigations of the source and disposition of several specific problems. In the final phase, each executive who participated in the study completed a questionnaire.

Pounds found the process of management difficult to describe in mathematical form. Management was viewed as the sequential execution of elementary activities. Elements of managerial activity were labeled *operators*, which transformed a set of input variables into a set of output variables according to some predetermined plan.

Problems were defined as occasions where there was a difference between some existing situation and the desired situation. Operators therefore could be used to solve problems. A decision was interpreted as being triggered by identification of a difference. Problem solving was interpreted as selecting operators to reduce differences.

Models were defined as mental constructs of the desired situation, which was compared with the existing situation. Recent past history was found to be a commonly used basis for a model. By their nature, models are simplifications. Examples of models aiding in problem identification were evaluations such as:

Why is inventory drifting out of line?

Why is our reject rate so high this week?

Why are so many deliveries late?

How can absenteeism be reduced?

Why is our safety record suddenly so good?

These models tended to be mental, without formal expression. However, these models were found to be strongly supported by routine reports, such as monthly profit-and-loss statements, weekly sales reports, daily reports of late deliveries, semiannual inventories, and so on. This information flows to the manager in a steady stream, with little meaning unless there is a historical reference.

Forty-two of fifty-two executives agreed with the statement that "most improvements come from correcting unsatisfactory situations," and most defined unsatisfactory situations as departures from historically established models of performance. Favorable departures from historical models were used to modify expectations within the model, as opposed to identification of a problem.

Historical models were also used extensively to devise future plans, which were converted into budget objectives. These budget objectives, in turn, became the bases for future models. **Planning models** were built by developing expectations over a long time horizon, typically five years. These projected models were used to evaluate managerial performances, as well as for other purposes. However, these planning models were not used to identify problems. Managers were given latitude to identify problems as they chose. Success was defined relative to the predictions of the planning model. Therefore, as you might expect, planning models tended to represent the minimum performance the manager could reasonably expect to attain. In turn, superiors could adjust planning models to gain further assurance of future success.

Other people's models were found to be important to decision makers as well. Higher-level managers may lack information, creating a problem for their subordinates. Employees may make personnel requests leading to problems. Organization structure exists to channel problems identified by its various members to individuals qualified to solve them.

Pounds found that these models explained most of the managers' activities. When asked to specify current problems, most managers mentioned five to eight problems. Later, each manager was asked to describe his or her activities for the previous week. These activities were all found to be related to the problems previously described.

Extraorganizational models come from outside the organization. Customers provide feedback on organizational performance relative to competitors. Trade journals report new practices. Many organizations provide managers with reports comparing the manager's group performance with those of similar groups. All of these sources provide additional means of evaluating comparative performance.

When extraorganizational models are used, their validity must be established. Other organizations and groups face different conditions of various types. Before jumping to conclusions, these other conditions must be considered.

Scientific models are available in the physical and social sciences, based on relatively precise relationships. These require little judgment based on experience. Water can be counted on boiling at 100 degrees centigrade at normal pressure. The lessons learned by scientists can be applied with high degrees of confidence.

Attempts continue to develop scientific models of business problem environments. This activity is a search for sounder mental models on an individual basis, and a scientific approach to management on a professional basis. However, the results of these efforts are not yet sufficient to cope with the time pressures of most business decisions. Whenever a problem is adequately described by a model, it can be labeled **structured.** Management science modeling, discussed in the next section, includes a variety of techniques that can aid in the evaluation of structured problems. Some of the models can be used to aid in the evaluation of less structured problems, as will be discussed in Chapter 4.

Business decision making is almost always a different case. Judgment is required to cope successfully with most decisions encountered. This judgment is almost always developed through experience.

Model Aid in the Development Phase

Mental models can be viewed as contributing to human generation of alternatives. If a decision maker has a theory of cause and effect relating to a problem, that understanding of the problem environment should trigger the imagination in developing potential solutions.

Often, however, business environments involve high degrees of complexity. Optimization models (such as linear programming) can be very useful in developing alternatives that humans cannot be expected to generate. If a company distributes 1,000 products to 2,000 customers, the combinations of distribution are far beyond the human capacity to control. Transportation or network models would be highly suitable in generating solutions that were very good on at least one dimension. Resource allocation problems also tend to be quite involved, and linear programming provides a valuable means of suggesting alternative decisions.

Supplemental Chapter 2 will explain the potential, assumptions required, and implications of linear programming. Often, real problems are more complex than linear programming assumes. However, by manipulating objective functions, a variety of solutions can be generated through linear programming, providing a valuable decision support tool.

Model Aid in the Selection Phase

Management science models have demonstrated their greatest value in this step of the decision-making process. Simulation models are very good at describing the possible outcomes of decisions. They have the benefit of allowing any assumptions whatsoever. Unfortunately, most realistic assumptions involve an infinite number of possibilities, and simulation analysis can become quite involved. The potential and implications of simulation will be discussed in Supplemental Chapter 3. Spreadsheets are a type of simulation as well. Financial models can be built including whatever decision makers want to assume. A benefit of spreadsheet models is that all of these assumptions can be clearly and concisely presented to the decision maker. As in simulation, assumptions can be changed, and the impact of changes can be seen by rerunning the spreadsheet model.

Optimization techniques can also aid the evaluation of alternatives. Often, real decisions involve the complication of a variety of objectives. Besides seeking increased profit, businesses need to develop markets, maintain cash flow, satisfy and develop the labor force, maintain a positive public relations environment, and a myriad of other objectives. Optimization models provide the best solution on any one objective. However, models can be used to optimize one objective and provide measures of attainment on the others. A variety of techniques are available to aid in reconciling multiple objectives. One means to evaluate solutions when considering multiple objectives is utility. The following section presents a technique that can aid decision makers in adding more structure to the evaluation step of the decision-making process.

Representing Mental Models with Cognitive Maps

One way of representing mental models is with **cognitive maps.** Cognitive maps are simply box-and-arrow diagrams in which boxes are used to represent variables and arrows represent relationships. They are useful in providing a "picture" of how the variables in a problem relate to one another. Figure 3.3 shows an example of a cognitive map depicting the variables and relationships in a business problem. Here, for example, additional advertising expenditures cause sales expenses to increase, which causes net sales revenue to decrease. However, additional advertising also causes sales volume to increase, which causes net sales revenue to increase.

Cognitive maps can also be represented in an "adjacency matrix," formed by creating a row and column for each variable in the problem. The numeral 1 is placed in each cell where there is an arrow from the variable in row i to the variable in column j. Zeros are entered in other cells of the matrix. Signs

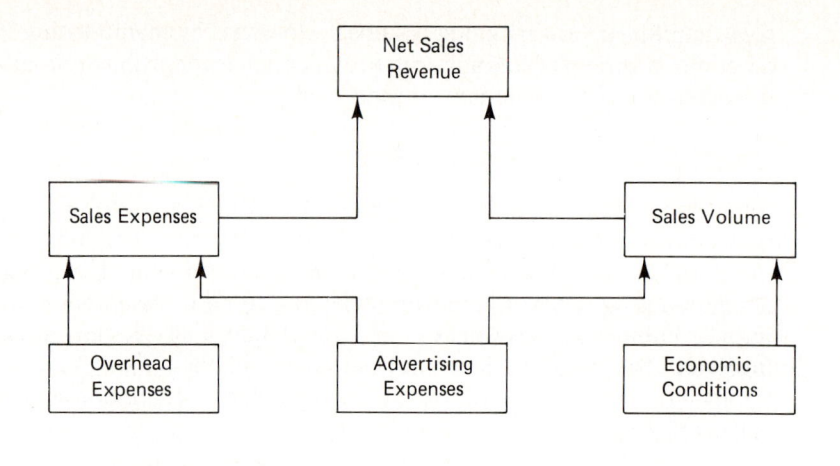

	NSR	SEXP	SVOL	OVER	ADV	ECON
NSR	0	0	0	0	0	0
SEXP	−1	0	0	0	0	0
SVOL	+1	0	0	0	0	0
OVER	0	+1	0	0	0	0
ADV	0	+1	+1	0	0	0
ECON	0	0	+1	0	0	0

Figure 3.3
(*top*) A cognitive map of variables in a sales problem; (*bottom*) a signed adjacency matrix for the preceding map.

may also be entered to indicate the direction of the relationship. In Figure 3.3, sales volume is expected to have a positive impact on net sales revenue, whereas overhead expenses are expected to have a negative impact.

Weights indicating the strength of the relationship may also be entered. If so, then the map is usually referred to as a structural model rather than a cognitive map. Various matrix modeling techniques are available to analyze structural models. Because these techniques are not commonly used, we will not discuss them further here.

Cognitive maps are useful as a first step in the development of a mathematical model of a problem. They are useful in that people can usually provide a list of variables existing in their mental model that they believe are important within the context of some problem. Given such a list, it is usually not difficult to specify what variable affects what other variables. That is basically all it takes to draw a map.

The cognitive map makes explicit a person's or group of persons' beliefs about variables and relationships that are important elements of a problem. This makes it possible for people to share and discuss their beliefs about causal relationships that are important to an organization. Maps can also be thought of as very useful organizational knowledge which has been made explicit. This knowledge can be stored in a computer system, manipulated to assist in decision making, and saved for future decision makers in the organization.

SUMMARY

Organizational decision making requires consensus and cooperation. The Mintzberg study indicates that decision making within organizations involves the need to monitor decision situations in order to respond to new situations. This can often lead to a great deal of adjustment of past decisions.

Two types of models are valuable in aiding decision making. Mental models are the basis of decision maker judgment, enabling humans to cope with complex decision environments. Understanding these mental models is key to aiding the decision-making process. Another type of valuable model is mathematical. A variety of useful techniques has been developed by management science. Although these techniques are most valuable for highly structured environments, they can also aid the decision-making process when less structure is present.

Management science is the application of scientific approaches to management decision-making problems. It has been very successful in some areas of business, such as logistics planning, resource allocation, and financial forecasting. However, there has been little impact in decision-making problems, where the problems do not lend themselves to explicit formulation, where there are ambiguous or overlapping criteria for action, or where the manager operates through intuition.

Mathematical modeling is fundamental to management science. Management science models have been valuable in situations where they describe a situation, aiding in the development of better decision solutions. They can also aid in predicting the results of decisions in the evaluation (selection) phase of decision making. Sometimes optimal solutions can be identified through models, aiding the alternative generation (development) step of decision making. However, the results of these models require a number of assumptions and estimates of relationships. In semistructured decision making, the focus of this book, models should be viewed as tools to aid decision maker learning, ultimately improving decision maker judgment. This means that decision makers should understand the assumptions of a model, as well as the parameters included in the analysis.

Cognitive maps, which portray variables and relationships in both diagrams and matrixes, are useful in representing mental models of organizational problems. These maps of expected impact among variables provide a means to develop problem structure, as well as to communicate the expected relationships between actions and results.

REFERENCES

Bonge, J. W. 1972. Problem recognition and diagnosis: Basic inputs to business policy. *J. Business Policy* 2 (3):45–53.

McKenney, J. L., and P. G. W. Keen. 1974. How managers' minds work. *Harvard Business Rev.* 52 (3):79–90.

Mintzberg, Raisinghani, and Theoret. 1976. "The structure of 'unstructured' decision processes." *Admin. Sci. Quarterly* 21 (2):246–75.

Pounds, W. F. 1969. The process of problem finding. *Industrial Management Rev.* 11 (1):1–19.

PROJECT IDEAS

Describe your mental model of the education process at your school. What decisions do you as a student have relative to obtaining your degree? What is your expected outcome of making different choices?

Describe your mental model of the job market. What decisions do you face in seeking employment opportunities? Describe the expected outcomes associated with each choice.

What is your view of a prospective employer's model of the job market? Organizations consist of many people. What kinds of mental models do interviewers seem to have? Do you expect these to coincide with the rest of the organization?

Represent the mental models in each of the preceding problems with cognitive maps.

CHAPTER FOUR

The Concept of Decision Support Systems

Decision support systems have been in existence for two decades. This period has seen dramatic changes in hardware (including the personal computer boom) and software (spreadsheets, word processing, databases). Furthermore, the computer literacy of people in business has increased significantly. Therefore, it should come as no surprise that the scope and variety of decision support systems have grown dramatically as well.

This chapter will answer the following questions:

- What constitutes a decision support system?
- What benefits have decision support systems demonstrated?
- What impacts have decision support systems had on central information systems?
  What role can central information systems play in building and operating decision support systems?
- What sorts of tools are available to build decision support systems?
- What kind of design strategy is appropriate for a DSS?
- What problems are typically encountered in justifying decision support systems?

To illustrate the concept of decision support systems, imagine a regional manager responsible for automobile rentals in the Colorado region of a national car rental company. This manager is given a number of assets, including offices, personnel, budget, and rental vehicles, and is responsible for generating profit, as well as developing the market in Colorado for the company. The manager faces an environment that involves some repetitive decisions and some constraints from national management. But the nature of this organizational level is that the manager is free to do many things. The primary concern of the company is that profits increase and market share grow.

Decisions

The manager faces a number of decisions. Some are generated by emergencies, others by problems slowly developing over time. Sometimes decisions are generated by the manager identifying opportunities. Almost all of these decisions are under unique circumstances. It is the manager's job to figure out what is different about each circumstance and take actions appropriate to the new environment. Decisions include personnel actions (hiring, firing, promotion), new outlet openings and old outlet closings, location decisions for new outlets, automobile inventory levels at each outlet, and advertising and promotion campaigns. All of these decisions are made under some constraints from the corporation. Budgets have been provided to the manager. Extra budget can be obtained if thoroughly justified. Management has overall plans guiding expansion or contraction of outlets, advertising and promotions, and personnel actions.

Monitoring

Computer systems provide a great deal of assistance to the monitoring function. The company's central management information system provides the manager with monthly reports, monitoring sales in Colorado by rental outlet. Profit-and-loss statements provide a financial picture of the region's contribution. Operationally, reservations are made on an automated national system, which not only keeps track of reservations, but also keeps track of the inventory of automobiles available by location. When a customer appears to pick up a rental vehicle, the computer system automatically generates the bill for services on preprogrammed forms. The jobs of personnel dealing with the public are made much easier, as normal operations require little effort, and they can focus on dealing with exceptions. Furthermore, the quality of service is improved through faster paperwork and more consistent service.

The regional manager can utilize statistical analysis to monitor his region's performance. Trend forecasts, based on extensions of time-series regression (a means of forecasting) of past performance, provide a means to predict future performance. The manager can also utilize regression of performance against other key variables, to try to objectively measure the impact of advertising, weather, convention traffic, and seasonal tourism, as well as identifying variables within the manager's control that would be useful (advertising campaigns).

The manager benefits as well from a **decision support system.** This system is custom designed for the manager, linked to the national computer system for retrieving data, as well as sending messages to national corporate personnel. The manager likes to keep track of business by type of automobile. The system is designed to speed the manager's access to key information. The current status of the rental business by type of vehicle and by location can be monitored. The manager also feels that economic conditions—both local and national—impact the company's business in Colorado. A microcomputer database system is used to keep track of economic indicators that the manager thinks provide an accurate forecast of business in the short run. National economic data is obtained from the *Wall Street Journal,* and local economic conditions are obtained from the *Denver Post,* both providing timely sources of the desired information.

The manager can also keep track of the performance of those reporting to him. The company computer system has personnel information. Furthermore, sales volumes by outlet are available. Although the company system keeps track of overall sales, a personal database is used by the manager to monitor sales in light of specific local conditions. Sales from the outlet in Pueblo may drop in January. The manager is responsible for identifying local conditions that affected rentals in Pueblo. Adverse weather may have closed the Pueblo airport for two weeks in January. The local outlet should not be expected to do as well under these conditions as the outlet did January a year ago. A contrary case may occur in Colorado Springs. A national convention in Colorado Springs is expected to increase rentals in April. Just knowing the volume of rentals is insufficient to manage the Colorado operations. The manager also needs to know special situations that occurred in order to evaluate local outlet performance.

Alternative Generation

Usually, the manager is responsible for generating alternative solutions for decisions. If a trend of rising sales in the Vail area is noted, the manager would consider opening new outlets in that area or expanding existing operations. If rentals in the Estes Park area increase less than the manager expected during the summer, the manager can consider additional training for existing personnel, reassignment of existing personnel, or identification of new personnel. Another alternative would be to increase advertising for potential customers in the Estes Park area. Because customers are liable to come from any area of the country, a number of decisions relating to specific areas and advertising media are necessary.

In addition to the manager's imagination, there are computerized sources of idea generation support. Graphical displays of statistical information (such as a map with sales by month by area) can be used to give the manager a clearer picture of what has happened. This, in turn, can trigger new ideas of managing the region's operations. Superimposed line graphs of rental volumes by outlet can give a clearer picture of which outlet is performing best (and which is performing worst). The manager can look for specific circumstances that may explain that outlet's performance. If a unique promotion campaign was used by a specific outlet, similar campaigns might be appropriate for other outlets.

An additional source of computer-generated alternatives is possible through linear programming. If a linear programming model accurately describing a specific system can be built, that system can be optimized. For complex systems, linear programming provides a means to generate complex combinations of variable values, which are beyond the capability of the manager's imagination.

Alternative Evaluation

A number of computerized systems provide the regional manager with the means to evaluate alternative decision options. We noted that **statistical** packages provide a means to objectively analyze regional performance versus uncontrollable and controllable managerial actions. Other modeling systems are available as well. **Spreadsheets** provide a valuable means to quickly list assumptions and extend these assumptions into the future. An example application could involve the evaluation of alternative advertising policies. Expected sales growth for each advertising policy requires a number of assumptions. The manager can model all of these assumptions, and the spreadsheet system can extend these assumptions into an expected performance for each alternative. **Optimization** packages provide managers with a means to identify the best way to proceed (for a well-defined system). An example would be an algorithm to identify the least cost plan to shuffle rental cars between outlets where a surplus of automobiles have been turned in, to those outlets where there are more requests than available cars. **Simulation** models are also quite often useful. Spreadsheet models are often simulations of a type, usually assuming specific growth rates and relationships. If probabilistic data is available, more realistic and comprehensive models can be evaluated, reflecting the degree of risk involved. For instance, forecasting demand involves a high degree of uncertainty. Statistical analysis can provide a picture of average growth rates, as well as their variance. Simulation models can be run (many times) to obtain a picture of possible outcomes, as well as an idea of their probability.

Models themselves are not all that is needed for a decision support system. Most models require some time to identify relationships and build the model in a form reflecting the particular decision. For repetitive decisions, such as determining advertising policies, assigning rental vehicle rerouting, or forecasting demand, the same models can be reused over time and refined. The old model can be called up on the terminal and modified. Models can be integrated. For instance, statistical analysis of rental volume can be automatically fed in to forecasting simulations.

Decision Support Systems

There are many definitions of what precisely a decision support system is. The broadest definition would be any use of readily available computer systems to aid decision makers faced with a decision (Figure 4.1). We lean toward this liberal interpretation. The following section will review academic definitions of DSS. This will be followed by review of actual decision support systems from published sources. Chapter 8 will examine seven different types of decision support systems.

The difference between a management science analysis and a decision support system is often blurry. The following example demonstrates the application of a management science approach to a problem, relying heavily upon data analysis and models. Over time, the initial success of the approach led to a

DATABASE
  Access to MIS
  PC packages
  Commercial sources
    of data

MODEL BASE
  Spreadsheets
  Optimization
  Simulation
  Statistical packages

USER INTERFACE
  Terminal
  Link to MIS
  Networks
  Graphics
  Word processing

Figure 4.1
Decision support system components.

system which was used by the organization on a regular basis, thus transforming an analysis using data and models to a decision support system.

MARKETING DSS
Gensch, Aversa, and Moore (1990)

ABB Electric was chartered in 1970 to design and manufacture medium-power transformers and other equipment for electrical distribution in the North American market. Its potential customers included four diverse groups. The primary initial market consisted of investor-owned utilities, although other types of organizations such as rural electrical cooperatives, municipalities, and industrial firms also generated and distributed electricity. ABB Electric's primary competition came from GE (General Electric), Westinghouse, and McGraw-Edison.

This industry was heavily impacted by the dramatic change in energy costs in 1973 (the price of oil skyrocketed). This created a need for ABB Electric, as a relatively new supplier, to carefully consider its marketing strategy. As is the case with many new businesses, ABB Electric had lost money during its first three years of operations, and this new price environment created a dangerous climate in which to operate. In 1974, ABB Electric commissioned a marketing information system with the intent of selecting new products to gain market share in a very competitive market. This system focused on analyzing the perceptions and preferences of potential customers, enabling ABB Electric to select target markets, identify

Figure 4.2
Customer preference
variables. (Based on
Gensch, Aversa, and
Moore [1990])

**Attributes most important in selecting
electrical distribution equipment**

Warranty
Energy losses
Appearance
Invoice price
Knowledgeable sales force
Maintenance requirements
Spare part availability
Bid document clarity

---

product features to emphasize in promotions, and aid in development of new
products and services.

Data

In order to determine current customer perceptions as well as customer
preferences, surveys were conducted asking potential customers to rate and
rank large sets of product and service attributes. Analysis of these survey
results determined a subset of variables that seemed to be significant. These
variables are presented in Figure 4.2.

It was also found that there was significant variance by customer type,
by geographic location, and by customer size. Therefore, the analysis was
conducted for each of 12 market segments.

Models

A multiattribute choice analysis was conducted, developing predictive
models of how customers would make their choices given available products.
Because people seem to make choices based on the attributes of available
choices, the idea of the model was to identify the important attributes, as
well as their relative importance. The model results indicated that actual
decisions were based on attribute weights different from those that the
customers indicated in the survey.

Because different market segments were expected to have different
weights on each attribute, a model was developed for each segment. This
allowed ABB Electric to determine the features important to each segment.
In addition, competitor strengths for each segment were identified. This
information was used to aid in preparing proposals in response to customer

calls for bids, as well as in designing future products to better match customer preferences.

The model was used to predict sales based on available product attributes and predictions compared with actual sales. ABB Electric had three sales districts. Two of the district sales managers were interested in applying the proposed program, whereas the third district sales manager was more skeptical. In 1974, a direct-mail marketing campaign emphasizing those ABB Electric product features matching average preferences in each market segment was administered in the two sales districts that had expressed interest.

After one year of implementation, the approach was evaluated for effectiveness. Total industry sales for transformers were down 15 percent over this year. ABB Electric sales in the sales districts where the focused advertising program was applied rose 18 percent and 12 percent, whereas sales in the district where the proposed program was not applied were down 10 percent. The model was used to predict what sales would have been without the focused advertising program, yielding estimates of a decline of about 10 percent in each district.

Because of the perceived success of this approach, a more widespread system was developed for use throughout the organization. Although this application was not presented as an example of a decision support system and its computer access features were not reported, it has the characteristics of a decision support system enabling ABB Electric to deal with a variety of decisions related to marketing.

Problem Identification

The primary decision to be made involved maintaining current customer business, as well as increasing the number of total customers. One focus of analysis was to classify customers. Another type of recurring decision was to design products to meet the needs of specific customers and to price these products in a profitable manner.

Data Collection

Purchasers of electrical distribution equipment were categorized into four groups: Those loyal to ABB Electric had a high probability of continuing to do business with the company; competitive customers had a slight preference for ABB Electric over competitors, but would require strong products and price; switchable customers were more likely to purchase from competitors, unless a strong proposal package was developed; and competitor-loyal customers were unlikely to purchase from ABB Electric. Purchasers of electrical distribution equipment were categorized into these groups on the basis of past purchasing behavior.

To deal with specific bid proposal requirements of customers, a database was developed reflecting product features available from competitors in each of the 12 market segments, as well as specific customer preferences within each of these market segments.

Alternative Generation

The system allowed ABB to better design products to meet specific customer requests, as well as assisting in effectively pricing products. The system also allowed ABB to develop a completely integrated power delivery system with improved safety, maintenance, and installation advantages over existing systems. This product was placed on the market in 1985.

The system was also used to provide the sales force with customer perceptions and preferences. In addition to providing the sales force with better information, sales promotion material was better designed, and direct-mail campaigns were managed in a more efficient manner by focusing on specific market segments.

Alternative Evaluation

By analyzing customer preferences, ABB made a strategic decision to provide a full five-year warranty on its products. This was a much longer warranty than the competition provided at the time. The impact of this strategy was that ABB developed a reputation for quality. This also meant that corresponding quality considerations needed to be incorporated into production. Adopting this strategy resulted in attainment of lower production costs partly because of the attention given to quality, and partly because ABB was better able to predict sales.

Whenever a specific customer request for bid to deliver a product was received, ABB was able to use the model to identify its competitive advantages. In effect, the system allowed ABB to custom-design products. Any modifications to production that would be required in order to meet customer specifications could be identified, and bid proposals could be developed. Product design could therefore be made that might better meet customer needs than the competition.

Additional modeling enabled ABB to determine the market equilibrium price for products having specific features. This information provided ABB with valuable information in pricing its bids.

Decision

As in most decision support systems, each specific decision is made by humans. But the decisions were made in light of thorough analysis of the market.

Implementation

The direct-mail survey in 1974 provided valuable information about the market that ABB serviced. The company was able to identify product features that were important to each segment of its market. Competitive advantages were identified, and marketing focused on those areas. This information and the models used in its analysis were the basis for changes in product design and production of these products, emphasizing quality at low cost. When the system had proved its effectiveness, it was developed into a marketing information system used on a wider basis throughout the company.

Monitoring

The effectiveness of the system can be inferred by ABB Electric market share performance. Starting with a 2 percent market share in 1971, ABB experienced a steady growth in market share up to 25 percent in 1983. After the power delivery system product was introduced in 1985, ABB market share grew to 40 percent in 1988.

This example demonstrates the evolution of a management science analysis, applying a scientific approach to a business problem through the collection of sound data and the development of models to explain that data, into a decision support system. This system became an integral part of the way in which ABB Electric approached marketing decisions. Although the interface features of the system were not discussed, they clearly are a necessary part of the way in which the system would be applied.

DSS CONCEPTS

One of the first discussions of DSS came from Little (1970), who primarily addressed the use of management science models to aid managers faced with decisions (Figure 4.3). Reviewing the business environment, Little noted that real decision making usually involved unstructured problems. This implies that decisions are often difficult to model, not always fitting the precise format of well-developed model types. Furthermore, management science approaches generally assume whatever data is necessary is available. In real life, data is often difficult to get, and that which is available is often less reliable than is desired. Furthermore, Little noted that managers do not often understand precisely what it is that these models do. Responsible managers can be expected to discount recommendations from models that are "black boxes."

Little's conclusions were that support of real decision making calls for simple, robust models. This aids management understanding of the analysis. Models should also be easy to control, so that if a particular manager does not agree with a particular assumption, the model can be changed to reflect the new

LITTLE (1970)
Model–based set of procedures to process data and judgments to assist decision making
– simple, robust, easy, adaptive

GORRY and SCOTT MORTON (1971)
Interactive computer–based systems to help decision makers use **DATA** and **MODELS** to solve **UNSTRUCTURED** problems

KEEN and SCOTT MORTON (1978)
Couple human intellectual resources with computer capabilities to improve decision quality in unstructured problem environments

BONCZEK, HOLSAPPLE, and WHINSTON (1980)
Language system, knowledge system, and problem–processing system

SPRAGUE and CARLSON (1983)
On–call computerized systems to **SUPPORT** rather than replace judgment for semistructured or unstructured decisions using **DATA** and **MODELS**
EFFECTIVENESS > EFFICIENCY

Figure 4.3
Definitions of decision support systems.

assumption. Models should be adaptive, or able to reflect new understandings of the analyzed system. Although all models are less than complete, models should be as complete as possible relative to important issues.

Gorry and Scott Morton outlined a framework for management information systems in their 1971 article (Figure 4.4). There are many dimensions to human decision making. *Structured* decisions are those for which clear, step-by-step procedures have been developed. Computers require a great deal of structure before they can function. A computer program is the structure the programmer wishes the computer to take. An example of a structured environment is the Army. When every action you take is laid out for you, your life is highly structured. Some decision environments in business are also structured. But many business decisions are much less structured. Simon (1960) described a spectrum of structure (structured, semistructured, and unstructured). Anthony (1965) noted different decision types within business (operational, managerial, and strategic). Some decisions involve day-to-day operations, dealing

ORGANIZATIONAL LEVEL

PROBLEM TYPE	Operational Control	Management Control	Strategic Planning
Structured	Accounts receivable	Budget analysis– engineered costs	Tanker fleet mix
	Order entry	Short–term forecasting	Warehouse and factory location
	Inventory control		
Semistructured	Production scheduling	Variance analysis– overall budget	Mergers and acqui- sitions
	Cash management	Budget preparation	New product planning
Unstructured	PERT/COST systems	Sales and production	R&D planning

Figure 4.4
Framework of information systems. (Reprinted from "A framework for management information systems," by G. A. Gorry and M. S. Scott Morton, *Sloan Management Review,* Vol. 13 No.1, 1971, pp. 56–70, by permission of publisher. Copyright 1971 by the Sloan Management Review Association. All rights reserved.

with problems that often become well known. At the other extreme, strategic decisions involve the long-range plan of the organization. Strategic plans occur much less often than operational decisions. Managerial decisions are usually required more often than strategic decisions, but not as often as operational decisions. Middle-level managers usually have more discretion than operational decision makers, but are constrained by strategic plans. Based on Simon's classification of problem structure and Anthony's classification of decision level, Gorry and Scott Morton developed a framework for computer support for decision making. They noted that most computer applications (at that time) were for structured classes of problems. As we discussed in Chapter 1, it made sense to use available computer resources on those problems that had an obvious payoff first. However, with the revolutionary growth in computer capabilities and computer access, it became possible to apply computers to problems with less structure. Typical problems were classified in the framework these authors developed. Gorry and Scott Morton also noted that the degree of structure for a problem changes, as decision makers learn more about problems.

Gorry and Scott Morton considered Simon's view of rational decision making, where a decision maker gathers intelligence to determine problems or opportunities, designs solutions to resolve these problems, and selects the alternative that seems to best resolve the problem. Decision quality was expected to improve as inputs (the relationship between actions and results) improved and as the decision process improved.

Keen and Scott Morton (1978) expanded these groundwork concepts to a comprehensive view of DSS. They viewed DSS as the coupling of the intellectual resources of individuals with the capabilities of the computer to improve decision quality. Totally structured problems usually do not require much decision maker analysis (in fact, they usually are well served by standard operating procedures for straightforward problems and expert systems for complex problem environments). Totally unstructured problems are difficult to support with computers and models, which by their nature require some structure. Keen and Scott Morton envisaged DSS applications to apply most often to semistructured problem domains.

Alter (1977) reported the results of an empirical investigation of 56 applications of DSS. Based on these observations, Alter classified seven types of decision support systems (Figure 4.5). He found that, in practice, humans use computers in a variety of ways, not necessarily concerned with academic classification systems. Whereas the original view of DSS was that the decision maker would personally use the computer, in the 1970s, very few managers were found to actually do this. Rather, their staffs would be the contacts with computer systems. Alter noted that for DSS applications, computer efficiency was distinctly less important than flexibility. Furthermore, whereas mainframe systems require thorough systems analysis and design, most DSSs seemed to evolve incrementally. Because the system was dedicated to a specific user (or the user's group), custom-designed features were often used. Software, graphics output, network connections, and other features were highly variable.

Bonczek, Holsapple, and Whinston (1980) focused on the evolving roles of models in DSS. Viewing a DSS composed of the user, models, and data, the

Figure 4.5
Alter's taxonomy of DSS benefits. (Based on Alter [1977])

FILE DRAWER
Query systems (look up answers)
Airline reservation systems **MIS**

DATA ANALYSIS
Exploratory statistical analysis
*Forecasting, relationship
 identification*

ANALYSIS INFORMATION SYSTEMS
Access to a series of databases and
 general models
Spreadsheet systems

ACCOUNTING MODELS
Calculate consequences of planned
 actions based on assumptions
Monetary simulations

REPRESENTATIONAL MODELS
Estimate consequences of actions
 based on less structured models
Simulation

OPTIMIZATION MODELS
Identify optimal solution
Linear programming

SUGGESTION MODELS
More structured models, concluding
 with a recommended action
EXPERT SYSTEMS

critical interfaces between these three components were used as the basis for designing effective languages, both for computation and for data retrieval. These authors considered the purpose of DSS to be flexible and exploratory. Their view of the future was that computer support to decision makers would continue to evolve from the explicit data needs of 1950 technology, beyond the 1970s ability to handle moderately structured data, to a future state where data approaching its rawest form could be transformed by the system into useful intelligence for decision making.

Keen (1981) reviewed the features and theoretical benefits of DSSs, as well as a number of actual applications from the first decade of their use. Features included an emphasis upon supporting judgment as opposed to automating decision making. A primary means of accomplishing this feature is by providing a means of examining more alternatives, stimulation of new ideas, and improved communication of analysis. A DSS was viewed as evolutionary, with no final system. A major emphasis of Keen's discussion was justification of DSSs, which will be discussed in more detail.

Key points in the planning and evaluation of decision support systems are the appropriate style of developing these systems (reliance on prototypes as opposed to the systems development life cycle common to other MIS applications), the limitations of traditional means of economic evaluation (such as cost–benefit analysis), and the evolutionary nature of DSS development. In order for a manager to decide if building a decision support system would be worthwhile, Keen focused on what the manager would need to know, how innovation could be encouraged while making sure money was well spent, and how some sort of figure could be placed on the value of effectiveness, learning, and creativity.

ISSUES INVOLVING DSS IMPLEMENTATION

The benefits of decision support systems have been well documented. They provide a means for decision makers to make decisions on the basis of more complete information and analysis. A review of Keen's list of benefits is given in Figure 4.6. An example of one organization's view of the value of this capability will be seen in El Sherif's presentation of the Egyptian government's system. We will also see other benefits of DSS found by Huff et al., as well as Hogue and Watson. The primary benefit of DSS is not to automate decision making, but rather to support decision maker(s) learning.

End-User Operation of DSS

One of the values cited as beneficial for DSS was the interactive use of the system by the decision maker. Early studies indicated a low level of user participation. Alter found that most systems were used by decision maker subordinates. The Huff study found only 14.5 percent of the applications surveyed were conducted by the decision maker alone.

It may make little difference whether the decision maker uses the system personally. Staff members who work closely with the decision maker generally are assigned to conduct analyses for two primary reasons: They have more expertise involved with technical analysis, and/or they have more time to devote to time-consuming tasks. Undoubtedly, early DSS use involved significant investments in time. Staff personnel were obvious candidates to operate DSSs. With the vast improvement in system usability we have seen in the 1980s, time is probably less important, and less computer expertise is required for DSS operation. Some systems, involving DSS generators, are probably going to be

Figure 4.6
Keen's list of DSS benefits.
(Based on Keen [1981])

1. **Increased number of alternatives examined**
   More expeditious sensitivity analysis
   Faster response

2. **Better understanding of the business**
   Enable decision makers to see relationships
   Can be used to provide an overall picture

3. **Fast response to unexpected situations**
   Easy revision of models
   Quick view of changes

4. **Ability to carry out ad hoc analysis**

5. **New insights and learning**
   Identify underutilized resources
   Stimulate new approaches

6. **Improved communication**
   Explain rationale

7. **Control**
   More consistent plans
   Standardized calculation procedures

8. **Cost savings**
   Reduced clerical work, less overtime

9. **Better decisions**

10. **More effective teamwork**

11. **Time savings**

12. **Better use of data resource**
    Allows quick browsing

used much more by decision makers themselves than other DSSs which require more system understanding.

An additional factor bearing on this discussion is the increased amount of participatory management styles. Governments usually involve more participation. But business is becoming more participatory, too. Group decision making becomes more important. The communications feature of DSS plays a crucial role in this participatory environment. When DSSs are used by a variety of people, they can become vehicles to better communicate more complex ideas.

Systems Development Practice

The traditional means of implementing a computer system is through the **systems development life-cycle (SDLC)** approach, where needs are thoroughly assessed, the system is thoroughly designed, and a coordinated effort is undertaken. Two characteristics of this approach are notable. First, precise cost estimates are needed. Second, the process takes more time because of more thorough analysis.

Keen (1980) advocated the use of an evolutionary approach for DSSs, because users very often do not know precisely what benefits or what features the DSS will provide them until they see it operating. A **prototyping** approach would involve building a small-scale initial system and allowing the ultimate user to try it out. The user could then ask for modifications based on a better picture of what the system would do. Although the SDLC makes a great deal of sense for large-scale systems serving the organization as a whole, DSSs generally involve much less investment and need to be built in much less structured decision environments. Therefore, it is almost impossible to thoroughly describe how the system is going to support the user. Prototyping is a much less thoroughly planned approach, but has the benefit of directly demonstrating the benefits of system features to the user. Prototyping also is usually much faster than a full systems development approach. This can result in much lower development cost and time, especially when there are many uncertainties about what the system should contain. If it were well understood what the system was to provide and how it would impact other systems, a systems development approach would be more efficient. But many DSSs involve features and applications that the user did not anticipate at the beginning of the project.

Both approaches have been used in evaluating DSSs. Both (or modifications of both) are appropriate, depending on a number of factors. Hogue and Watson found one-third of the systems they examined used evaluation techniques closer to the systems development approach, and two-thirds used evaluation techniques closer to the prototyping approach. They pointed out that whenever there is interaction with the central data processing system, the systems development approach is probably appropriate, because of the impact on other systems.

Cost Justification

One of the major issues in deciding upon development of a DSS is cost justification. It would be unsound management to adopt every possible application. If the value of a system exceeds its cost enough to make it an attractive investment, economic theory would indicate that the system should be adopted. Benefit/cost analysis provides a means to aid the decision to adopt a system. A benefit/cost ratio is simply benefits divided by costs (both in net present value terms for long-range projects). If this ratio is greater than 1, the project would be beneficial. The ratio can also be used to rank alternatives if a number of alternatives exist. This approach requires accurate estimation of benefits and costs. The decision is viewed as a capital investment.

There usually is something of a dilemma in deciding whether or not to develop a DSS. The primary problem is that the benefits of a DSS involve giving decision makers better tools to make decisions. It is not easy to place a dollar value on this ability.

Keen (1981) states that whereas traditional cost–benefit analysis is effective for many computer-based systems, it is not appropriate for innovative systems such as DSS. Innovations involve speculation, such as research and development. Keen suggests the use of **value analysis** for assessing DSS proposals.

Value analysis focuses on benefits and estimates the costs of attaining those benefits. Rather than calculating a highly subjective benefit/cost ratio, the system can be evaluated in terms of improving the decision-making environment versus the cost in dollars. The decision maker can then make the purchasing decision on this basis. Keen (1986) gives the principles of value analysis as:

Separating benefit from cost

Establishing what quantifiable benefits are worth (in terms other than dollars)

Determining how much you would pay for that benefit

Identifying qualitative benefits

Rank-ordering benefits (including both quantitative and qualitative benefits)

Defining indicators with which qualitative benefits can be evaluated

Identifying a rough estimate of needed benefits for project adoption, as well as likely benefits

Prototyping is an important systems development style for this approach. The benefits of the system can best be evaluated by seeing what it can do in real terms. Uncertainty and risk would be enhanced by being able to see a small version of the system before the full amount of cost is expended. Furthermore, the ultimate user of the system can look at what the prototype does, and be in a position to suggest modifications before full development effort is expended.

The steps involved in value analysis are:

Stage I

1. Define the benefits
2. Determine a cost threshold

   Define the maximum amount you would be willing to pay for a system delivering the benefits
   Evaluate if a prototype can be built that delivers the necessary capabilities

3. Build a prototype

Stage II

4. Assess the prototype

   Review the benefits and revise to match new expectations
   Define the functional capabilities of the full system

5. Establish the cost of Version 1 of the full system
6. Determine the benefit threshold

   What level of benefits would be required to justify the expenditure

Adoption

7. Build Version 1
8. Continue to revise

   Review usage, evaluate new capabilities

Whereas DSSs benefits are difficult to estimate, not all DSS ideas will be worthwhile. Value analysis and prototyping provide a means to rationally assess their value.

STUDIES OF DECISION SUPPORT SYSTEMS

Three studies are presented here. The first, by Huff et al. empirically examined the state of DSS in Canada in the early 1980s. It should be noted that the use of DSS will be expected to change with time, because the development of computer technology changes rapidly. Thus, whereas Alter found one picture of DSS usage, the Huff study provides something of a different picture. Alter found systems used primarily by individual decision makers. The Huff study found more use in groups, which we interpret as a growth in system sophistication. Hogue and Watson surveyed the decision makers in 18 decision support systems, focusing on the relationship of central MISs to the development and operation of DSSs. The role of decision style, user involvement, central information system involvement, and use of DSS tools were reviewed. The third study presents a specific organization's use of DSS. That application is an attempt to incorporate DSS throughout an organization, which El Sherif terms **institutionalization.**

DSS USE
Huff et al. (1984)

n=131

This study examined 131 decision support systems used in Canada. Although Alter's study was more case oriented, the Huff study was able to build on past theory development to measure various aspects of DSS use. Huff et al.'s objectives were to gather descriptive data about DSS usage patterns, to study the appropriateness of Alter's taxonomy, to explore the role data processing (DP) centers played in DSS implementation and development, and to attempt to measure the impact of DSS upon the decision-making process within organizations.

The Huff study found 37 percent of the systems surveyed included interactive systems. Only 3.1 percent utilized graphics capabilities, which had been emphasized in theoretical work. On the other hand, 94 percent of the systems included analytic models. Furthermore, whereas theoretically a DSS would be under the personal control of the user (or the user's staff), data processing departments were often involved in the development or operation of decision support systems.

Decision Types

Decision support systems were found in a wide variety of economic sectors. The manufacturing sector was found to have the largest percentage of DSSs, followed by financial institutions. Both of these sectors have many unstructured problems, and these would be the sectors where more applications would be expected. Also notable was the high proportion of DSSs found in government and utilities. Usually, public sector decisions are highly complex, because the political element is highly important, resulting in many decisions with low levels of problem structure.

The kinds of decisions supported were found to vary widely. Although DSSs would be expected to be applied to less structured (and therefore less operational) decisions, the results of the Huff study were:

Type of Task	Percentage
Operational control	30.0
Resource allocation	14.6
Annual budgeting	11.5
Long-range planning	37.7 ←
Other	6.9

Over one-half of the operational control and resource allocation systems were used daily. Annual budgeting systems, of course, were used less frequently.

Users

One of the theoretical definitional features of a DSS is interactive computer use. A minor issue is who precisely uses the DSS. Theoretically, it was expected that decision makers (generally viewed as one individual) would directly use the system. The Huff study found that more decisions were made by groups. Over 47 percent of the applications were conducted by subordinates, confirming Alter's findings that staffs used DSSs heavily. But the Huff study found that over one-third of the applications were for the purpose of supporting group decisions. Only 14.5 percent of the applications were to support decisions made by the user without consultation.

Types of Systems

One of the objectives of the Huff study was to examine how well Alter's taxonomy matched actual use. The seven categories of Alter's taxonomy were used, in addition to an eighth "other" category. They found that the "other" category was not used by any of the 131 respondents, indicating that the taxonomy is reasonably exhaustive. All of the seven categories were used, although there were different densities. The categories were not found to be mutually exclusive, with 51 of 131 respondents listing more than one category as appropriate. The numbers of systems by category were:

Category	Primary Category	Secondary Category
File drawer	8	7
Data analysis	44	19
Analysis information system	5	14
Accounting model	26	4
Representational model	23	2
Optimization model	22	0
Suggestion model	3	2

Note that the categories increase with sophistication down the list. File drawer systems have functions highly similar to MISs, whereas suggestion models have many of the features of expert systems. Neither of these extreme categories had relatively high densities. Part of the explanation for the low use of suggestion models would be that the software capable of supporting this application was not yet widely available in the early 1980s. Although neither file drawer systems nor suggestion models may fit strict definitions of DSS, the fine distinction of academic definitions is not always useful in practice. The use of both extreme categories is helpful in aiding decision makers, and practitioners would tend to view them as means to support decisions.

Benefits and Problems

System benefits were found to include speed of use, with some perception of added accuracy. Slightly over one-sixth of the users noted the ability of considering more alternatives, whereas other benefits cited included gaining more and better information and greater flexibility. A small proportion of the users identified better control of the decision-making process outcome and better understanding of decisions.

(Problems in using systems were most often related to analytic models, followed by problems in using the system and problems related to data.) Model-related problems included system inflexibility, insufficiently sophisticated models for the problem, or models that were too complex and difficult to understand. Given that 94 percent of the systems incorporated models, these findings would seem to indicate that model selection is a very important element in designing a DSS. *only if lots of people found problems w/ them*

Definition of DSS

The Huff study was interested in validating the definitions of DSS. They considered six definitional features and asked respondents questions testing each of these features.

The purpose of the system is to support managers in a specific decision task. This question was asked directly. Ninety-two percent of the systems were said to have been developed for specific decisions.

DSS are usually interactive, frequently using graphics, and are usually operated by the user or an assistant. Only 37 percent of the systems were used in a direct, interactive manner. This varies from most definitions, but matches Alter's findings. (Nearly 90 percent of the systems were used on an ad hoc basis, emphasizing the need for flexible systems. Graphics use was much lower than expected, appearing in only 3.1 percent of the surveyed systems.

DSS frequently involves some types of analytical models. A high proportion (94 percent) of the respondents used analytical tools.

DSS put major emphasis on present and future decisions. Based on written comments, the study found strong evidence that this is a characteristic common to all DSSs in the sample. Many were described as systems to aid forecasting or determining the impact of decisions on the future of the organization.

DSS are often developed by users or with users providing the main driving force. Only 38 percent of the sampled systems were initiated by users (or their predecessors). It was found that a number of users were not in their current job position when the system was developed. Of those who were, 85 percent participated significantly in system development, and 9.1 percent developed the system entirely by themselves. We would interpret this as indicating a broader organizational context for DSS than the original theoretical expectation. A large proportion of decisions in practice require consultation with others. Therefore, custom-designed systems for one specific user are probably less appropriate than originally anticipated.

Role of DP Department in DSS Development

The role of data processing departments is probably dynamic. Original DSSs saw much less involvement of DP departments. Keen and Scott Morton (1975) state: "None of the systems with which we are familiar have been built within the main EDP department. In several of the systems, the organization's EDP group was seen as the 'enemy'."

The Huff study found:

Department	Development Responsibility	Implementation Responsibility
User department	55.7%	64.9%
DP department	23.7%	19.1%
Joint user and DP	4.6%	5.3%
Consultant or vendor	7.7%	0
Other (head office, other)	8.4%	10.7%

Note that although DP departments were not the primary developers or implementers, they were involved much more than was found to be true in the early 1970s. One reason is that DSSs benefit from access to corporate databases. There is a motivation to provide DSSs with this access because the interference with DP operations is less, and the technology to accommodate this application is widely available.

DSS IMPLEMENTATION
Hogue and Watson (1985)

Eighteen organizations with DSSs were surveyed through field studies. The highest-ranking individuals of each organization who used DSSs heavily were surveyed.

Development Approach

Hogue and Watson used a seven-point scale, with 1 representing the systems development cycle and 7 a totally evolutionary approach.

Development Approach		Number
1	(SDLC)	1
2		2
3		3
4		0
5		5
6		4
7	(evolutionary)	3

Although SDLC and related approaches were used in one-third of the systems surveyed, two-thirds were more evolutionary. Several factors were found to be important in the degree of SDLC use in DSS development. If the DSS supports the entire company or requires company-wide data, more SDLC would be appropriate. This approach, however, greatly lengthens development time. **DSS generators** are software (sometimes including hardware) that give users the ability to quickly build a DSS. IFPS (Interactive Financial Planning System) is an example of a DSS generator. The use of DSS generators makes an evolutionary approach attractive. Less basic development is required when DSS generators are used. Nine of the eighteen companies used a DSS generator in their systems, including such products as SIMPLAN, Profile, EIS, Micro DSS/F, and IFPS. The other companies put the systems together with more fundamental tools. A number of companies combined generators and other tools.

Another important factor is the ability to specify information requirements in advance. When that is not possible, the evolutionary approach is almost mandatory. Hogue and Watson found that when specialists developed the system, SDLC tended to be used more. This was attributed to work habits developed over time. More strategic decisions usually involve less structure, leading to an emphasis on the evolutionary approach. Additionally, higher-cost systems are usually subjected to closer review, making the SDLC approach more appropriate.

User Involvement in Development

A number of conventional DSS development stages were described in the interviews. Company officials were asked to indicate participation of various levels of management at each stage.

	Management Level			18 Total
Stage	**Lower**	**Middle**	**Top**	**All**
Idea	0	10	10	18
Information requirements	0	12	10	18
Building	2	13	1	14
Testing	2	13	1	15
Demonstration	2	14	4	16
Acceptance	0	13	11	18

There was at least moderate user involvement of middle management in all stages. Top management was usually involved initially and at the acceptance stage, but there was little involvement in the building, testing, and demonstration stages. Lower management was seldom involved, which Hogue and Watson attribute to the middle and/or top management decisions supported by these systems.

The availability of a DSS generator was found to increase the amount of user involvement. More structured decision-making tasks tend to lead to less user involvement, because their input is not as critical. Because group decision making normally involves more discussion than individual decision making, DSSs supporting groups tend to require greater user involvement.

Incorporation of Decision Style

The study found that in 8 of the 18 companies, an attempt was made to custom-design the DSS to match a user's decision-making style. However, attempts to fully replicate a user's decision-making process were rare. More often, custom-design efforts focused on information requirements and data manipulation methods. In 13 of the 18 systems, the DSS supports more than one user. Therefore, custom design is less useful.

The study found that 14 of the 18 companies used staff intermediaries to use the DSS at least occasionally. In six cases, the decision maker and staff intermediary worked on the system together. In eight of the companies, the decision maker used the system alone at least occasionally. The intermediaries generally worked in close proximity to the decision maker, with a close working relationship involving easy access. There seems to be little need to match specific decision maker styles.

The Role of Central Systems and OR/MS Groups

Central computer system support was frequently involved in developing DSSs, but seldom in a leadership role. More typically, this group was used in the role of consultant or team member, with the user group taking the leadership role.

Hogue and Watson noted that even though users and their staffs do most of the work with the DSS, there was a high need for technical assistance. Central computer system personnel are usually necessary to provide this expertise, especially relative to data networking.

Although models are important in most DSSs, they are normally created by personnel in the user's organizational group rather than OR/MS professionals. Only one of the eighteen companies had the DSS project led by the OR/MS group, and in only one other company did the OR/MS group serve as a consultant.

The next section presents a more recent example of incorporation of DSS within an organization. In this case, the motivation for developing the system came from the top of the organization, through recognition that increased use of DSS would be expected to improve the effectiveness of the organization. In addition, the case emphasizes the role of group decision making.

INSTITUTIONALIZATION
El Sherif (1990)

In late 1985, the Cabinet of Egypt initiated a program to improve strategic decision making. Decision support systems were established in different ministries, sectors, and governates. These systems supported decisions in debt management, public sector performance evaluation, customs reform, energy pricing, and general administrative decision making. It is presented here not as a specific decision support system, but as an example of an attitude of incorporating DSS philosophy within an organization.

El Sherif noted four areas of challenge in incorporating DSSs in the Egyptian Cabinet strategic decision-making system:

1. Strategic decision making is an ill-structured process, often involving long time frames, with many participants and stakeholders, high conflict and crisis management, and a turbulent, dynamic environment.

2. Applying DSS requires a focus on particular decisions, with the intent of supporting the process rather than concluding with a decision. In group settings, there is a wide variety of individual decision-making styles. Data from both organizational sources as well as external sources is useful and often necessary. There is a need to consider the appropriateness of the models to be used and to continually examine model assumptions. Development of a DSS is usually incremental, involving prototyping approaches linking changing user needs to the implementation process. In addition, application of prescriptive models to descriptive organizational decision-making processes requires care.

3. Implementing management science models has long been a problem. Models require accurate data for accurate results. Real data is often unavailable at the time it is required and often is less complete than desired. Problem definitions are often inadequate and often result in incomplete models. It is important to involve users in model development. Top management support is essential, as group participants vary in resistance to change. Some systems require extensive effort to develop software, DSSs, or other tools, and these are often poorly documented. Inflexible models, unsuitable information and data representation, and linguistic problems often make systems unusable by decision makers.

4. Institutionalization of DSS requires adopting new processes within the organization. Challenges include overcoming resistance to change, formulating procedures in order to develop models, changing standard procedures, training organization members, and monitoring system adoption and its impact.

The Cabinet of Egypt is the highest executive body in the country, consisting of 32 ministers headed by the prime minister. Each minister is responsible for a given sector, such as energy or agriculture. Multisectoral issues, policies, and programs are addressed by the cabinet. The cabinet's agenda is set according to urgency.

In late 1984, the Minister of Cabinet Affairs expressed interest in exploring the use of DSS to aid cabinet strategic decision making. Areas of concern included improving effectiveness in agenda preparation, consideration of issues, the decision-making process, information quality and reliability, and decision-making time.

A preliminary project plan based on policy needs and national development priorities was developed. The objective of a decision support center (IDSC) was to develop systems for the cabinet and top policymakers in Egypt, to support establishment of decision support centers in ministries to more effectively and efficiently use available information resources. An additional objective was to encourage more use of computer resources in the Egyptian government.

The plan included a center to support the cabinet, with nodes throughout the government to link ministry and agency systems. Telecommunications access to international sources of information and databases were included. In November 1985, the IDSC consisted of three people. By March 1989, the IDSC included over 180 specialists. By early 1987, 24 projects were in progress. El Sherif found institutionalization of DSS far more challenging than implementation of a DSS itself.

Three examples of DSS application were presented.

Customs Tariff Policy

A new customs tariff was considered by the cabinet in early 1986. In April, the main features of the intended legislation were leaked to the press, followed by stagnated business awaiting the new tariff. In August, the new tariff was formally announced. In the four-month interim, many conflicts arose between six ministries.

A DSS was developed with the objectives of achieving a consistent tariff structure, aimed at increasing government revenue while minimizing the burden on low-income groups. A team headed by a representative of the Ministry of Finance was formed to interact with ministers from key sectors to build a model to predict the impact of various tariff policies. After one month, the conflict was resolved, and the cabinet unanimously endorsed a model-based proposal. This proposal led to new legislation supported by the business sector, as well as the government.

Based on this experience, a permanent body was proposed to monitor this DSS and make any needed changes. Government approval was obtained. After one year, following adjustments in the currency exchange rate, a new custom tariff structure was required. Model assumptions were reexamined and data updated. However, almost the same development procedure was required because the system had not been institutionalized. This led IDSC to formulate a plan to include intensive training on using microcomputer systems. About 30 staff members were thoroughly trained in system use.

Customs revenue over a $2^{1/2}$ year period in the late 1980s resulted in increased customs revenue from $56 million (U.S.) the first year, $167 million (U.S.) the second year, and $127 million (U.S.) for the first six months of the third year. The customs tariff system is now fully integrated into the Finance Ministry's operations.

Debt Management

Egypt has accumulated a foreign debt over the years, which impedes economic development and implementation of its five-year plan. This debt was necessary to rebuild the Egyptian economy during the last two decades. Prior to this project, transactions were handled on a loan-by-loan basis, with over 5,000 loans. This made it very difficult to monitor and manage the country's debt, to include locating funds, renegotiating terms and interest rates, and scheduling payments.

In 1985, Egypt faced economic pressure. Resources (oil, the Suez Canal, foreign remittances, and tourism) were shrinking, and creditors were refusing to provide additional loans. A World Bank expert estimated the cost of debt service to be $1 million (U.S.) every six hours. In September 1986, a debt-management system was initiated. Originally, it was perceived as a database system. This was expanded to include a forecasting and sensitivity analysis model to support the process of rescheduling debt payments. The negotiations were successful, and Egypt's foreign debt was rescheduled. After this experience, the cabinet requested a simulation of future debt burden, including scenarios and strategies. This successful system also resulted in increased requests from other ministries for access to the system. This led to adaptations to link the central base to the major banks in Egypt. Soon the tracking function of the project was overloaded.

A training and education plan was implemented as part of a plan to institutionalize the system. There has been a growing commitment and involvement by members throughout the government hierarchy for this DSS, including a monthly impact assessment process on DSS delivery and use.

DSS for the Ministry of Electricity and the Ministry of Irrigation

In August 1987, the Minister of Electricity and Energy requested a DSS to aid in dealing with strategic issues. Electricity costs were increasingly contributing to the national budget deficit and balance of payments.

A pricing model was embedded in a DSS, allowing users to generate scenarios and alternatives. The model evolved over several versions, allowing the ministry to generate new tariff policy scenarios. A new tariff policy was developed, increasing revenue by 160 million Egyptian pounds in its first year of implementation. This tariff policy is periodically monitored.

Based on this successful experience, the Minister of Electricity and Energy assigned personnel to develop a joint team with IDSC to establish an information and decision support center for the ministry. Teams were assigned to develop DSSs for pricing, debt management, energy production and consumption, project monitoring, capital goods, legislation, and studies. These systems included an Arabic language interface to increase accessibility. A process of institutionalization, including training both staff and top management, redesigning organizational structure, and incorporating an incentive system, was adopted.

After the DSS was implemented, the Nile water level declined in 1988, threatening the level of power generation from the Aswan Dam. This created a crisis in both energy and irrigation, as Nile water is essential for agricultural production.

The water planning group of the Ministry of Irrigation joined in using the previously built water planning model. A simulation of Lake Nasser and an optimization model of the Aswan High Dam were developed, based on updated data. The results of these two models were used to present several policy alternatives to the cabinet to illustrate the effects of different release policies, as well as their future impact on the hydraulic performance of the reservoir. This information aided the cabinet in its decision for water release.

Institutionalization

El Sherif cites the use of DSS as resulting in significant improvement in the strategic decision-making process. He is most impressed by the need to foster institutionalization. In order for DSSs to be successful, they must be used. In these examples of government implementation, systems need to be adopted and trusted throughout the organization, because there is not one specific decision maker. Group decisions involve convincing a great many organization members, as well as implementing executives, of the appropriateness of a specific decision.

SUMMARY

Decision support systems come in many forms. Their primary feature is harnessing computer power to aid decision maker learning about decision environments. Huff et al. found the primary benefits to be speed and accuracy. DSSs generally accomplish this through access to data and models appropriate to the decision. But a loose definition of DSS seems appropriate, because decision makers should not be constrained in their use of computer systems.

When DSSs first appeared, they were developed independent of central information systems. Keen (1981) noted that there was little connection between DSSs and central systems in the 1970s. Originally, central information systems may have viewed this uncontrollable use of computer systems as inefficient meddling by computer-illiterate novices. However, common sense on both sides seems to have prevailed. Huff et al. found about one-fifth of the systems involved central systems, especially in development and operation. Hogue and Watson found central systems frequently provided technical support and networking access. We would expect that any arrangement leading to more effective application of computer systems will prevail. If DSS benefits are experienced in one area of a company, there is a strong motivation to expand its use. El Sherif presented a more contemporary concept, institutionalization of DSS throughout an organization. Although this concept also undoubtedly has limits, we would expect that in the future, there will not only be more use of DSSs, but more integration of systems as well.

The use of components and tools to aid DSS is also interesting. Originally, it was expected that heavy use of graphics would be appropriate. Graphics provide a means to explain situations to the user much more rapidly than text. However, Huff et al. found only 3.1 percent of the systems they surveyed used graphics. We would expect that this was a function of cost-effective availability. With the explosive development in personal computer systems, work stations, and software, we expect that graphics use will increase significantly in the near future.

A heavy use of models was found by Huff et al. (94 percent of those surveyed). Chapter 8 will provide a more complete picture of what models can do within decision support systems. It is important to recognize that the focus is on effective modeling of the decision problem rather than sophisticated algorithm use. Although some DSSs include advanced models, the next chapter will include examples of model use where it is necessary that users understand *how* the computer comes to its conclusions. It is notable that Hogue and Watson found very little interaction with operations research/management science departments. Most models were user generated. Widely available tools make this possible. Fourth-generation languages, applications generators, and inexpensive yet powerful commercial packages such as Lotus, IFPS, linear programming, statistical systems, and many other applications make user construction of a DSS very reasonable.

A related concept concerns the use of DSS to support groups. We will discuss this topic more thoroughly in Chapter 9. However, what we have seen in this chapter bears on the concept of DSS. Although the original concept was custom-designed support for an individual decision maker, actual practice seems to indicate much more group involvement. This may be a function of changes in the way organizations make decisions. Electronic communications and more thorough analysis available from computers may have had an impact in increasing consultation with others before making decisions. Huff et al. found over one-third of the systems they examined involved a group decision (as opposed to 14.5 percent individual decision making). This may be biased in that many of the systems examined in the Huff study were in the public sector. But Hogue and Watson found 13 of 18 systems involved group decisions as well.

El Sherif proposed an institutional-wide system of DSSs. There is a difference in the kinds of interactive support required when considering multiple users. The theoretical focus in the 1970s was on matching individual decision-making styles. If many people are going to be involved with using a DSS, it would seem more important to design the system around the problem environment than around specific individuals. There are other considerations that need to be addressed in this organizational (as opposed to personal) environment. There is a need to provide effective training. Furthermore, inevitable organizational resistance to change needs to be addressed by the demonstration of system effectiveness.

Chapter 8 will examine seven DSSs in some depth. These systems are all real applications, taken from a journal that requires user certification prior to publication. These systems were selected because we felt they demonstrated some of the advanced possibilities of DSS. They tend to be fairly complex and involve more advanced model types. This should not be interpreted as a necessary condition for a DSS. First, there is a certain bias. Journals do not publish what the editorial staff considers to be a mundane application. Advanced and complicated systems tend to get more notice. We would like you to remember that simple systems can be built by anyone with access to a personal computer and software. We tend to feel that there is more net benefit to society from a large number of small, uncomplicated systems than any one blockbuster system. Decision support is available throughout business. We look forward to impressive advances in DSS use in the near future.

REFERENCES

Alter, S. L. 1977. A taxonomy of decision support systems. *Sloan Management Rev.* (Fall):39–56.

Anthony, R. N. 1965. *Planning and control systems: A framework for analysis.* Cambridge, MA: Harvard Business School.

Bonczek, R. H., C. W., Holsapple, and A. B. Whinston. 1980. The evolving roles of models in decision support systems. *Decision Sci.* 11 (2):337–56.

El Sherif, H. 1990. Managing institutionalization of strategic decision support for the Egyptian Cabinet. *Interfaces* 20 (1):97–114.

Gensch, D. H., N. Aversa, and S. P. Moore. 1990. A choice-modeling market information system that enabled ABB Electric to expand its market share. *Interfaces* 20 (1):6–25.

Gorry, G. A., and M. S. Scott Morton. 1971. A framework for management information systems. *Sloan Management Rev.* 13 (1):56-70.

Hogue, J. T., and H. J. Watson. 1985. Current practices in the development of decision support systems. *Information and Management* (April). 205–212.

Huff, S. L., S. Rivard, A. Grindlay, and I. P. Suttie. 1984. An empirical study of decision support systems. *INFOR* (February): 21–39.

Keen, P. G. W. 1980. Adaptive design for decision support systems. *Data Base* 12 (1–2): 15–25.

Keen, P. G. W. 1981. Value analysis: Justifying decision support systems. *MIS Quarterly* 5 (1):1–16.

Keen, P. G. W. 1986. *Competing in time: Using telecommunications for competitive advantage.* Cambridge, MA: Ballinger.

Keen, P. G. W., and M. S. Scott Morton. 1978. *Decision support systems: An organizational perspective.* Reading, MA: Addison-Wesley.

Little, J. D. C. 1970. Models and managers: The concept of a decision calculus. *Management Sci.* 16 (8): B466–B485.

Simon, H. A. 1960. *The new science of management decision.* New York: Harper & Row.

Sprague, R. H., Jr., and E. D. Carlson. 1982. *Building effective decision support systems.* Englewood Cliffs, NJ: Prentice Hall.

PROJECT IDEAS

How can a PC system, including a database package, a spreadsheet, and a word processor (or an integrated system), be used to develop a DSS?

What does El Sherif mean by "institutionalization"? What bearing does the concept of institutionalization have on DSS design and use?

How can decision support systems aid decision maker learning?

In 1982, there was a debate in *Interfaces* concerning the concept of DSS. Naylor (1982) argued that DSS was simply an extension of traditional management science analysis. Blanning (1983) and Watson and Hill (1983) begged to differ. Review these articles and discuss the two positions.

Blanning, R. W. 1983. What is happening in DSS? *Interfaces* 13 (5):71–80.

Naylor, T. H. 1982. Decision support systems or whatever happened to M.I.S.? *Interfaces* 12 (4):92–94.

Watson, H. J., and M. M. Hill. 1983. Decision support systems or what didn't happen with MIS. *Interfaces* 13 (5): 81–88.

There are many commercially available systems that are advertised as DSSs. One of these is IFPS, which we will present in Chapter 7. There is a choice available to DSS builders, in that they can develop systems from scratch or they can purchase generic systems. Discuss the benefits and relative deficiencies of these two extreme approaches.

CHAPTER FIVE

Data Collection

The focus of this chapter is on how to access raw data. A discussion of intelligence, the processing of data into human understanding, is presented, along with two real examples where data collection, turned into intelligence, played a useful role. The types of data useful to business decision making are addressed, and sources are discussed. Currently developing technology, to include commercially available electronic databases and CD-ROM disks, is reviewed, along with the need to develop electronic and model assistance in dealing with data. An Appendix gives some published sources of data.

This chapter will answer the following questions:

- □ What is meant by intelligence in data collection terms?
- □ What types of data are needed in business?
- □ What sources exist to obtain this data?
- □ What kinds of commercially available electronic databases exist?

There is more data in the world than anyone can hope to digest. A major role of a management information system is to store essential data in an easily retrievable way. Libraries perform the same function for the general public. Many agencies, public and private, generate and store data on special topics. In all cases, there is far more data than is demanded. Computers have played a major role in the enormous growth in data available and in allowing humans to cope with it.

The management problem in coping with data is what to keep and how to keep it. A general fact of life is that you never know what data is going to be useful in the future. Life is interesting because you never know what problems you will face tomorrow. One extreme approach to data management is to keep it in its rawest form, so that you can retrieve and manipulate it to the form you desire whenever you identify a problem. This is an expensive way to operate, because it requires a lot of capability in manipulating data. This approach also costs a lot in storage. The other extreme is to compress data, in the form of averages or unit costs. This saves a lot of storage, but loses a lot of information. Emphasis upon efficient computer system operations leads to the second extreme. Custom-designed decision support systems would tend to keep data in less aggregated form, with detailed information on *selected* topics to allow more flexibility. However, detailed information can only practically be stored and recovered for limited items of data. The value of microcomputer databases is that an individual decision maker can access such data on call, as well as store his or her own data, without the need of burdening an overloaded central information system.

INTELLIGENCE

Having a lot of facts and numbers does not by itself impart knowledge. One of the problems in today's business world is that we have so much data available that we have difficulty making sense out of it. We need a means of converting raw data and bits of facts into something useful.

A series of definitions might explain the process of intelligence (here intelligence refers to learning about a situation, not human ability to think, although they are related). **Data** consists of sets of facts or numbers. Computers are very good at storing and organizing facts and numbers. **Information** is a meaningful conclusion drawn from facts and data. We can view **knowledge** as human understanding. Sound human understanding is gained through *inference, insight,* and *learning.* Having more data should enhance knowledge. But knowledge is not gained by osmosis. **Intelligence** can be defined as the wisdom gained from knowledge, which is only recognized when it is communicated to other people.

Intelligence systems are a means of examining a problem, seeking to apply an approach as scientific and objective as possible to make sound conclusions. A view of an intelligence system would be:

Identification: What information is required?

Acquisition: Obtain the required information.

Storage: Computer information systems perform very well in this area. More than simply placing data and information in databases is required, however. Computer systems need to consider comprehensiveness, as well as efficiency. The more information that is stored, the more difficult it is to retrieve.

Evaluation: Knowledge is gained when data and information are converted into something meaningful to a human. One of the roles of a decision support system is to expedite human evaluation by improving access to key information and providing appropriate models to evaluate through experiment. When this evaluation is automated, the characteristics of expert systems are present.

Application: Although knowledge itself is a worthwhile goal, it does no good to a business unless it is applied. In a DSS, humans hopefully make better decisions because they have gained knowledge and converted it into intelligence. Expert systems can be programmed to go beyond evaluation to application.

There are a number of categories of important intelligence in business. The Jamaican example will demonstrate the importance of **scientific and technological** intelligence. This form of intelligence refers to things the organization does. **Economic and financial** intelligence relates to external and internal business conditions. Externally, it is important to know how the market for the organization's product is doing, both now and in the future. Internally, it is important to have a good idea about product profitability and financial management. **Market** intelligence relates to customer trends, as well as competitor trends. More and more it is necessary to gain **government** intelligence as well, as regulations enforce new programs to accomplish new societal goals. **Negotiation intelligence** is another critical element in many business operations. Knowing what the other side will settle for would have a dramatic impact on the profitability of any particular deal.

Two examples follow that demonstrate the value of intelligence.

JAMAICAN BAUXITE INSTITUTE
Ventura (1987)

The aluminum industry involves significant capital investment and technical expertise. The industry is an oligopoly, with a limited number of multinational producers dominating the market. World War II saw this industry grow substantially, with requirements for vehicles and munitions. Deposits in Europe and the United States were soon depleted, and the multinational companies developed bauxite deposits, the raw material that is processed into aluminum, worldwide.

Many new deposits were located in the Caribbean. Jamaica is one of the largest sources of bauxite in the world. As might be expected, multinationals held significant control over the management and royalty reimbursement of bauxite depletion.

In 1972, Jamaica elected a new government, which was interested in obtaining more control over bauxite mining in Jamaica. Bauxite was a major element in the Jamaican economy, providing most of the funds necessary to conduct the government. When the new Jamaican government met with aluminum producers operating in Jamaica, the government found that it was at a disadvantage because the companies had all of the technical and most of the accounting data available to them, whereas the Jamaican government had to operate without this information.

A training program was instituted to develop Jamaican bauxite specialists. By 1972, a mineralogy laboratory was established. The Jamaican Bauxite Institute was formed to gather as much detailed intelligence on the aluminum economy as possible. This included:

> Technical information (the multinationals had cited substitutes for aluminum as a reason for keeping costs, and thus royalties, down; the multinationals had also indicated that there was only a 25-year mining reserve in Jamaica)

> Economic information (the multinationals used internal accounting to determine the royalty they paid to Jamaica)

> Political information (the multinationals were based in the United States and Canada, and there was concern about the response of these countries to unilateral actions by Jamaica)

A number of interesting conclusions were reached by the Jamaican Bauxite Institute. Although a number of alternatives to bauxite as a source of aluminum exist, none of these alternatives are economically competitive. Furthermore, it was found that a 100-year reserve at current production existed in Jamaica. Politically, it was found that the Canadian and U.S. governments were sympathetic to Jamaica's position and would not interfere with actions under consideration.

Jamaica was instrumental in the formation of the International Bauxite Association (IBA), a cartel of bauxite-producing countries. This cartel was modeled after OPEC, seeking to gain international control over a resource critical to most of its members. This political power, coupled with the technical and economic intelligence gathered, enabled Jamaica to deal with the multinationals from a position of strength.

A number of strategies were adopted by IBA members. Guyana nationalized all operations. Surinam let multinational companies continue to operate, but formed a government agency to make all production and construction decisions. Jamaica's approach was to obtain a majority interest in all bauxite and alumina operations. The IBA was able to negotiate new terms for royalties, basing the royalty on final aluminum content rather than on the aluminum company's valuation of bauxite. The U.S. dollar was used as a basis for royalty payments.

By the end of the 1970s, Jamaica was able to increase its revenues while slowing the depletion of its resources. Ventura cites the social intelligence gathering efforts of Jamaica as playing a primary role in gaining control over its resources.

To follow up this story, major changes have occurred in the aluminum industry. The economic hold on the market of the multinationals was broken. However, the IBA has not maintained its hold either. The price of aluminum was very low in the early 1980s, making it difficult to operate at cost. Because of the large capital investments required, production continued despite losses. This led to significant curtailing of aluminum production in the Caribbean, with operations closing in Haiti and the Dominican Republic. Multinationals quit operating in Guyana, and operations in Surinam and Jamaica dropped substantially.

At the same time, operations in Brazil and Venezuela, which had not been large producers, grew a great deal. Neither Brazil nor Venezuela had joined the IBA. Australia, which had joined the IBA, but whose local governments, which controlled royalty policies, did not support the IBA, became the world's largest producer despite inferior ores. These events have led to a Jamaican depression during the 1980s.

Certainly, the case demonstrates the extreme importance of intelligence in all forms. Negotiation is crucial, not only in international affairs, but in all businesses. Negotiating without knowledge is a sure path to failure. Knowledge is required in technical areas, economic considerations, and political factors. Jamaica did a very good job gathering intelligence in all of these areas.

Negotiation requires more than intelligence, however. Jamaica may have overreacted somewhat. Although the multinationals undoubtedly had not shared the fruits of mining as equitably as possible, Jamaica's actions ultimately resulted in harm to both the multinationals and Jamaica. Others have stepped in, resulting in a much more diversified world aluminum industry. Although Jamaica benefitted a great deal in the short run, it took much less time than expected for the economic system to react.

An additional example, more general in nature, but also more successful, concerns the international grain industry.

GRAIN TRADERS
Blanc (1987)

The world grain trade is dominated by five multinational corporations: Cargill (United States), Continental Grain (United States), Louis Dreyfus (France), Andre (Switzerland), and Bunge (Argentina). This industry is notable for its secrecy. Grain-trading multinationals have been in business for a long time and have maintained their control over the industry. Because of its profitability, all firms are closely held, without the need to obtain capital in open markets such as the stock exchange. This means that they do not have to disclose operational matters.

Blanc studied this industry and found that one of the secrets to its success is its mastery of intelligence gathering and interpretation. Although none of the intelligence the multinationals keep is confidential in any way, and all of it ultimately becomes public knowledge, the important aspects are instant worldwide communications of sound information. Blanc stated that they run their intelligence services all over the world like private news agencies that never print a word.

The grain industry is characterized by highly volatile prices. The ability to obtain immediate information is crucial. We all can read what markets did yesterday, and ticker tapes can tell us what they did a few moments ago. But by the time we take action, the market may well have changed. Cargill has 140 affiliates or subsidiaries in 36 countries. Its Minnesota headquarters operates a network of offices overseas, with a private computerized telegraph system linking 250 North American locations and 60 overseas. This provides Cargill critical access to any information affecting the world grain market. Information from multiple sources is coordinated.

Although access to information is necessary, it is also necessary to have people with the expertise to interpret the data. Company experts are well versed on crop conditions worldwide, making them sound sources of demands for grain throughout the world. By electronic linkages, these experts can keep on top of a very complex market.

Tools

Grain companies invested in telecommunications early in the century. Recently, they have integrated space technologies and computers in their daily operations. Satellites and remote sensing provide a means to monitor crop acreage throughout the world. This is especially valuable in monitoring developing countries, where alternative sources of information may not be available.

Computer models are also used to predict crop production and for econometric forecasting. These computer models were cited as among the most powerful tools for grain intelligence ever developed. An example is the AgServe program developed by Control Data Corporation. This model combines a sophisticated agricultural database with crop modeling techniques, a weather database, statistical tools, and connections with demand models from Wharton Econometrics. Again, whereas all of the raw information is public knowledge, the model's ability to conduct complex analyses quickly makes it a valuable resource.

Conclusions

This example demonstrates the value of intelligence. Raw data becomes intelligence when it is processed. Millions of bits of data are available, but they need to be put into some order to enable valid conclusions.

Computer systems make this possible. There is a need to store and manipulate vast quantities of data in databases. There is a need to process this data, sometimes with statistical procedures, sometimes by filtering out qualitative data to present essential information to humans. Computer systems also make it possible to build models that translate intelligence into predictions of future events. When these models are used in decision support systems, what-if scenarios can be conducted.

Analytic models are by definition abstractions of reality. There are always details left out. However, very often the details left out of MIS reports and databases are crucial to the intended use of the analytic model. Therefore, it is often necessary to scratch up data beyond what is readily available in reports. This activity is called research.

SOURCES

There are a number of methods available to accomplish such research. The primary source of information within a company would be expected to be the management information system. Another source of data is observation, or time study. Surveys are also useful means of obtaining data. For data concerning an industry in general, one can often rely upon private agencies that collect and publish information concerning industry-specific operations. Governmental agencies also provide excellent sources of data for general economic conditions. There are other less direct methods of data collection as well. Many people have been hired for the primary reason that they are very familiar with a competitor's operations. We will not discuss more covert means of data collection.

Many decisions are well supported simply by obtaining a crucial bit of information. Data is also crucial in the use of models, which we will discuss in later chapters. All of them are sensitive to some degree upon the accuracy of input data. Garbage in yields garbage out. This makes data collection a crucial element of the overall decision-making process. It also tends to be the most time-consuming element.

Six major sources of decision support system information are reviewed (Figure 5.1).

Figure 5.1
Sources of business data.

Management Information Systems

Time Studies

Surveys

Industry Publications

Government Publications

Commercial Electronic Databases

Management Information Systems

The primary source of internal company data is the MIS. One of the roles of an MIS is to serve as a database, providing consistent information for all managers within the company. Computers have made this function extremely efficient relative to precomputer systems. Database management is a growing area of importance.

But not all desired information about company operations will be found in the MIS. New problems often call for new data. Although cost data is often found in the database, the explanation of specific circumstances resulting in cost performance is not usually stored. Another problem is that analytic models often need time data, which may be random variables rather than constants. Knowing the mean value will not always provide all the information required for analysis. It often is necessary to go beyond the MIS database to obtain the required data.

Time Study

The term *time study* is used here to apply to collection of data by observation. There are many benefits to time study as a means of data collection. First, one can control the quality of the data collected, because scientific principles can be applied. This means that the observer can also note factors that cause particular times to vary. When key information is not known, sometimes it can be gathered by observing actual operations. It is also possible to conduct experiments to generate this unknown information. Valuable knowledge about the causes of problems often can be found by watching the operation. This can sometimes lead to a quick solution to the decision problem. Another major benefit is that the analyst can obtain a much better understanding of the important elements in the process being analyzed.

The actual time study is not that complex. All that is necessary is a watch, a clipboard to record data, and a good view of the operation. Time study simply involves recording all events that happen, when they start, and when they stop. Time study has some costs, however. It is very tedious work. In addition, once the raw data is collected, a lot more work is involved in processing it. It is relatively expensive, due to the time required. Furthermore, as in any process of scientific observation, large samples are required to obtain a complete picture.

Time studies are not always socially acceptable. People tend to behave differently when they are being watched. In a strict union shop, the observer is often viewed as a spy. Besides the social dangers, work tends to take longer than it normally would. At the other extreme, workers may feel they should work faster. Either behavioral modification distorts the data measuring business operations.

There are short-cut methods for time study. Work sampling is a term for a spot-check time study. In this approach, the observer does not spend the entire time recording events, but pops in to observe at periodic intervals. This is more like statistical sampling, whereas a continuous time study would be more akin to a population survey.

Computers have recently been used for time study purposes. As the trend to automatic machinery (robotics, numerical controlled machinery, computer-assisted manufacture, etc.) has developed, operators on the production floor are now assigned more to monitor the operation and correct problems as they arise. They are often able to record the beginning and ending times of production events at terminals located at the work stations, or computer systems can automatically record these times. Either is a very useful means of collecting data on operations.

Surveys

Many questions involving new operations or products cannot be observed. The future must be predicted. The expert opinion of a number of different sources can be obtained by asking. For new products, no one should know more about customer preferences than those customers. For new operations, people who have worked in the area under question have knowledge that can be tapped. Experts may be people within the company or professional experts outside the company. In all cases, survey questionnaires provide a useful means of obtaining predictive information. Most marketing research is of this type and can even be expanded to include controlled experiments. Professional experts have been used to predict future events, sometimes through application of the Delphi technique, a process of interactive expert opinion to be discussed in Supplemental Chapter 1.

A potential problem with surveys is that one should expect those being surveyed to look out for their vested self-interest. Customers may have a tendency to lead the producer to expect higher demand, resulting in larger supply and thus lower prices. Experts internal to the company are often held responsible for production. They may include a bias toward a pessimistic estimate of required times and resources. Sales managers, seeking to satisfy the customers they have to deal with, may have a more optimistic bias.

Industry Publications

Most industries have associations that provide a variety of services to their members. These services include lobbying efforts, educational programs to inform the public of industry products, and pooled advertising to increase demand. Another common service is the collection of industry-specific data. For instance, blue books are often available for specific industries, such as automotive repair, providing standard fees for specific services. Blue books are also available for the rental of various types of equipment and many other items.

A major change in technology is the use of compact disk–read only memory (CD-ROM) as a means to distribute information. Gale GlobalAccess (Mitchell and Harrison 1989) is one source for many types of information that can be obtained on CD-ROM. Companies can and do use this technology for parts manuals. Furthermore, schools and libraries use this technology as well. A CD-ROM's capacity is up to 600 megabytes of data. CD-ROMs have been cited as having the capacity to handle 18 volumes of printed material. Compact disk drives can be obtained providing users the ability to search vast amounts of data. Because these systems are read only, they are not storage devices. However, they provide a revolutionary means of distributing data. Data suppliers typically revise disks on cycles of about six months, redistributing updated information.

A future development will probably be the incorporation of multimedia technology. These systems would require both audio and visual data simultaneously. Compact disks were initially designed for audio systems, as most of you undoubtedly have experienced. Thus the technical capability exists. Gale cites the current problem of fitting additional channels into a computer system (two for sound, one for video, and one for data) which must be interleaved properly.

The major advantage of CD-ROM is the large physical size capacity (over 250,000 pages of text per disk). This would save many trees. Furthermore, CD-ROMs are highly durable. However, these systems currently have high prices, as does the software to efficiently retrieve data.

Government Publications

There are many governmental agencies at the state and federal level with responsibilities for collecting and reporting data. One very positive feature about our federal bureaucracy is an extremely well developed statistical capability. All governmental agencies pump out reams of detailed measurements of some aspect of our society. Of particular interest to businesses are Department of Commerce and Department of Labor documents. Most university libraries include a government documents section. This general source of information provides valuable measures of the general economy. Most states have a bureau of business research which provides similar measures of that state's economic activity. A list of some useful federal sources of data relative to economic performance are given in the Appendix, as well as a few other sources. One of the most complete sources of economic performance is the *Survey of Current Business*, which continues the *Business Conditions Digest* data series.

Commercial Databases

A major growth area in the U.S. economy is the development of commercial databases (Figure 5.2). A wide variety of governmental measures of the economy are available on tape or disk. International organizations provide similar

COMPUSTAT: Financial database providing extensive statistics of financial operations of over 12,000 companies over time. Bibliographic data banks for news and references are available through **COMPUSERVE**

DRI (Data Resources, Inc.): Statistical data banks in agriculture, banking, commodities, demographics, economics, energy, finance, insurance, international business, and other

Dow Jones Information Service: Statistical data banks on stock market and other financial activities, as well as company financial statistics. A news retrieval system provides bibliographic data banks

Interactive Data Corporation: Statistical data bank covering agriculture, autos, banking, commodities, demographics, economics, energy, finance, international business, and insurance

Lockheed Information Services: Over 150 data banks in agriculture, business, economics, education, energy, engineering, environment, news, governments, patents, science, and other

Mead Data Central: **Nexis** provides a full text bibliographic database of over 100 newspapers, magazines, and other news publications
Lexis: Provides a bibliographic database of legal cases

Figure 5.2
Representative commercial database services (From Turban [1990], p. 241).

(although less developed) data for worldwide activities. These applications are part of the governmental responsibility to measure and report how well the economy is doing. But commercially viable operations have been developed for applications such as the *Dow Jones Information Service,* providing stock market data and in-depth financial statistics on corporations. *Mead Data Central* provides major bibliographic data banks, one covering legal information and articles and the other covering news by topic (to include the *Encyclopaedia Brittanica*). These are only two sources for a true growth industry in providing information. Statistical data banks are available for agriculture, banking, commodities, demographics, economics, energy, finance, insurance, international business, and specific industries. It is now possible to have your computer monitor the stock market during the day while you are at work, to have a program scan stocks to identify performances matching specifications you have selected, to develop a plan of action for the morning, and to allow you to review the options and select your stock dealings for tomorrow. Electronic communications facilities can then be used to contact your broker so that your decision can be implemented.

The explosion in available data has resulted in a booming industry in keeping track of it. Daniells (1985) has published a source book of business information sources, categorizing available data by topic (such as basic U.S. statistical sources, foreign statistics and economic trends, industry statistics, and functional topics, such as accounting, computer information systems, finance and banking, insurance and real estate, international management, and marketing).

The *Encyclopedia of Business Information Sources* (Woy 1988) gives approximately 20,000 citations on about 1,000 business-related subjects. This publication is designed to provide a quick survey of key sources about a subject, as well as specific references to sources for more detailed information. Entries are arranged by subject (such as absenteeism or the battery industry) and further subdivided by type of source and publication.

The *Encyclopedia of Information Systems and Services* (Lucas 1990) provides an index system to identify sources. The master index covers all sources arranged alphabetically by name of organization. The database index provides information about machine-readable files (including on-line and CD-ROM modes). The publications index lists printed sources. The software index reports products available for data management and manipulation. Furthermore, organizations and services are indexed by means of data delivery, the personal name index identifies human contacts, and sources are indexed geographically. Finally, there is an index to general and specific subject interests.

ACCESSING DATA

Technological development in data storage and delivery has been an area of astounding progress. A major idea behind decision support systems is to provide decision makers the means to cope with this vast amount of data. It is crucial for decision makers to develop the means of identifying the information that would enable them to make better decisions.

Little presented a plenary session of the 1990 Joint Meeting of the Operations Research Society of America and the Institute of Management Sciences October 29, 1990. Little was one of the early proponents of using computers to aid decision makers, focusing on the use of models in the functional area of marketing. Some of his comments are reviewed below to demonstrate the value of system support to focus on key information for decision making.

INFORMATION TECHNOLOGY
Little (1990)

Little noted that we are entering an era in which a large portion of business activity will involve the interaction of computers across organizations. A major challenge is to develop equipment, as well as models, to extract decision-making information from massive amounts of automatically collected data. The effectiveness of workers is expected to be impacted significantly by their ability to use these tools. Little also emphasized the need to remember scientific principles, by approaching problems with an attitude seeking theories and mental models explaining what is occurring within organizations, testing theories and models with observed data, and learning through theory revision.

Little focused on the specific topic of marketing consumer goods. Sales of these products were cited as being about $280 billion per year. Marketing these goods costs manufacturers tens of billions of dollars per year, allowing many opportunities to improve efficiency and effectiveness.

Bar coding, similar to what we see in grocery stores, has created many opportunities for efficiency. Not only does it take much less time to get through a checkout line, but vast amounts of information can be obtained immediately. Bar coding started in 1974, and its initial growth was relatively slow. In 1979, Information Resources (IRI) applied bar coding technology in the area of marketing research. Test market sites in Pittsfield, Massachusetts, and Marion, Indiana, were selected, because of their high rate of cable TV usage. IRI placed bar code scanners in all supermarkets in these cities, recording sales and price data. Furthermore IRI recorded all newspaper advertising and all special store displays. In each market, 3,000 to 4,000 households were recruited, and a special device was placed on their TV sets. Members of these households identified themselves whenever they went through a grocery checkout counter to enable automatic detailed data collection about their purchases. The devices on the test group's TV sets were used to send different commercials in order to obtain a controlled study of their impact. This use of technology, including bar codes, computers, and cable TV, allowed an extremely powerful laboratory for marketing research.

By the mid-1980s, scanners were used on a wide enough basis to permit a national sampling of 2,500 or more supermarkets. Major data services were developed by Nielsen as well as IRI. The impact of price and promotion can be evaluated very effectively throughout the distribution chain, from manufacturer through wholesale and retail centers to the customer.

However, Little noted that the amount of data available is enormous, roughly 100 to 1,000 times what manufacturers had previously experienced. This makes identification of detailed information difficult. Little noted the need to get data under control. Models and analysis were cited as necessary tools to avoid failure. Furthermore, market response models to measure marketing variables such as price and promotion of various kinds are necessary. Given the vast quantities of data, automation is a must. An example study of coupon effectiveness reported by Abraham and Lodish (1987) was reviewed.

In 1988, about 220 billion coupons for product price reduction were distributed. About 3 percent of these coupons were redeemed. Distribution, handling, and redemption cost manufacturers about $4.7 billion. Although the number of coupons redeemed was available, it was not known how many of these customers would have purchased these items anyway. To study the impact of this promotion device, the purchase histories of 60,000 households in 25 markets were collected. Models were developed to measure the true impact of coupons. In the test, models of sales for tested items were calibrated for a period of time before coupons were distributed. The models were then used to project sales in the absence of coupons. Then actual sales in the presence of coupons were monitored. The difference between forecast and actual sales measured the amount of sales attributable to the coupon promotion.

Little emphasized the major problem facing business in the current data-rich environment. Vast quantities of data exist, providing the ability to more thoroughly understand what goes on in a business. However, the ability of humans to manually cope with this data has been exceeded. Computer databases can be invaluable in storing information. But the larger these databases become, the more difficult it is to retrieve particular items of information.

Business decision makers do not need to be swamped with information. There are certain key bits of information that would enable them to better understand what is happening. Little proposed the need for computer systems and models to condense vast quantities of data into key information. Little cited the use of models and expert systems by salespeople in the field to produce analyses of customer benefits for that customer's specific situation. Another example was the use of work stations within home improvement stores, allowing customers to design their particular project on the computer, which would develop a bill of materials and its cost as the project was designed.

Much of what Little proposes is being incorporated into commercial databases. Lockwood (1989) reports on two of these systems where the need to provide information to executives quickly is addressed. DowQuest, a service sold by Dow-Jones to provide information on articles published on various topics, allows executives to enter a word, phrase, or question. A search algorithm automatically scans through the database of 185 publications and retrieves articles meeting the criteria selected by the user. Nexis, the news service discussed before, offers software for about $50 which provides menu interface and prompts the user to create searches off line and download results automatically. All search items can be seen on the screen (if they fit). Other software products are available to aid database searches, and new products are being introduced on a regular basis.

SUMMARY

It has been said that we have entered the information era. The amount of data available has exploded. How to access this data is of major concern. Computer systems provide a means to not only store vast quantities of data, but to manipulate this data (through models and expert systems) into meaningful intelligence as well.

It is true that tremendous potential exists. Many people are concerned with this ability to move into the "Big Brother" era. The problem posed to society and business is to harness the power of computer databases and intelligence systems while obtaining rational controls on this power.

Time study provides a valuable approach to experiment and observe the impact of proposed changes to operations. Other experiments can be devised to obtain new knowledge about the business as well. A general scientific approach is valuable, in accessing and generating knowledge relative to a systematic theory of how the business functions.

Consideration of data is often given little notice. It is primarily a matter of hard work, with the need to apply objectivity as often as possible. There are many sources of data within an organization. General sources for obtaining business data were discussed. These sources cover both measures of internal operations (MIS, time study, surveys) and the environment external to the business (surveys, publications to include CD-ROMs, commercial databases). The potential of converting data into intelligence was demonstrated with two examples. Knowing where to find key information is a very valuable skill. The ability to generate additional information is even more valuable.

REFERENCES

Abraham, M. A., and L. M. Lodish. 1987. PROMOTER: An automated promotion evaluation system. *Marketing Sci.* 6 (2):101–23.

Blanc, G. 1987. The grain traders: Masters of the intelligence game. In *Intelligence for economic development: An inquiry into the role of the knowledge industry,* ed. S. Dedijer and N. Jequier, 139–57. New York: Berg.

Daniells, L. M. 1985. *Business information sources.* rev. ed. Berkeley: University of California Press.

Little, J. D. C. 1990. Operations research in industry: New opportunities in a changing world. The 1990 Philip McCord Morse Lecture, ORSA/TIMS Joint National

Meeting, Philadelphia, October 29, 1990. The Operations Research Society of America.

Lockwood, R. 1989. On-line finds. *Personal Computing* (December):79–84.

Lucas, A., ed. 1990. *Encyclopedia of information systems and services.* 10th ed. Detroit: Gale Research, Inc.

Mitchell, J., and J. Harrison. 1989. *CD-ROM directory 1990.* 4th ed. London: TFPL Publishing.

Turban, E., 1990. *Decision support and expert systems: management support systems.* 2nd. ed. New York: Macmillan.

Ventura, A. K. 1987. Jamaica's bauxite battle. In *Intelligence for economic development: An inquiry into the role of the knowledge industry,* ed. S. Dedijer and N. Jequier, 111–27. New York: Berg.

Woy, J., ed. 1988. *Encyclopedia of business information sources.* 7th ed. Detroit: Gale Research, Inc.

PROJECT IDEAS

A useful short project would be to have students explore the library for electronic databases.

A subsequent exercise would be to have students actually use the databases that are located.

Time-Study Possibilities

There are many operations involving customer arrival and service. Examples include post office operations or bank teller windows. To understand what is involved, the student needs a clipboard, a watch with a second hand, and a block of free time. Gather data by recording when a customer arrives (could have started service if the server was not busy), when service starts, and when service ends. Other events worth recording are when a service element stops service for whatever reason. Once data is collected (at least one hour, at least 30 observations), the data needs to be analyzed to determine the time between arrivals and the time for each service. These measures then can be plotted to estimate the distribution.

Government Data Collection

The students can be assigned to gather data on some measure of the economy, such as the gross national product or the unemployment rate. The measure could be annual, quarterly, or monthly. It may be used to add to an existing data set on the computer system used. Students should find what the definition of the series is, as well as historical data dating back to a time compatible with the existing data set. Hopefully, this will require digging through back issues including historical updates.

Surveys

Students can develop a survey questionnaire and seek information concerning some issue of interest. Using other students as subjects is usually workable, especially if there is an issue of interest to students, with some expected significant difference of opinion. In conjunction with the gathering of survey opinion, the student might check with authorities or other sources of information.

APPENDIX: Data Sources

Federal Publications

Business Conditions Digest (Department of Commerce) (**discontinued March 1990**)—monthly report of a number of data series focused on forecasting U.S. GNP

Survey of Current Business (Department of Commerce) (**continues *Business Conditions Digest* in short form**)—monthly, general business conditions

Monthly Labor Review (Department of Labor)—monthly employment statistics (a journal with articles)

Employment and Earnings (Department of Labor)—monthly, more detailed than *Monthly Labor Review*

Other

International Monetary Fund—report of balance of payments, including currency rates, for participating countries

Moody's—a series of manuals including abstracted information and balance sheets of most large U.S. corporations, intended for investors

Standard & Poor's—annual, updated report of financial stability of most U.S. corporations

Advertising Age—marketing newspaper, with a great deal of data on marketing

Annual Editor & Publisher Market Guide—annual report of marketing information by SMSA (standard metropolitan statistical area)

Indexes

Business Information Sources. 1985. rev. ed., ed. L. M. Daniells. University of California Press. Categorization of databases by functional area of business

Encyclopedia of Business Information Sources. 1988. 7th ed., ed. J. Woy. Gale Research, Inc. Bibliographic guide on about 1,000 business subjects, including on-line databases

Encyclopedia of Information Systems and Services. 10th ed., ed. A. Lucas. Gale Research, Inc. Descriptive guide to databases in electronic form

The CD-ROM Directory. 1990, 1989. 4th ed., ed. J. Mitchell and J. Harrison. TFPL Publishing. Index of CD-ROM databases

CHAPTER SIX

Database Management

Current, accurate data is a fundamental prerequisite to effective decision making. Almost all the techniques described in this book depend heavily on the appropriate data. Organizations have realized that data is a valuable asset, and in the past few years they have developed techniques for managing data resources effectively. Computer database systems provide a means to organize data and to access this data electronically. Courtney and Paradice (1988) discuss the use of database systems to aid business decision making.

Large organizations generate tremendous amounts of data that can only be managed with the aid of computers. Effective computer databases require careful planning, design, development, and operation. All of these functions have been studied by data management specialists, and specific techniques have been developed for planning, designing, implementing, and operating database systems.

Our perspective here, however, is that of the user of organizational databases. Thus our main concern will not be so much with how databases are built, but with how to use them.

This chapter will discuss:

□ The purposes, types, and objectives of database systems
□ The concept of relational database systems
□ The Structured Query Language

TYPES OF DATABASES

There are three primary means of organizing databases typically used today. We will focus on **relational** databases. Two other approaches are the **network** and **hierarchical** models. Network and hierarchical models will be briefly described, because they occur widely in organizational data processing, especially at the operational level of the firm, where efficiency is more important than flexibility.

Relational databases are probably the most popular form of database today. Thus we will describe them and the Structured Query Language (SQL) because it has been chosen by the American National Standards Institute as the standard query language for relational database systems. SQL is a fourth-generation language (4GL) as discussed in Chapter 1. The developers of most major database packages now provide SQL interfaces. By 1987, there were already over 50 SQL software packages available for various and sundry computer systems. Today, these packages probably number in the hundreds. Ageloff (1988) provides a useful demonstration of SQL.

THE OBJECTIVES OF DATABASE SYSTEMS

The main goal of an organizational database system is to collect the data necessary for running the enterprise and making that data accessible to those who have a legitimate need for it. The same data is often useful to many people both inside and outside the organization, and if so, access to that data should be shared.

For example, a retailing company needs information on its sales to bill its customers, to decide what items to order, and to know how its main function, selling, is performing. Sales data is useful to sales managers, general managers, purchasers, accountants, and many others in the firm. That same information, when amassed for all retailing firms in the country, is useful to the federal government in determining how the retailing sector is performing. This information may be crucial to decisions of the Federal Reserve Board in its attempts to influence the economy by managing interest rates. Investors also have a legitimate need to have sales information on firms in which they own shares or firms in which they might invest.

For several reasons, it makes sense to collect this data once, store it in one place, and then disseminate it to those who have a legitimate need for it. If the data is stored in one place, it makes it easier to update if the values change or if an error has occurred. If the same data value is scattered around at several different locations (either different areas of the storage devices of one computer or on different computers), it is costly and inefficient to have to search for all the locations where a number might be stored in order to change it. If one or more locations were missed during an update operation, then we would end up with inconsistent data. Some users would be using one number, and others would use a different number for the same thing. If this data were used to drive decision models, it would probably lead to incorrect decisions for some users. So for shared data, the objective is to have one location for each data value.

In a database environment, it is imperative that the data be protected from unauthorized access and malicious or unintentional damage. This is especially true because so many people have access to the database. There are many measures used to provide data security. Two of them, views and access privileges, are described later in the chapter. Several other techniques are also commonly used, but they are rather technical and we will not discuss them.

Finally, let us point out that many users will always have specialized data needs for models, reports, or some other purpose unique to one person or a few people at a localized site. If the data is not useful to others in the organization, then it does not make sense to include it in the organizational database system. Chapter 5 described the need for such data and how it can be collected. Network and hierarchical database management systems will be discussed next. The remainder of this chapter deals with relational databases and how to manage and access data with SQL.

NETWORK AND HIERARCHICAL DATABASES

In the hierarchical and network approach, it is useful to distinguish **record types** from **record occurrences**. A **record type** is a named set of data items corresponding to some type of entity, such as an employee, a customer, a student, a machine, a product, and so on. Thus we might have an employee record type, a customer record type, a student record type, and so forth. A **record occurrence** consists of the data values for a specific employee (say, James Olson), student (Courtney Paradice), machine (serial number 007), and so on. In other words, a record occurrence is just the data for one record of a given record type.

In hierarchies, record types are thought of as being arranged in "trees" or levels of record types (Figure 6.1). The topmost level or "node" is called the "root node," because the data organization starts here. In Figure 6.1, the root

Figure 6.1
A hierarchy.

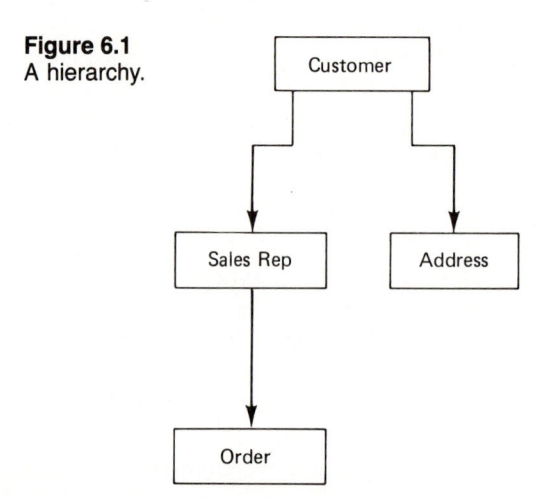

node is customer. Customers have sales reps, which occur at the level below customers. The customer record type is said to be the "owner" or "parent" of the sales rep record type. The sales rep record type is said to be the "child" of the customer record type or a "member" in the sales rep–customer set. (The terms owner and member were defined by the Conference on Data and Systems Languages, CODASYL, for short, which is an industry-wide committee that sets standards for network databases.) Notice that customers also "own" an address record type. Customer addresses and sales reps are called "siblings" because they occur at the same level in the tree and have the same parent.

The type of relationships occurring between record types is what distinguishes hierarchies from networks. In the database in Figure 6.1, it is assumed that a given customer, say Norma Gaiter, is always serviced by the same sales rep, say Bill Trotter. However, one sales rep, Bill Trotter, may service many different customers, say Norma Gaiter, James Olson, and Courtney Paradice. This is an example of a one-to-many relationship. One sales rep services many customers. This is permissible in hierarchies, as are one-to-one relationships. If customers were large companies, say IBM, Dow Chemical, and Exxon, and one salesrep were assigned to a single company, then that would be a one-to-one relationship between companies and sales reps. Say IBM was handled by Norma Gaiter, Dow by Ajay Zork, and Exxon by Lisa First. There is one rep to one company, and vice versa. Finally, a node in a hierarchy may have only one parent node, which is the case in Figure 6.1.

One-to-one and one-to-many relationships are relatively easy to handle in database systems. IBM has had a hierarchical database package called IMS on the market for over 20 years. Thousands of databases built on IMS are still in use today. Some process hundreds of thousands of transactions per day. Such databases are very efficient in handling routine transactions such as retrievals about a specific part, employee, student, and so on. They are not very effective at dealing with unanticipated queries such as those arising in the DSS environment. Relational databases are the choice in such circumstances, which is why we concentrate on them in this book.

Remember that in a hierarchy, each node could have only one parent node (Figure 6.2). If a node has two or more parents, but only one-to-one or one-to-many relationships exist between parents and children, then the situation is called a **simple network.** To illustrate simple networks, suppose we rearrange the entities and relationships in Figure 6.1, as shown in Figure 6.2. Now customers "own" orders directly, and sales reps also "own" orders. Thus the orders record type has two parents making this a simple network.

If we have a situation wherein a customer calls in an order and the order is taken by any sales rep that is available, then we have a many-to-many relationship. This occurs because one customer may be handled by many different sales reps (on different calls), and one sales rep handles many different customers.

Figure 6.2
A simple network. This is a simple network because the order record type has two parents, Customer and Sales Rep.

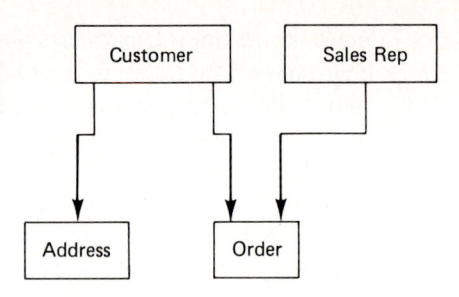

This is a more complicated relationship to represent and is referred to as a **complex network.**

There are numerous database packages in existence that can handle networks, both simple and complex. Software packages conforming to the CODASYL specifications, for example, can handle networks. Many of these packages have fourth-generation languages suitable for end users. However, these languages have no standard specifications. The CODASYL committee has published standards for a "data manipulation language" which is designed for use in conjunction with COBOL. This language is obviously intended for use by programmers and is beyond the scope of this book.

RELATIONAL DATABASES

In a **relational database,** data is thought of as being arranged in simple tables with rows and columns. We will use an example database that is a partial implementation of the Fisher-Price executive information system (EIS) described in Chapter 10. The example database is shown in the appendix to this chapter. (*Note:* The data in this table has been devised by the authors. Fisher-Price may not sell the products described here.)

Relational databases are founded on the mathematical theory of sets or relations (hence their name). We will not be concerned with the theory; we will just focus on how to use SQL to create, implement, and modify relational databases. Much of the literature on relational databases uses the terms *relation* to refer to a table, *attribute* to refer to a column, and *tuple* to refer to a row. We will use the more common terms *row, column,* and *table.*

Each table in a relational database is given a name. Likewise, each column in a table is also named. The actual data is stored in the rows. In a properly designed relational database, each table corresponds to a set of entities or objects often called an **entity class.** An entity can be just about anything—for example, a student, an employee, a vehicle, an insurance policy, a dog, a joke, or a security. All students, employees, vehicles, and so on, taken together, constitute the entity class. The table name is, of course, based on the entity class stored in that table. Therefore, we might have an Employee table, a

Student table, an Auto Policy table, or a Dog table. The entities in the Fisher-Price database are products, sales representatives, customers, and orders. Notice that there is a table for each of these entity types.

Entities have characteristics or **attributes** (hence the name of columns in relational databases). Employees have social security numbers, phone numbers, salaries, job titles, and so on. Jokes have punch lines, subjects, and so forth. The type of attribute in a column, then, determines the column name. For example, we might have columns with names such as Social Security Number, Spouse, Policy Number, Vehicle Number, Color, Breed, and so forth.

Values for attributes are selected from a **domain,** which is simply the set of permissible values that the attribute can have. The set of nine-digit integers is the domain for Social Security Number. The set of all dog breeds is the domain for the attribute Breed. The domain concept is one way of helping to assure accuracy (usually called **data integrity**) in relational databases.

It is necessary to be able to identify each row in the database, and in order to do this each row must have an identifier called a "key." The key is usually a data item such as Social Security Number or Student ID. Sometimes two or more columns are required to form a unique key for each row. If so, this is called a combined key. We will see an example shortly.

The design of relational databases with efficient update properties is a rather complex process. The design goal is to avoid mixing data about different entity types in the same relation, except where we need information on the relationships between entities. For example, in the Fisher-Price database, we have tables defined for the entities mentioned previously, but we also have special tables set up to indicate the relationships between customers and orders (the CUSTOMER_ORDER table) and sales reps and orders (REP_ORDER).

This organization of the data makes updating and maintenance efficient, but may be a nuisance to users when data is retrieved, because we may have to pull data from several different tables to get what we need. There is a way around this problem by using what is referred to as a "view" of the database. For the time being, we will illustrate SQL with the database in the appendix. Views will be discussed later.

The Structured Query Language

As mentioned previously, SQL is the standard retrieval language for relational databases. Standards for the language have been published by the American National Standards Institute (1986). Standards are helpful in making it easier for users to implement different packages. Once the standard language has been learned, all one has to do to use a different package is to learn its particular nuances (probably no package conforms precisely to the standards). This is certainly much easier than learning a completely new language.

Perhaps the easiest way to describe SQL is through examples. The Fisher-Price database will be used to illustrate SQL.

Defining an SQL Database

To define relations in SQL, the CREATE TABLE operation is used. A CREATE TABLE statement is used to name each table in the database, specify its columns, and denote the type of data each column contains. The statement may also contain the keywords NOT NULL and UNIQUE to ensure that a unique key exists for each row.

The most common data types are CHARACTER (abbreviated CHAR), DECIMAL, and INTEGER. To see how these are used, let us look at the CREATE TABLE statement that would be used to define the PRODUCT table:

```
CREATE TABLE PRODUCT
(ITEM#          CHAR (11) NOT NULL,
 DESCRIPTION    CHAR (20),
 PRICE          DECIMAL (6,2),
 ON_HAND        INTEGER,
 UNIQUE         (ITEM#) )
```

Notice in this example that the maximum length of character data is given in parentheses following the keyword CHAR. ITEM# is the key attribute for the table, so it is specified to be NOT NULL in its entry and the last clause requires that it be UNIQUE. Decimal entries, such as that for price, are given a length and number of decimal positions in parentheses. A length is not specified for integers, such as the quantity on hand. Integers may range roughly from -2 billion to $+2$ billion. There are other data types for large real numbers and small integers, but we will not discuss them.

By the way, the previous CREATE TABLE statement was indented to improve its readability to people. It could have been strung out on two or three lines for the computer. The same is true for all the following SQL statements, but we will indent to help you see the way the statements are structured.

A combined key is illustrated in the ORDER table, which requires a combination of ORDER# and ITEM# to identify each row. The correct statement is

```
CREATE TABLE ORDER
(ORDER#       CHAR (5) NOT NULL,
 ITEM#        CHAR (5) NOT NULL,
 QUANTITY     INTEGER,
 DISCOUNT     DECIMAL (3,2),
 UNIQUE       (ORDER#, ITEM#) )
```

Here the UNIQUE clause specifies that the combination of order number and item number must be unique.

To add rows to a table, the INSERT operation is used. For example, to add the first row to the PRODUCT table, the appropriate statement is

```
INSERT
INTO     PRODUCT
VALUES ('A0001', 'Ninja Turtle Doll', 29.95, 1052)
```

Any item not declared to be NOT NULL may be omitted from the list of values, but then the column names for which values are given must be included in parentheses after the table name in the INSERT clause. To see this, assume that the quantity of fuzzy dice on hand is not known. Then the statement to insert the known values would be

```
INSERT
INTO     PRODUCT (ITEM#, DESCRIPTION, PRICE)
VALUES ('C0373', 'Fuzzy Dice', 10.95)
```

Retrieving Data from One Table

Most of the features of SQL will be illustrated by retrievals that deal with only one table, as this will simplify the discussion. Of course, it is essential to be able to combine data in different tables and this will be described later in the chapter.

The most basic form of an SQL retrieval statement is

```
SELECT   (list of columns)
FROM     (table name)
```

For example, to retrieve salesrep name and region, the query and corresponding output would be

```
SELECT   NAME, REGION
FROM     SALESREP
```

	result:	NAME	REGION
		Chavez	Southwest
		Conaway	Texas
		Hathaway	West
		Aaron	Northeast
		Gonzales	Southwest

If all the columns in a table are desired, an asterisk (*) follows the SELECT keyword, rather than typing every column name:

```
SELECT   *
FROM     SALESREP
```

	result:	SS#	NAME	REGION
		252-75-3781	Chavez	Southwest
		255-89-7221	Conaway	Texas

372-75-8388	Hathaway	West
388-62-3241	Aaron	Northeast
457-25-3891	Gonzales	Southwest

Suppose we want a list of regions as given in the SALESREP table, so we enter the query:

```
SELECT    REGION
FROM      SALESREP
```

> result: REGION
> Southwest
> Texas
> West
> Northeast
> Southwest

Notice that SQL displays every occurrence of region, including duplicate values (Southwest is the only region duplicated). In a case such as this, we probably only want to see unique region names, not duplicates. If so, we need to use the keyword DISTINCT before the list of column names, as follows:

```
SELECT    DISTINCT REGION
FROM      SALESREP
```

> result: REGION
> Southwest
> Texas
> West
> Northeast

Notice now that the duplicate value for the Southwest region has been eliminated from the output. DISTINCT may be used only once in a given SELECT clause.

WHERE Clauses

There are many extensions to the basic SQL retrieval statement. Probably the most common is the WHERE clause, which is used to specify conditions on data values to be included in the output. The general form is given as follows:

```
SELECT    (list of columns)
FROM      (table name)
WHERE     (condition)
```

To illustrate, suppose we want to know the price of a Bat Mobile. The query is

```
SELECT     PRICE
FROM       PRODUCT
WHERE      DESCRIPTION = 'Bat Mobile'
```

result: PRICE
          42.95

Notice that the product description Bat Mobile is enclosed in single quotation marks ('). In addition, this query uses the equal (=) comparison operator. Other comparison operators are $<$, $>$, $<=$, $>=$, and $<>$ (not equal). The query to list all product descriptions with prices less than or equal to 29.95 is given as

```
SELECT     DESCRIPTION
FROM       PRODUCT
WHERE      PRICE <= 29.95
```

result: DESCRIPTION
          Ninja Turtle Doll
          Baby Rattle
          Fuzzy Dice

AND and OR

Additional conditions may be given by using the logical connectors AND and OR. Suppose we want to retrieve product descriptions where the price is less than or equal to 29.95, and quantity on hand is less than 2,000 units. We would enter

```
SELECT     DESCRIPTION
FROM       PRODUCT
WHERE      PRICE <= 29.95
AND        ON_HAND < 2000
```

result: DESCRIPTION
          Ninja Turtle Doll
          Fuzzy Dice

An OR is required if we want to know the price of both nuclear tanks and baby rattles:

```
SELECT     DESCRIPTION, PRICE
FROM       PRODUCT
WHERE      DESCRIPTION = 'Nuclear Tank'
OR         DESCRIPTION = 'Baby Rattle'
```

result: DESCRIPTION   PRICE
          Nuclear Tank   54.95
          Baby Rattle   5.95

IN and NOT

The previous query may be shortened by using the operator IN, which is used to specify a set of values, any one of which may satisfy a WHERE clause. This is done by substituting IN for = , dropping the OR, and putting the set of values in parentheses following IN:

```
SELECT    DESCRIPTION, PRICE
FROM      PRODUCT
WHERE     DESCRIPTION IN ('Nuclear Tank', 'Baby Rattle')
```

result:

DESCRIPTION	PRICE
Nuclear Tank	54.95
Baby Rattle	5.95

Suppose we want to know the price of every item *except* nuclear tanks and baby rattles. This can be done by using the NOT operator before IN:

```
SELECT    DESCRIPTION, PRICE
FROM      PRODUCT
WHERE     DESCRIPTION NOT IN ('Nuclear Tank', 'Baby Rattle')
```

result:

DESCRIPTION	PRICE
Ninja Turtle Doll	29.95
Remote Control Car	249.95
Bat Mobile	42.95
Fuzzy Dice	10.95

LIKE

The operator LIKE is used to retrieve data when an exact match of a character string is not needed, but rather a general pattern is desired, such as all the names that begin with A or all the product descriptions that include "Remote Control." In specifying strings with LIKE, the underscore (_) stands for any single character, and % stands for any character string of any length (including zero length). To illustrate, suppose we want to find the name of a sales rep and all we remember is that the name begins with "C." This requires matching a string of arbitrary length, so % will be used. We can list all sales reps' names starting with C, by using the following syntax:

```
SELECT    NAME
FROM      SALESREPS
WHERE     NAME LIKE 'C%'
```

result:

NAME
Chavez
Conaway

If we want the names with six characters, beginning with C, we follow the C in the query above by five underscores, instead of a %:

```
SELECT      NAME
FROM        SALESREPS
WHERE       NAME LIKE 'C_____'
```

result: NAME
            Chavez

BETWEEN

If we want to retrieve values that lie within a range (some upper and lower bound), we may use the BETWEEN operator. (We could use ANDs, but BETWEEN is shorter.) For example, if we want the product description and price of any product whose price is in the range 29.95 to 54.95, inclusive, we could use the phrase:

```
WHERE       PRICE >= 29.95
AND         PRICE <= 54.95
```

Using BETWEEN and showing the whole query would be expressed as

```
SELECT      DESCRIPTION
FROM        PRODUCT
WHERE       PRICE BETWEEN 29.95 AND 54.95
```

result:

DESCRIPTION	PRICE
Ninja Turtle Doll	29.95
Nuclear Tank	54.95
Bat Mobile	42.95

In using BETWEEN, the lower bound must be given first (before AND), and values matching the upper or lower bound are included in the output.

To show that character data can be used in a BETWEEN clause, assume that we want a list of all customers whose name begins with one of the letters between A and M. The query is

```
SELECT      NAME
FROM        CUSTOMER
WHERE       NAME BETWEEN 'A%' AND 'M%'
```

result: NAME
            Cheslow
            Kim

ORDER BY

Many times we may want to have output sorted into ascending or descending order by a column such as customer name, product description, social security number, or item number. SQL offers the ORDER BY clause to sort output. Results are placed in ascending order, unless descending is specified. Suppose we want to see a list of customer numbers and names, in alphabetic (ascending) order by name. The query demonstrated yields

```
SELECT      CUSTOMER#, NAME
FROM        CUSTOMER
ORDER BY    NAME
```

```
result:    CUSTOMER#      NAME
           C010           Cheslow
           C001           Kim
           C025           Silver
           C007           Walters
```

If we want the same information in inverse alphabetic order, then we must use the descending (DESC) option, yielding:

```
SELECT      CUSTOMER#, NAME
FROM        CUSTOMER
ORDER BY    NAME DESC
```

```
result:    CUSTOMER#      NAME
           C007           Walters
           C025           Silver
           C001           Kim
           C010           Cheslow
```

Computed Values

Simple computations can also be performed in SQL statements. The operators $+$, $-$, $*$, and $/$ are used to indicate addition, subtraction, multiplication, and division, respectively. In evaluating a mathematical expression, multiplication and division are performed first, then addition and subtraction. Parentheses may be used to control the order of evaluation. As an example, suppose we want to know the market value of the inventory of nuclear tanks (price $\times$ quantity on hand).

The appropriate query is given as

```
SELECT      ITEM#, (PRICE*ON_HAND)
FROM        PRODUCT
ORDER BY    DESCRIPTION = 'Nuclear Tank'
```

```
result:    ITEM#      (PRICE * ON_HAND)
           A0007      97426.35
```

Functions

Several mathematical functions are included in the SQL specifications. These include COUNT, SUM, MAX, MIN, and AVG (average). To compute the total market value of all items in inventory, we could use the SUM function as shown:

```
SELECT      SUM(PRICE*ON_HAND)
FROM        PRODUCT
```

result: SUM(PRICE*ON_HAND)
            1050501.40

If we wish to count the number of regions, we would use:

```
SELECT      COUNT (DISTINCT REGION)
FROM        SALESREP
```

result: COUNT (DISTINCT REGION)
            4

Notice the use of DISTINCT here. Without the DISTINCT keyword, we would have obtained a count of 5.

To count the total number of rows in a table, we would use COUNT (*). So the adjacent query would count the number of rows in the ORDER table:

```
SELECT      COUNT (*)
FROM        ORDER
```

result: COUNT (*)
            7

GROUP BY

Simple reports may be produced with SQL by using an operation known as grouping. To illustrate, assume that we want a report giving the total number of units on order for each item appearing in the ORDER table. The operator GROUP BY, which is always used in conjunction with a function, gives us the capability to do this rather easily. The proper statement is

```
SELECT      ITEM#, SUM (QUANTITY)
FROM        ORDER
GROUP BY    ITEM#
```

result: SUM (QUANTITY)
ITEM#
A0001   110
B0008   120
C0373   10
A0007   50
B0192   60

ORDER BY can be used to sort output in a GROUP BY operation, but ORDER BY must follow GROUP BY:

```
SELECT      ITEM#, SUM (QUANTITY)
FROM        ORDER
```

```
GROUP BY    ITEM#
ORDER BY    ITEM#
```

result: ITEM#   SUM (QUANTITY)
           A0001   110
           A0007   50
           B0008   120
           B0192   60
           C0373   10

In addition, conditions may be specified on the GROUP BY clause by giving the conditions in a HAVING clause that directly follows GROUP BY. To give an example, assume that we want to limit the output of the previous query to only those items with total orders exceeding 100 units. The statement changes as is demonstrated:

```
SELECT      ITEM#, SUM (QUANTITY)
FROM        ORDER
GROUP BY    ITEM#
HAVING      SUM (QUANTITY) > 100
ORDER BY    ITEM#
```

result: ITEM#   SUM (QUANTITY)
           A0001   110
           B0008   120

In a query such as that previously given, WHERE can still be used to specify row conditions. If so, WHERE precedes GROUP BY, as in the next query, which restricts the output in the preceding statement to only those items whose numbers begin with the letter B:

```
SELECT      ITEM#, SUM (QUANTITY)
FROM        ORDER
WHERE       ITEM# LIKE 'B%'
GROUP BY    ITEM#
HAVING      SUM (QUANTITY) > 100
ORDER BY    ITEM#
```

result: ITEM#   SUM (QUANTITY)
           B0008   120

Retrieving Data from Multiple Tables

When the data that we wish to retrieve resides in different tables, then the tables, or parts of them at least, must be combined somehow. This is referred to as a "join," which is performed by connecting the tables on the basis of columns in each table containing a common element of data. In relational database parlance, we are referring to the columns whose data come from a common domain. For example, the ORDER table and the PRODUCT table have

ITEM# in common. The CUSTOMER_ORDER table and the REP_ORDER table have ORDER# in common.

To illustrate a join with two tables, suppose we want to know the name of the sales rep who took order number Z272A. This requires a join over data in the REP_ORDER table and the SALESREP table. As before, we specify the columns we want displayed in the SELECT clause, the tables (more than one now) in the FROM clause, and use WHERE to specify the conditions. The query to get the desired data is

```
SELECT    NAME
FROM      SALESREP, REP_ORDER
WHERE     ORDER# = 'Z272A'
AND       SS# = REP#
```

result: NAME
           Aaron

Here the join operation is specified in the AND clause, which requires that the social security number must equal the sales rep number. Even though the column names are different, these columns contain the same data (the data comes from the same domain).

To see another join, suppose we want to know the item numbers of the items that were ordered by customer number C010. This requires combining data from the CUSTOMER_ORDER table and the ORDER table, as shown:

```
SELECT    ITEM#
FROM      ORDER, CUSTOMER_ORDER
WHERE     CUSTOMER# = 'C010'
AND       ORDER.ORDER# = CUSTOMER_ORDER.ORDER#
```

result: ITEM#
           A0001
           B0008
           C0373

Notice that the table names have been prefixed to the column names in the AND clause. This is necessary to eliminate ambiguity, as otherwise we would enter ORDER# = ORDER#, which would not make sense to a nonthinking computer.

To illustrate a join involving three tables (a "three-way join"), assume that in the previous query we wanted to see both item numbers and item descriptions. The description is stored in a third table, PRODUCT. The appropriate query is

```
SELECT    PRODUCT.ITEM#, DESCRIPTION
FROM      ORDER, CUSTOMER_ORDER, PRODUCT
WHERE     CUSTOMER# = 'C010'
```

```
AND        CUSTOMER_ORDER.ORDER# = ORDER.ORDER#
AND        PRODUCT.ITEM# = ORDER.ITEM#
```

result:

PRODUCT.ITEM#	DESCRIPTION
A0001	Ninja Turtle Doll
B0008	Baby Rattle
C0373	Fuzzy Dice

There is another way of performing joins in SQL databases. This involves what is called a "nested query" or "subquery." Nested queries are connected via the IN operator described earlier. In a join over two tables, a subquery is used to define a set of values, which are then fed to the "main" query via IN. The subquery follows the main query and is placed in parentheses. This may sound like a complicated operation, but it really is quite simple. An example will help clarify the process. Let us see how to use a subquery to retrieve the name of the sales rep who took order number Z272A. (We did this previously using WHERE and AND.)

```
SELECT    NAME
FROM      SALESREP
WHERE     SS# IN
    (SELECT REP#
     FROM REP_ORDER
     WHERE ORDER# = 'Z272A')
```

result:

NAME
Aaron

In the previous statement, the subquery in parentheses is performed first and defines a "set" containing only one value, sales rep number C007, who took the order. The sales rep number C007 is fed to the main query via the IN operator, and the sales rep's name is found in the SALESREP table. Here again, SS# and REP# come from the same domain.

Next, we will use a subquery to find out what items were ordered by customer number C010. The correct statement is

```
SELECT    ITEM#
FROM      ORDER
WHERE     ORDER# IN
    (SELECT ORDER#
     FROM CUSTOMER_ORDER
     WHERE CUSTOMER# = 'C010')
```

result:

ITEM#
A0001
B0008
C0373

Finally, we will do the three-way join described previously. This will require nesting queries two levels deep:

```
SELECT    ITEM#, DESCRIPTION
FROM      PRODUCT
WHERE     ITEM# IN
    (SELECT ITEM#
    FROM ORDER
    WHERE ORDER# IN
        (SELECT ORDER#
        FROM CUSTOMER_ORDER
        WHERE CUSTOMER# = 'C010'))
```

	result:	ITEM#	DESCRIPTION
		A0001	Ninja Turtle Doll
		B0008	Baby Rattle
		C0373	Fuzzy Dice

Updating SQL Databases

Organizations exist in dynamic environments, and it is necessary to keep the database current. We have already seen how INSERT is used to add data to the database. Two other operations, UPDATE and DELETE, are available to change and remove data, respectively. Some examples of these operations are given next.

UPDATE
Suppose that the customer named Kim moves from Seoul to College Station. The UPDATE operation to reflect this move is

```
UPDATE    CUSTOMER
SET       CITY = 'College Station'
WHERE     NAME = 'Kim'
```

result: 1 record updated.

Notice that the *table name,* not the column name, follows the word UPDATE, and the keyword SET is used to give the new data value. This statement assumes that there is only one person named Kim in the database (or that all customers named Kim are moving to College Station), because all the rows where Kim occurs in the CUSTOMER table will be changed.

DELETE
To illustrate a delete operation, assume that order number Z358R has been filled, and we wish to remove it from the database. The appropriate statement is

```
DELETE
FROM       ORDER
WHERE      ORDER# = 'Z358R'
```

> result: 1 record deleted.

No column names are specified, as DELETE removes an entire row from the specified table.

Different People, Different Perspectives: Views and Security

In a large organization, many people may need to access a particular database. However, most users will need to access only a part of the database, and each person will have his or her own perspective or "view" of the data. Views provide a way of restricting the data to only that portion of the database needed by specific users. Views may also be used to make retrieval operations simpler for many users. As mentioned previously, good relational database design usually results in spreading the data out over numerous tables. Joins may be used to reintegrate the data, but this is often a cumbersome process. Joins may be embedded in views that are accessed by users in such a way that users may never know exactly how the data is organized.

CREATE VIEW

To define a view, a CREATE VIEW operation is required. To illustrate this operation, assume that we want to create a view called SW_REP for the manager of the Southwest region, which includes data only on the sales reps in that region. The definition of this view is

```
CREATE VIEW    SW_REP AS
     SELECT    *
     FROM      SALESREP
     WHERE     REGION = 'Southwest'
```

We can then use this view to retrieve data (not necessarily to update, however) just as if it was defined in a CREATE TABLE statement. So, for example, we could use the syntax:

```
SELECT   *
FROM     SW_REP
```

> result: SS#   NAME   REGION
>   252-75-3781   Chavez   Southwest
>   457-25-3891   Gonzales   Southwest

Because REGION is now redundant as a column, we may wish to exclude it from the view. To illustrate that we can also rename and exclude columns, we will also rename SS# as REP# and NAME as LAST_NAME and drop REGION. The statement for this is

```
CREATE VIEW    SW_REP (REP#, LAST_NAME) AS
       SELECT SS#, NAME
       FROM SALESREP
       WHERE REGION = 'Southwest'
```

Now if we SELECT * FROM SW_REP, we get the result:

REP#	LAST_NAME
252-75-3781	Chavez
457-25-3891	Gonzales

To illustrate how join operations may be embedded in views, making the join virtually transparent to users, we will create a view called ORDER_DATA that has the columns REP#, REP_NAME, CUSTOMER#, CUSTOMER _NAME, and ORDER#. The required view definition is

```
CREATE VIEW ORDER_DATA (REP#, REP_NAME, CUSTOMER#,
CUSTOMER_NAME, ORDER#) AS
SELECT    SS#,    SALESREP.NAME,    CUSTOMER.CUSTOMER#,
CUSTOMER.NAME, CUSTOMER_ORDER.ORDER#
       FROM       SALESREP, CUSTOMER, CUSTOMER_ORDER,
                  REP_ORDER,
       WHERE      CUSTOMER_ORDER.ORDER# =
                  REP_ORDER.ORDER#
       AND        CUSTOMER.CUSTOMER# =
                  CUSTOMER_ORDER.CUSTOMER#
       AND        SALESREP.SS# = REP_ORDER.REP#
```

As you can see, joins can become rather complex in an SQL environment. Imagine having to key this in each time you wanted this data!

GRANT

Views provide one means of limiting access to data, thereby protecting it somewhat. The GRANT operation provides a more powerful means of controlling access to the database.

GRANT is used by the database administrator (the person responsible for managing the database) to specify what type of access privileges each user has for the database. Privileges are associated with users via some sort of user identification procedure that may be unique to the host computer system or the SQL package in use. We will refer to this as a userid. GRANT has the simple form:

```
GRANT     privileges
ON        table or view
TO        userid
```

In this operation, privileges may consist of any combination of SELECT, INSERT, DELETE, or UPDATE. The keyword ALL can be used to authorize all four of these operations. PUBLIC may be used to grant the privilege to anyone who has a userid for the database.

Suppose the person holding userid TERMINATOR is to be given authorization only to retrieve data from the SALESREP table. The appropriate GRANT operation is

```
GRANT     SELECT
ON        SALESREP
TO        TERMINATOR
```

For example, say that the holder of userid DIEHARD should be able to retrieve and perform all update operations on the PRODUCT table. The statement is

```
GRANT     SELECT, INSERT, UPDATE, DELETE
ON        PRODUCT
TO        DIEHARD
```

or, equivalently,

```
GRANT     ALL
ON        PRODUCT
TO        DIEHARD
```

Suppose the sales manager for the home office is assigned userid GOSELL, and she is to have retrieval-only privileges on the view ORDER_DATA defined previously. We would enter:

```
GRANT     SELECT
ON        ORDER_DATA
TO        GOSELL
```

Finally, say the sales manager for the Southwest region holds userid HAVASUPI and he is to have all privileges on the SW_REP view. The statement to allow this is

```
GRANT     ALL
ON        SW_REP
TO        HAVASUPI
```

A Note on Other SQL Features

There are several other features of SQL, mostly used by database personnel. For example, it is possible to embed SQL statements in programs written in a host language such as COBOL, FORTRAN, or C. Such features are clearly not intended for the ordinary user and will not be described in this book.

SUMMARY

The current business environment includes many items of data that can be accessed electronically. Databases provide the means to organize this data effectively and to allow its retrieval in an efficient manner. There are a number of ways to organize data in databases. The primary types of database systems have been presented.

This chapter has focused on data management with the Structured Query Language. Data is a valuable asset that organizations should manage effectively. Data useful for one person in an organization is very often useful to many other people, both inside and outside the organization. Such data should be collected, managed, and shared. Those are the main objectives of database systems.

Relational databases organize data into tables with rows and columns. The Structured Query Language is designed to manipulate data in a relational database. The chapter has described the most important features of SQL from a user's point of view.

REFERENCES

Ageloff, R. 1988. *A primer on SQL*. St. Louis: Times Mirror/Mosby College Publishing.

American National Standards Institute. 1986. Database language SQL. *Document ANSI X3* 135.

Courtney, J. F., and D. B. Paradice. 1988. *Database systems for management*. St. Louis: Times Mirror/Mosby College Publishing.

APPENDIX: Relational Database for Fisher-Price EIS

CUSTOMER

CUSTOMER#	NAME	CITY
C001	Kim	Seoul
C007	Walters	Ledoux
C010	Cheslow	Richmond
C025	Silver	New York

CUSTOMER_ORDER

CUSTOMER#	ORDER#
C007	Z272A
C010	X075Y
C025	Z358R

SALESREP

SS#	NAME	REGION
252-75-3781	Chavez	Southwest
255-89-7221	Conaway	Texas
372-75-8388	Hathaway	West
388-62-3241	Aaron	Northeast
457-25-3891	Gonzales	Southwest

REP_ORDER

REP#	ORDER#
252-75-3781	X075Y
255-89-7221	Z358R
388-62-3241	Z272A

PRODUCT

ITEM#	DESCRIPTION	PRICE	ON_HAND
A0001	Ninja Turtle Doll	29.95	1052
A0007	Nuclear Tank	54.95	1773
A0059	Remote Control Car	249.95	2928
B0008	Baby Rattle	5.95	5728
B0192	Bat Mobile	42.95	3272
C0373	Fuzzy Dice	10.95	1379

ORDER

ORDER#	ITEM#	QUANTITY
X075Y	A0001	10
X075Y	B0008	20
X075Y	C0373	10
Z272A	A0007	50
Z272A	B0192	60
Z358R	A0001	100
Z358R	B0008	100

CHAPTER SEVEN

Modeling Support

Chapter 5 discussed how to access raw data. Chapter 6 looked at how this data can be organized and accessed electronically. This chapter focuses on how to analyze data in order to draw conclusions.

One of the most valuable analytic tools to arrive with the microcomputer revolution is spreadsheeting. There are many analyses that took great persistence and ability with a calculator that are now available to everyone with access to a spreadsheet. Spreadsheets give the ability to organize numbers and manipulate them to whatever degree desired. The arithmetical inaccuracies that usually existed in manual operations are gone. (You can still be inaccurate, but it takes effort.) Spreadsheets also include many useful functions and subroutines, making formerly complex operations like net present value calculation, amortization, and depreciation very easy. Furthermore, most spreadsheets have graphics capabilities, making presentation and communication of ideas much more complete, professional looking, and generally more effective.

DSS generators are software packages providing capabilities to develop a specific DSS quickly. This would include the ability to access data, develop a model representation of the decision problem, display results to the user effectively, and provide a means to generate effective reports. Spreadsheets are good examples of general DSS generators.

This chapter will answer the following questions:

- What capabilities do spreadsheets have as general tools?
- What value is this tool in a DSS?
- What differences exist between Lotus 1-2-3 and IFPS?
- What features of IFPS make it a fourth-generation language and a DSS generator?

There are many spreadsheets available. The most widely used on microcomputers is Lotus 1-2-3. There are also mainframe versions, such as the

Interactive Financial Planning System (IFPS). (IFPS has recently been written for microcomputers.) Most students have some familiarity with Lotus, and it is very valuable. This chapter will focus on IFPS. There are some differences in operation, which make it slightly difficult to switch back and forth. But technically, anything that can be done with Lotus can be done with IFPS, and vice versa. IFPS is designed with corporate reporting in mind, and the data entry is by row. Lotus was designed for more general use, and data entry is cell driven. This is the primary difference. IFPS has some very positive features for budget analyses of many varieties. IFPS is self-documenting, thus helping to prevent errors in large, complex applications.

The value of spreadsheet analysis can be demonstrated to some degree in the following actual application of a DSS. Although the analysis involves more than the spreadsheet, hopefully you can see some of the potential of applying a spreadsheet within an overall analysis to aid decision making. IFPS clearly fits the idea of a DSS generator. Lotus is also a DSS generator, but its flexibility sacrifices some of the ease of generating reports that exists in IFPS. Both packages have graphics capabilities that are easy to use.

LA QUINTA MOTOR INNS
Kimes and Fitzsimmons (1990)

La Quinta Motor Inns is a mid-sized hotel chain. This industry has experienced increased competition. Profitability of sites is a function of competitive, demographics, market awareness, demand, and physical variables. One of the most important decisions facing La Quinta is the decision of new site location. The ability to select good sites more accurately and more quickly than the competition provides a significant competitive advantage.

Problem Identification

When competition sought to compete with the special niche La Quinta had developed, La Quinta began by examining what had happened in past location decisions, with the intent of developing a model to aid in future location decisions.

Location decisions at La Quinta were made by several people, including the director of marketing research, the vice-president for development, the vice-president for real estate, the president of the firm, and four site evaluators. The final decision was the president's.

Data Collection

Data was collected on 57 mature inns. Demand generators and competition within a four-mile market area of each hotel were identified. Demographic information and market awareness data were collected from chambers of commerce, tourist bureaus, and the Bureau of the Census.

In addition to collecting data on past performance, models built by others were reviewed. It was found that most of these models were appropriate only for services drawing business from the immediate surrounding area. However, hotel clients are generally attracted to a hotel by its convenience to other travel needs.

Another study conducted for the chain found that 80 percent of its clients visited destinations within four miles of the hotel. This led the analysts to consider a four-mile market area.

Alternative Generation

The decision in this case is an ongoing one, with real estate acquisition opportunities arising for a variety of reasons. In this application, the evaluation system is available to support site location decisions as they arise.

Alternative Evaluation

The basis of the evaluation advisor is a regression model. This model was (is) used to predict performance of a potential hotel location.

The dependent variable selected was operating margin, defined as profit plus depreciation and interest expenses as a percentage of total revenue. Total revenue and total profit were rejected as too highly correlated with hotel size. Occupancy was rejected because it was unstable, especially during turbulent economic periods.

The original analysis was conducted in 1983. That study considered independent variables including six measures of competitive factors, eighteen demand generator variables, three demographic, four market awareness, and four physical variables. Correlation analysis found that hotels tended to do better in areas where the brand had high market penetration and awareness. Demand generators, such as the amount of hospital space and the local population, had positive effects on profitability. Areas with low unemployment tended to do better, because higher prices could be charged. Site accessibility, office space in the downtown area, sign visibility, and traffic count were other important variables.

In 1986, other variables appeared to have stronger correlation with profitability. The number of college students, proximity to military bases, lower median incomes in the market area, and higher competitor room rates had significant correlations with the dependent variable of profitability.

Several variables were found to be significant in one year, but not the other. In 1983, profitable hotels were located in areas with lower airport volume, near to hotels in the same chain, with better sign visibility. In 1986, hotels nearer downtown areas, in higher local population areas, in locations with high traffic counts, and in market areas with more office space were more profitable.

After extensive diagnosis to avoid collinearity and outlier problems, a model was built based on standardized data (mean of 0 and standard deviation of 1) to eliminate scaling problems. The final model included independent variables of state population per inn, price of the inn, square root of the median income of the area, and the number of college students within four miles.

This regression model implies that profitability is affected by market penetration and higher prices (in turn, a function of the competitive room rate in the area). The higher the median income in the area, the lower the profitability expected. The location of colleges nearby had a positive effect.

Rather than attempt to accurately predict profitability, it was considered more important to be able to predict either profitability or unprofitability. A decision rule was developed that would classify sites as good (profitable) or bad (unprofitable) based on criteria selected by management. To be classified as a good site, an expected operating margin of over 35 percent was required. This cutoff was selected by management. The cutoff giving the best results for predicting success or failure (by management's definition) was identified. The firm was more concerned with avoiding bad sites than with missing out by rejecting good sites.

A *spreadsheet system* was used to implement the model. Information on each of the independent variables is entered, and the system standardizes the data and calculates predicted profitability with the regression equation. The decision rule is then applied.

Furthermore, guide sheets for use in the field by site selectors were developed, listing desirable ranges of values for a number of variables.

Decision

The president of the firm has the final decision at La Quinta. La Quinta's president formerly visited each potential site personally. The models have proven valid to the point where this is no longer the case. But the original intent, and current application, of the system is a tool to aid decision makers rather than replace them.

Implementation

The model system has been validated and extended with more sophisticated extensions of locations identified by the regression model as highly probable of profitability. System development was a three-year project, in a period with changing economic conditions and increased competition. The system was modified to account for changes in the external environment.

Monitoring

The president of La Quinta Motor Inns certified the *Interfaces* article with a statement that the model is currently used to aid the site selection process and identified several sites La Quinta was considering as involving too much risk. The model continues to be used and updated.

Comments

This example demonstrates the use of computerized systems, applying both data and models, to a decision. It has characteristics of a **data analysis** type of system in Alter's classification, but characteristics of an **analysis information system** as well.

Usually, we think of a decision as being made by one individual. Technically, that is also true in this case. However, this case demonstrates what probably happens in most situations. Although there is one ultimately responsible individual, most decisions seem to involve the input of a lot of people.

The case also demonstrates the importance of solid scientific analysis. Sound regression procedure was used by the consultants in this case, who were very careful to develop a robust model, avoiding many known pitfalls possible in regression analysis. Logical variables were identified, data collected in as accurate a manner as possible, and thorough regression model design applied.

The importance of continuing to monitor the problem environment is demonstrated. After three years, the economic situation was quite different than had been the case after initial analysis. The model was refined to be robust under both kinds of economic conditions. The company continued to monitor model performance and further refine the system.

IFPS (INTERACTIVE FINANCIAL PLANNING SYSTEM)

IFPS was one of the first (if not the first) products using the term **decision support system.** It is a fourth-generation computer language. Essentially, models can be built algebraically, using variable names that are meant to be helpful to those who did not build the model. The intent was that decision makers could directly build models without technical help.

Model building in IFPS is a matter of formulating a situation, to include identifying objectives and relevant variables. Variables in the model are tied together through algebraic relationships. Once such a model is built, it can be treated very much as a simulation model, although generally spreadsheet models do not involve random numbers (they can). Different decision alternatives can be designed and results compared. As in simulation, each decision alternative must be modeled. The steps of simulation are appropriate, in that the model needs to be validated (the answers you get make sense). In practice, it is very easy to validate IFPS models, because the definitions of variables are very self-descriptive. An easy check is to verify the first two columns or so to assure relationships are working correctly. A key feature of IFPS is WHAT-IF analysis. In effect, sensitivity analysis can be conducted with spreadsheets by making temporary assumptions for selected variables. These are not permanently changed in the model, but reports are generated making these temporary assumptions, and decision makers thus have the ability to see what impact various assumptions would make. IFPS has other features designed to aid decision makers as well. A GOAL-SEEKING analysis is available to allow the modeler to see what conditions would be necessary to obtain specified results. An EXPLAIN module gives the user the ability to diagram relationships, see which variables impact others, and even ask why a particular function peaked or troughed at a particular time.

An example application of IFPS use follows. The oil industry involves high degrees of uncertainty. With the price of oil fluctuating wildly over the last 20 years, sudden losses can be incurred, but opportunities for tremendous profits can arise as well. This example demonstrates the use of IFPS to aid decision making in an oil company.

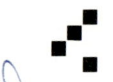

PENNZOIL PRODUCTS COMPANY
Wysocki (1988)

Pennzoil Products manages the production and marketing of lubricating oil and specialty products. It is aided by a sophisticated planning system that forecasts market demand by product group and distribution area, as well as assisting in determining the price of each product. This system is based on the IFPS/Plus system, a menu-driven modeling and spreadsheet package.

One of the system's outputs is the Logistics Division's portion of the annual profit plan. The Operational Planning System forecasts monthly operating statistics for supply, distribution, purchasing, and seven packaging plants. The distribution of lube base oils produced at Pennzoil refineries is also suggested, along with forecasts of finished product costs for marketing and monthly income statements by plant for finance. In addition to these primary functions, the system also provides essential data used for many operational decisions.

The system is flexible, allowing special reports in response to requests, such as reports on volumes by location or updated cost reports. A valued feature noted by the users of the system was the user-friendly interface allowing generation of new reports in very short time periods.

Pennzoil Products' Lube Supply and Distribution Department began computerized generation of the annual profit plan and mid-year update in the mid-1970s. In 1988, they redesigned the system based on IFPS/Plus, because the old system had become so complex through additions and changes that there was concern about the ability to generate the mid-year update to the annual profit plan. The new system's first actual test was to generate the update, which was accomplished on time with fewer complications than ever experienced with the old system. As often happens, when the plan was submitted, higher management asked for a change. With the new system, this change was easily accomplished. With the old system, a great deal of complication and trouble would have been encountered.

The perceived benefits of the redesigned system included the ease of data management (requiring only initial data entry). The system was found to be easy to use, based on menus and prompts. Although modeling capabilities were not directly required for the primary purpose of generating the annual plan, they were desired for future expansion.

IFPS MODELING

To Build a Model

The IFPS system varies with computer system, but, in general, there are two types of files you will want to use, an input file, containing one or more models, and an output file, containing reports. Both types of files are created within IFPS.

To build a model, the command is **MODEL name**. An IFPS model looks very similar to a BASIC program, in that a line number determines the sequence of the report. Note that it is not necessary, as would be the case in a BASIC program, that sequential logic exist. You have the ability in IFPS to define variables in terms of other variables that have *not* yet been defined. Ultimately, each variable used must be defined. But the model is compiled by the package after it is completed, and the order of variables is meant to determine the order of the report.

An optional first entry is the AUTO command. The AUTO command automatically numbers lines for you. You can specify the starting line number and the increment, such as **AUTO 10 10**. This would start the numbering system with line 10 and increment by 10. **AUTO 8 3** would label the first line 8, the second 11, and so on.

IFPS modeling is very straightforward. The rows of the model are used to define variables. The first variable in a model defines the columns. COLUMNS is a key word, which cannot be used as a variable name. The COLUMNS variable can be numbers (each column is indexed, first–last column) or a name, which can be entered in sequence, separated by commas:

COLUMNS 1–5

or

COLUMNS YR1,YR2,YR3,YR4,YR5

Other variables are entered as you desire for the report. If you use the AUTO command, the number will be there. You simply name a variable, followed by an =, and define it. There are a number of optional means of defining variables. Note that upper- and lowercase letters can be used, but that IFPS will treat X as a different variable than x. In addition, note that the apostrophe (single quote) is a continuation symbol, should a definition be longer than one line. Do not use the continuation in the middle of a variable name.

1. Simply enter constants, separated by columns:

    X = 5,5,5,112,42

    If you define fewer constants than you have columns, the default will be to the last entry. The word FOR can be used:

    X = 5 for 3,112,42

2. The PREVIOUS statement is extremely useful, especially when there are growth rates:

    X = 100,previous*1.05

    The PREVIOUS statement will take the last entry in the column and perform the prescribed operation. You can also use the PREVIOUS statement to manipulate some other variable:

    X = 100,100 + previous Y

    or

    X = 100 for 2,100 + previous 2 Y

3. Very often, variables are represented as algebraic manipulations:

    X = Y/Z + (W-V)

    The standard basic arithmetical conventions apply. Note that variables do not have to be spelled out, but can be referred to by L###, the line number where the variable was defined.

4. Variables can also be defined through subroutines, covered shortly.

Spaces or comments in the report can be obtained by typing * at the beginning of a line. If nothing follows the *, a blank line will be inserted in the report. Comments and headings, or theoretically even prose, can be inserted following the *. IF-THEN-ELSE contingent variable values can be entered in a straightforward manner. Relationship conventions follow FORTRAN, with .LT. for strictly less than, .LE. for less than or equal to, .EQ. for equals, .GE. for greater than or equal to, and .GT. for greater than. The IFPS syntax is:

    X = If A .GT. B then C else D

To finish a model, type **END OF MODEL**. This model can then be listed or edited. To list, simply type **LIST**. The currently active model will be listed, or you will be informed that there is no active model. To activate a model, type **MODEL** modelname.

Editing

To edit a file, type **EDIT** modelname. There are a few key editing commands we will cover. Note that there are more editing commands available in the references.

Delete #D—where # is the line number to be deleted.

Insert #line—you can insert a line anywhere you want, as in BASIC. The line number determines where it goes.

Replace #line—if you insert a line with the same number as an existing line, the old line is replaced.

Change #C/old/new—the old string in # is replaced by the new string.

SAMPLE MODEL

A simple model is presented, starting with the output (Table 7.1), which seems to be the easiest means to explain what is desired, and then showing the model that would generate that output. The scenario is a straightforward situation where revenue is generated from sales, which grow at the rate of 10 percent per year. There are a number of cost elements. Net profit is sales less the total of these expenses. In this case, depreciation is treated in the cost accounting sense. The model would be as shown in Table 7.2.

Table 7.1

	YEAR1	YEAR2	YEAR3	YEAR4
Sales	100000	110000	121000	133100
Cost of sales	45000	50000	55000	60000
Gross profit	55000	60000	66000	73100
Salaries	40000	41000	42000	43000
Benefits	4000	4100	4200	4300
Administrative expense	5000	5200	5408	5624
Depreciation	8000	8000	8000	8000
Interest	2000	2000	2000	3000
Total expenses	59000	60300	61608	63924
Earnings before tax	− 4000	− 300	4392	9176
Growth	1.1	1.1	1.1	1.1

Table 7.2

	MODEL GOLD
	AUTO 10 10
10	COLUMNS YEAR1,YEAR2,YEAR3,YEAR4
20	*
30	Sales = 100000,previous*Growth
40	*
50	Cost of Sales = 45000,previous + 5000
60	*
70	Gross Profit = Sales-Cost of Sales
80	*
90	Salaries = 40000,previous + 1000
100	Benefits = Salaries*.1
110	Admin Expense = 5000,previous*1.04
120	Depreciation = 8000
130	Interest = 2000 for 3,3000
140	Total Expenses = L90 + L100 + L110 + L120 + L130
150	*
160	Earnings before tax = Gross Profit-Total Expenses
170	Growth = 1.1
180	END OF MODEL

FUNCTIONS AND SUBROUTINES

Functions

There are a number of useful functions available on IFPS. We will look at the financial functions. There are also statistical and mathematical functions. Functions are differentiated from subroutines in that functions return a single value. Therefore, functions can be used in variable definitions:

    X = NPVC(a,b,c)

Net Present Value

One of the most useful functions is net present value. Net present value is the worth, in today's value, of a stream of cash flow. The key word calling this function is NPVC. There are three arguments necessary for its calculation: a stream of cash flow, the discount rate, and the original investment. These can be entered as variables:

    X = NPVC(stream of cash flow, discount rate, investment)

Stream of cash flow will usually be a collector variable, which adds together all transactions (net) occurring at the end of a time period. Note that IFPS assumes the conventional application, where a sum of money is invested at the beginning of operations and returns on the investment flow in over time. Therefore, the package is programmed to assume returns occur at the end of the time period.

Discount rate is the cost of capital (borrowing cost, opportunity cost, or other appropriate value) reflecting the time discount. The discount rate is entered in decimal form (10 percent is entered as .1). This value can be entered as a constant, although creating a variable makes what-if analysis easier.

Investment is assumed to occur at the beginning of a period. Note that a variable is usually necessary, because if you enter a constant in the function, IFPS will assume you reinvest that amount every period. If there is a one-time investment at the beginning of operations, that variable needs to be set to 0 after the first period. The sign of investment is programmed in IFPS to be opposite to the stream of cash flow.

There are many more flexible things you can do with the net present value function. You can model assumptions different than those given if you remember cell 1 discounts at the end of the period and cell 3 discounts at the beginning. If you are calculating net present cost (both stream of cash flow and investment are cash outflows), you need to change the sign of either cell 1 or cell 3. Through the use of variables, you can model a changing discount rate, as well as collect quite complex streams of cash flow.

Net Terminal Value

Net terminal value is the same as net present value, except the perspective is at the end of the planning horizon. It returns the value of a stream of cash after n time has past. The key word is NTV, and the same three parameters are required as for net present value:

X = NTV(stream of cash flow, discount rate, investment)

Internal Rate of Return

Internal rate of return is the discount rate that will yield a net present value of 0 for a stream of cash flow. (Note that there may be multiple values—the largest positive value is returned here.) There are only two parameters required. The key word is IRR:

X = IRR(stream of cash flow, investment)

Benefit/Cost Ratio

The benefit/cost ratio (BCR) is the ratio of discounted benefits to discounted costs. If the BCR is less than 1, the returns are not worth the cost. If the BCR is greater than 1, it is worthwhile. BCRs can be compared as a gauge of the relative value of alternative investments. The higher the BCR is, the better. The key word is BCRATIO:

X = BCRATIO(stream of cash flow, discount rate, investment)

Subroutines

Subroutines differ from functions in that multiple outputs are obtained. Therefore, you model the variables implicitly in the subroutine itself and do not define a variable as being equal to anything. We will look at depreciation and amortization subroutines.

Depreciation

Depreciation is a valuable concept, both for tax calculation, as well as for cost accounting. The concept is that an investment in some asset is not really an expense, but rather a conversion of an asset from cash into something useful. However, such assets tend to wear away. Depreciation provides a means of estimating how much such assets decline in value over a period of operations. There are a number of forms of depreciation. IFPS has the capability of supporting the standard forms.

> **Straight line:** This is the most straightforward estimate of depreciation. It is assumed that an asset will be held for n time periods, after which it will be salvaged for x amount of cash. The difference between investment and salvage is equally prorated over all periods. The key word is STLINE DEPR:
>
> STLINE DEPR(investment, salvage fraction, asset life,'
> PERIOD DEPRECIATION, BOOK VALUE, ACCUMULATED DEPR)
>
> The first three entries are inputs. The last three entries are outputs, new variables created. If you do not desire the third output, simply omit defining it in the statement. If all you want is the first output, STLINE DEPR(a,b,c,m). Note that the **salvage fraction** is the proportion of salvage to investment.
>
> **Declining balance:** This form of depreciation uses an acceleration constant, resulting in greater depreciation in early periods. The IFPS subroutine allows switching over to either straight-line or sum-of-years-digits forms. This switchover occurs when accelerated depreciation would be less than the switchover method. The key word is DECBAL DEPR:
>
> DECBAL DEPR(investment, salvage fraction, asset life,'
> acceleration constant, switchover, PERIOD DEPRECIATION,'
> BOOK VALUE, CUMULATIVE DEPRECIATION)

The possible switchover codes are:

> 0—no switchover
>
> 1—switchover to straight line
>
> 2—switchover to sum of years digits

Sum of years digits: This method provides an accelerated method, although less than declining balance. The key word is SUM DEPR:

SUM DEPR(investment, salvage fraction, asset life,'
PERIOD DEPRECIATION, BOOK VALUE, CUMULATIVE DEPRECIATION)

ACRS: The accelerated cost recovery system follows the change in the federal income tax law passed in 1982. Note that this was superseded in 1987. The key word is ACRS DEPR:

ACRS DEPR(category, purchase year or month, investment,'
PERIOD DEPRECIATION, BOOK VALUE, CUMULATIVE DEPRECIATION)

Amortization

Loan amortization is a very useful spreadsheet capability. The inputs of the subroutine are the amount of the amortized loan, the annual interest rate, the loan life, the start column, and the number of payments per column. The outputs are the payment amount per time period, the portion of that payment applied to interest, the portion applied to principal, and the loan balance. The key word is AMORT:

AMORT(amortized loan, unamortized loan, annual interest rate, loan life,'
start column, payments per column, TOTAL PAYMENT,'
PAYMENT TO INTEREST, PAYMENT TO PRINCIPAL,'
LOAN BALANCE)'

REPORTS

To obtain an output report, you must use the RECORD command. Note that if you enter RECORD, nothing will happen. On a mainframe system, you will be opening a buffer which you later can name. The reason you do not name the output file at this stage is that occasionally, the model is not worth saving or you may note a defect in the model. If you have used the RECORD command, when you QUIT, you will be asked to either name the output file or dump the buffer. If you did not RECORD, there will be nothing to save.

SOLVE Options

To run a model, the first command necessary is SOLVE. A model has to be active, either one you have just built or one from a file. There are a number of options available.

WIDTH

You can control the way the report looks with a WIDTH option. Width options must be redone every IFPS session, although they remain active for the entire session unless changed. You can control the overall width of the report, the variable width, the column width, and the number of decimals used in the report. This indirectly allows you to control the number of columns per page (Table 7.3). The defaults assume an 8½-by-11-inch paper for the report. The label width determines how many characters you can have in a variable name. More complete and descriptive reports require longer variable names, in general.

If you have wide printer paper, you can use wider report widths. This makes it easier for you to read reports for those models involving more than six columns. You can specify a subset of these four parameters, as long as they are specified in the order given. For a report with 10 years of data, on a wide printer,

WIDTH 130 30 10

would yield a report 130 characters wide. Thirty spaces are reserved for variable names, leaving 100 spaces for numbers. You specified 10 characters per column, meaning you will get 10 columns per report page. Note that IFPS will wrap fractional columns if a fractional column is left over, which does not look nice. In this case, decimal places were not specified, so the default of float is used.

The next SOLVE option tells IFPS which part of the model is to be included in the report. The options available are:

ALL—the entire report is given.

variable,variable, . . . —the report includes only those variables specified by name.

L###,L###,L###, . . . —the report includes only those variables defined in the lines specified.

La THRU Lb, etc.—the report will list lines a through b.

WHAT-IF Analysis

One of the distinctive features of IFPS is the WHAT-IF command. This option gives the model user the ability to temporarily change assumed values and obtain as much of the report as desired for the specified changes, without distorting the original model.

The WHAT-IF command can be activated any time a model is active. You are asked to enter statements of temporary change. In order to indicate you have made all the changes you desire, you need to type SOLVE when you have

Table 7.3

	Default	Maximum	Minimum
Report width	78	132	20
Label width	24	100	1
Column width	9	32	1
Decimal places	Float	9	−1 (for none)

completed your changes. Then you are given the opportunity to specify which lines you want reported. In the sample model given earlier, the impact of a growth rate of 11 percent (rather than the original 10 percent) could be quickly generated with a WHAT-IF statement:

```
?                       model GOLD
?                       WHAT IF
ENTER STATEMENTS
?                       Growth = 1.11
?                       SOLVE
ENTER SOLVE OPTIONS     ALL or other specifications
```

The resulting Earnings before tax would be

	YEAR1	YEAR2	YEAR3	YEAR4
Earnings before tax	−4000	700	6602	12839

Multiple WHAT-IF statements can be used prior to the SOLVE statement.

GOAL SEEKING

GOAL SEEKING lets you solve the model backwards. You specify a goal value for a particular variable and select one variable that is allowed to change in order to accomplish the goal. If the decision maker desired to see what salaries could be afforded while keeping total expenses at a 2 percent growth rate, the following syntax would apply:

```
?                       model GOLD
?                       goal seeking
ENTER NAME OF VARIABLE(S) TO BE ADJUSTED TO ACHIEVE
        PERFORMANCE
?                       Salaries
ENTER 1 COMPUTATIONAL STATEMENT(S) FOR PERFORMANCE
?                       Total Expenses = 59000, previous*1.02
ENTER SOLVE OPTIONS
?                       Salaries
```

	YEAR1	YEAR2	YEAR3	YEAR4
Salaries	40000	40891	41796	41806

EXPLAIN

The EXPLAIN feature is a very good feature for exploring a complex model. It is interactive, so if you type EXPLAIN, the package will guide you through the available features. Useful elements include DIAGRAM which sketches inputs and outputs for a variable, OUTLINE which provides a display of all direct and indirect inputs to a variable, DEFINITION FOR which repeats a definition for a variable, and WHY DID or WHY IS in conjunction with variable names, alternative comparisons, columns, and cases. For additional information, see the *IFPS/Plus User's Manual* published by Execucom Systems Corporation, as well as Gray (1983, 1988) and Hayen and Callen (1985).

LOTUS 1-2-3

The most popular form of spreadsheet is undoubtedly Lotus 1-2-3. This product and its clones have become a staple form of microcomputer application. There are many books available to explain this product in detail. One example of an analytical application is given by Winter (1989). There are many other applications as well, as Lotus is easy to use, relying upon menus to steer users through model building. Lotus is very flexible and can be used for a variety of purposes.

Our intent is not to provide the means to become expert in Lotus. However, we can show how the same models built in IFPS can be built with Lotus. MODEL GOLD, presented in the previous section, can be developed on Lotus as follows.

To begin a Lotus session, access the software (usually this involves typing LOTUS). You will be given a blank worksheet consisting of cells, with columns labeled alphabetically and rows labeled numerically. You can begin by directly entering numbers, character strings, or formulas in each cell. Lotus also includes a copy command which makes model building very easy.

We can begin by defining the headings of our report. We want the labels given in the IFPS section on the left. Some of the variable names are long. Therefore, we will reserve columns A, B, and C in our report for these row labels. To enter these, simply move the cursor to the appropriate row and type in the variable name as you wish it to appear. If we want spaces, we can simply leave a row or column blank. We want to have column labels for the first row. These can be entered in the same manner as the row labels (Table 7.4). We can enter the model by beginning with column D (YEAR1). Many of the variable values for subsequent columns in this model can be generated efficiently with the copy procedure. Note that to indicate to Lotus that you want variable

Table 7.4

Cell	Entry	Cell	Entry
A3	Sales	D1	YEAR1
A5	Cost of sales	E1	YEAR2
A7	Gross profit	F1	YEAR3
A9	Salaries	G1	YEAR4
A10	Benefits		
A11	Administrative expense		
A12	Depreciation		
A13	Interest		
A14	Total expenses		
A16	Earnings before tax		

numbers, precede a numeric entry with a + or −. Some entries in the first year can be expressed by formulas (Table 7.5).

Copy Procedure

The ability to copy formulas makes model building in Lotus 1-2-3 very efficient. There is, however, a need to be careful. There are a number of different cases represented in this small model. However, the only real problem will be in row 13, where the rate of growth in expenses for interest changes in the fourth year.

The fastest way to generate the third and fourth year entries is to use the copy procedure. This can be accessed by placing the cursor at the beginning of the block to be copied, entering the slash key (/) to obtain the worksheet menu, typing C for copy. Then move the cursor to the bottom of the block you want copied. The block will be highlighted on the screen. (If something should go wrong, you can always use the escape key to get back to the menu, and following the prompt FROM, type the beginning cell, two dots, and the ending cell. Here that block would be **E3..E16.**) Hitting the return should give the prompt TO and the cell where the cursor currently is located. You can enter the beginning and ending cells separated by two dots to indicate where you want the block copied. In this case, that is **F3..G16.** The proper numbers will then appear in columns F and G (YEAR3 and YEAR4). However, note that the entry for variable Interest in year 4 is wrong. This can be corrected by moving the cursor to cell G13 and entering + 3000. The entire report will now adjust to this new entry and will look exactly like the IFPS output for MODEL GOLD.

Functions

Lotus, like IFPS, includes many functions. In Lotus, functions are called by the @ symbol. Financial function syntax is presented in the following discussion.

Net Present Value

In order to obtain the net present value of a stream of cash flow, the syntax is

@NPV(discount rate,range)

Table 7.5

Cell	Entry D	Entry E
D3	+ 100000	+ D3*1.1
D5	+ 45000	+ D5 + 5000
D7	+ D3 − D5	+ E3 − E5
D9	+ 40000	+ D9 + 1000
D10	+ D9*.1	+ E9*.1
D11	+ 5000	+ D11*1.04
D12	+ 8000	+ D12
D13	+ 2000	+ D13
D14	+ D9 + D10 + D11 + D12	+ E9 + E10 + E11 + E12
	+ D13	+ E13
D16	+ D7 − D14	+ E7 − E14

The **discount rate** is the cost of capital, expressed in decimal form, as in IFPS. Note that the Lotus function will treat all cash flow entries within the given range as occurring at the end of the period. If some cash flow elements occur at the beginning of the period, rearrangement of cells will still allow the desired calculation. If the only beginning cash flow element is the initial investment (call this INVEST), this can be modeled as:

INVEST + @NPV(discount rate,range)

Future Value
The Lotus terminology for net terminal value is future value. The syntax for an annuity with equal payments for a number of equal time periods at a given discount rate is

@FV(payment,discount rate,periods)

The equivalent present value can be obtained by

@PV(payment,discount rate,periods)

Internal Rate of Return
The internal rate of return for a range of cash flows in Lotus requires an initial estimate (guess) of this value. The syntax is

@IRR(guess,range)

Payments
The periodic payment necessary to finance a loan at a given interest rate for a given number of equal time periods is

@PMT(principal,rate,periods)

This is not as complete as the IFPS AMORT subroutine, but is more flexible in that with IFPS you get an entire row of calculations and need to look for the final value, whereas with Lotus you can place the single-cell net present value anywhere you want in the report.

IF-THEN-ELSE
Another useful function in Lotus is the @IF function. This allows the modeler to contingently define cell entries. This function may be stated, @IF(condition,true,false).

@IF(A,B,C)

The function requires three entries: A, B, and C. If A is true, then B is the entry. If A is not true, then C is the entry.

SUMMARY

IFPS is a very useful spreadsheet for business reports, especially those related to pro forma analysis, cash flow analysis, or budget reports. The package emphasizes quality output and is built around the idea of self-documentation, as the variable names are meant to be self-descriptive. The order in which variables are defined determines the order of the report, releasing the modeler from the need to define things in serial order. The WHAT-IF feature was instrumental in the marketing of the concept of DSS.

It must be noted that there are many extensions of the package available. There is the capability to work with databases, and many companies have applied IFPS to develop standard reports and tap individual department data files to generate a series of reports. Furthermore, there is a personal computer disk available. It is not popularly priced, but a student version is available, with limited characteristics. Note that there is a significant difference in the PC operation and the mainframe version. Once computer system characteristics are identified, however, the modeling concepts are the same.

It is this user's impression that anything that can be done with IFPS could be done with Lotus, and vice versa. However, there is a drastic difference in approach. It is also this user's impression that the types of reports suitable for IFPS are much easier on IFPS. This is probably a matter of personal style. On the other hand, more flexible applications are generally easier on Lotus.

REFERENCES

Execucom Systems Corporation. 1987. *IFPS/Plus user's manual.* Release 3.5 (2 vols.). Austin, TX: Execucom.

Gray, P. 1983. *Guide to IFPS.* New York: McGraw-Hill.

Gray, P. 1988. *Guide to IFPS/Personal: The interactive financial planning system for personal computers.* New York: McGraw-Hill.

Hayen, R. L., and R. W. Callen. 1985. *IFPS: An introduction.* Englewood Cliffs, NJ: Prentice Hall.

Kimes, S. E., and J. A. Fitzsimmons. 1990. Selecting profitable hotel sites at La Quinta Motor Inns. *Interfaces* 20 (2):12–20.

Winter, F. W. 1989. Market segmentation using modeling and Lotus 1-2-3. *Interfaces* 19 (6):83–94.

Wysocki, A. 1988. Pennzoil Products one step ahead with IFPS/Plus. *Planner* (Summer):5–7. Austin, TX: Execucom.

PROJECT IDEAS

Housing Decision

Housing is an investment/cost we all face. The decision to buy or rent is complex. The arguments realtors give are that buying a house is an investment (equity tends to grow—at least until recently, you get a tax deduction for interest and taxes, and your quality of life increases because you become a homeowner).

Houses are expensive and time consuming. You have much less time because you become responsible for maintenance. You have less money because payments, utilities, and maintenance eat up your paycheck. On the other hand, rent can be more uncertain, and although it may be less expensive, many of us do not have the discipline to save the difference.

Assume you have $10,000. Conduct a comparative analysis between renting and buying.

House Purchase Assumptions

Purchase price of $75,000.

Take the $10,000 available and make a downpayment of $8,000, plus closing costs of $2,000. Amortize the $67,000 balance over 20 years at 10% to get the principal and interest.

House tax payments of $1,000 per year, growing at 3% per year.

Insurance payments of $300 per year, growing at 6% per year.

Maintenance expense of $1,000 per year, growing at 2% per year.

Utilities expense of $2,400 per year, growing at 7% per year.

Calculate tax refund, based on a 28% tax bracket. Deductions for a given year are the previous year's interest, plus the house taxes paid into escrow *two* years prior, less $3,000 (what your standard deduction would have given you anyway). The minimum tax deduction would be 0.

The value of the house will grow at the rate of 4%.

Rent Assumptions

Assume rental payments of $7,200/year, growing at 4% per year.

Utilities expense of $1,200/year, growing at the rate of 7% per year.

Savings account of $10,000 initially, plus the difference in house payment (principal, interest, taxes, and insurance) and rental payments, with a rate of interest of 7%.

(Disregard utilities and maintenance for savings—assume you would spend it. Assume you would also spend any tax refund from the house.)

Compare the value of the house with the value of the savings account, and total cumulative expenses (including utilities, maintenance, and tax refund) for both alternatives. Conduct a what-if analysis assuming realty inflation of 5% (value of house, rental payments).

Make or Buy Decision

You are consulting with a company with a large truck fleet. The company has paid a lot of money recently for repairing flat tires and wants to analyze three options for repairing these tires. Currently, the company has tires repaired on the open market (the nearest tire dealer). A major tire dealer has offered the company a 5-year contract to repair tires at a fixed cost over the entire 5-year period. A third alternative is for the company to create a new department to do this work internally, charging other departments at cost.

The volume of work to be done is currently 10,000 tires changed per year. Most people in the company expect this volume to grow at the rate of 10% per year. There is some disagreement, with growth rate estimates as low as 5% per year and as high as 15% per year.

Alternative 1: The current situation is to repair tires on the open market. This price is expected to grow at the rate of 5% per year.

Alternative 2: A contract can be signed which commits a tire company to the fixed rate of $24/tire. This would remove the uncertainty of price increases.

Alternative 3: A project has been proposed and estimated to construct and operate facilities to change tires. This project involves an initial investment of $100,000 and a salvage value of $20,000 after 5 years. Operating cost per tire change is estimated at 10 per tire, with an inflation rate of 6% per year. Overhead for this operation is expected to be $40,000 per year with an inflation rate of 6%.

There is a need to consider after-tax comparisons because of depreciation. The first two alternatives would simply be tax-deductible expenses. The tax rate for the company is 34% of taxable income. The proposed project (alternative 3) would involve investment, and thus depreciation. The company uses straight-line depreciation. The assignment is to identify cash flow, with primary interest in net out-of-pocket expense (the company is concerned with running out of cash), as well as final net present value. Both cash flow and net present value need to be identified for each alternative. (Cash flow has a time element—in this case, a row of five values. Net present value compresses time into one number—the equivalent value of the entire cash stream in terms of today's dollars.) Assume a cost of capital of 10%.

Conduct a "what-if" analysis reflecting 5% and 15% rates of growth in flat tires to compare with the most likely 10% rate of growth.

To run:

IFPS	accesses the package
FILE1	opens file FILE1 which contains models
MODEL sample	creates model named sample (or whatever you call it)
AUTO 10 10	automatically numbers lines beginning with 10, increments of 10
COLUMNS 1-*n*	defines *n* columns (you can also give column names)
Enter model	
END OF MODEL	
RECORD	to record output, use command RECORD to open buffer (name later) this can be done any time in the session—everything that happens after you open the buffer is saved

You can now edit, or solve models. When you are done,

QUIT	IFPS will ask if you want to save updated models—if you created a model, or made corrections, you do.
	IFPS will ask if you want to name the output file, or forget it. If you want to save the output, name the output filename.

Solve commands:	SOLVE	asks for solve options
	WIDTH	allows you to control output
	ALL	runs model
	WHAT-IF	allows you to change variable(s) without changing the model (after WHAT-IF statements, type SOLVE)

Width options:	Default	Maximum	Minimum
Report width	78	132	20
Label width	24	100	1
Column width	9	32	1
Decimal places	float	9	− 1 (for none)

Functions (var = functional result)	Net present value	NPVC
	Net terminal value	NTV
	Internal rate of return	IRR
	Benefit/cost ratio	BCRATIO

Subroutines (multiple output variables)	Depreciation	STLINE DEPR (ACRS, etc.)
	Amortization	AMORT

Based on Gray (1986).

CHAPTER EIGHT

Example Decision Support Systems

Chapter 4 included a discussion of Alter's taxonomy (Alter 1977) of decision support systems. This chapter examines examples of each type of DSS in that taxonomy. These are presented with the idea of giving you a picture of the variety of decisions supported and the variety of approaches used, both in development and modeling. Note that they are all taken from *Interfaces,* a journal with the purpose of presenting real applications of management science models. This has the benefit of focusing on real applications. However, it may give a false impression concerning the depth of sophistication required for a DSS. As we stated in Chapter 4, model sophistication is not a necessary condition for effective decision support systems. The Huff study discussed in Chapter 4 found 11 percent of the systems to have file drawer characteristics, and 23 percent of the systems to be accounting models (like the example in Chapter 7). It is not necessary for an effective decision support system to include management science models. However, management science models can be very effective components of decision support systems.

The example systems will be presented following the decision-making process framework presented in Chapter 1. In addition, implementation issues will be discussed, along with conclusions about the salient points from each example. Although Alter's taxonomy is used as the basis of this chapter, you should not feel that every system will precisely match that set of definitions. Note that many of the systems have features of more than one element of that taxonomy.

This chapter should provide you material to see more completely:

- Real examples of each type of system in Alter's taxonomy
- How these decision support systems aid each step of the decision-making process
- The role the user interface, data, and models played in each of these systems

□ Group decision-making aspects that were present

The following examples demonstrate a broad range of decision types that are supported, from administration of a public program, to evaluation of a one-time site location decision. A variety of degrees of interaction, data needs and treatment, and analytic approaches were used. Both public and private sector decisions are represented.

Alter categorized DSSs into seven categories:

File drawer—systems where the user can look up facts

Data analysis—supporting exploratory statistical analysis

Analysis information systems—accessing databases and general models

Accounting systems—calculating the financial impact of planned actions

Representational models—calculating the expected consequences of less structured models

Optimization models—suggesting the optimal solution to a model

Suggestion models—presenting recommended solutions

The problem background and implementation sections in the following examples provide interesting pictures of how different organizations apply decision support systems (Table 8.1). Group decision making predominates in these examples. As we discussed in Chapter 4, we see decision support systems as providing a means to consult with more people, which should enhance decision making through better problem understanding, generating more complete alternatives, and estimating decision impacts more thoroughly. Some aspects of implementing decisions reflect the need to convince other people to cooperate in decisions.

File drawer systems focus on query capability. Many applications, such as airline reservation systems, provide valuable support to decisions by allowing organization representatives to check the real-time status of available resources. The first example provides a case where an agency of the government of India applied this type of system.

Table 8.1

DSS Type	Organization	Reference
File drawer	Indian government	Ramani and Bhatnagar (1988)
Data analysis	Finnish Parliament	Hamalainen (1988)
Analysis information system	Syntex Laboratories	Lodish et al. (1988)
Accounting model	L. L. Bean	Andrews and Parsons (1989)
Representational model	AT&T	Spencer et al. (1990)
Optimization model	American Airlines	Tedone (1989)
Suggestion model	San Francisco Police Department	Taylor and Huxley (1989)

FILE DRAWER SYSTEM: GOVERNMENT OF INDIA
Ramani and Bhatnagar (1988)

The government of India introduced a public distribution system in 1954 to distribute essential commodities at reasonable prices through retail outlets (fair-price shops). The objective was to deliver essential foodstuffs to urban and rural poor, as well as to those living in inaccessible areas. The government also hoped to influence market prices for food. Any household could join the system to purchase food at fixed prices, considerably lower than the open market. By 1985, this system had grown to a network of about 320,000 shops, with 6,000 warehouses. The Central Ministry of Civil Supplies set policies concerning what was to be sold where, as well as prices. Central government agencies were responsible for procuring, storing, and transporting goods. Within each state, State Ministries of Civil Supplies administered the program. States are divided into many districts, which are further divided into many talukas (counties).

Each fair-price shop maintains a list of its card holders, who are entitled to purchase a monthly allotment of each commodity. Ministries estimate the quantity of each commodity (usually below demand) and formulate plans for allotting commodities to states. States further allocate commodities to talukas, which allocate to each fair-price shop. Each fair-price shop picks up its allotment from warehouses and distributes food to card holders.

An MIS to support long-term planning of production and procurement, coordination of central procurement agencies, and coordination of shipments was designed. The impact of the public distribution system on open-market prices was also to be monitored, as well as delivery of food to inaccessible regions and the poor.

Problem Identification

This system supports a wide variety of decisions. The authors identified the major problem areas as:

Local production lower than anticipated

Shipment of needed food across states

Hoarding and artificial shortages

Low central allocation to a state

Inability to pick up allotted quantities

In-state allocation mismatched with need

Leakage of supplies by fair-price shop

Leakage from warehouses

Poor scale of distribution

Lack of public distribution system facilities

Overstocking at warehouses and high cost of operation

Data Collection

The analysts made field visits to study record-keeping systems at fair-price shops, warehouses, and state governments, as well as existing planning and monitoring processes. The existing system was found to be unable to adequately identify weaknesses in food movement or allocation. Most reports were in response to specific requests from senior officers who had received complaints. Allocation planning was not based on data. Basic reports from fair-price shops and warehouses were proposed. In addition, subunit performance indicators and feedback reports to field units were designed, along with formats for planning.

The developed system provides monitoring and control reports on each commodity by fair-price shop and on each warehouse. The fair-price shop reports provide the amount each fair-price shop picked up from a warehouse in a month, as well as the total quantity distributed to card holders. The percentage of card holders served and quantity distributed per person are identified. Days out of stock are reported, along with the end-of-month inventory. These fair-price shop reports are consolidated for talukas, districts, and states. Monthly warehouse reports focus on stock positions and transportation efficiency. Yearly reports focus on the coverage of the population under public distribution system.

Implementation

A pilot system was developed and applied to a few talukas from one state to create a sample database. Information was provided in either tabular or pictorial form. The user could focus the report on a month, a commodity, a fair-price shop, a warehouse, a taluka, or a district and could choose the format of the report using a menu-driven user interface.

It was determined that microcomputers would be useful at the district level in order to process basic data from fair-price shops and warehouses and to compile reports for inspectors, talukas, and the district. Furthermore, daily reports of warehouse receipts and issues to fair-price shops could be planned. Additional databases on commodities to include market prices, production, and availability in order to identify future supply-and-demand trends were identified as useful additions to the system.

Comments

This application is a management information system. Regular reports are provided. However, there is query capability beyond that traditionally available in most MIS systems. As in many cases, the distinction between an MIS and a DSS is blurry. The argument for including it as a DSS is that it represents what could be done with Alter's classification of **file drawer** systems. File drawer systems can be extremely useful for a broad variety of problems. As in this case, standard internal information often needs to be supplemented. For instance, monitoring open-market prices is an important consideration in the public distribution system. This information is not available internally, but the need for such a data bank was identified.

The total decision-making process is not necessarily supported by file drawer systems. Their primary focus is on identifying problems. They often involve a great deal of data, expediting the data collection phase in the decision-making process. Alternative generation is left to human users, along with alternative evaluation and decision making. Implementation would be a problem-specific function. However, these systems provide a great deal of support in monitoring the impact of specific decisions.

An evolutionary step beyond query capability is the capability to conduct data analysis in order to measure what actually is occurring, either within the organization or within the set of customers served by the organization. Data analysis can involve a variety of functions, including descriptive statistics, forecasting (covered in Supplemental Chapter 1), or identification of relationships. The following example focuses on identifying the will of the citizens of Finland on a controversial and important issue.

DATA ANALYSIS SYSTEM: PARLIAMENT OF FINLAND
(Hamalainen (1988)

Evaluation of energy generation alternatives is one of the most commonly analyzed decisions throughout the world. This decision is highly important because of the extremely high cost involved, its long-range impact (power plants may last 50 years or more), and the dynamic environment in the industry (fuel prices fluctuate drastically and new technologies are regularly developed). In addition, nuclear power has advantages relative to pollution generation and renewable resource depletion, but involves additional risk which many perceive as unacceptable.

Because of its northern location and large density of heavy industry, Finland has a high per-capita consumption of energy. Four nuclear power plants provide 17 percent of Finland's energy. The Finnish Parliament has final authority to accept or reject licenses for nuclear power plants. The Finnish Department of Energy conducted studies indicating that new sources of power would be needed by the mid-1990s at present growth rates. If the economy stagnated, this demand for new capacity would be delayed until the year 2000. Other studies indicated large nuclear and coal-fired plants to be the most economical sources of new power. There was an additional policy option requiring no new large plants, but rather a mix of conservation measures and decentralization of small and medium-sized plants. Nuclear plants require eight to ten years to construct.

Problem Identification

A 1983 poll indicated fewer than 50 percent of the population supported nuclear power. In 1984, two power companies announced an interest in applying for a license to construct nuclear plants. Parliament was split on this issue. The issue was also considered technically difficult, with a continuous flow of new and often contradictory information. Both Parliament and the electrical utilities wanted to identify the outcome before the fact, because a negative vote would impact future proposals.

The analyst in this case was independent of the decision makers. The project was funded by the Academy of Finland, which had no involvement with the decision. This made the analysis independent of any of the different stakeholders in the issue.

In this case, a microcomputer-based decision aid was used by the Parliament of Finland when planning national energy policy. Hamalainen provided the users the analytic hierarchy process (AHP) software. AHP is a means of developing a formula based on subjective information, described in Chapter 2.

Data Collection

The aim of the project was to help structure the parliamentary energy debate through the use of a decision aid. Each political party was contacted, explaining the project, principles, and goals. Each party was asked to select one or two members of Parliament to participate. All parties except one participated, and twelve members worked with the decision aid, one at a time. Each participant completed the decision analysis session in less than two hours.

An analytic hierarchy process model was developed based on the factors identified in this phase of the analysis. Top-level factors were **national economy; health, safety, and environment;** and **political** factors, each with subelements as shown in Figure 8.1. The hierarchical weightings of Parliament members and energy experts were analyzed, and a comprehensive report on the results was prepared and published in the fall of 1984.

Alternative Generation

In this case, the alternatives were for Parliament to approve a 1,000-megawatt nuclear plant, two 500-megawatt coal-fired plants, or adopt the philosophy of conservation and no large plants.

Alternative Evaluation

The second phase of the project was to use the framework of the decision aid to structure the debate in Parliament and in the Finnish media. Top-level

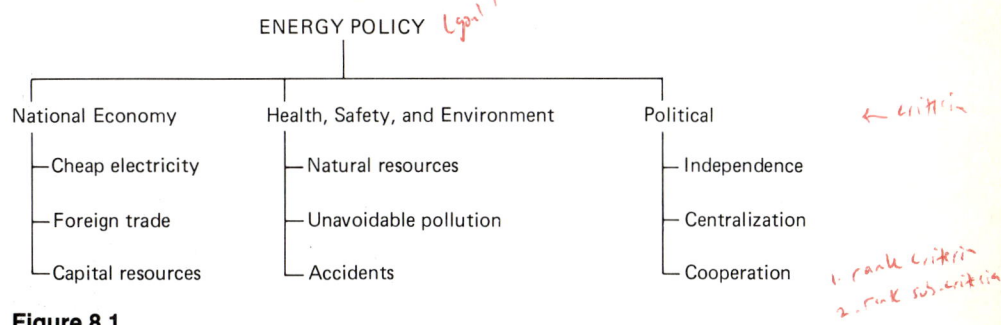

Figure 8.1
(Based on Hamalainen [1988])

experts from government, power companies, and research institutions were invited to evaluate the model. The major antinuclear group in Finland was invited as well, but chose not to participate.

Four widely divergent views among parliamentary members were identified. It was noted that these same four classes of emphasis were shared by technical experts, indicating that additional knowledge was not required. The debate therefore centered on differences in values among parliamentary members.

Decision

The decision analysis indicated that the nuclear power and no large plant options emerged as the primary alternatives to be discussed. It turned out that no decision was ever required. The power companies delayed their formal application until early 1986, shortly before the Chernobyl accident. After that incident, the application was withdrawn.

Implementation

Measures were taken to increase imports and begin construction of medium-scale peat and coal plants. Hydroelectric possibilities are being explored.

Monitoring

The politicians who worked with the model were positively impressed with the analysis. The consensus was that the decision aid helped clarify the issue for individual decision makers and provided deeper understanding of alternatives. The public was given an overall framework for the energy problem. The analytic hierarchy process technique was originally chosen because it was easy to understand and lived up to this expectation. AHP was found to present the issue with such clarity and simplicity that all participants, regardless of computer or mathematical background, felt at ease when using it.

There was some negative response to the idea of members of Parliament using computer support. One commentator called the project a threat to democracy and a dangerous step toward a technocrat-and computer-controlled society. This minority view was not shared by those who used the model.

Comments

This example is different on a number of features. First, it turned out that no decision was ever made, but rather evolved by default. Although this may seem unique, we would expect that this happens rather often, especially on strategic issues. Conducting the analysis may make the decision obvious. A second feature is that the analysis was provided unsolicited by the decision makers. In the political environment, this may be an advantage, because objectivity can be claimed more convincingly.

This system seems to fall in the class of **data analysis** following Alter's taxonomy. There was no exploratory statistical analysis, but rather identification of important decision factors as well as subjective opinions of various groups.

Analysis information systems extend beyond the focus upon data to the use of general models. Not only is data accessed, but the data is used to conduct analysis estimating the impact of decisions. The following example demonstrates these features, although as is the case with most real applications, other features appear as well.

ANALYSIS INFORMATION SYSTEM: SYNTEX LABORATORIES
Lodish et al. (1988) see Little

Syntex Corporation began making products for dermatologists in 1940. It has grown into an international company developing, manufacturing, and marketing a wide range of health and personal care products. Syntex Laboratories is the U.S. human pharmaceutical sales subsidiary, the largest subsidiary of Syntex Corporation. In 1981, Syntex Laboratories was growing at an extremely high rate, both in sales and profitability.

Syntex Laboratories products were grouped into four categories: non-steroidal antiarthritic drugs, analgesics, oral contraceptives, and topical steroids. There were seven major products, including the antiarthritic drug Naprosyn, its largest and most successful product.

The sales force for Syntex Laboratories visits physicians and encourages them to prescribe Syntex drugs. Marketing elements include advertising in medical journals, direct mail, physician samples, medical symposia, and convention booths.

Decision

In 1982, Syntex Laboratories needed to decide how large its sales force should be and how it should be deployed. This decision was complicated, because the size of the sales force made a great deal of difference in the

$\pi(\text{size of sales force, deployment})$

deployment decision. The response of profit to sales force is mitigated by market factors such as pricing, advertising, distribution, demand, and competitive behavior. Furthermore, sales force decisions are biased upward. In downturns, it is more difficult to reduce sales force than it is to increase it in times of an increasing market. Before the study, the practice was to increase the sales force a small amount, primarily based on budget constraints. Sales management wanted a more rational basis for determining sales force size. Furthermore, corporate management was beginning to require more thorough analysis in justifying increased expenditures.

Data Collection

Data was available on the sizes of each of the segmented physician specialties (family practice, general practice, internal medicine, orthopedics, and other categories).

Other information was not available. The number of prescriptions written by physician, as well as willingness to try new products, was unknown. Furthermore, when a physician writes a prescription, it is difficult to predict where the prescription will be filled. This makes it difficult for a salesperson to know whether a sales call was successful or not.

The consultants to Syntex identified the need for the following information in order to accurately estimate sales response to different sales force sizes:

> Where the increase or decrease in sales force personnel would be employed
>
> What products would have more or less effort applied to them
>
> Which market segments would receive more or less effort

A direct estimate at the microlevel would involve hundreds of estimates for each product, region, and specialty.

A **Delphi analysis** (a means of obtaining a forecast from multiple experts—see the description in Supplemental Chapter 1) was conducted to determine the expected response of sales to sales force increases. The personnel involved included the senior vice-president of sales and marketing, the vice-president of sales, two representatives of the market research department, two product managers, two regional sales managers, and two salespeople. A meeting was held with the purpose of reaching a group consensus on the likely response of each Syntex product and physician specialty to sales representative effort. Initially, each participant was asked to estimate the change in sales for each of the seven products and nine physician specialties that would result from different levels of sales representatives. These estimates included expected sales under conditions of: (1) no sales effort, (2) one-half of current effort, (3) 50 percent greater sales effort, and (4) a saturation level of sales effort. Following the Delphi procedure, initial estimates were obtained without participants consulting each other. Responses of the group were summarized, including quartiles, medians, and minimum and maximum answers to each question. The group then discussed these summaries, and those with extreme estimates were asked to explain their reasons. This procedure was found to make critical assumptions easy to identify. Therefore, the competitive situation, the role and ability of the sales force to influence physicians, and the environmental effects were thoroughly discussed. Each participant then redid their estimates, resulting in a group consensus.

Alternative Generation

Computerized models were developed to take response functions developed for both product and segment allocation. The first model sought to identify the optimal number of sales presentations to be allotted to each product. The second model sought to decide the number of sales representative visits by physician specialty. Two models were used to obtain independent estimates of sales force size to reduce the risk of error. Response curves were fitted by a smooth curve.

A computer program was developed which identified the maximum rate of change in marginal contribution per representative by product. The program allocated the number of representatives at this rate, and then continued to add representatives by change in marginal contribution until this rate became negative.

The system produced a plan involving over 700 representatives, compared with the current sales force size of 433.

Alternative Evaluation

Model output was presented during the three-day national sales meeting. The planning group reconvened and discussed the output. A small amount of fine tuning was conducted. Although the model was not expected to be perfectly accurate, it impressed management as being based on the input of the most knowledgeable people in the company, backed by a very thorough discussion.

The strategic implications obtained from the model provided Syntex with a basis for increasing the size of its sales force and a plan for the sales force's allocation. A strategy for product emphasis was identified as well.

Decision

The results of the analysis were presented to senior management and the board of directors of the corporation. During the next three years, about 200 sales representatives were added. This was less than the model recommended because of constraints on training and deploying representatives.

Implementation

It was difficult to reorient the sales force toward the general practitioner segment, but some change was noted. An unexpected impact of the analysis was that R&D and Marketing developed a similar model to evaluate the marketing strategy of new products.

Monitoring

One year after the original analysis, a more detailed model was developed and run based on subjective estimates of the same group. The previous results were corroborated.

Over the three-year period following the analysis, sales were $25 million higher than the strategic plan forecast. These changes were in the direction forecasted by the model and directly related to changes in sales force deployment. However, it took over a year for impact to appear. The return on investment in added sales force was at least 100 percent, with expectations that this improvement would continue.

This analysis cost $30,000, a small investment for an ongoing additional annual revenue stream of $25 million.

Comments

This analysis represents Alter's category of a **data analysis** system. Exploratory statistical analysis was conducted to determine the expected relationship between actions and results. It also has some of the characteristics of an **analysis information system,** because the output was presented in a format somewhat similar to a spreadsheet and was applied to another problem within the corporation.

This example involved an unstructured problem. The analysis was supported by data development and application of computer models. The system was not interactive, relying upon outside consultants. In principle, of course, this *could* have been automated. Whether it specifically is a DSS is not terribly important. The example, at a minimum, demonstrates a potential application of a DSS.

This case also demonstrates the group nature of most business decisions. Large organizations rarely involve one-person decisions of significant magnitude. There are a number of other organizational members who generally need to be consulted for approval before major changes can be made in strategic decision making. This application also underscores the need for software specifically designed to support group decision-making processes, a topic to be discussed in Chapter 9.

One of the most useful developments leading to widespread use of microcomputers in business was the spreadsheet. A common use early in the development of spreadsheets included a variety of financial analyses, such as pro forma budget analysis and balance sheets, supporting traditional accounting practice. This allows calculation of the expected consequences of planned actions, with a clear statement of the assumptions (see Chapter 7). Although the following example does not employ a spreadsheet, it does focus on estimating the financial impact of the alternatives considered by the user.

ACCOUNTING MODEL: L. L. BEAN
Andrews and Parsons (1989)

L. L. Bean uses telephone order-taking operations for catalog and mail-order sales. L. L. Bean designed its telephone service centers around a trunk configuration, where calls pass through trunks without delay so that queuing takes place only at the operator level. Both part-time and full-time workers were used, with about 350 employees total.

Problem Identification

L. L. Bean identified two major concerns in its telephone agent operations. It wanted to balance the cost of furnishing quality customer service with the cost of losing customers, and it needed to know what resources were required to meet its target service levels.

Specific scheduling of agents for 24 hours, 7 days a week was a short-range decision. Schedules were prepared on Wednesdays for the work week running from Monday through Sunday. L. L. Bean had a current system, but wanted to evaluate four vendor systems that would aid specific scheduling.

Data Collection

In order to make a sound scheduling decision, an accurate forecast of workload, on an hourly basis, was required. The scheduling decision is complicated by the need to accommodate overlapping shift schedules. Shift lengths were different, and schedules needed to consider lunch and rest breaks, days off, and starting times. Data was available on historical operations, as well as from vendors.

Alternative Generation

Four commercially marketed systems were considered, in addition to L. L. Bean's current system. In this case, alternative generation was a function of human imagination.

Alternative Evaluation

An evaluation model was built to enable evaluation of the five systems under consideration. This model allowed entering actual call volumes by hour, along with staffing levels recommended by the alternative systems. The problem being scheduled was a classical waiting-line system with multiple servers. Total costs are a function of labor cost (increasing with more servers) and lost revenue (decreasing with more servers).

A cost–benefit evaluation based on expected total costs was developed and verified. An hour-by-hour report was generated by the system, providing servicing levels as well as expected costs. A weekly summary was also produced.

This system was test-run on actual operations data, to validate the system. This system was then used to evaluate the five alternatives, resulting in a measurable comparison for management in terms of total costs. The total analysis included judgmental, objective, qualitative variables in addition to vendor price, software quality, system flexibility, and other factors.

Decision

Given this analysis, management was in a position to make its decision based on more complete information.

Implementation

The Director of Order Processing and Telecommunications of L. L. Bean stated that the underlying cost–benefit approach was adopted by L. L. Bean in development of its own capacity determination tables. L. L. Bean developed a system for scheduling staffing on half hour intervals.

Monitoring

L. L. Bean estimated over $100,000 per year saved in staffing costs alone. Furthermore, by using the automated scheduling system, there was a significant reduction in the clerical effort required to prepare the schedule each week.

Comments

This example is another case where the strict definition of DSS is hard to fit. The analysis described was a one-time analysis, including automated elements. The resulting system becomes a DSS once it is accepted by management. Note that by Simon's definitions, the decisions supported by these first four systems are all semistructured or unstructured.

The analytic model used (queuing analysis) is an example of an analytic technique without optimization capability. This system, like spreadsheet modeling and simulation, requires human generation of alternatives. The overall analysis has the features of Alter's **accounting model** category, in that the consequences of planned actions (based on stated assumptions) are calculated in monetary terms.

The next category involves use of more formal modeling. Representational models allow decision makers to obtain estimates of the consequences of actions. A common type of representational model is simulation (Supplemental

Chapter 3). Note that spreadsheet models can be used for simulations, as well as a variety of other approaches. Linear programming is an optimization tool, generally used for the next category of DSS. But linear programming requires satisfaction of strict assumptions for optimality to be guaranteed. These assumptions cannot often be met in practice. Linear programming can still be useful as a means of generating alternatives.

REPRESENTATIONAL MODEL: AT&T
Spencer et al. (1990)

There are over 180,000 telemarketing centers in the United States which produced over $118 billion in revenues in 1986. This is a major growth industry, as only 1,650 companies had telemarketing programs in 1980. The 800 number service, allowing customers to call into the telemarketing center at no customer cost, was introduced in 1967. In 1988, 46 AT&T customers used the system to determine site locations. They spent an estimated $20 billion on telephone services in 1986, expected to grow 10 to 15 percent per year through 1990. The four major categories of telemarketing are order processing, customer service, sales support, and account management.

AT&T is perceived to be the highest-priced vendor. It has adopted the strategy of stressing extra value, to include telemarketing consulting at no additional cost. As part of this program, AT&T develops DSSs for its consultants to use in dealing with customers. Site location is a major decision in the telemarketing industry, and a DSS to aid telemarketers in finding good locations for telemarketing centers is part of the AT&T program.

A number of factors are involved in site location. In the early years of telemarketing, the cost of the 800 service was the major factor. However, communications costs are down, whereas labor costs are up.

Problem Identification

Telemarketing customers need to consider a number of factors in locating service centers, including labor markets, real estate values, regional accents, and education levels. As part of its service, AT&T seeks to provide a useful telemarketing center site location system.

Data Collection

In 1985, AT&T undertook a study to determine the primary cost elements in this site location problem. Fifty major customers were interviewed. The three primary operational costs were communications, labor, and real estate.

Based on this initial research, in 1987, AT&T developed brochures to inform customers of the costs involved in site locations. In January 1987,

AT&T learned that a major national retailer was reorganizing its catalog operation. AT&T decided to establish a special study team to develop a system capable of aiding network design, number of centers, and locations that would be best for each customer. A meeting with the major retailer was arranged, and that retailer was included in the system design team.

During the ensuing month, this team determined the economic, demographic, and AT&T internal data needed for site selection.

Alternative Generation

Candidate sites are generated by the customer, as well as by potential enumeration of Standard Metropolitan Statistical Areas (SMSAs). In the pilot study, the customer chose to have one location in Texas, selecting Dallas and Houston as candidates. The model evaluated 13 Texas SMSAs, and identified San Antonio as the optimal Texas site. The other nine locations desired by the customer were chosen by several runs of the model, coupled with feedback from the customer.

Alternative Evaluation

The evaluation of alternative sites is supported by using a linear programming model of the communication network to determine the optimal site and up to five next-best sites. Once these locations are determined, a more detailed analysis of both quantitative and qualitative factors is conducted.

The optimization system uses a mixed integer programming model (explained in Supplemental Chapter 2), with a report writer added on. Initial run times were excessive, so heuristics (modifications to the algorithm not guaranteeing optimal solutions) were incorporated along with different computer support, and run time was improved substantially.

The system provides answers to the questions:

1. How many telemarketing centers should be opened?
2. Where should the centers be located?
3. What geographic region will be served by each center?
4. How many attendant positions are required at each location?

Decision

After the quantitative and qualitative analysis, the retailer chose the San Antonio site in Texas, as well as the nine locations in other states.

Implementation

Because of the need to build an effective system quickly, a prototype system was created and refined as needs were identified. After the initial application, a more user-friendly version was developed, including a front-end, system database in FOCUS and a matrix generator in FORTRAN. A report writer was coded as well. A PC-based graphics system was used for the interface.

Evaluation and refinements to the system continued. In November 1987, field trials with a variety of customers with diverse requirements were conducted. Several enhancements to both the user interface as well as the linear programming algorithm were made. The system was released in February 1988.

Monitoring

Constant feedback from customers was received. Based on this feedback, additional demographic categories and economic forecasts were incorporated into the system, as well as a geographic mapping program to visually display model recommendations. A PC version, PC-SITE, was tested in February 1989.

Comments

This system represents a large class of DSSs not often recognized in the theoretical literature. Commercial DSSs deliver standard analytic methods to whomever purchases (or as with AT&T, whoever is a general customer) the service. There are many other examples, which have been in existence for nearly two decades, including IFPS (see Chapter 7). What makes these decision support systems is that they are custom designed for specific classes of problems. Here, too, rigid definitions are a little confining, because IFPS can be used for many kinds of decisions. But these systems all have the ability to incorporate databases and model bases in an interactive setting.

This type of DSS is analogous to expert system shells, which are software packages providing frameworks that the user can adapt to specific applications. A great deal of user development time is saved by using these kinds of systems. The limitation is that shells, as well as commercial systems like the AT&T application, may have some rigidities. More thorough expert systems can be built from scratch with LISP or PROLOG. More thorough DSSs can be built from scratch, as AT&T did here. But the final product is capable of servicing many customers in addition to the original one.

This system uses linear programming, but as an evaluator, not as an optimizer. The system has the features of a **representational** DSS.

Optimization models provide decision makers with powerful tools, capable of identifying the best possible solution for a model satisfying the required assumptions. Linear programming models usually are associated with optimization. Well-developed software is widely available to solve linear programming models of a variety of types.

OPTIMIZATION MODEL: AMERICAN AIRLINES
Tedone (1989)

American Airlines maintains an inventory of repairable spare parts to support its fleet of over 400 aircraft. American Airlines has developed a PC-based DSS called RAPS to forecast part demand, recommend least cost allocations of parts to airport locations, and calculate the optimal solution's availability level for each part.

Mechanical part inventory management is a very important element in the management of any business with large volumes of equipment. American Airlines uses two categories of spare parts. Rotable parts are generally high in value and have been chosen to be recycled. Expendable parts, on the other hand, are generally much less expensive and are readily available on the open market. American Airlines manages over 5,000 rotable parts, ranging from landing gears to altimeters. These parts cost approximately $5,000 each, although some parts, such as avionics computers, may cost over $500,000.

As all airline passengers expect, departing aircraft must have fully functional parts. If a part is found defective before departure, it is replaced. It is most efficient if the replacement parts are available on site. Whenever a rotable replacement part is used, a message is sent up the hierarchy. Exchange bases warehouse parts and replenish the site stock. When the unserviceable part is received at the base, the nonworking part is diagnosed and repaired. Repaired parts are returned to the base inventory.

The cost of repair parts management consists of holding costs plus shortage costs. Holding costs are easily identifiable. Shortage costs require more analysis. In this application, corporate data sources were tapped to obtain average lost revenue, crew costs, and loss of good will due to canceled flights. Negative costs of fuel savings due to canceled flights were included as well.

Problem Identification

The problem is to find the allocation of parts to exchange between bases and warehouses that would yield the least total cost.

Preliminary investigations indicated that too many rotable parts were being stocked. In the mid-1970s, American Airlines developed a materials management planning system to forecast and monitor rotable parts requirements. However, that system was mainframe based and could only be run overnight. Sensitivity analyses were very difficult under those conditions, and very few model parameters could be changed by the user. There was also declining confidence in the forecast accuracy of that system.

Data Collection

The location and disposition of each rotable part is recorded on a real-time computer system RCS (rotable control system). Whenever a part is removed, a tracking record is created, maintaining the history of the unserviceable part from removal to repair, as well as the history of the serviceable unit sent to replace it. The RCS system provides the RAPS system with information on transit and repair times, part removal histories, and current allocation levels. Other corporate databases provide specific supply part information.

The old mainframe system was examined, and mathematical and technical deficiencies were identified. The forecasting module of that system used only time-series methodology and was therefore slow to respond to changes in aircraft utilization or fleet expansions. A heuristic had been used to generate the solution, which was not guaranteed to be optimal.

A critical element of the system is forecasting expected demand. The system forecasts in two phases. The first phase calculates total system demand for each part for the entire organization. Linear regression is used to identify a relationship between monthly part removals and functions of monthly flying hours. Rolling 18-month histories of removals and flying hours are updated, with the most recent month's data used in the regression. The second phase is to allocate this total demand to each site.

Alternative Generation

The new system incorporates a linear programming system, capable of identifying the optimal allocation of spare parts. The objective function of the model is total cost. The availability of parts is uncertain, thus making the model nonlinear. A two-phase linear programming procedure was incorporated into the system. This algorithm requires less than two minutes for solution on a PC/AT.

Alternative Evaluation

The RAPS system includes a number of modules. In addition to the optimized plan, personnel can use the system to determine the number and locations of rotable parts and to examine the consequences of changes in the basic allocation assumptions.

In addition to identification of the optimal plan, the system makes it possible for inventory managers and analysts to determine the impact of new fleets on part allocations, in making surplus and purchase decisions, evaluating vendor proposals, forecasting future demand, and anticipating allocation behavior through sensitivity analysis.

Implementation

The system is operated with a menu-based interface, making it possible for users in the field to utilize all modules and tap the large quantities of data required.

Monitoring

Although linear programming is used as a tool, the model is stochastic (includes uncertain elements). Because of the uncertainty of stochastic models, it is possible that particular sites can have an unplanned surplus or critical shortage of particular parts. A related system, DRS (dynamic redistribution system), identifies conditions of critical shortage prior to a site running out of a part. The DRS would recommend a transfer shipment from a site with a surplus in the event a critical shortage was identified.

The RAPS system has been estimated to have saved American Airlines $7 million in a one-time savings, as well as a recurring annual savings of nearly $1 million. In addition, the productivity of parts management analysts has been improved, as they can now analyze many more parts per day. RAPS also provides an audit trail, recording the dates and times of part analyses. Because of the ease of making an allocation, allocations are made more often, meaning more current data is used as the basis for the decision.

Comments

This case provides an example of the advancement of computer support to management. In the 1970s, most systems were heavily used mainframes, meaning that real-time analysis was impossible. PC systems provide means to do much more. The system is an **Optimization** system.

Another common situation is the high investment many companies have in repair parts. Inventory management is critical, because whereas the holding cost of any one item is generally very low, the masses of volume add up to significant sums. Computer technology allows more accurate management of repair parts. Similar systems can be applied to other inventories, such as retail goods.

The last category of a DSS seeks to provide decision makers with suggested solutions to more complex decision problems. This approach blends with the concept of expert systems. The following example involves a case where optimization is not possible, because the decision involves a variety of factors that are not well captured by formal models. Solutions are heuristically generated, and the system is focused on allowing users to better evaluate the features of the resulting solution.

SUGGESTION MODEL: SAN FRANCISCO POLICE DEPARTMENT
Taylor and Huxley (1989)

Because of having to meet a variety of resident needs, deployment of patrol officers is a difficult problem. Citizen safety, cost, and officer morale need to be balanced. San Francisco has a population of about 700,000 and a police force of 1,900 officers, of whom about 850 perform patrol duties. Patrol coverage of the nine police districts in San Francisco accounted for $79 million in 1986, out of a total budget of $176 million.

San Francisco Police Department (SFPD) management felt the demands of San Francisco residents could better be served if more than one officer per car were used. The Police Officer Association (POA) wanted four 10-hour shifts per week as opposed to five 8-hour shifts. Other variables were rotating versus fixed schedules. With fixed schedules, officers work the same shift on the same days every week. Rotating schedules involve more variety. Additional constraints to the decision were that there must be at least a minimum number of officers on duty at all times and that nonpatrol duty (training, station duty, etc.) must be taken into account.

A task force was formed composed of officers from the POA, patrol management, and technical support. This task force decided to seek a new system, with the criteria that the system must:

1. Use computer-aided dispatching data on service calls to establish workload by day of week and hour of day
2. Generate optimal and realistic integer schedules on a microcomputer system
3. Allow easy adjustment to accommodate human considerations without sacrificing productivity
4. Create schedules in less than 30 minutes and make adjustments in less than 60 seconds
5. Perform both tactical scheduling and strategic policy testing in one integrated system
6. Have a flexible, easily used interface

Problem Identification

The traditional means of scheduling patrol officers is to develop schedules manually, relying upon learning through experience. But manual methods could not easily or accurately measure the impact of changing shift spaces. Previous attempts to adopt the four 10-hour shift system had met with failure because manual scheduling was unable to effectively adapt to that new environment. Therefore, SFPD needed a new scheduling system.

The scheduling problem is complicated in that the decision includes identifying how many officers begin work on given days and hours. The measure of effectiveness is comparing the scheduled number of officers on duty to the number of officers needed during each hour of the week by precinct. The long-term goal is to minimize the number of officers needed to achieve a desired level of protection, while balancing the workload among officers.

Data Collection

SFPD had a sophisticated computer-aided dispatching (CAD) system, which provided a large and rich database on resident calls for service by precinct. This system dispatched patrol officers to calls and maintained statistics on call types, waiting times, travel times, and total time per call. The system that was developed included a forecasting module that taps the CAD data for requirements for each hour of the week.

Alternative Generation

A search of the available systems identified the commercial products available on the market. No integer or continuous linear programming optimization models were found in use. Currently available software was evaluated to be inadequate in meeting the SFPD requirements. Taylor and Huxley were contacted and worked with the task force for about 10 months before an agreement to develop a system was reached.

Alternative generation is automatically developed by the computer system, to include a personal schedule for officers (typically 90) of a precinct. The starting solution is generated by the forecasting module, which identifies the number of officers required each hour of the week. These values are adjusted to allow for nonpatrol duty requirements and for trends in calls for service. A table and graph showing the number of officers needed each hour of the week for a precinct are developed.

Scheduling is accomplished by an integer search procedure to seek the best fit of hourly requirements. The objective function is to minimize shortages and to minimize the maximum shortage. This function is nonlinear. A linear programming model is solved with variables of shift start times and the number of officers starting in each time period. Constraints include limitation on the number of officers available, minimum staffing requirements for each hour, and soft constraints on the number of officers needed each hour. There are a limited number of start-time groups.

It is desirable that schedules not change drastically from week to week. Therefore, the starting schedule for each period is the last period's schedule. The starting schedule is modified step by step, while certain changes are vetoed, until the objective function is no longer improved. A new schedule is therefore generated in an intelligent manner.

Alternative Evaluation

The system provided graphical displays of solutions to explain to users why the solution was good or bad and why some policies were superior to others. Users have the ability to fine-tune the solution interactively. Alternative schedules can be entered, and the system will evaluate these alternatives.

Decision

As with all DSSs, human decision makers have final responsibility for the decision.

Implementation

To test the model, a battery of schedules were developed and compared with continuous linear programming solutions. The linear programming solutions were not necessarily integer, but provided a lower bound on optimality. In all cases, the system solutions were within 1 percent of the lower bound. Furthermore, the LP models took up to nine hours, at least 10 times longer than the system required.

The system was also tested against manual schedules. The system reduced by about 50 percent the shortages and surpluses of patrol officers assigned relative to designed limits.

Because of labor relationship conflicts, there was some difficulty in implementing the system, despite POA participation in starting the project. Therefore, the system was phased in one station at a time. This pilot application began November 1986. Further pressure arose from the city's insistence that empirical evidence be presented before additional patrol cars, needed to implement the one officer per car approach, be funded. The results of the pilot study did demonstrate to the city that the investment would be cost effective.

User acceptance and training were enhanced through animation and three-dimensional graphics. Furthermore, graphics were very useful in communicating system solutions to the user. Training time for police officers averaged two days.

Monitoring

SFPD estimates that this system added 176,000 productive hours to the patrol staff per year. This generates a savings of $5.2 million per year through improved scheduling. SFPD found the system to be well received by officers, with sick leave decreasing by about 50 percent. Response times to calls decreased about 20 percent. Citation revenues increased dramatically. Productivity in meeting calls for services improved about 25 percent. The system is credited with increasing officer morale, decreasing response time, improving revenues, and decreasing sick leave. The system was viewed as paying for itself almost immediately.

Comments

This system incorporates a heuristic capable of generating a good schedule very quickly, matching a variety of constraints. It is a type of expert system (**suggestion** system in Alter's taxonomy), in that logical actions humans would take have been incorporated to identify the schedule. It fits the concept of decision support system especially well, as the intent is to allow users to develop and evaluate alternative schedules rapidly.

SUMMARY AND INFERENCES

These studies provide an opportunity to compare a number of DSS features. Two of the systems seem to be DSSs in a marginal sense. The Indian government system (file drawer example) is primarily an MIS, although it is utilized in a menu-driven system by users in the field. The L. L. Bean model verges on a consulting analysis for a one-time decision, but the decision is ongoing, and the general features of an accounting model are demonstrated. These systems were applied to a variety of problem areas (Table 8.2).

These example DSSs involve a variety of decision-making environments. The user interfaces varied widely. The Finnish example could be supported by one small PC system. The American Airlines system involves distributed processing, with users in the field capable of entering data, as well as making queries. The San Francisco Police Department system allows heavy interactive use by decision makers. Data treatment also varies widely. AHP provides a means of eliciting subjective ratings. Some data was obtained from outside of the organization, some from within the MIS itself.

Model use seems to be the determinant characteristic of Alter's taxonomy. File drawer systems do not include analytic models. For the other categories, descriptive statistics are useful either in developing the models used or as part of the analytic procedure. Spreadsheet support is very useful in systems ranging from data analysis (as a means of displaying results) to the basis of the system itself (analysis information systems and accounting models) and even in representational model systems. Linear programming is generally associated with optimization model systems, but can also be used to generate alternatives in representational model systems or suggestion model systems. The use of the system in the decision-making process is the important factor in decision support systems (Table 8.3).

All of these systems involved some flavor of prototyping. Initial systems were built, with the system demonstrated to the user. User suggestions generated enhancements and modifications to each system. This is a useful means to build better systems, but even more benefit comes from convincing users that

Table 8.2

System	Problem	Group	Benefit
Indian government	Food distribution	Government	Efficient operations
Finnish Parliament	Energy policy	Government	Informed decision
Syntex Laboratories	Sales force size	Company division	$25 million sales/year
L. L. Bean	Schedule telephone agents	Management group	$100,000/year
AT&T	Site selection	Consultant	Informed decision
American Airlines	Forecast inventory	Maintenance group	$1 million/year
San Francisco Police Department	Schedule patrol officers	Police precincts	$5.2 million/year

Table 8.3

Study	Interactive	Data	Models
Indian government	Field users	System focus External needed	None
Finnish Parliament	Personal PC use	Opinions (AHP)	Subjective (AHP)
Syntex Laboratories	No	External needed Subjective (Delphi)	Curve fitting Custom designed
L. L. Bean	No	From MIS	Forecasting, queuing, cost/benefit
AT&T	Product is interactive DSS	Survey customers External data added	Mixed integer LP
American Airlines	Field users	Internal (from MIS)	Probabilistic, LP
San Francisco Police Department	Field users	Internal	Scheduling

the system is worthwhile. The Indian government system, American Airlines system, and San Francisco Police Department system were all designed to be used by individuals in the field. Ease of use and training are important considerations in such an application. The police department scheduling system incorporated heavy use of graphics in order to communicate the implications of each schedule to the user. In that case, it was not only necessary to generate a useful solution, it was necessary to demonstrate that solution's superiority to alternatives. Graphics provided a means to communicate efficiently.

In these examples, there was limited interaction with central information systems. Central information systems supplied crucial data in a number of cases (Indian government, L. L. Bean, American Airlines, and San Francisco Police Department). This should not be taken to imply that a larger role is not often encountered in most applications. These cases were special by their nature. Conventional applications generally are not published. Central systems not only provide the necessary data, but can be a source of technical expertise as well.

These examples represent only some of the potential problem areas that can be supported by decision support systems. Current computer technology, both hardware and software, is vastly improved over what existed a decade ago. The near future promises even more dramatic enhancements to the possibilities of applying computer systems to aid human decision making.

REFERENCES

Alter, S. L. 1977. A taxonomy of decision support systems. *Sloan Management Rev.* (Fall):39–56.

Andrews, B. H., and H. L. Parsons. 1989. L. L. Bean chooses a telephone agent scheduling system. *Interfaces* **19** (6):1–9.

Hamalainen, R. P. 1988. Computer assisted energy policy analysis in the Parliament of Finland. *Interfaces* **18** (4):12–35.

Lodish, L. M., E. Curtis, M. Ness, and M. K. Simpson. 1988. Sales force sizing and deployment using a decision calculus model at Syntex Laboratories. *Interfaces* **18** (1):5–20.

Ramani, K. V., and S. C. Bhatnagar. 1988. A management information system to plan and monitor the distribution of essential commodities in India. *Interfaces* **18** (2):56–63.

Spencer, T., III, A. J. Brigandi, D. R. Dargon, and M. J., Sheehan. 1990. AT&T's telemarketing site selection system offers customer support. *Interfaces* **20** (1):83–96.

Taylor, P. E., and S. J., Huxley. 1989. A break from tradition for the San Francisco Police: Patrol officer scheduling using an optimization-based decision support system. *Interfaces* **19** (1):4–24.

Tedone, M. J. 1989. Repairable part management. *Interfaces* **19** (4):61–68.

CHAPTER NINE

Group and Organizational Decision Support Systems

As many of the DSS examples presented in this book demonstrate, although the original intent of DSS was to support individual decision makers, the actual practice has almost always involved group decisions. This is probably because most decisions in organizations are *not* within the complete discretion of any one individual. Although small businesses may involve the owner making all the decisions, contemporary businesses have grown to often mammoth size. Although captains of industry in the 19th century were able to run their businesses by dictatorship, modern business involves obtaining cooperation by persuasion rather than coercion. Dennis et al. (1988) reported that general managers spent from 30 to 80 percent of their time in group activities. We suspect the change from centralized decision making to group decision making has been underway for a long time and increases with every decade.

Two categories of decision support systems are discussed in this chapter. **Group decision support systems (GDSS)** are designed to help relatively small groups arrive at a consensus for decision more effectively. **Organizational decision support systems (ODSS)** extend beyond this focus on specific decisions involving groups and move toward the institutionalization presented by El Sherif in Chapter 4. These systems focus on the organization rather than on the individual (as with DSS) or the group (as with GDSS).

This chapter will:

□ Describe group decision support systems (GDSS)

□ Discuss the differences between GDSS and DSS

□ Present multiple-criteria GDSS concepts

□ Describe negotiation support systems

□ Describe organizational decision support systems (ODSS)

□ Discuss the value of institutionalization of computer systems to aid decision making

Decision making involves a number of environments and factors. Individuals bring their own value systems to bear and are able to identify their preferences without much difficulty. They may not be able to explain precisely why they prefer one solution over another, but they usually know what they want. Group decisions require communication, as well as a means of reconciling differences if there is conflict. Organizational decision-making processes have unique features of their own. First, most organizations are collections of a number of groups. So one unique feature is that the complexity of going from individual decision making to group decision making is magnified by extending beyond groups to organizations. There is also a very real possibility that representatives of some groups will tend to act in the interests of their group rather than in the interests of the organization.

The theoretical features of decision support systems are slightly different when group or organizational contexts are considered. Ad hoc query capability, access to quantitative and qualitative models to generate information from raw historical data, integration of external and internal sources of information, and flexible access to the system are still important in the group environment. But group environments emphasize other characteristics as well.

GROUP DECISION SUPPORT SYSTEMS

In group decision making, there is not as much clarity in the characteristics of the "right" answer. Identifying member opinions, as well as unifying them into a consensus, are additional elements of the decision-making process. Decision makers need to consider the perceptions of others. Sometimes, lack of knowledge exists. Computer systems can help through queries and model analysis. Other times, there are fundamental differences of opinion. Computers can do little to change people's minds on some issues, but differences can be identified, and leaders can more efficiently focus their efforts to guide group consensus to implement joint decisions. Communications capabilities are much more important in group environments than in more centralized decision making.

Although models can play a useful role, models are convincing only when they are understood. In group environments, this is less likely to be the case than in centralized decision-making systems. There may be fundamental disagreements concerning model assumptions or disagreements about the appropriateness of using a particular model. The added dimension of different group concerns is going to make for less uniform environments and therefore less repetition of decision procedures. There generally is less use of models in GDSS than in DSS.

This more dynamic decision-making environment requires stronger computer support. Access to accurate and current data, as well as to flexible and understandable models, are needed. Communication and coordination across organizational levels is going to become more important. An added task that could use innovative support is negotiation, to reconcile divergent group opinions.

A number of GDSSs have been built in the last 10 years. These systems appear to lead to better decision quality, increased participation by group members, and less group domination by a few vocal members. A goal of these systems is to gain consensus. The GDSSs built to date will not guarantee consensus, but they do create a climate making consensus more likely.

Levels of Group Decision Support

DeSanctis and Gallupe (1987) identified tasks where group decision support systems could aid the decision-making process on three levels.

The focus of level 1 GDSSs is to improve the decision-making process by facilitating information exchange among members. Computer system features that would aid this process were:

Electronic messaging or other information exchanges between group members

Networks linking each member's personal computer terminals to those of the other group members

A public screen at each group member's terminal

Anonymous input of ideas and votes to enhance participation of those group members with low perceptions of their group status

Active solicitation of ideas or votes from each group member to encourage participation

Summary and display of ideas, including statistical summaries and vote displays

A blank agenda that can be completed by the group to aid initial organization of meetings

Continuous display of the agenda, as well as other functions, to keep meetings on schedule

Level 2 GDSSs would add many of the decision-making aids of traditional DSSs to the level 1 features.

Planning models

Utility and probability assessment models

Budget allocation and cash flow models

Social judgment models

Delphi or nominal group technique support to aid in idea gathering

Level 3 GDSSs would add rules of order to the features found in the level 1 and level 2 systems. These rules could determine the order in which participants could address the group.

Automated rules of order

The ability to build a rule base for rule selection and application

Automated counseling to advise on available rules and how they might be used

Automatic filtering and structuring of group communication

We view the group decision-making process as being much the same as the decision-making process presented in Chapter 1, with the added complication that consensus (or at least synthesis) is desired. Gaining consensus is much more complicated than drawing an individual conclusion. The group process is likely to involve even more looping and backtracking, as different group members develop their perceptions of the problem. GDSSs can aid the group decision-making process through a number of features. The potential benefits of each of these features are presented in Figure 9.1.

The impact of GDSS has been examined in a number of studies. Because the field is relatively new, no generalizations can yet be drawn. However, most studies have found that participation increases when GDSSs are used, and decision quality seems to improve. There have been mixed results concerning the impact of GDSSs on increasing consensus, confidence, and satisfaction. Some studies have found these three factors to be improved through GDSS, with more focus on the group task. Other studies have found that increased participation often increases conflict and political behavior by group members. A key variable in these different results may be the nature of the group. If group members share the same general goals, consensus will be much easier to reach than cases where group members are negotiating a hostile settlement.

A Group Decision Support System: PLEXSYS

An example of an existing group decision support system is PLEXSYS (Nunamaker, Applegate, and Konsynski 1987a, 1987b). A decision room has been built at the University of Arizona, equipped with 16 computer terminals used by group members to input ideas, comments, votes, or electronic messages to other group members. Terminals are networked through a host computer, giving group members the ability to constantly exchange information. Large, centrally positioned projection screens allow display of information pertinent to all group members.

Computer software is provided, giving the ability to retrieve data from a variety of sources, including national dial-up data networks. Group members are able to access data analysis tools, including both quantitative and qualitative models. The decision-making session can be organized based on enumeration of issues by group members, as well as identifying assumptions affecting decisions. Group members can use the same system to agree on decision criteria. Information can be stored for future reference.

PLEXSYS consists of a session planning module, four process modules, and a means to accumulate and represent knowledge.

Feature	Potential Benefits	Decision Phase Support
Anonymity	Reduce individual inhibition Focus on ideas	Problem recognition & diagnosis
Simultaneous input	More efficient information generation Less domination by influential members	Problem recognition & diagnosis
Electronic recording & display	More efficient information manipulation Enhanced group memory	Alternative generation/ evaluation
Group process structuring	More effective use of group process structuring techniques (e.g., Delphi, nominal group technique) More task–oriented interaction Better adherence to meeting agenda	Evaluation
Information processing enhancement	Easy access to modeling tools Easy access to data and communications Quick and efficient access to group member opinions	Problem recognition/ Alternative generation/ Evaluation
Electronic voting	Quick aggregation of votes Anonymous voting possible	Evaluation/ Synthesis

Figure 9.1
Common GDSS features and benefits. (From Kim [1990])

Session planning: The meeting agenda can be created, with time frames for each agenda item. When an activity's time is nearly gone, the group can be prompted. Agenda templates are provided to aid in structuring the agenda for a specific meeting.

Idea generation: This module collects comments from group members and functions as a brainstorming tool. Each group member can enter ideas and comments relative to the issue at hand. This input can be anonymous. Additional response solicitation methodologies include software to support the Delphi technique (see Supplemental Chapter 1) and nominal group technique, a similar procedure without the preservation of anonymity.

Idea organization: This module provides tools that can be used to consolidate and analyze ideas and issues emerging from the idea generation session. Group members can retrieve information from external sources to support member arguments. The aim of this module is to generate a mission statement through iterative change, seeking consensus.

Voting: The voting tool gives group members the ability to register their preferences on an issue on a variety of preference scales. Options include a for/against binary vote, a Likert scale vote, rank ordering, and multiple choice. Votes can be counted anonymously, with results displayed to the group. Several models used to evaluate alternatives are provided in this module to allow group members to examine possible outcomes based on different decision criteria, as well as different environmental scenarios.

Issue exploration: This module allows participants to focus on emerging issues by exchanging comments. Information can be selectively reviewed on relevant topics. A stakeholder identification tool can retrieve and anonymously analyze and display information about various assumptions. The positions of other group members can be identified, allowing identification of those alternative solutions that are unacceptable to specific members of the group.

Knowledge accumulation and representation: This module manages the database operations of the system. Data is accumulated and made available within the session, as well as preserved for future sessions and for report generation.

Because it includes the means of structuring group meetings, the means to enhance communication between group members, and the tools for data analysis, PLEXSYS is a level 2 GDSS.

An example use of a group decision support system follows. This system was applied to a common problem area, demonstrating some of the possibilities of harnessing computers to aid highly unstructured decision environments.

LOUISVILLE PUBLIC PLANNING
Taylor and Beauclair (1989)

A volunteer group called Third Century, which consists of nearly 500 community members encompassing a wide variety of neighborhoods, educational levels, and business or private sectors, meets regularly to identify major issues confronting the city. They conduct open forums to discuss critical issues, gather data seeking better understanding of problems and solutions, and sponsor meetings and festivals with the aim of revitalizing the downtown area. A major goal is to develop a set of policy priorities for the future of the community.

Reaching consensus on major policy issues is a major challenge. The

University of Louisville was approached by Third Century leaders for help in designing an effective and representative means of reaching community consensus on education issues. The University of Louisville suggested a GDSS approach.

Fifty individuals were identified by Third Century as potential participants in a program to reach consensus. The group included a U.S. senator, school superintendents from public and private schools, university administrators, teachers, community leaders, neighborhood advocates, minority leaders, and citizen activists. Because of scheduling constraints, four sessions of seven participants each were conducted.

GDSS Design

The GDSS design aimed to assure that all leaders had an opportunity to present their cases in setting educational priorities. A flow chart (whose elements are given in Figure 9.2) was programmed into a usable computer code. Because of cost limitations, this was done by university personnel. The system was designed to allow each viewpoint to be presented, but in a nonthreatening way. One approach with this end in mind was to present issues in a generic form without attribution to particular individuals.

Representatives from Third Century visited each group leader. A list of the 10 most frequently cited educational concerns was identified, and each of these issues was rephrased as an action item (a short statement clarifying each main concern). Because implementation of each of the 10 items was far beyond the community's ability to fund, priorities had to be established. Some action items depended on adoption of other action items.

---

[1] Present issues
[2] Individual rank order of issue importance
[3] Calculate mean of group rankings
[4] Present mean rankings to group
[5] Discussion
     First iteration–enter comments individually)
     First iteration–aggregate group comments)
[6] Present comments
If scheduled time gone, quit.
If consensus not reached, return to [2].

Figure 9.2
Flowchart of GDSS. (Based on Taylor and Beauclair [1989]). Reprinted with permission. *DSS-89 Transactions: Ninth International Conference on Decision Support Systems,* George R. Widmeyer, Editor. Published by The Institute of Management Sciences, 920 Westminster Street, Providence, Rhode Island 02903.

Implementation

Each of the four sessions (seven participants each) started with a brief orientation (about one hour), with each of the 10 issues discussed. Although many participants advocated specific positions during these sessions, the main intent was to develop a common understanding about the nature and scope of the issues (Figure 9.3). Sessions were scheduled for three hours each.

Sessions were held in the GDSS research room on campus. Groups were limited to seven participants each because that was the maximum number of participants the GDSS room could support. The University of Louisville provided facilitators and technical assistants to expedite the process, as well as reduce fears of using computers by those with little experience.

In the first iteration, participants were asked to rank-order the 10 issues, with a value of 10 assigned to the most important, and a value of 1 assigned to the least important. The system collected that information and calculated mean ranks for the group. A consensus list was displayed with these ranks. Group members were then asked to enter comments about their rankings relative to the group ranking for each issue. These comments were stored in the system. Comments were presented to the group by issue, followed by lively discussion. The first iteration generally took about one hour.

The participation was found to be very fruitful. The focus of the first iteration was on what could realistically be done. Each issue was presented

Issue	Rank
Funding	1
Early childhood education	2
Corporate and community involvement	3
Curriculum	4
Literacy	5
Professional teaching issues	6
Reducing dropout rates	7
Research and technology	8
Higher education	9
Responsiveness to student needs	10

Figure 9.3
Louisville group issues. (Based on Taylor and Beauclair [1989]). Reprinted with permission. *DSS-89 Transactions: Ninth International Conference on Decision Support Systems,* George R. Widmeyer, Editor. Published by The Institute of Management Sciences, 920 Westminster Street, Providence, Rhode Island 02903.

without disruption. There seemed to be a greater degree of understanding about other viewpoints and a willingness to consider changing positions after the first iteration.

The second iteration had participants prioritize the issues on the basis of the prior discussion. The second iteration found a greater degree of consensus. A brief discussion was held, but comments were not collected electronically. This iteration took about 30 minutes.

A final iteration allowed participants to prioritize issues again. In each case, there was a surprising degree of consensus. Participants indicated that they felt the session was worthwhile. A final discussion was held to talk about the final rankings.

Discussions after the exercise were positive in terms of ease of use, benefit of output, and reduction in time to complete the task. Participants liked the anonymity of advocacy, the forum for discussing specific issues, and the nonthreatening environment for reaching agreement. Plans were adopted for applying the same procedure to establish economic development priorities for the community.

The size of the groups was constrained by the size of the GDSS room. It would have been better to have all leaders participate in the same session. Slight deviations in rankings were found between the four groups, but they were minor and did not alter the final priority list of action items.

This example provides a demonstration of the possibilities of aiding group decision making. The application involved the opportunity for some conflict, although group members were unified by a joint concern for educational issues. Steps were taken in implementing the process to reduce conflict. Other situations involve high degrees of conflict by their nature. Computer systems can also be used to aid this type of environment as well.

A NEGOTIATION SUPPORT SYSTEM: MEDIATOR

Jelassi and Foroughi (1989) describe negotiation support systems as special cases of GDSSs, emphasizing computerized assistance for situations in which strong disagreement on factual or value judgments exists between group members. Negotiation support systems focus on enhancing the prospect of consensus, with the intent of making compromise more possible.

The system uses a series of representation spaces to allow group members (parties) to present their views of the problem. Three of these representation spaces are used. Control spaces allow parties to present their views of solution characteristics. These can be mapped to goal spaces, which display each party's view of the contribution of alternative solutions to goal attainment. A microcomputer program providing a utility assessment procedure (PREFCALC) is used to allow parties to translate goal attainment levels to their utility. MEDIATOR also provides a means to calculate the relative contribution of each solution to goals. A means to generate a compromise solution by minimizing the maximum distance to an ideal solution (an ideal solution is an infeasible solution that has the best characteristics on all goals) as a potential solution for consideration.

The functional aspects of MEDIATOR include the ability of each team to formulate and store issues of importance to them and the ability for each party to display selected information on a public screen. Limited "what-if" analysis is available, with the intent of identifying compromise alternatives. The system also includes agenda development features and allows time constraints per agenda item.

These systems demonstrate the potential to support group decision making, even in antagonistic environments. In order to develop improved computerized group decision support systems, research is proceeding on a number of fronts. Understanding individual processes is difficult. The added dimension of group behavior adds to this difficulty.

There are a number of common characteristics of groups involved in decision making. Group size often ranges between five and twenty individual members. The output of group decision making tends to be more intellectual and less concrete than the output of individual decision making. Groups can consist of a variety of types of members, from cooperative efforts commonly found within business organizations (subject to the normal presence of competitive elements), to antagonistic parties seeking to negotiate a decision. Action in the group process can be accomplished through a process of give and take, or it can be imposed by a group leader. Therefore, the nature of the group is important in considering ways to aid their decision-making process.

MULTIPLE-CRITERIA GDSS

Group decision making by its nature increases the likelihood of conflicting, multiple objectives. Most of the discussion in this chapter is based on the viewpoint of computer systems. There has also been interest in group decision support from those whose focus is on multiple-criteria mathematical models. This section presents group decision support from that point of view.

The following study is presented to demonstrate the nature of many group decisions. It demonstrates the existence of multiple objectives (or criteria) in most real decisions. Although a GDSS was not used, many of the features of GDSS were applied, such as exchanging information and using computer support to try to identify the tradeoffs among objectives. Computer support was successfully applied to help each individual group identify the relative weights of importance that reflected that group's preferences among objectives.

DUTCH ENERGY PLANNING
Kok (1986)

The Energy Study Center in the Netherlands developed a model of the Dutch energy system. Five organizations with a major influence on Dutch energy policy were represented in a series of meetings applying multiple-objective analysis. These organizations were the Federation of Netherlands Industries, the Netherlands Trade Union Federation, the Center for Energy Conservation (an environmental research group), the Ministry of Housing, and the Ministry of Economic Affairs.

The intent of the study was to compare the application of five different multiple-objective selection techniques. The intent was not to identify a compromise solution satisfactory to all groups, but rather to develop the preferred solutions for each of the five groups individually. The interest here is the reaction of the group to a complex decision environment with a number of objectives when diverse group interests are represented.

The first stage of the study spent a great deal of time carefully defining the feasible alternatives in the Dutch energy system. The model variables, including prices of oil, coal, and uranium and energy demand, were explained. The group was asked to develop objectives and debated the objectives that were included. There was disagreement concerning the future price of nuclear energy, so different prices were considered. After three iterations, nine objectives were identified, presented in Figure 9.4.

The model was used to calculate the Dutch energy environment for the year 2000. A tradeoff table (identifying the optimal feasible solution for each of the nine objectives, also measuring the attainment on each of the other eight objectives for each of these nine solutions) was presented to the group. Some of these solutions coincided, so six unique solutions were obtained by this initial procedure. It was noted that some of the objectives, es-

---

Minimization of capital+operating costs
Minimization of SO_2 emissions
Minimization of NO_x emissions
Minimization of nuclear energy capacity
Maximization of renewable energy
Maximization of profits from Dutch natural gas
Minimization of Dutch natural gas utilization
Minimization of net oil imports
Minimization of fossil fuel use

Figure 9.4
Dutch energy objectives. (Based on Kok [1986])

pecially minimization of cost and minimization of nuclear energy, were highly conflicting.

The divergence of opinions was found to be very high. Four objectives, maximization of profits and minimization of utilization of Dutch natural gas, minimization of oil imports, and minimization of fossil fuels, were all given low priority by each group representative. Therefore, these four objectives were dropped in a follow-up experiment several months after the first experiment. However, divergence in group relative weights increased. A problem noted was that groups were not willing to compromise the use of nuclear energy. Groups either were insistent that nuclear energy not be used or insistent that it be used.

Interactive multiple-objective techniques were found capable of generating solutions reflecting the preferences of each of the groups. Two to four iterations were required. The techniques were viewed as valuable in learning about the tradeoffs between objectives. It is interesting that the econometric model itself was largely ignored because of disagreement about the cost of nuclear power plants. But the exercise did demonstrate the ability of multiple-objective techniques to aid decision maker learning about objective function tradeoffs, and allowed each group to identify its relative preference among objectives.

Lewandowski and Wierzbicki (1989) of the Institute of Automatic Control in Warsaw viewed decision support systems from a multiple-objective perspective. This perspective emphasizes DSS models as aids to the decision-making process. Every decision-making process is part of a longer process of learning on the part of decision makers. This learning leads to the decision maker becoming a master expert. When a decision maker becomes expert, the decision-making process is characterized by shorter processing time, and as structure of the problem is developed in the decision maker's mind, uncertainty is reduced. A large number of these decisions make up the learning process. A theoretical aspect of importance to this view is that under conditions of learning, consistency is not a necessary condition.

Therefore, DSSs have dynamic value functions in the decision-making process. These value functions help decision makers learn, as well as fill in details of the outlines of decisions suggested by decision makers.

Humans have a much stronger ability to learn than do computers. Lewandowski and Wierzbicki viewed many decisions as incapable of being totally automated. The initial phases of the decision-making process can be supported by central information systems. However, interpretation of this information requires formal problem recognition, interpretation, and diagnosis. These mental processes are well served by decision support tools. This, then, is the first function of a decision support system: to aid model formalization and analysis. DSSs should include a directory of models along with a database of the results of the experiments conducted with these models. This ability to review experimental results is necessary for the phase of generating solutions, as well as for evaluation of these solutions.

Modes of Rationality

Rational decision models generally assume well-expressed objectives, which usually involve decision maker analysis of tradeoffs. If this is the case, decision maker choices can be viewed as transitive and accurately represented by a preference cone logically extending prior choices to previously unevaluated alternatives. However, if decision maker choice is implicit (i.e., existing in the logical processes of the decision maker, but not expressed or even directly considered by the decision maker), transitivity of choices may not be totally accurate.

A primary means of reflecting decision maker preference is through a continuous utility function. This would exist if there were no strict hierarchy of values between decision outcomes. Utility has many drawbacks as a predictor of individual behavior in complex situations (see Chapter 2). Identification, or even estimation, of a utility function requires a heavy burden of questions and answers from the decision maker. Because of these factors, Lewandowski and Wierzbicki concluded that the DSS approximation of utility should change over time in order to account for learning.

An alternative approach to utility optimization is **satisficing** [settling for less than the optimal solution (Simon 1955)]. Originally, satisficing was justified because of the difficulty of optimization, the uncertainty involved in most decisions, and because of decision complexity. March (1978) termed this environment **bounded rationality.**

Lewandowski and Wierzbicki proposed the concept of **aspiration levels** for decision outcomes as a means of identifying complex tradeoffs. When an aspiration level for a good is obtained, by this theory the decision maker would cease to optimize. Aspiration levels represent values of decision outcomes acceptable to the decision maker.

Wierzbicki (1985) proposed principles of quasisatisficing decision making. One or more decision makers, representing some perspective of rationality, with the right to change their minds due to learning and the right to stop optimization for any reason (such as improving a negotiating stance), were assumed. In this method, the user evaluates possible alternatives based on a set of attributes. These attributes can be expressed on a numerical scale (quantitatively) or verbally (qualitatively). Constraints on objective attainments can be included. The user can characterize objectives in one of four forms: maximization, minimization, stabilization, or free.

Specification of these aspiration levels for each objective is one of the basic means of communication from the user to the DSS. Two types of aspiration levels can be included. Aspiration levels can be the objective levels desired, or they can be the reservation levels (the worst acceptable case).

The suggested decision support system should use this guiding information, along with other information in the system, to propose one or more alternatives to the decision maker that best satisfy the decision maker's specifications. If a suggested alternative is unsatisfactory to the user, the aspiration levels can be modified, leading to the system suggesting alternatives. The process is repeated until the user learns enough to be comfortable making a decision. The DSS can develop an order-consistent achievement function reflecting the system's estimation of the decision maker's utility function.

This proposal attempts a significantly more powerful group DSS, directly addressing the underlying preference structure of the decision makers. Although promising, such systems are more complex and therefore more difficult to apply. However, they offer a highly attractive means of incorporating multiple criteria into group decision making.

The next case applied multiple-criteria analysis in a group decision situation. A complex set of objectives existed. AHP (see Chapter 2) was used to develop an additive function combining all of these objectives. An interesting feature was that the group was used to develop this additive function. The decision was also complex, in that there were many options, and a mathematical programming model was used to identify the solution that yielded the highest additive function value.

CANADIAN FORCES MAINTENANCE
Mitchell and Bingham (1986)

The Canadian Forces had a major equipment maintenance responsibility. Equipment ranged from tanks and computers and laser equipment, to laundry equipment. The Director General of Land Engineering and Maintenance was responsible for approximately 600,000 labor-hours of repair and overhaul work per year.

The organization of this work involved a number of options. Work could be assigned to a depot, to Canadian industry, or to sources in the United States and Europe. Military maintenance systems operated by assigning particular responsibilities to various sources, with the intent of obtaining competent repair in a timely and cost-efficient manner. These particular responsibilities were called work packages, and maintenance management included the decision of allocating work packages to one of six sources. The six sources in this example were the depot, the original equipment manufacturer, a Canadian industrial contractor, a U.S. army depot, and two other sources.

The central depot was a large facility, capable of performing a variety of maintenance tasks. About 300 workers were employed. The depot had relative efficiencies, based on advanced tools, assembly-line techniques, and test equipment. However, there was an aging work force, and difficulties were encountered in recruiting and retaining qualified personnel. There also had been a large amount of new, sophisticated equipment added to the Canadian Forces, primarily a new tank and a family of armored vehicles with sophisticated electronics and optical systems. Therefore, a study was funded to recommend allocation of all Canadian Forces maintenance work, focusing upon what work should be assigned to the depot.

Objectives

A number of objectives were important in the study. There were six operational objectives (maintain short-term readiness, develop long-term readiness, minimize repair time, maintain materiel reliability, ensure materiel compatibility, and develop technical capability), two depot objectives (develop depot capability and efficiently utilize its capacity), two cost factors (R&D costs and administrative costs), and an industrial benefits objective (foster Canadian industry).

Decision Makers

A large group was involved in the decision. Thirteen senior decision makers were involved, as well as fifteen managers of specific major equipment programs. Twenty-one contract officers were responsible for specific classes of materiel.

Analytic Model

An AHP model was used to identify the relative importance of the 11 objectives. The additive model weighting these objectives was then used as the objective function in a zero–one linear programming model, which included constraints on depot capacities. There were 225 work packages to be assigned, with six options for each of the 225 packages.

Process

A three-day workshop was used to develop managerial judgment, through the AHP model. The consultants led the group through a structured procedure to judge the relative importance of the objectives and the work package attributes in measuring the effectiveness of the possible allocations of work packages. The pairwise comparisons developed by this procedure were used to obtain the relative weights through AHP.

On the first day of the workshop, 50 decision makers and technical personnel were briefed on the overall purpose and approach. The structure of the model was developed, objectives identified, and relative weights for the top-level objectives obtained (operational requirements, efficiency and effectiveness, administrative objectives, and Canadian industry emphasis).

Once objectives were identified and the relative weights of the top-level objectives developed, the executives involved were released. The remaining analysis was performed by middle-level managers and senior staff. The second day, the weighting process was completed by evaluating the relative importance of various work package and contractor attributes to achieve overall objectives. This yielded the additive weighted function.

The third day was devoted to obtaining rating information for all possible assignments of the 225 work packages to each of the six options. This completed the AHP model.

Linear Programming Model

A zero–one linear programming model was developed focusing on the relative advantage or disadvantage of assigning a work package to the depot. This yielded a much smaller zero–one model, making it feasible to obtain an optimal solution. The linear programming model constrained total depot capacity, as well as minimum hours by trade. The objective function coefficients for each work package were obtained by multiplying the hours of work in a work package by the relative AHP advantage (or a negative value for disadvantage) of doing that work package in the depot. A second model was run without minimum shop hours.

Results

A long-range plan for allocating future overhaul work was developed, improving the allocation of one-fourth of the existing work by moving it to different contractors. The depot was scheduled more efficiently, with about 40 percent of the current work reallocated in the long-range plan.

A secondary result was a long-range plan for developing resources and facilities at the depot. Personnel needs in the long run (15 years) were identified, making it possible to identify what new facilities and capital equipment would be needed.

An estimated 15 percent improvement in calculated effectiveness was obtained over existing work allocations. If new work was allocated more efficiently through the model, the improvement in effectiveness was expected to be in the 15 to 30 percent range. This was calculated to be between $3.6 million and $7.2 million per year of added value out of a $24 million per year direct cost for maintenance work.

This case demonstrates a number of points. First, AHP is again seen to be very usable in a group setting involving multiple criteria. In this case, it was possible to use a linear programming model in a decision support context as well. The process involved a fairly large group, representing organizational values. The feasibility of AHP in a group DSS was demonstrated. There are clearly organizational DSS features as well.

Multicriteria models can be very useful in aiding decisions. Multicriteria theory comes from a normative background. Decision support is based on nonnormative approaches. But there is potential to combine the ideas and techniques of each of these two approaches, yielding improved techniques in both fields. Minch and Sanders (1986) presented a framework applying DSS techniques to multicriteria analysis. Lewandowski and Wierzbicki considered the emphasis from the other direction.

GDSS RESEARCH

GDSSs commonly support a number of tasks. These tasks include accessing stored information, generating new information, sharing information, and utilizing information to reach consensus on issues under consideration.

Dennis et al. (1988) proposed a framework for GDSS research. They considered a variety of group characteristics, task characteristics, and decision contexts. The focus of that research was identification of how these factors lead to different outcomes when different problem characteristics are present.

Group variables: A number of group characteristics can be present in group decisions. These include member proximity, as well as the timing of the decision. Group size, as previously noted, can vary widely. The history of the group can also vary. Sometimes, groups are together for the first time. Decisions over time can involve a number of members of the same organizational element. Some groups are formal (specifically charged with a decision task), whereas others are informal. Group duration can vary from one-time decisions to an ongoing assignment. We have seen an example of a cooperative group (in Louisville) and a group with divergent goals (the Netherlands). Group members may have a variety of degrees of experience with computer support systems.

Task variables: The nature of the task can dramatically affect decision-making process outcomes. Some tasks call for expert "rational" judgment, whereas others may call for the development of politically based decisions. Tasks can vary in complexity, from simple decisions about scheduling Little League baseball games, to summit meetings between heads of state.

Context variables: Group decision-making contexts can vary from contrived experimental situations (gathering data on student responses to artificial decision-making situations) to the complex interrelationships of real decision making among a variety of conflicting stakeholders. Individual incentive or reward systems can vary. If stakeholders have a financial stake in the decision, they may behave differently than they would if they did not. Organizational cultures can vary, with some groups being influenced by organizational norms or expectations. External environmental pressures can vary as well. Negotiating parties seeking to settle a strike which shuts down vital services can receive intense pressure to come to a settlement. In other environments, nobody may be able to recognize a strike is underway.

GDSS variables: The presence or absence of GDSS features is a key variable for the study and development of computerized support systems. Some systems use computers primarily to expedite communication between group members. Others, such as MEDIATOR, include model support. A focus of research in GDSS is to identify relative effectiveness of different features in different situations and seek new and better configurations. The field is still quite young, and many developments are expected while effective systems are being identified.

Group process variables: These variables represent different leadership traits or degrees of conflict among group members. Process variables include the degree of group structure. Highly structured groups would be expected to use different processes than unstructured groups. The number of group sessions may vary. Groups meeting in multiple sessions might be expected to find GDSS more useful than groups meeting once. The time available to make a group decision may be important. Extended sessions imply a greater need for evaluation and larger amounts of data, or at least the need to share viewpoints more completely. Different voting systems are possible, with some systems applying the one-person–one-vote principle, whereas other systems have been developed to reflect recognition of greater expertise of some group members.

The value of anonymity in GDSS is unclear. Anonymity has been found to encourage participation. The degree of participation can be important in the effectiveness of a group decision. However, anonymity may also increase conflict between group members, as participants are less inhibited from making extreme statements. Some studies have controlled the variable of anonymity of group member comments. It has usually been found that anonymity leads to more comments, but that these comments tend to be more critical.

Outcome variables: These variables measure the success of the decision-making process. A variety of measures exists, including group satisfaction (with the process as well as with the decision), decision quality, time required, number of alternatives identified, amount of participation induced, attainment of consensus, and perceived confidence in the final outcome. Obviously, some of these variables are not easily measured.

These variables can be examined in efforts to determine the appropriateness of a variety of GDSS features. They have been used in comparing the use of **local area decision networks** (computer conferencing) as opposed to **decision rooms,** where group members are brought to the GDSS technology, or group decisions without computer support. Many decision room configurations are possible.

Dennis et al. reported that groups using computer conferencing generated decisions of equal quality as those in conventional face-to-face meetings (unsupported by computers), but were less likely to reach consensus and took longer to reach a group decision. On the other hand, those using computer conferencing were found more likely to participate equally.

ORGANIZATIONAL DECISION SUPPORT SYSTEMS

The focus of organizational decision support systems is on aiding the decision-making problems faced by organizations. According to Hackathorn and Keen

(1981), the focus of organizational support is providing computer information support to decisions involving a sequence of operations and actors which must be coordinated to solve problems. Communication and coordination are two primary functions to be aided by organizational support.

The general field of MIS has always claimed this role, providing information through reports and databases that are shared by organizational members. However, traditional MIS does not generally focus on aiding the decision-making process directly. A good MIS will provide accurate information quickly and efficiently. How it is used is not the focus. Decision support provides tools more directly focused on aiding learning.

ODSSs seek to coordinate and disseminate decision making throughout the organization (across functional areas and across hierarchical levels). These systems can result in decisions more focused on organizational goals. Furthermore, management as a group can more consistently interpret the competitive environment through a GDSS. If the same analytic tools are used repetitively, analysis will be better understood. If common data sources are used, these data sources will tend to improve in quality, because erroneous data identified by one organization member will be corrected for use by everyone in the organization.

El Sherif and El Sawy (1988) presented an organizational decision support system (discussed in Chapter 4). The system was constructed for the Egyptian Cabinet, linking decision support systems with common model bases and data. This system provided a means to apply DSS analysis throughout the organization. A major benefit of this approach was that all organization members became familiar with the analytic techniques of other organization members, thereby improving communication. This system also provided a data framework that could be used to keep track of critical information.

Another ODSS example is the Enlisted Force Management System (EFMS) developed by Walker (1990) and others for the U.S. Air Force. This system helped Air Force staff make decisions impacting enlisted personnel. The system was developed starting in 1981 and initially implemented in 1986. EFMS supported functions that were the responsibilities of five major, relatively independent, units in dispersed locations. Major components were the model base (linking a series of small models), the database (centralized input for models, output for reporting, and support to answer queries), and the user interface (designed to be uniform to allow access to many users). Users at dispersed sites could interact with the database and models through high-level (English-like) language on microcomputers. The central processing unit was a mainframe computer.

George (1990) reported other ODSSs similar to the Air Force system. Pagani and Bellucci (1988) presented a system to support corporate strategic planning. This system augmented existing DSSs and included a model base, databases (common and individual), communications capabilities, and word processing and graphics support. Dondi et al. (1988) reported an ODSS to support five-year plans for contracts in foreign markets for an Italian firm. This system included capabilities to support analysis involving resource planning with flexible constraints, and it supported several organizational units in a partially unstructured strategic environment.

SUMMARY

The concept of DSS in the 1970s focused on aid to individual decision makers. In the 1980s, there has been growing recognition of the importance of group aspects in decision making. A number of systems have been developed that were designed specifically for groups.

DSS can aid organizational development through a number of features. Probably one of the greatest advantages is the institutionalization of computer use to improve decision analysis. When an organizational system is used, benefits come from enhanced communications, sounder data (because data crucial to organizational decisions is examined by a number of organization members, and therefore data is more thoroughly corrected), and increased use of models (whose results are often shared throughout the organization). The benefits of individual DSSs would not have to be sacrificed, because individual users can still maintain their own databases for their personal information and can add whatever models they want to their own systems. ODSSs can even enhance personal use, by demonstrating new techniques throughout the organization and creating a climate where computerized decision support is the standard approach to decision-making analysis.

The group decision-making process is more complex than individual decision making. Models of rationality have been very difficult to develop for individuals. It is even more difficult to extend these ideas to groups. Political and negotiation models seem more promising than rational models. However, efforts continue to develop more appropriate rational models, represented in part by the work of Lewandowski and Wierzbicki.

Institutionalization of computer usage throughout an organization holds great promise. A number of governmental examples were presented, but many commercial applications also exist. The Fisher-Price example in Chapter 10 was presented as an executive information system, but was an organizational-wide system as well.

Although useful group, negotiation, and organizational support systems have been developed, there are many interesting unresolved research questions. Current systems vary widely in the degree of automation, in cost, and in effectiveness. Merely spending money is not the solution. The future promises higher degrees of decision support in these areas with new and imaginative applications expected. A key to better systems is understanding the decision-making processes involved at all levels: individual, group, and organizational.

REFERENCES

GDSS

Dennis, A., J. George, L. Jessup, J. Nunamaker, and D. Vogel. 1988. Information technology to support electronic meetings. *MIS Quarterly* (December):591–624.

DeSanctis, G., and R. Gallupe. 1987. A foundation for the study of group decision support systems. *Management Sci.* **33** (5):589–609.

Jelassi, M., and A. Foroughi. 1989. Negotiation support systems: An overview of design issues and existing software. *Decision Support Systems* **5**:167–81.

Kim, J.-D. 1990. The effects of decision schemes on small group decision processes and outcomes. Ph.D. diss., Department of Business Analysis & Research, Texas A&M University.

Kok, M. 1986. The interface with decision makers and some experimental results in interactive multiple objective programming methods. *European J. Oper. Res.* **26**:96–107.

Lewandowski, A., and A. P. Wierzbicki. 1989. Decision support systems using reference point optimization. In *Aspiration based decision support systems,* 3–20. New York: Springer-Verlag.

March, J. G. 1978. Bounded rationality, ambiguity, and the engineering of choice. *Bell J. Economics* **9**:587–608.

Minch, R. P., and G. L. Sanders. 1986. Computerized information systems supporting multicriteria decision making. *Decision Sci.* **17** (3):395–413.

Mitchell, K. H., and Major G. Bingham. 1986. Maximizing the benefits of Canadian Forces equipment overhaul programs using multi-objective optimization. *INFOR* **24** (4):251–64.

Nunamaker, J. F., Jr., L. M. Applegate, and B. R. Konsynski. 1987a. Computer-aided deliberation: Model management and group decision support. *Oper. Res.* **36** (6):826–48.

Nunamaker, J. F., Jr., L. M. Applegate, and B. R. Konsynski. 1987b. Facilitating group creativity with GDSS. *J. Management Information Systems* **3** (4):5–19.

Simon, H. A. 1955. A behavioral model of rational choice. *Quart. J. Economics* **69**: 99–118.

Taylor, R. L., and R. A. Beauclair. 1989. GDSS as a tool in public policy: The Louisville experience. In *DSS-89: Transactions of the Ninth International Conference on Decision Support Systems,* ed. G. R. Widmeyer, 271–76. Providence, RI: The Institute of Management Sciences.

Wierzbicki, A. P. 1985. Negotiation and mediation in conflicts: Plural rationality and interactive decision processes. In *Lecture notes in economics and mathematical systems,* ed. M. Grauer, M. Thompson, and A. P. Wierzbicki, vol. **248.** New York: Springer-Verlag.

ODSS

Dondi, C., P. Migliarese, G. Moia, and G. Salamone. 1988. An organizational decision support system for Italtel projects and internal resource planning. In *Organizational decision support systems,* ed. R. M. Lee, A. M. McCosh, and P. Migliarese, 43–58. Amsterdam: North-Holland.

El Sherif, H., and O. El Sawy. 1988. Issue-based decision support systems for the Egyptian Cabinet. *MIS Quarterly* **12** (4):551–70.

George, J. F. 1990. The conceptualization and development of organizational decision support systems. Working Paper, Department of MIS, University of Arizona.

Hackathorn, R. D., and P. G. W. Keen. 1981. Organizational strategies for personal computing in decision support systems. *MIS Quarterly* **5** (3):21–27.

Pagani, M., and A. Bellucci. 1988. An organizational decision support system for Telettra's top management. In *Organizational decision support systems,* ed. R. M. Lee, A. M. McCosh, and P. Migliarese, 3–13. Amsterdam: North-Holland.

Walker, W. E. 1990. Differences between building a traditional DSS and an ODSS: Lessons from the Air Force's Enlisted Force Management System. *Proceedings of the Twenty-Third Annual Hawaii International Conference on System Sciences* 3:111–19. Los Alamitos, CA: IEEE Computer Society Press.

PROJECT IDEAS

What added complications are involved in group decision-making processes as opposed to individual decision-making processes?

Discuss whether you would expect more individual or group decisions in an organization.

How can computers be used to reduce conflict? What impact does anonymity have on reducing conflict?

Views of GDSS from the perspective of business computing were presented, along with a view from multiobjective mathematical programming. Discuss differing approaches to rationality presented by these two viewpoints.

How do these different perspectives lead to different uses of computer resources to aid group decisions?

Discuss computer support available to support negotiations.

CHAPTER TEN

Executive Information Systems

The development of computer technology in recent times has made the concept of the computerized executive a more realistic goal. Managers have to synthesize a multitude of data and weave this data into useful information enabling them to identify and evaluate problems. This chapter discusses concepts in applying information systems to aid top executives in running their businesses.

This chapter will provide you:

- □ Definitions of executive information systems
- □ Technologies used in these systems
- □ Examples where systems have been developed and implemented
- □ Differences between these systems and other system types
- □ A view of future possibilities

CONCEPTS

We will review four articles, ranging in publication dates from 1976 to 1988, concerning the use of computers by managers. You will see that there have been major changes in the way in which managers access computers. There have also been major changes in the computer support available. The early articles focus on possibilities, the later articles focus on actual practice.

Alter (1976)

Alter studied 56 firms using computerized decision support systems. At that time, very few management functions had actually been automated. Alter commented that all indications were that most could not be. However, many applications were being developed and used to **support** decision making, as opposed to replacing human decision making.

Three major hurdles were identified. Managers and computer users at that time were familiar with only a few of the available systems. Most ideas for computer applications came from lower levels of the organization. These developments tended to focus on technical functions. Alter noted that most innovative proposals were not adopted, because the impetus for change came from sources other than the user.

The primary benefits from these systems were enhanced communications. A common conceptual basis for decision making was often obtained. Impacts of alternatives on marketing, production, and finance could be predicted in terms all groups could more readily understand.

Despite recognition that the needs of the users were crucial in the development of successful systems, users initiated less than half (25 of 56) of the systems studied, and they had even lower participation in system development (18 of 56). A higher proportion of implementation problems were encountered in those systems that did not have user participation.

In this period (the early 1970s), Alter viewed an environment where managers did not become involved with computers. Mainframe systems were too busy with data processing and clerical activities, and microcomputers were not yet commercially developed. Managers had little access to computers. The required software to aid decision making also did not exist, because there was not yet a market for it.

Rockart and Treacy (1982)

Rockart and Treacy presented a visionary view of the potential for executives to directly use computers in order to obtain the data they needed. Chief executives traditionally obtained information from staffs. However, improving computer technology and more powerful analytic software made it possible to see a future where chief executives could directly access data, as well as conduct deeper analyses.

Cases were cited where such use was already being made. One chief executive usually spent a few hours a day at a computer terminal, accessing reports and conducting original analyses. Another executive had a system incorporating graphics to enable quick generation of information about financial developments. A third CEO used an on-line database for his company's operations, as well as those of competitors. Another company president wrote programs to immediately obtain data about a variety of operations. Sixteen companies were studied by Rockart and Treacy where at least one of the three top officers directly accessed and used computer-based information on a regular basis.

One reason for this growth was attributed to be the availability of user-oriented computer facilities at relatively inexpensive prices. Another reason was the increasingly competitive environment, making it necessary to use the strongest tools possible to maintain competitive advantages. Executive use of computers can also encourage broader computer use throughout the organization. One CEO noted that when employees saw the terminal on his desk, it was a clear message to the rest of the organization to increase its use of similar tools.

Based on these observations, Rockart and Treacy saw a number of common features to executive information systems. The central purpose of each system was *to more effectively provide planning and control information*. CEOs needed to better understand their company's operations, and computer systems provided a means to improve this understanding. Each system had *data on important business variables*. Each key variable was *tracked over time* and *by business unit*. This enabled a greater use of comparative evaluation. When possible, executives extended key variables to include data on major competitors, key customers, and important industry segments. They often purchased well-developed computerized databases.

Executive information systems were used for two diverse applications. They provided timely access to the current status and projected trends of the business. These systems also allowed the executive to personally apply analytic methods that the executive understood and trusted.

Although it was admitted that most top managers in the United States in 1980 did not have any terminal access, Rockart and Treacy felt that competitive pressure, along with ease of use, would lead to a dramatic increase in executive information systems. One expected hurdle was a traditional view of role playing, where using a keyboard was considered beneath top executives. In addition, it was often difficult to justify expenditure on benefits that were so hard to justify in concrete terms. However, the benefits noted even at that early stage of EIS development were seen to be strong enough to lead to an increase in their use.

Fersko-Weiss (1985)

This article reported the results of *Personal Computing*'s survey of the chief executives of 500 large companies. Fifty-nine of these CEOs reported personal business use of computer systems. Some of these executives went to schools to learn to use computer systems more effectively. A trend of note was the hiring of MBAs by companies to train CEOs to use personal computers.

A number of notable example applications were given. The CEO of Mack Truck acquired a personal computer to keep track of highly involved labor negotiations. But during gaps in the negotiations, that CEO learned other things to use it for, and quickly became a heavy personal computer user. This executive instituted a program to give every manager a personal computer or a work station. A similar approach was adopted by the CEO of Centel, who began using a personal computer for personal finances at home, but became so impressed with the opportunities that about 700 personal computers were acquired for staff, managers, and engineers.

The CEO of Beneficial Corporation spent about 95 percent of his time in communications. Electronic communications provided a means to send messages instantaneously. In addition, he used a personal computer at home, so that if he was in a productive mood, he could send instructions or request research at any time of the day.

The CEO of Carrier Corporation also used a computer at home. He felt that many of his best ideas occurred in the middle of the night and were often forgotten. With a computer system available, he was able to send an electronic message and gain a sounder night's sleep.

The CEO of Procter & Gamble viewed computer use as a mind expander. He built his own financial models, in addition to programming other applications. His view was that if his staff built his systems, he would not gain as much understanding of the analysis. One program he wrote was given to the MIS department to enable employees to evaluate their retirement compensation plans, allowing them to enter estimates of future variable values and see the effect on their retirement benefits.

The president of Boeing used his personal computer to write speeches. In addition to being much more effective in organizing his thoughts, as well as being able to add and change ideas, the system enabled him to refer to past speeches that were saved on file. The Boeing president cited an example computer success story. A wing flap malfunction developed on a Boeing aircraft in Kenya. The traditional way of dealing with the problem would have been to send an engineer on site, which would have involved a number of days. But an engineer located in Kenya electronically sent a view of the wiring system to Seattle, where the problem was recreated on-line, and the computer automatically suggested a solution (an expert system). The wing flaps were able to be repaired in a matter of hours.

Brody (1988)

Brody reviewed actual executive information systems commercially available in early 1988. These are given in Table 10.1. Sales of these systems were reported to be about $30 million in 1987 and were expected to be about $115 million in 1990.

Most of these systems consisted of mainframe software that summarized information from a variety of sources and presented it in an easy-to-comprehend format on a personal computer. On-line information sources could be obtained, including the commercial databases discussed in Chapter 5.

High-tech interfaces were emphasized, including touchscreen, mouse, or infrared controllers (the things that make VCRs and TVs work remotely), along with menu systems. Heavy use of graphics to condense data and make it easier to understand was emphasized. The systems were built to require minimum training and use of manuals.

Executive information systems rely heavily upon exception reporting, eliminating the need for vast amounts of information where operations are proceeding as planned. Some systems display statistics falling outside of desired ranges (set by the executive) in different colors.

In addition to providing executives with access to operations, a typical system allows **drilling down,** or accessing detailed statistics that were initially summarized. Drilling down is available for a number of levels of detail. As executives identify a problem area, they can explore the detail for additional information, leading to a more complete diagnosis of problems.

Another feature is electronic mail. Meetings can be more expeditiously scheduled, through quick communication of available times. In addition, records of communications can be kept.

These articles provide a picture of the growing field of executive information systems. Figure 10.1 demonstrates a dynamically growing use of computers by executives. An MIT group found that only 10 percent of the senior executives of major corporations had computers on their desks in the late 1970s. Because of new executive-friendly systems, that figure was hypothesized to be as high as 70 percent by the mid-1990s.

Another source estimated about 800 to 900 executive information systems in use in 1988. About 100 of these were estimated to have been purchased from commercial vendors. One problem was price. Vendor software cost about $100,000 per system, but implementation usually cost another $100,000. Many companies feel they can build systems internally for that much. Vendors cited the lack of user-friendliness in internal systems. However, at least two companies that had developed their own systems entered the commercial market with their products. Although commercially available systems varied significantly in sophistication, the consensus was that the price of executive information systems would decline as all other computer technology products have.

Frenkel (1990)

This article reported a growing use of executive information systems. Chevron Corporation's use of such a system during an attempted takeover in late 1988 was reviewed. The chief financial officer of Chevron (along with 45 other

STUDY	PUBLISHED	OBSERVED
Alter	1976	limited
Rockart and Treacy	1982	growing
Fersko–Weiss	1985	59/500
Brody	1988	many
Frenkel	1990	more

Figure 10.1
Executive use of computers.

Chevron senior executives) had EIS links to stock market operations, as well as electronic mail linkages. By being able to monitor Chevron stock transactions in real time, to analyze these transactions, and to immediately communicate with each other, Chevron was able to fend off the takeover bid.

Chevron reported that its EIS pulled together marketing, manufacturing, and personnel information systems, making it possible to present information better, allowing more analysis, and enhancing communication. Note that in this application, one of the valuable features of the EIS was the ability to share the system with other decision makers.

Confirming Brody's article, Frenkel reported that Comshare and Pilot Executive Software dominated the vendor share of the EIS market, although about 50 percent of EISs were estimated to be developed by companies for their own use. Additional vendors reported were Execucom, Information Resources, Computer Associates, IMRS, and Metapraxis. New products reported have been included in Table 10.1.

Trends seem to include experimentation with local area networks to enable communication through personal computer systems and a growing use of hypertext technology. The cost of systems was reported to be substantial, with established products ranging from $150,000 to $300,000.

Definitions

Executive information systems, like decision support systems, are not restricted by definitions. Most definitions have been proposed by commercial vendors, who have obvious biases to have definitions include unique features that their products possess. But a general concept emerges from looking at the examples we have seen. Turban (1988) described the characteristics of an executive information system. Foremost, they should be **consistently used by executives.** They should have **tailored databases,** providing executives access to past data, current data (like yesterday's operations), and a means to project future data. Access to commercial databases for key external information can often be useful. They should have **easy access,** allowing executives to expeditiously identify the current status of operations, as well as exhibit projected trends. They should **fit the user's style.** Executives vary in the kinds of information they desire. The EIS should be designed to provide the executive with the information desired, without burdening the executive with extraneous material. **Extensive graphics support** is a common characteristic, taking advantage of the quick content communication available from graphics. A recent technology is **hypertext,** which allows computer users to apply menu systems and immediately call up programmed information. This technology allows much more responsive interface between the user and the computer. **Hypermedia** extends this technology to include various forms of output, such as television, audio, or any other media. **Electronic mail** capabilities are an essential feature, allowing executives to communicate quickly with other important actors in the business's operations. Rockart and DeLong (1988) defined executive support systems as routine use of a computer system, usually with direct access to that system, custom designed for the senior manager. See Figure 10.2 for a summary of the features of executive information systems.

The objectives of executive information systems are to produce insights and understanding on the part of executives (aid in developing their mental models of their businesses). These systems should include expeditious means of exploring, in order to give the executive additional insight. This exploring can be in terms of searching the database through drilling down in order to get specific details for an identified problem area. Exploring could be supported by analytic models as well, although models do not fit the concept of executive information systems nearly as much as they do for decision support systems.

COMMERCIALLY AVAILABLE PRODUCTS

Brody (1988) reported ten commercially available systems. Two of these systems were developed as in-house systems and later marketed. Frenkel (1990) reported additional systems.

Two examples are presented in order to further clarify what executive information systems are and some of the benefits involved. The first example demonstrates development of an in-house system, which can be expected to better match the specific needs of the organization. The second example demonstrates building an EIS around a commercially available product, which can be expected to be much faster and may satisfy the needs of most applications. Both systems seem to be effective, demonstrating something of a view of the future use of computers in organizations.

Figure 10.2
EIS features.

ON LINE
  Easy access
  Heavy use of menus common

SUMMARIZED CURRENT DATA
  Tailored focus on key variables
  Graphics useful
  Trend analysis
  Drill–down capability

ELECTRONIC MAIL

Table 10.1

Company	Installations (Brody 1988)	Product
Comshare	80	**Commander**—mainframe based **One-Up**—PC linkage
Execucom	?	**Executive Edge**
Forthright Systems	<20	**Vantage Point** interface allowing user-built EIS (sold to Execucom in 1989)
Forum Systems	90	**PC/Forum**
Information Resources	About 10	**Express** database access
IMRS		**On Track** financial reports **Fastar EIS** ad hoc drill-down
Interactive Images	20 to 25	**Easel** interface
Lincoln National	160	**Office Productivity Network** (in-house product)
Metaphor Computer Systems	112	Work stations and software
Metapraxis		**Resolve**—stand-alone PC system
Pilot Executive Software	>80	**Command Center Advantage**—mainframe based **Multipath**—ad hoc drill-down
Southern Electric Intl.	11	**Cadet** system networks PCs (in-house product)

FISHER-PRICE
Volonino and Drinkard (1989)

Fisher-Price manufactures, markets, and distributes infant, traditional, and promotional products. The two principal product lines are toys and juvenile products.

Fisher-Price has successfully integrated various management information and support systems into its strategic business plans. Its information systems objective has been to develop innovative uses of computer and communications technologies for strategic advantage and, where necessary, for defensive competitive action. Fisher-Price has incorporated DSSs as well as executive information systems (EIS) as part of its long-range plan of contemporary management.

The president of Fisher-Price and the vice-presidents of information systems and sales and marketing have been prime EIS sponsors and users. A senior project analyst was assigned to handle the daily details associated with EIS development. The EIS development team included executives, an executive staff, and systems analysts, providing thorough knowledge of the firm's business and data sources.

Objectives

The objectives of the EIS were:

To provide all levels of management and the sales force with appropriate and current information

To provide management with enhanced control reporting on customer and territory experience

To develop accounting reports accurately reflecting summaries of transactions, appropriate to meet management planning, monitoring, and control needs

To reduce dependence on customer service personnel to answer questions (reduce personnel and reduce telephone bills)

To reduce requests for systems to generate ad hoc reports

To reduce paper and printing expenditures, along with mail and handling costs

System Components

The system consisted of five components (one under development and one to be built).

The **Sales Information Link** provided numerous screens and reports that could be obtained from a main menu. Information concerning customers, products, sales, shipments, and orders could expeditiously be obtained. Hundreds of summary-level records were available through the menu-driven system, allowing management to drill-down to appropriate and current information. Documentation and the table of contents were easily obtained through HELP. Levels of information were available by individual product, product category, business group, salesperson, and customer by geographic region.

The **Distribution** module was added to the system, as it became apparent that the sales force required significant amounts of this information. The **Historical Plan/Planning** module was added to support and monitor short- and long-range planning, as well as forecasting. Two modules were under development: the **Human Resources** and **Retail** modules.

Because of industry trends toward quick response, Fisher-Price felt the need to reduce its finished-goods inventory through joint systems with customers. Through electronic data interchange, Fisher-Price could monitor production and closely coordinate shipping when its retailers demanded quick response. Fisher-Price has been able to capture 65 percent of its purchase orders electronically, leading to reduction of processing time. In turn, invoices were electronically delivered to customers, reducing paperwork and errors.

Before the development of Fisher-Price's EIS, information requests required a 30-day lead time. With the EIS, information was available the same day. Managers throughout the organization became daily hands-on users. Senior managers could investigate business dynamics, giving them more time for analysis.

Fisher-Price improved its competitiveness through integration of its EIS with strategic planning. The EIS and electronic data interchange systems provide Fisher-Price the ability to respond to rapidly changing markets.

GENERAL DYNAMICS
Evans, Gray, and Rhodes (1989)

A General Dynamics division vice-president responsible for a major new manufacturing project recognized the need for an executive information system in his division. Data needs were outlined, and the information systems staff given responsibility for the EIS development.

EIS software was not available, and the information systems staff did not have previous experience with EIS. Claremont Graduate School was known to have an installation utilizing PILOT software. It was agreed that Claremont faculty and students would develop a prototype which was to be evaluated in aiding the decision of developing a full EIS for General Dynamics. This prototype was to give access to information of daily production operations.

Manufacturing EISs need to be able to provide the types of information common to all EISs, in addition to tracking parts and the dollar costs of production. Needed data should be captured on the factory floor, including nonquantitative information such as explanatory memos. Information requirements for the General Dynamics system were developed through meetings with the manufacturing team, interviews with project executives, and feedback from users based on early prototype demonstrations. A set of dummy raw data was developed simulating the manufacture of 18 parts (including a hierarchy of parts) over a two-year period. This data was used to develop a sample database. Software was built providing information about parts status, parts tracking, production events, and parts costs. About 185 discrete screens were developed.

Two software products from PILOT Executive Software were used. Command Center is a fourth-generation language system with menu control, graphics, database, and data import and export ability. The menus are arranged in hypertext-like form allowing drilling down, as well as lateral movement throughout the system. ADVANTAGE is a generalized package allowing rapid creation of menus. Templates act as rapid applications generators. The templates were modified for the manufacturing environment.

Application

Four primary dynamic menus were developed for the system, designed to provide drill-down capability, trend analysis, status–cost reporting, events reporting, parts tracking, and exception reporting.

The STATUS menu displayed actual versus planned production information. Planned production units for the month were available, along with month-to-date production (both completed work and work in process). The plan for the following month is also available.

The TRACKING menu displayed the last reported operation on an assembly and the number of days the assembly had been in process. All serial numbers of an assembly were displayed, along with color coding to indicate whether a component had been authorized for use in a part prior to qualification testing. Therefore, the user could quickly determine the location of each unit in the manufacturing and testing process.

The EVENTS menu displayed key operational and testing action groups for a unique assembly. Total units processed by step were available on a month-to-date and daily basis. Information on test failure rates was also available. This information allowed the user to identify operations with excessive backlogs, as well as locate quality control problems.

The COSTS menu displayed the costs of operations, material, and support. Costs for the original manufacture, rework, and assembly could be identified. In addition, costs for assemblies by serial number were available. The user could therefore compare actual and standard costs and determine the degree of rework being done.

Five demonstrations were conducted in the first half of 1988 in order to validate the EIS with its potential users. Later demonstrations convinced General Dynamics executives that the system met requirements. The success factors cited included strong executive sponsorship, as well as the use of the prototype approach. The EIS project manager had technical knowledge, as well as business knowledge and the ability to communicate effectively with senior management. Organizational resistance was overcome by involving a broad range of people in the design process and providing them with a sense of ownership.

Note that both of these examples extend beyond support to an individual executive to more of an organization-wide focus. This, in part, is because individual systems are not that justifiable. Systems involve significant investment, and support of just one individual is not merited. Most companies invest to support positions, not individuals. Furthermore, it seems silly to develop a state-of-the-art system for the chief executive when the CEO cannot communicate expeditiously with the rest of the organization. In addition, if the information is worthwhile to the CEO, it is also worthwhile to others throughout the organization.

DIFFERENCES BETWEEN EIS AND OTHER SYSTEMS

All of the systems we look at in this book seek to use computers to aid decision making. Executive information systems are similar to management information systems, in that they seek to deliver needed information to the organization's decision makers. The distinctive feature of executive information systems is that the latest in computer technology is tapped to deliver key information as accurately and rapidly as possible. Because this generally implies added expense, the obvious initial focus is on systems supporting top executives. As both of the examples we have just presented demonstrate, this can lead to a system supporting the entire organization.

Executive information systems focus on reporting key information, as well as the capability of expanding information to answer executive questions about details. The focus is on obtaining an accurate and current view of organizational performance. This aids in the decision-making steps of identifying problems or opportunities. The means to generate data also exist, but thorough data collection activities would usually involve a longer process delegated to staff. Later steps in the decision-making process, such as alternative generation and alternative evaluation, also require greater investment in time than the executive may have available. However, when executive information systems are used on a wide scale, communication and understanding are enhanced through electronic transmission of reports, as well as familiarity with a common system. During the alternative evaluation phase, executive decision makers can use EISs to make last-minute comparisons with organizational performance, as well as answer other questions through drill-down capability. But the difference between executive information systems and decision support systems seems clear. Decision support systems generally involve more detailed analysis of a specific decision. Executive information systems provide valuable means of identifying the need for decisions.

Once decisions are made and the results of a policy are understood (through monitoring), it is possible in some types of repetitive decisions to structure a problem through an expert system. Most expert systems (rule-based systems) provide a means for businesses to administer policies through preprogrammed decision making.

Our view is that these systems provide support at various phases of problem structure. Management information systems provide the ongoing repetitive status reports and database of company operations to allow monitoring company performance over time. Executive information systems enhance this capability by focusing on key issues, to enable identification of problems or opportunities calling for a decision. Decision support systems provide the ability to analyze decisions in depth, developing better understanding of a problem (adding structure through learning). If a decision environment becomes more structured, an expert system can be developed, reducing the burden on human decision makers.

An important aspect of the executive information system is identifying those indicators that tell the executive how the organization is performing.

CRITICAL SUCCESS FACTORS
Rockart (1979)

Late in the 1970s, Rockart noted the flood of paper reports flowing to executives, which tended to tie the executive up rather than aid his or her decision-making capability. Very often, executives received too much of the wrong information. There was also uncertainty about what data the executive needed for effective decision making.

A research team at MIT developed the **critical success factor** approach to aid executives in identifying the kinds of information they needed. After identifying goals, critical success factors in accomplishing those goals can be identified. An important element is to identify measures of performance of these critical success factors. Then reports can be organized to give the executive data that can more directly measure organizational progress in attaining the executive's goals.

Existing approaches to providing information to senior executives include the by-product technique, the "null" approach, the key indicator system, and the total study process. Each of these will be described briefly.

The By-Product Technique
In the by-product method, the organization's information system is designed to meet the day-to-day needs of line managers. Information for senior management is considered a by-product of the line managers' information system. Summary, detail, and exception transaction processing reports are generated and made available to executives.

The focus here is upon electronic data processing or transactions processing. It was perhaps the most widely used approach in the late 1970s. This approach fails to consider the need for external information at the top of the organization and produces a huge quantity of data. It fails to address directly the information needs of senior management.

The Null Approach
As the name implies, the null approach is not really an approach at all. It argues that the information needs of executives are so subjective, immediate, and dynamic that they cannot be anticipated or designed for. Furthermore, proponents would argue, the information needed by top management cannot be generated from operational systems. Thus this is a "throw up your hands" type of approach.

This position fails to recognize that some external information needs of executives can be anticipated and managed. In addition, it does not recognize that some operational information is valuable. This was a commonly held position of MIS personnel at the time of Rockart's writing.

The Key Indicator System
The key indicator method is somewhat similar to the critical success factor method discussed later. This method involves three basic concepts:

1. The selection of key variables or "indicators" of the health of the enterprise
2. The establishment of baselines or target values for each of these indicators, so that exception reports can be generated when an indicator's value is significantly different from its norm
3. The use of flexible visual displays and graphics

The most significant differences in the key indicator method and the CSF approach is that the former deals almost exclusively with financial statement data and financial ratios and may involve numerous indicators. For example, the system by Gould, Inc., provided data on 40 operating factors, whereas less than 10 or so elements would be included in a system designed using the CSF approach.

The Total Study Process

The total study process was popularized by IBM and involves the analysis of the information needs of all managers in at least a large segment of the organization. These are large-scale projects and involve months or years of effort to design and implement. Systems designed in this fashion are costly, and projects may run into millions of dollars. These systems are typically aimed at middle management not senior management. The goal is to develop a better understanding of the organization, the information necessary to manage the organization, and currently available information. Then a system is designed and implemented that provides all possible relevant information, in addition to that already available.

Although this approach may be necessary in providing middle-level systems, it is expensive, tends to focus on a single level, and often ends up being a glorified by-product approach. Systems designed with this approach tend to be costly to change and hence tend to be static in nature.

The Critical Success Factor Method

Critical success factors are the limited number of areas in which results *must* be satisfactory for the organization to compete successfully and flourish. If performance in these areas is below standard, then the organization's performance as a whole will be less than adequate. Thus critical success factors denote areas of activity where managerial attention should be focused and concentrated. Performance with regard to CSFs should be constantly monitored and controlled.

Critical success factors should be closely aligned with the goals of the organization. Goals are the end results that management hopes to attain in particular planning periods. Successfully managing critical success factors should ensure that goals are achieved.

Because the CSF method is concerned with the information needs of senior executives, especially the chief executive officer, there are necessarily only a few people involved as the ultimate "end users" of information in the EIS. Thus the EIS can be tailored to the needs of these individual managers and their particular styles and desires.

Sources of Critical Success Factors

Rockart recognizes four prime sources of critical success factors: the industry, the competitive strategy of the organization, environmental factors, and time. For example, in the supermarket industry, any firm must be careful to manage its product mix, inventory, sales promotions, and price. In the automotive industry, some critical success factors include styling, an effective dealership system, cost control, and meeting energy standards (at least in the late 1970s and perhaps in the 1990s as well).

The competitive strategy may determine critical success factors because the particular market niche of the organization may force it to concentrate on a specialty of some kind. Perhaps the firm concentrates on quality in its product or service, or cost, or geographic location.

Factors in the environment are in continual change and may become critical success factors at various points. Rockart mentions the Arab oil embargo of 1973, which suddenly made energy management a critical area for many organizations. A similar situation occurred in the early 1990s in the Persian Gulf area. Similarly, the economy, the society in general, and various governmental agencies may change in such a manner as to make a particular factor critical for a period of time.

Temporal factors are areas internal to the firm that may be critical for a period of time. These often result from some element of the firm that is so unusually far out of control that the attention of top management is required. Examples would include severe shortages or surpluses of inventory, a plane crash resulting in the loss of several key personnel, or some similar crisis. These factors differ from environmental factors because they are primarily the result of internal forces, not external ones.

Measuring Critical Success Factors

As opposed to key indicators which are usually stated in monetary terms, critical success factors are often stated in rather subjective terms. Yet it is essential to provide objective measures of CSFs, so that the organization has a firm, unbiased handle on how well it is performing in critical areas. Thus ways of measuring performance in these critical areas must be developed.

These are usually not all that difficult to define. Rockart gives an example of applying the CSF approach at Microwave Associates, working with Larry Gould, formerly its president. Gould identified the seven critical success factors listed in Table 10.2. The company is in a high-tech industry where technological reputation is important, and in which it must bid competitively on orders required by customers. Notice that the CSFs are rather subjectively specified, but both "hard" and "soft" measures are given.

Table 10.2
Microwave associates CSFs and measures

Critical Success Factor	Measure(s)
1. Image in financial markets	Price/earnings ratio
2. Technological reputation	Orders/bid ratio
	Interview results
3. Market success	Market share
	Growth rate in new markets
4. Risk management in bids	Experience with product
	Experience with customer
5. Profit margin	Profit margin
6. Company morale	Turnover, absenteeism
7. Cost management	Budgeted to actual cost

Based on Rockart (1979).

The critical success factor method offers advantages to EIS design because it specifically addresses the information needs of senior executives. Furthermore, it concentrates on the few areas in which good performance is necessary to ensure successful operation of the enterprise. It addresses corporate goals, the critical factors that must be managed to attain those goals, and ways of measuring goal attainment and management of critical factors. This information on goals, CSFs, and measures can be used to design an appropriate executive information system for the organization. Use of the approach results in systems that provide executives the information needed to manage the organization from the top.

FUTURE POSSIBILITIES

The focus of executive information systems is on providing quick and accurate reports of organizational performance, along with the ability to explore key data in greater depth. The previous section discussed the identification of key indicators, enabling an EIS to be efficiently designed to accomplish these purposes. The potential to aid executives in developing strategies also exists. This section presents a proposal to accomplish this aim.

STRATEGIC OPTIONS GENERATOR
Wiseman and MacMillan (1984)

The *strategic options generator* was proposed by Wiseman and MacMillan for identifying opportunities to gain a competitive advantage through the use of information systems. The strategic options generator consists of answering five questions, each of which has several possible answers:

1. What is the strategic target?

Suppliers   **Customers**   **Competitors**

2. What strategic thrust can be used against the target?

Differentiation   **Cost**   **Innovation**

3. What strategic mode can be used?

Offensive   **Defensive**

4. What direction of thrust can be used?

Usage   **Provision**

5. What information skills can be used?

Processing   **Storage**   **Transmission**

Strategic Target

A first step is to focus on what the organization seeks to accomplish. The target may be suppliers, customers, competitors, or any combination of the three.

Suppliers: Equitable Life Assurance had an inventory control and purchasing system that contained information on prices charged by vendors of their supplies. It gave them leverage in dealing with vendors. The company estimated it saved over $2 million with this system.

Customers: Wetterau, the fourth-largest food wholesaler in the United States, was forced to switch from independent supermarkets to chains as the number of independents dwindled. They were able to enter this new market by offering point-of-sale terminals coupled with sophisticated inventory control software that assisted in ordering, pricing, and many other functions. The target was a new customer base.

Competitors: American Airlines developed its Sabre reservation system in the mid-1970s. Although the information on competitors' flights was included in the system, American flights were displayed first, even when other carriers provided better connections or cheaper tickets. This system was so successful that Braniff Airlines claimed it was one reason for its financial difficulties.

Multiple Targets

Most systems targeted at customers are also indirectly targeted at competitors, because new customers must often be taken away from another firm (although it is possible to bring an entirely new set of customers into an industry). Metpath, a large clinical laboratory, gained an advantage over its competitors by installing terminals linked to its computers in physicians' offices. Physicians could retrieve test results as soon as they were known. Once the customers (doctors and their staffs) had learned the system, it became difficult for competitors to regain them. Thus the system was also targeted at customers. Similarly, American's Sabre system was also targeted at gaining travelers via the provision of better service to travel agents.

Strategic Thrust

The thrust may be differentiation, cost, or innovation.

Differentiation: Differentiation is distinguishing the firm from its competitors through the use of information systems. Again, American Airlines has successfully done this with travel agents by providing the Sabre reservation system.

Innovation: Innovation is providing a new service through the use of information technology. Merrill Lynch announced a new service called the Cash Management Account in 1977. Investors using this service were provided with credit through a margin account, managed investment of cash and dividends, and access to cash via check and debit cards. This service resulted in the addition of more than 450,000 new customers. It took competitors years to catch up.

Cost: Equitable's inventory control and purchasing system allowed it to reduce the cost of acquiring supplies.

Strategic Mode

The strategic mode is either **offensive** or **defensive.** If competitors have already taken some action to which you are responding, then you are in a defensive mode. Merrill Lynch's competitors were placed in a defensive mode by its Cash Management Account service. Conversely, Merrill Lynch was in an offensive position. American Airlines took an offensive mode, forcing its competitors into a defensive posture.

Direction of Thrust

The direction of the thrust is either internal **usage** of the system or **provision** of information technology to customers or vendors. American Airlines provided terminals and access to schedules and fares to ticket agents. Merrill Lynch provided the Cash Management Account to investors. Metpath provided terminals and access to data to physicians. Equitable used its system internally to capture data and use it in negotiations.

Information System Skills

Three basic categories of information system skills can be used: **processing, storage,** or **transmission.** Actually each is used to some extent in any system for strategic advantage. National Decisions Systems introduced a product called "1980 Data Census" consisting of five volumes of statistical data from Census Bureau computer tapes, adding software to generate analyses and displays. This product allowed users to process data. Ford Motor Company developed an auto parts inventory system for its dealers, allowing them to search stored inventory data. Dun and Bradstreet developed a delivery system for its on-line databases, allowing users to access transmitted data.

The American Airlines reservation system used databases very extensively and transmitted that data to ticket agents. Decision support systems such as those described in Chapter 8 process data extensively.

Wiseman and MacMillan emphasized several points in the development of information system opportunities. A competitive strategy must systematically explore all options. Active participation of information system personnel is needed, because such systems require significant resources, and expertise is needed for implementation.

SUMMARY

Executive information systems emphasize easy access, summarizing important current data, and using computers to give the executive the ability to obtain needed information, as well as to communicate electronically. The focus of executive information systems is on current reports on key information and the ability to drill down to answer executive questions about specifics. These systems can be very expensive, but very effective.

A very important element in the use of executive information systems is identification of the information required for decision making. Rockart's critical success factors provide a means to aid in identification of key indicators and their measures.

The focus of existing systems is on reporting, accessing data, and responsive interfaces. The potential for enhancing these systems to aid strategy development also exists. The concepts are suitable for use throughout the organization, but the current high cost means starting at the top. Some organizations, like Fisher-Price, have integrated these systems throughout the organization.

There are choices available in building executive information systems. A cost–time tradeoff exists between the two general means of developing EIS. They can be developed in house, providing greater control, as well as the ability to custom-design systems for an organization's specific needs. There are also a number of commercially available systems that can be the core of an EIS. Commercial systems would provide faster development, especially if there is little experience with these systems within the organization. Commercial systems may include features that an organization originally did not specify, but which they may find useful.

The primary difference between EIS and DSS is the focus on models. Executive information systems typically do not include models, although they could be incorporated. The focus of EIS is on problem identification and data collection. Mathematical models are not as useful in supporting these stages of the decision-making process. Executive information systems can contribute a great deal in developing the executive's mental model of the organization's progress.

REFERENCES

Alter, S. L. 1976. How effective managers use information systems. *Harvard Business Rev.* (November–December):97–104.

Brody, H. 1988. Computers invade the executive suite. *High Technology Business* (February):41–45.

Evans, W. F., P. Gray, and J. E. Rhodes. 1989. Executive information systems for manufacturing: A case study. In *DSS-89: Transactions of the Ninth International Conference on Decision Support Systems,* ed. G. R. Widmeyer, 46–52. Providence, RI: The Institute of Management Sciences.

Fersko-Weiss, H. 1985. Personal computing at the top. *Personal Computing* (March):68, 70–71, 73, 75, 77, 79.

Frenkel, K. A. 1990. The war for the executive desktop. *Personal Computing* (April 27):56–59, 61, 63–64.

Rockart, J. F. 1979. Chief executives define their own data needs. *Harvard Business Rev.* (March–April):81–93.

Rockart, J. F., and D. W. DeLong. 1988. *Executive support systems.* Homewood, IL: Dow Jones–Irwin.

Rockart, J. F., and M. E. Treacy. 1982. The CEO goes on-line. *Harvard Business Rev.* (January–February):82–88.

Turban, E. 1988. *Decision support and expert systems: Managerial perspectives.* 1st ed. New York: Macmillan.

Volonino, L., and G. Drinkard. 1989. Integrating EIS into the strategic plan: A case study of Fisher-Price. In *DSS-89: Transactions of the Ninth International Conference on Decision Support Systems,* ed. G. R. Widmeyer, 37–45. Providence, RI: The Institute of Management Sciences.

Wiseman, C., and I. MacMillan. 1984. Creating weapons from information systems. *J. Business Strategy* **5** (2):42–49.

PROJECT IDEAS

Students can be sent to the library to identify current commercially available executive information systems. A search of the *Reader's Guide to Business Periodicals* may also yield success or failure stories.

Students can be assigned to find articles comparing the relative advantage of in-house or commercial products.

Discuss the aid of EIS to problem identification, data collection, and implementation steps of the decision process.

The authors do not expect much EIS support to alternative evaluation. Why not?

In practice, organizations often blend EISs with MIS. Why?

CHAPTER ELEVEN

Expert Systems: Introduction

Probably the fastest area of growth in business is the application of artificial intelligence to business problems. These systems harness computers in innovative ways, providing a means to more consistently deal with repetitive problems in effective ways, as well as developing new techniques for operating businesses. This chapter:

- Describes expert systems
- Presents example business applications of expert systems
- Provides a broad overview of how expert knowledge can be acquired, how this knowledge can be represented, and how computer systems can use this knowledge to arrive at recommendations
- Discusses the relationship of expert systems to the decision-making process
- Discusses appropriate problem characteristics for fruitful application of expert systems

Many decisions can be automated. When problem environments (or domains, in expert system terminology) are highly structured and rigid policies are to be followed, computers can do as good a job at decision making as humans. Examples include writing paychecks and paying bills. If employee time is verified, computers can be trusted to multiply time by the rate of pay, subtract taxes at the prescribed rates, take away prescribed payroll deductions, and print a check. If a service or product is verified as received, computers can take the amount billed and write another check. Other decisions involving less structure require judgment and learning. We have presented a number of such decisions dealt with through decision support systems. These decisions tended to be unique, because a new environment could be present each time a decision was called for. Still other decisions are more repetitive but complex. Space shuttle flights are controlled by computers, because there is a very high degree of complexity involved. The structure of this complexity has been mathematically described. Business also involves many problems where some complexity is involved (but NASA-level funding is not generally appropriate). One approach is to develop standard operating procedures. The IRS involves a high degree of structure, in that theoretically each situation has a precise answer. But the domain is highly complex. Rational prudent taxpayers often make mistakes. Tax domains have been automated, but judgment is still required.

Many individuals have developed a particular area of expertise. A few individuals are recognized the world over for their ability to deal with a particular class of problem. At one time, at least, Henry Kissinger was considered the world's expert at diplomacy. Napoleon was considered an expert in military strategy. Lyndon Johnson was considered an expert at a number of political skills.

There are many domains in business where individuals have developed the expertise for dealing with specific complex situations. Scheduling work in a plant that produces a variety of products can be a very difficult task. It is not hard to develop a schedule, but a schedule that is efficient is rare. Over the years, some people have developed a knack for coping with scheduling problems in plants. Another difficult business decision is pricing. Price a product too high, and nobody buys it. Price it too low, and either you go broke with a high volume or customers start to think the product is cheap and quit buying it. Many businesses have particular individuals who have developed a successful knack at setting prices. In both of these examples, the business expert may not be able to explain why the schedule or the product price works. Usually experience has taught these people, in the school of trial and error.

Expert systems are computer programs emulating human experts within a specific domain. Expert systems involve artificial intelligence, in that computers can be programmed to emulate human thinking. Expert systems seek to develop the factors experts use in dealing with a problem and arrive at the same conclusions the experts would. This can involve following rules for conclusions. The chapter will discuss other means of programming computers to apply expert knowledge as well.

AN OVERVIEW OF EXPERT SYSTEMS

Expert systems provide a way to preserve this valuable, but perishable, expertise. If the expert can describe how all possible situations are dealt with (**knowledge acquisition**), a set of rules can be programmed. This may have a number of advantages. Expertise can be preserved, even after the expert retires or quits. The expertise can be multiplied, by applying the computer program for that type of decision throughout the organization. Instead of having to fly the expert around the world to wherever the organization has a problem, either the program can be sent or, better yet, data can be transported electronically. See Figure 11.1 for a brief summary of expert system capabilities.

Figure 11.1
Expert system capabilities.

Preserve perishable expertise

Solve complex problems quickly

Provide answers rather than data

Provide explanations

There are many business benefits to expert systems. (Figure 11.2) There are monetary savings if the expertise is effective. Quality will also improve, if the expertise is effective. Expert systems free experts from routine tasks. Expert systems are usually programmed to explain the logic behind recommendations, thus matching the style of most managers. In addition, expert systems can be used as training vehicles, allowing the organization to develop as many experts as it desires.

There are limitations to expert systems. They have required intensive development costs in the past. When expert systems were first applied to business, they often took extensive periods of time (usually about six months) for the expert and a knowledge engineer to identify what the expert would do in specific situations. Another extensive period (again, usually about six months) was often required to write the code containing this expertise and prompting users for questions identifying the necessary information to apply the programmed expertise. Expert systems are still focused on very specific problems. They often cannot be applied out of a very narrow problem domain.

Figure 11.2
Expert system benefits.

Monetary savings

Improved quality

Compatible with common managerial style
(based on JUDGMENT)

Training vehicles

Free experts from routine tasks

Preserve expertise

Definition

Expert systems are computer programs with the characteristics including *the ability to perform at the level of an expert,* representing domain-specific knowledge in the manner in which the expert thinks, and incorporating an explanation of program logic. Expert systems can deal with uncertain data, and they can also deal with problems where knowledge can be represented symbolically.

Expert systems differ from conventional computer programs primarily by being more tolerant of imperfect knowledge and by the separation of knowledge (the **knowledge base**) from the reasoning routine. This allows applying the expertise to new problems, by inserting a new knowledge base.

Components

Expert systems consist of three major components. The **dialogue structure** is the means by which a user can access the expert system. The user usually inputs particular circumstances through interactive answers to the system's questions. Most expert systems also include an explanation capability, explaining to the user the chain of logic used by the system to reach its conclusions.

The **inference engine** is the program that can infer facts from the information in the knowledge base. A variety of means of organizing logical rules have been developed. The two most common are **forward chaining** and **backward chaining.** Forward chaining involves making inferences as soon as information is received. Rules are tested to obtain a match between the current state and the rule's conditions. If the conditions are true, the conclusion is added to a list of known facts. Forward chaining is data driven. Problems involving monitoring are often dealt with through forward chaining. However, forward chaining is often very inefficient. A great deal of computation time can be absorbed exploring possible situations when future information would make much of this effort unnecessary. Backward chaining is goal driven. A goal or hypothesis is the starting point. The program then works backwards, seeking necessary information in order to draw conclusions. In backward chaining, questions are asked as they are needed to draw conclusions. This can be a much more efficient process for most business applications. It is efficient if there are a limited number of possible goal values. In some large problem domains, these techniques can be combined, often yielding a more efficient program.

Expert systems represent knowledge in a **knowledge base.** A number of knowledge-based forms exist, ranging from predicate calculus, production rules, frames, and semantic networks. Most business applications are rule based, because rule bases are easy to understand and are appropriate for recording expertise.

Predicate calculus is a system of formal logic based on determining whether a given proposition is true or false. This approach allows relationships between propositions to be specified, thus allowing the system to reach conclusions.

Production rules are of the form IF (condition) THEN (conclusion), appropriate for domains where the decision is to be determined by the existence of a specific situation.

Frames are an alternative means of representing knowledge, using data structures where all knowledge about a particular object is stored in one location. Frames are used for declarative knowledge, which is more descriptive than procedural.

Semantic networks organize knowledge around objects as well, but through nodes in a graph rather than through a data structure. Relations between objects are represented by arcs (links). These arcs, or links, relate objects and their descriptors. Arcs can be definitional and can identify relationships. As with frames, all relevant information about a specific object is stored in one place.

Production rules are widely used in business applications and are quite efficient in diagnosis problems. Rule-based systems are appropriate for encoding heuristic (rule of thumb) knowledge used by human experts. The other forms have potential use in more sophisticated systems that seek to develop relationships automatically.

Knowledge Validation

We must stress that the validity of the knowledge in any system is crucial. If erroneous information is computerized, nothing is improved (decision errors will just be made faster). Therefore, it is important to check the validity of the expert system. There are two sources of error. First, not much may be known about the problem domain. If the expert system is not performing well, the error in this case would be that additional knowledge needs to be obtained. Second, the environment in which the decision is being made may be changing. This often happens in business, because business performance depends on human behavior, which we all know changes with time. It would be wise to consider the impact of a changing environment in all of the following examples. The stock market is known for its changing environment, and, in fact, computerized trading may be causing some of the change. Telephone sales is a relatively new field, where the response of customers can be expected to change. An example expert system supporting form completion is provided. Here, the regulations behind the form can change over time. The last example deals with commercial loan analysis, where recent years have seen radical change in the environment concerning the availability of credit and the need to worry about collateral value (such as oil and real estate assets).

Knowledge validation refers to checking the accuracy of an expert system. This should be done by extensive testing before the system is applied, of course. However, it is also important to watch for changes in the problem environment which make past expert rules less effective. The stock market is one example of a changing environment, where many program trading sets of rules that were effective in the past may well be less effective in the future. Expert system effectiveness should be monitored after the system is applied, to ensure that the rules that proved effective during system testing are still valid.

Knowledge representation types will be explored in more detail in Chapter 14. This chapter will look at some examples of knowledge representation.

Example of a Production Rule-Based System

A stock trading example from a Shearson Lehman broker (Leinweber 1987) will be used to outline a set of rules leading to a recommendation. Note that a database of stocks traded on a continuous basis is required to identify candidate purchases.

Rule 1: Is this stock moving opposite to its industry group?

> **NO**—forget it, there are other stocks to consider
>
> **YES**—explore this stock further

Rule 2: Is the volume for this stock today higher than average?

> **NO**—forget it, the movement is likely an anomaly
>
> **YES**—explore this stock further

Rule 3: Is the price for this stock over the last 10 minutes

> **RISING**—conclude mild evidence of a long position (consider buying)
>
> **FALLING**—conclude mild evidence of a short position (consider selling now, buying later).

Rule 4: Has the stock price moved up relative to its industry group in the last 10 minutes?

> **YES** (UP)—conclude additional evidence for a long position
>
> **NO** (DOWN)—conclude additional evidence for a short position

Rule 5: Has the stock price moved up since the start of trading today?

> **YES** (UP)—conclude stronger evidence for a long position
>
> **NO** (DOWN)—conclude stronger evidence for a short position

Rule 6: Have there been price reversals for this stock today?

> **YES**—forget it, the trend is probably over
>
> **NO**—keep going

Rule 7: IF rule 3 gave mild evidence of a position, but rule 4 did not confirm this evidence, conclude **considering** this stock.

Rule 8: IF rule 3 gave mild evidence of a position, and rule 4 confirmed that position, but rule 5 did not, conclude **advising** this stock.

Rule 9: IF rule 3 gave mild evidence of a position that was confirmed by both rules 4 and 5, conclude **strongly advising** this stock.

Note that this set of rules must be exhaustive in order to guarantee a conclusion. One approach to designing such a system would be to develop a **decision table,** enumerating all possible combinations of answers to the first six rules. Because there were two possible outcomes to each of these rules, this would mean 64 possible combinations. There are four possible recommendations (including forgetting the stock). The expert's job is to fill in the conclusion for each of these 64 combinations of outcomes.

Three examples of expert system applications follow. The first is a rule-based system, representing knowledge through production rules, to provide assistance to the growing area of telephone sales.

Example of a System Tied to a Database

TELEPHONE SALES
Conlin et al. (1987)

TeleStream is a knowledge-based decision support system improving the utilization of database information for telephone sales. The system operates by aiding understanding of transaction goals and retrieving needed information quickly on prospect qualifications, buying patterns, sales promotions, pricing margins, and possible product substitutions.

Many organizations, including those in banking, manufacturing, sales, and credit checking, depend on large databases as a critical component of the business. The databases supporting these functions often include a large amount of information, and therefore timely retrieval of needed information can be difficult. This is especially a problem for business activities requiring timely information, as well as systems where users may lack complete information about what the database contains.

Telemarketing utilizes telecommunications to apply personal selling. A common example is a distributor selling to retailers. Often prices are negotiated, and special promotions applied. The salesperson should know the goals of the organization, steps associated with selling, and product management. Databases supporting telemarketing usually contain information about technical product data, shipping schedules, inventory levels, customer order histories, purchase orders, pricing, discount, and promotion data. Distribution firms often have hundreds of customers and thousands of products. Therefore, the required databases are often very large. They can inform the salesperson about particular product inventory levels, identifying cases where substitute products are required. Discount and promotion information can be used to help sell more products. However, because of time constraints during telephone sales calls (35 calls per hour per salesperson are not uncommon), as well as salesperson inexperience, these features are often not used.

TeleStream is a knowledge-based system applying artificial intelligence to improve the power of a financial control and distribution management software product. TeleStream is given a customer identification and identifies the customer's technical and time constraints, and then presents the salesperson information pertinent to the sale, allowing the salesperson to focus on the telephone conversation.

The steps taken by experienced salespeople were incorporated into the system. The normal plan of action is to:

Identify customer qualifications: Provide the salesperson with account history, credit limits, and sales potential.

Define product demand: Identify products the customer is interested in, including relevant information about parts included, their use, and usual quantity.

Pricing: Previous price quotes, promotional packages, and quantities required for discounts are provided.

Sales configuration: Inventory stockage of the desired products and available substitutes are provided, along with needed accessories. Alternative product configurations can be proposed for negotiation.

Order submission: If the sale is made, the system places the order.

TeleStream consists of two major components. **Sales Advisor** accesses the database and is the decision-making part of the system. This component develops sales proposals that meet the needs of the customer, while also meeting the objectives of the firm. The system is capable of suggesting promotional products and suggesting products related to prior purchases. **Sales Assistant** provides the user interface.

The two components operate independently. This allows the salesperson to enter or request information without waiting for the system to complete its current activity. The two systems are capable of communicating with each other. The salesperson is always informed of the status of requests.

The TeleStream system uses a **blackboard** control architecture. This architecture is made up of independent modules, each with the capability to display and read messages. This feature facilitates communication between independent knowledge sources.

Sales Advisor consists of three major components: goals, controller, and knowledge sources.

Planning goals reflect the general plan of action, such as identifying the customer, identifying information the customer wants, and identifying quantities, delivery times, and prices. The system can also propose a product, negotiate terms, propose accessory products, and record sales. Focus goals prioritize activities based on strategic goals. This is important when multiple activities are being processed. Strategic goals are long-term organizational goals, such as maximizing sales volume or maximizing profit. Tactical goals are short-term goals, such as selling a currently overstocked product or selling a product being promoted.

The controller manages the Sales Advisor by searching for information posted by the other modules. This enables the system to display priority activities, identify and activate appropriate knowledge sources, and search for messages from the Sales Assistant.

The knowledge base consists of rules, incorporating expertise in a narrow area of the problem domain. Sources include inventory, product, price and discount, and promotion information. The system can also develop proposals for the salesperson to present to the customer.

This example demonstrates the diversity of activities to which expert systems can be applied. As with most business applications of expert systems, it is rule based. Other forms of knowledge representation can be used in business as well. The following example incorporates frames in a business setting. Note that although technology exists for frame-based systems, business applications (outside of production) are limited. This is probably because of the difficulty in identifying applications where frames are appropriate, as well as the effort required to develop them. The example is quite old, but deals with a problem domain where benefits exist.

TRAVEL FORM SYSTEM
Fikes (1981)

This application is a frame-based system using object-oriented programming to aid in planning business travel. The domain knowledge is the trip structure, the steps involved in trip preparation, dates, times, cities, airports, and other elements. The frames describe the structure of the database. Several forms containing overlapping information are used. The system has the ability to expedite repetitious tasks. The object-oriented programming style is well suited for creating internal representation of forms, creating a task database and embedding domain knowledge in the system.

When a user requests aid in planning a trip, the system displays a menu containing entries, including Request Advance, Plan Travel, Plan Lodging, Request Reservations, and Plan Day. A form is associated with each of these entries. The information entered on these forms is used to build a database describing the trip plan. The database is relational, allowing update of the entire database as information changes are made. The system fills in form fields with data retrieved or derived from other forms, as well as from general databases such as personal profiles. Ambiguities are resolved and inconsistencies recognized. When changes are made, the implications are displayed, or if ambiguities exist, the user is queried for resolution.

When the system is activated, the user is asked for a trip name. A Planning Steps menu is displayed, listing trip planning steps. If an advance is requested, the proper form is displayed. The user's personal profile is used to complete whatever form items about which the system has knowledge. Form items that the system cannot complete are highlighted. The user can change entries assumed by the system. Another form is used for travel planning. Travel steps are requested. Information from the advance request is used to complete whatever information is available. Past travel habits are assumed, with the user having the ability to make changes.

The information about the trip can be viewed in a variety of ways, using relational database capabilities. The trip can be viewed as a travel itinerary or a schedule of daily activities. When travel changes are made, the entire system is checked for necessary changes, such as new accommodations or travel connections.

The system allows forms to be modified when travel plans change. Forms serve both as input and output devices for the database describing the trip. The database consists of descriptions of travel steps, lodging stays, day activities, and other information. Knowledge about the structure of trip elements is used to infer the data required. An example is that travel steps on succeeding days imply the need for lodging between the two steps.

A dependency maintenance facility allows the system to operate without key information. When an action cannot be completed because a needed value is missing, a flag is attached to the slot where the information is missing. When the missing value becomes available, the action is retried.

A number of means of dealing with incomplete database descriptions are used. The system is designed to make as many deductions as possible with the information currently in the database. If two or more forms provide the same information, the system checks for conflict and merges the data if it is redundant. The user is asked for clarification if there is conflicting information. Information about the trip is sorted and merged, to provide a complete itinerary.

Frames were found useful for this application, because the system could be designed in terms of data-type taxonomies. Active data structures can respond to messages, react to new data, supply default data when needed, and compute or search for requested data.

Schwarz (1987), an official with the U.S. Environmental Protection Agency, argued for application of expert systems as a means of replacing paper, to at least some degree, for collecting information (government forms). His argument was that paper involved high processing, storage, and access costs, as well as high degrees of unfriendliness. Computer systems based on human information collecting methods would be able to more clearly ask for required information, identify needed questions, check for errors and inconsistencies, perform all required calculations, and provide feedback. The cost of the expert systems was estimated at $5,000 to $25,000 per page of paper form replaced. The benefits would include user satisfaction, as well as a reduction in many of the costs associated with paper form processing, storage, and access. Schwarz roughly estimated government employee cost at $25 per hour, and paper forms take roughly one hour per page. The expert systems would pay for themselves about the 750th time they were used.

Example of a System Using Links

The following example demonstrates some of the characteristics of semantic networks.

COMMERCIAL LOAN ANALYSIS
Duchessi, Shawky, and Seagle (1987)

Commercial loans are granted after analysis of the performance of the applying company. Analysis begins with an evaluation of general trends in sales, operating income, net income, expenses, cash flow, and working capital. The loan officer evaluates whether or not the company's performance is improving, stable, or deteriorating in each of these categories. Next, credit, collateral, and capital analyses are conducted using the most recent year's data. The company's efficiency is compared with industry averages in categories such as inventory turnover, receivables, fixed assets, and total assets. Efficiency ratings typically are strong, normal, weak, or poor. Strong and poor ratings usually require no additional consideration. But normal and weak ratings lead to additional analysis. Loans can be granted with varying stipulations or covenants restricting the loan.

GEN-X is a knowledge-based system to support this analysis. The **knowledge base** includes the rule base and other facilities for reasoning about the problem. The **data files** contain financial data that is examined by the knowledge base during execution. Output is stored in separate files for report generation. The **interface** gives users a means of entering data, obtaining reports, responding to queries, and receiving feedback. A spreadsheet layout is used with rows representing financial statement line items and columns representing years. Reports summarize the loan analysis and list recommended loan covenants. Firm and industry financial data is available by report.

Knowledge Representation

Knowledge is represented as a network of interrelated components. The nodes of the network represent facts, entities, and procedures. Links between nodes describe the relationship between node items. Some links take on values, if they link a variable node to a procedure. An example is the value that links the node inventory turnover trend with the node trend procedure.

The system consists of modular components that can be developed separately and later integrated. Major components are credit, collateral, capital, and capacity.

An IF-THEN table allows many rules to be easily formulated from a collection of facts. The loan analysis begins with a decision tree retrieving all standard financial facts from a file that has been produced by the spreadsheet program. These facts are true–false values, such as whether or not a firm's debt ratio is better than the industry average for firms of its type. Next, key general financial trends of the firm over the last five years are examined, including sales, net income, and working capital. The tree structure identifies facts needing to be established. The spreadsheet program makes all required calculations, which are fed to the IF-THEN rules to establish facts.

These three examples apply a variety of different knowledge representation forms. The telemarketing system used production rules, the travel reimbursement system used frames, and the loan analysis system had some of the features of semantic networks. Note that hybrids of these three approaches are often used. Chapter 14 will focus on the relative advantages of the major types of knowledge representation in expert systems.

To demonstrate the potential for application of expert systems in business, the following section will summarize the financial applications reviewed by Leinweber (1987).

EXAMPLE APPLICATIONS IN FINANCE

Many financial expert systems are being built, serving as expert assistants in banking, insurance, treasury service, and securities analysis. Real-time expert systems support traders, who operate in wider markets with more opportunities than ever before. Racioppo (1987) cited a number of fundamental changes in the securities industry, including elimination of fixed commissions in the United States and Britain, large numbers of mergers and consolidations, entry of banks into the securities markets and insurance and retail firms into brokerage, globalization of capital markets, increased competition, and new trading techniques. A market somewhere in the world is open 24 hours a day. Because many of these markets are new to many traders, there is far more complexity than existed in the past.

A number of expert system products have been developed for the financial market.

Insurance

Of the 28 largest insurers in the United States, Leinweber noted that 12 were engaged in expert system R&D, whereas 10 others were implementing operational systems in 1987. Applications included underwriting, claims processing, reserving, and auditing.

Underwriting entails determining the amount of risk involved in writing insurance. Expert systems have been applied to improve consistency in applying company standards to assess the degree of exposure to various risks by industry. Knowledge bases include industry-specific information about safety equipment and risk reduction techniques.

Claims Processing

Expert systems can quickly evaluate a claim by referring to previous claims on the same policy or by family members of the insured. Efficiency in detecting missing or suspicious information is vastly improved. An area of particular value is in fraud detection in medical claims. Blue Cross/Blue Shield reported an 80 percent reduction in labor costs for claims processing following application of an expert system. Lockheed Corporation has applied an expert system to detect overcharging and fraud in medical insurance programs. Every evening, its system retrieves the approximately 800 medical claims received during the day. A claim is processed by the expert system in about 25 seconds. Suspicious-looking claims are reported.

Reserving

Reserving involves deciding how much current revenue to set aside for payment of future claims. Expert systems provide a means to comprehensively and consistently plan reserves to meet uncertain demands.

Auditing

In order to limit risk and provide adequate control, auditing resources must be used carefully. The Equitable Insurance Company has developed an expert system to aid its internal auditors in selecting business units for audit. A number of subtle factors are considered, including management team experience, performance of internal controls, and external changes in the market or industry.

Consumer Credit Services

Servicing loan applicants is a major problem for financial institutions. Applications have increased much faster than organizations have been able to train qualified personnel to process. Institutions try to avoid accepting bad loans, while retaining qualified applicants. A number of lending and credit advisory systems have been built. American Express has developed a system to aid loan authorization. American Express cards have no fixed limit, so each time a card holder uses his or her card, in effect, a loan is being applied for. The system approves routine charges automatically. Unusual purchases are referred to a human authorizer, who evaluates the charge based on previous purchases and payments, as well as other data. Up to 12 screens may be used. Approximately 800 forward-chaining rules are used in the system evaluation. Other systems are also being used by other consumer credit institutions.

Loan officers often find they spend a great deal of their time tracking down additional information or verifying items on the loan application. An expert system has been developed that identifies those situations that are almost satisfied, but lack one or two conditions. These cases help loan officers by identifying needed information, focusing their attention on more fruitful search activities. Again, expert systems can apply more thorough and consistent analyses to loan applications than would be expected by humans.

Banking

Banks apply expert systems for a number of services, including credit authorization as outlined in the previous section. They have also used expert systems to support funds transfer and trading activities, particularly of foreign exchange. The Athena Group Foreign Exchange Advisor is used by several banks to qualitatively evaluate currency option strategies over a range of market conditions. The expected result of various strategies over a wide range of possible market conditions are reported to the user.

Portfolio Management

Security selection and portfolio insurance are two other areas supported by expert systems. In 1987, there were over 20,000 stocks and 60,000 bonds available for purchase. There are many data services and programs to support securities analysts. There is more information than could possibly be digested. The Athena Group Portfolio Advisor is an expert system that can assist financial professionals in applying qualitative techniques to compare many hypothetical portfolio designs satisfying legal and strategic constraints. The impact of individual variables is analyzed and the analysis explained.

Portfolios can be much more complicated than holding a set of stocks. Put and call options can be purchased or written with the intent of limiting risk or generating additional income. The number of financial instruments available and their complex interrelationships are increasing at a rapid pace. There are varying margin requirements, liquidity, and price relative to theoretical values. Instruments can be combined to hedge against market risks. Furthermore, there are foreign markets available, as well as domestic markets. There is a need for many expert systems in this area.

Trading

A number of expert systems have been developed to aid trading. Applications include arbitrage, hedging, and other trading environments. Pattern recognition capabilities are especially suited for this environment. An expert system to support trading requires timely information (in real time). Because of the multitude of available markets, multiple data sources need to be integrated. This data can be used as the basis for developing system indexes to gauge relative market strength or weakness. Trading rules are developed on the basis of identification of patterns indicating whether a security should be bought or sold. Once trade recommendations are given to the user, timely execution is important. Electronic communication with brokers is required to implement recommended strategies.

An example set of rules that could be incorporated was suggested by a Shearson Lehman broker (cited above with the intent of showing how rules could be applied).

THE ROLE OF EXPERT SYSTEMS IN THE DECISION-MAKING PROCESS

Expert system support to decision making is different than that provided by MIS, DSS, or EIS. MIS and EIS focus on providing decision makers with tools to identify problems or collect data to more fully understand problem environments. DSSs have some supplemental capabilities in these areas, as well as tools to allow decision makers to explore ideas more fully. All three of these systems focus on developing human learning. Expert systems, on the other hand, focus more on taking what has been learned and automatically applying this learning to a situation.

The decision itself does not have to be delegated to the computer. MYCIN (Harmon and King 1985, Chapters 2 and 6) is an example where an expert system is used to aid diagnosis and treatment of meningitis and bacteremia infections. No one seriously suggests automatically prescribing treatment on the basis of MYCIN results. The intent in that application is to suggest ideas to humans, whose judgment is preferred to that of the computer system.

There are artificial intelligence tools to aid in identifying problems. Chapter 13 will discuss computerized problem diagnosis. Data collection can be expedited as well. The TeleStream example involves computerized scanning of a large database to provide salespeople with information that is likely to be important. Expert systems can be viewed as capable of generating alternatives, by presenting recommended solutions to problems. When using an expert system, solution evaluation is primarily a human responsibility, although the ability of most expert systems to present their chain of logic aids this step of the decision-making process as well. Decisions could in concept be turned over to expert systems. Usually, most business applications find them used in an advisory role rather than as a decision-making entity. It is always good to have human veto power over computers.

VP-EXPERT

A number of expert system shells exist, making it possible for users to develop expert systems for many simple rule-based situations. VP-EXPERT is one of those shells. The next chapter provides a brief explanation and some rudimentary instructions are appended to that chapter for using this package. A more complete reference (Hicks and Lee 1988) would provide you the ability to become expert at its use.

Here we will show how this shell can be used to build an expert system. The scenario is a bank considering a loan application. This bank is fairly conservative and tries to be very selective in accepting loan clients. Three factors are considered in evaluating the loan application. These include age, income, and risk. Age categories are young (under 30), middle aged (between 30 and 60), and old (over 60). Income levels are low (less than $30,000 per year), average (between $30,000 and $80,000), and high (over $80,000). Risk is defined relative to the loan request. If current debt exceeds assets, risk is high. If the requested borrowed amount exceeds the amount of debts less assets, risk is considered medium. If assets are more than debt plus the amount of the borrowing request, risk is rated low.

Figure 11.3 gives conclusions for all categories of these three factors. The

GROUP	INCOME	RISK	LOAN
Young	low	high	0
Young	low	medium	0
Young	low	low	Asked
Young	average	high	0
Young	average	medium	.5*Asked
Young	average	low	Asked
Young	high	high	.3*Asked
Young	high	medium	Asked
Young	high	low	2*Asked
Middle	low	high	0
Middle	low	medium	.7*Asked
Middle	low	low	Asked
Middle	average	high	.2*Asked
Middle	average	medium	.6*Asked
Middle	average	low	Asked
Middle	high	high	3*Asked
Middle	high	medium	3*Asked
Middle	high	low	5*Asked
Old	low	high	0
Old	low	medium	0
Old	low	low	Asked
Old	average	high	0
Old	average	medium	0
Old	average	low	Asked
Old	high	high	0
Old	high	medium	.5*Asked
Old	high	low	Asked

Figure 11.3
Loan decision table.

VP-EXPERT knowledge base is given, as well as an outline of rules fired by the backward-chaining VP-EXPERT system. The rule outline is for input of a 35-year-old loan applicant with $30,000 income per year seeking a $20,000 loan. Assets are $50,000, and debts are $40,000. The final loan authorization is $12,000.

```
ACTIONS
REPORT Logic
DISPLAY "Welcome to the 7th County Bank of Aberdeen loan department."
DISPLAY "I understand that you were proposing we loan you some money."
FIND Risk
FIND Loan
DISPLAY "The amount we are able to loan you is: {Loan}.";
RULE 1
IF Age < 30
THEN GRP = Young;
RULE 2
IF Age > = 30
     AND Age < = 60
THEN GRP = Mid;
RULE 3
IF Age > 60
THEN GRP = Old;
RULE 4
IF Income < 30000
THEN INC = Low;
RULE 5
IF Income > = 30000
     AND Income < = 80000
THEN INC = Avg;
RULE 6
IF Income > 80000
THEN INC = High;
RULE 7
IF Assets > 0
     AND Debt > (Assets)
THEN Risk = High;
RULE 8
IF Assets > 0
     AND Want > 0
     AND Debt < (Assets)
     AND Debt > (Assets-Want)
THEN Risk = Med;
RULE 9
IF Assets > 0
     AND Want > 0
     AND Debt < (Assets-Want)
THEN Risk = Low;
```

RULE 10
IF GRP = Young
    AND INC = Low
    AND Risk = High
THEN Loan = 0
BECAUSE "You need the money!";
RULE 11
IF GRP = Young
    AND INC = Low
    AND Risk = Med
THEN Loan = 0
BECAUSE "You owe too much!";
RULE 12
IF GRP = Young
    AND INC = Low
    AND Risk = Low
THEN Loan = (1*Want)
BECAUSE "Glad to help out the
young!";
RULE 13
IF GRP = Young
    AND INC = Avg
    AND Risk = High
THEN Loan = 0
BECAUSE "You need to discipline
your spending.";
RULE 14
IF GRP = Young
    AND INC = Avg
    AND Risk = Med
THEN Loan = (.5*Want)
BECAUSE "We are willing to share
your burden.";
RULE 15
IF GRP = Young
    AND INC = Avg
    AND Risk = Low
THEN Loan = (1*Want)
BECAUSE "Any time you need money,
let us know.";
RULE 16
IF GRP = Young
    AND INC = High
    AND Risk = High
THEN Loan = (.3*Want)
BECAUSE "You need to develop
more savings.";

```
Testing LOAN.kbs
(=yes)
!     Risk
!     !        Testing 7
!     !        !       Assets
!     !        !       !        (=50000)
!     !        !       Debt
!     !        !       !        (=40000)
!     !        Testing 8
!     !        !       Want
!     !        !       !        (=20000)
!     !        (=Med)
!     Loan
!     !        Testing 10
!     !        !       GRP
!     !        !       !        Testing 1
!     !        !       !        !       Age
!     !        !       !        !       !        (=35)
!     !        !       !        Testing 2
!     !        !       !        (=Mid)
!     !        Testing 11
!     !        Testing 12
!     !        Testing 13
!     !        Testing 14
!     !        Testing 15
!     !        Testing 16
!     !        Testing 17
!     !        Testing 18
!     !        Testing 19
!     !        !       INC
!     !        !       !        Testing 4
!     !        !       !        !       Income
!     !        !       !        !       !        (=30000)
!     !        !       !        Testing 5
!     !        !       (=Avg)
!     !        Testing 20
!     !        Testing 21
!     !        Testing 22
!     !        Testing 23
!     !        (=(.6*Want))
```

Figure 11.4
VP-EXPERT loan sequence.

RULE 17
IF GRP = Young
    AND INC = High
    AND Risk = Med
THEN Loan = (1*Want)
BECAUSE "Remember to deposit early and often.";
RULE 18
IF GRP = Young
    AND INC = High
    AND Risk = Low
THEN Loan = (2*Want)
BECAUSE "Any time we can be of assistance,
be sure to call.";
RULE 19
IF GRP = Mid
    AND INC = Low
    AND Risk = High
THEN Loan = 0
BECAUSE "Get out of the bank, the city,
and the state!";
RULE 20
IF GRP = Mid
    AND INC = Low
    AND Risk = Med
THEN Loan = (.7*Want)
BECAUSE "You need a better job.";
RULE 21
IF GRP = Mid
    AND INC = Low
    AND Risk = Low
THEN Loan = (1*Want)
BECAUSE "You have demonstrated great thrift.";
RULE 22
IF GRP = Mid
    AND INC = Avg
    AND Risk = High
THEN Loan = (.2*Want)
BECAUSE "You are an obvious spendthrift!";
RULE 23
IF GRP = Mid
    AND INC = Avg
    AND Risk = Med
THEN Loan = (.6*Want)
BECAUSE "You need to learn to live
within your income.";
RULE 24
IF GRP = Mid
    AND INC = Avg

What is the value of your assets (in dollars)?

How much do you owe (in dollars)?

How much was it you wanted to borrow?

What is your age (in years)?

What is your annual income (in dollars)?

Question order determined by need of backward–chaining inference engine to determine rule conditions.

Figure 11.5
VP-EXPERT questions.

Input

Assets	50,000
Debt	40,000
Want	20,000
Age	35
Income	30,000

Results

GRP	Mid
INC	Avg
Risk	Med

"The amount we are able to loan you is $12,000."

Rationale
"You need to learn to live within your income."

Figure 11.6
VP-EXPERT results.

```
      AND Risk = Low
THEN Loan = (1*Want)
BECAUSE "Make sure you pay by the fifteenth of every month.";
RULE 25
IF GRP = Mid
      AND INC = High
      AND Risk = High
THEN Loan = (3*Want)
BECAUSE "We sincerely want your business!";
RULE 26
IF GRP = Mid
      AND INC = High
      AND Risk = Med
THEN Loan = (3*Want)
BECAUSE "We like to have Yuppies as customers!";
RULE 27
IF GRP = Mid
      AND INC = High
      AND Risk = Low
THEN Loan = (5*Want)
BECAUSE "Are you available for dinner?";
RULE 28
IF GRP = Old
      AND INC = Low
      AND Risk = High
THEN Loan = 0
BECAUSE "Old folks belong in the Old Folks Home.";
RULE 29
IF GRP = Old
      AND INC = Low
      AND Risk = Med
THEN Loan = 0
BECAUSE "You need to save up for retirement, not go around borrowing.";
RULE 30
IF GRP = Old
      AND INC = Low
      AND Risk = Low
THEN Loan = (1*Want)
BECAUSE "Make sure you deposit the deed in our vault.";
RULE 31
IF GRP = Old
      AND INC = Avg
      AND Risk = High
THEN Loan = 0
BECAUSE "You're old enough to know better.";
RULE 32
IF GRP = Old
      AND INC = Avg
```

```
        AND Risk = Med
THEN Loan = 0
BECAUSE "The golden years are time to read a lot of books at home.";
RULE 33
IF GRP = Old
        AND INC = Avg
        AND Risk = Low
THEN Loan = (1*Want)
BECAUSE "Make sure to keep up your life insurance payments.";
RULE 34
IF GRP = Old
        AND INC = High
        AND Risk = High
THEN Loan = 0
BECAUSE "Don't you think you're a little old to act 20?";
RULE 35
IF GRP = Old
        AND INC = High
        AND Risk = Med
THEN Loan = (.5*Want)
BECAUSE "At your age, you need to slow down a bit.";
RULE 36
IF GRP = Old
        AND INC = High
        AND Risk = Low
THEN Loan = (1*Want)
BECAUSE "We are looking for an additional member of our board.";
ASK Age: "What is your age (in years)?";
RANGE Age: 0,100;
ASK Income: "What is your annual income (in dollars)?";
ASK Debt: "How much do you owe (in dollars)?";
ASK Assets: "What is the value of your assets (in dollars)?";
ASK Want: "How much was it you wanted to borrow?";
```

This small example can help explain how VP-EXPERT works. The shell is **nonprocedural** (until arithmetic operations are used), meaning that the order in which rules are entered does not matter. The program is more efficient in a nonprocedural mode. The inference engine is **backward chaining,** because the sequence of the program is determined by assuming a condition for the goal variables (in this case **Risk** and **Loan**). Because the shell was asked to determine **Risk,** the first rules tested are those which could classify risk. The first rule giving a conclusion about **Risk** is rule 7. In order to determine if **Risk** is high, **Assets** and **Debt** need to be known. These are not in the system, so the shell asks the user for a value for **Assets** (50,000 assumed) and **Debt** (40,000 assumed). Because the conditions of rule 7 are not met, the program seeks another rule defining risk. Rule 8 is tested, requiring a value for **Want** (20,000 assumed). All of the conditions of rule 8 are met. Therefore, the system concludes that **Risk** is Med (medium).

The next variable to be determined is **Loan.** The first rule with a conclusion for this variable is rule 10. In order to make a conclusion, age group (**GRP**) is required. Rule 1 has a conclusion for **GRP** and is tested. Rule 1 requires **Age,** so the system asks the user his or her age (35 is assumed). The condition of rule 1 is not satisfied. The next rule with a conclusion for **GRP** is rule 2. The condition of rule 2 is satisfied, and **GRP** is concluded to be Mid (middle aged). This information does not satisfy the conditions of rule 10, so subsequent rules with **Loan** conclusions are tested. Rules 11 through 18 all fail, because they require **GRP** to be young.

Rule 19 is tested, satisfying the **GRP** condition. Income category (**INC**) is required, leading to rule 4. Rule 4 requires knowing **Income,** which is requested from the user. The condition of rule 4 is not satisfied. Rule 5 is the next rule with a conclusion for **INC.** Rule 5's condition is satisfied, and **INC** is concluded to be Avg (average). This means that rule 19's conditions are not met. Neither are rules 20 through 22. Rule 23's conditions are all met, and the conclusion for **Loan** is .6 times **Want.** Therefore, the expert system has successfully identified a conclusion for all requested variables, and it reports the authorized loan to be $12,000 (60 percent of the $20,000 requested).

The knowledge base includes explanation. In this case, the explanation is that "You need to learn to live within your income." VP-EXPERT does not print this message out automatically, but the information can be sent to a file to explain the outcome to the user.

This example gives you a picture of the operations of a rule-based knowledge base. This type of system can be used for a variety of useful applications, providing greater consistency, as well as valuable advice for humans learning new responsibilities. There are other means of storing knowledge. Frames are more like database packages, suitable for applications involving queries and searches through a large number of possible entities. Semantic networks can be used to trigger a variety of procedures, expanding the possibilities of expert system application.

SUMMARY

Expert systems are appropriate for a limited number of problem domains. The problem should involve a well-bounded task, because expert systems cannot deal with problems where there are a very large number of event combinations. They are suitable for tasks that are substantive in real life. This means that if the real problem can be adequately dealt with in a few minutes by the average human employee, it is not worth developing an expert system. Expert systems *are* appropriate for these problems if there is a great cost if a human makes an erroneous decision. Expert systems should be applied to repetitive problem domains. If a problem occurs only once and is not expected again, it is really not worth the cost to develop an expert system. There should also be a significant difference between the best solution and the worst solution. Organizations can live with poor solutions if there is no cost for being wrong. Test data should be easily available in order to validate the expert system, and there should be general agreement about the system's conclusions. There are many complex problems where expert systems would be appropriate. However, in order to be built, recognized expertise is necessary. There should be a consensus that the expert being modeled is effective at coping with the problem domain. In addition, the effectiveness of the expert system should be evaluated on a continuous basis, because the problem domain for which it was designed may have changed.

Expert system development is often very time consuming, both for the expert whose knowledge is being captured, as well as for the system builders (knowledge engineer, programmer, etc.). Expert systems usually involve a **prototype** construction style, where a number of iterations are applied seeking to capture all of the possible sets of circumstances in the problem domain. This construction time can be reduced drastically through use of one of the many expert system shells available (including VP-EXPERT). Shells, however, are often limiting, in that the system has to be built in a form for which the shell was designed. Often, domains are more complex than the shell can support. Companies seeking to develop expert systems face the decision of buying a shell and living within its constraints or building the system from scratch, generally using a suitable programming language such as LISP or PROLOG. Building the system from scratch can be time consuming. Barrett and Beerel (1988) give the general rule: "Use a shell if you can, an environment where you should, and an AI language when you must."

REFERENCES

Barrett, M. L., and A. C. Beerel. 1988. *Expert systems in business: A practical approach,* 124. New York: John Wiley & Sons.

Conlin, M., G. Strohm, A. Sathi, A. Pinkus, and F. Dumont. 1987. A goal directed approach to data access organization in telemarketing. In *Proceedings of the First Annual Conference on Expert Systems in Business,* ed. J. Feinstein, J. Liebowitz, H. Look, and B. Silverman, 45–53. New York: Learned Information, Inc.

Duchessi, P., H. Shawky, and J. P., Seagle. 1987. Commercial loan analysis: An application of knowledge based systems. In *Proceedings of the First Annual Conference on Expert Systems in Business,* ed. J. Feinstein, J. Liebowitz, H. Look, and B. Silverman, 55–62. New York: Learned Information, Inc.

Fikes, R. E. 1981. Odyssey: A knowledge-based assistant. *Artificial Intelligence* 16: 331–61.

Harmon, P., and D. King. 1985. *Expert systems: Artificial intelligence in business.* New York: John Wiley & Sons.

Hicks, R., and R. Lee. 1988. *VP-Expert for business applications.* Oakland, CA: Holden-Day.

Leinweber, D. 1987. Expert systems for financial applications. In *Proceedings of the First Annual Conference on Expert Systems in Business,* ed. J. Feinstein,

J. Liebowitz, H. Look, and B. Silverman, 121–44. New York: Learned Information, Inc.

Racioppo, S. 1987. Expert systems in global financial markets. In *Proceedings of the First Annual Conference on Expert Systems in Business,* ed. J. Feinstein, J. Liebowitz, H. Look, and B. Silverman, 201–8. New York: Learned Information, Inc.

Schwarz, D. S. 1987. The problem of collecting information: The expert forms solution. In *Proceedings of the First Annual Conference on Expert Systems in Business,* ed. J. Feinstein, J. Liebowitz, H. Look, and B. Silverman, 219–28. New York: Learned Information, Inc.

PROJECT IDEAS

Select any decision area where you are an expert. Develop a rule-based system capturing your expertise. If an expert system shell is available, develop the system.

Expert systems in engineering and the physical sciences sometimes involve knowledge representation schemes other than production rules. Business applications are dominated by production rule systems. Discuss why this is so.

Describe the difference between backward-chaining and forward-chaining inference engines.

Rule-based systems involve following programmed rules through identifying a set of circumstances and then applying the programmed conclusion. Describe how this applies artificial intelligence.

Prototyping is an alternative procedure to the traditional method of systems design. Discuss why the traditional methods of system design are less appropriate than prototyping in expert system development.

CHAPTER TWELVE

Expert Systems with VP-EXPERT

VP-EXPERT is an example of an expert system shell. Shells, as discussed in the previous chapter, make it easier and faster to build expert systems. As with all software packages, the more power the package has, the more little details are present. This chapter seeks to walk through some of the features of VP-EXPERT, with the intent of giving you the ability to start developing expert system applications. More thorough documentation of the package is available from Hicks and Lee (1988).

Many other shells are currently available. These shells all have some differences, although all are relatively easy to use. Other shells could be substituted for VP-EXPERT, using the same problem scenarios presented in this chapter.

This chapter presents:

- Basic VP-EXPERT system features
- How to create a VP-EXPERT knowledge base
- Running an expert system on VP-EXPERT
- Use of the induction feature
- Review of confidence factors

The VP-EXPERT knowledge base consists of three blocks. The **Actions** block contains procedural directions, including specification of a report file for explanation of conclusions (the BECAUSE statements), setting monitor colors, and initial displays to introduce systems to the user. The **Rules** block contains the inference engine of the system. IF, THEN, and ELSE conditions are prescribed, with optional BECAUSE statements. Note that ELSE is a dangerous condition and, except for special situations, should be avoided. The **Statements** block provides questions guiding the user in identifying variable input values. Choices can be used when a finite number of options are appropriate. Ranges can be specified for continuous variables between limits.

We will introduce VP-EXPERT through a simple expert system. Assume an economic advisor, willing to provide advice on product pricing, given various supply and demand conditions. Any sophomore with one week of economics knows that if you are selling all you have available, prices should be raised (*ceteris parebis*). If you are not selling all of your products, prices should be lowered. In this expert system, all that is necessary is to know the current price, supply, and demand (over the last month). We will assume a conservative economist, who is willing to recommend price changes of 10 percent.

VP-EXPERT SYSTEM ACCESS

Given the software and site-specific drive situations, the package is accessed by typing VPX. A series of menus is encountered. The first menu (Induce) includes options to *induce* a knowledge base from decision tables built prior to the session, an Edit option to build a new file, a Consult option to run the active file (after it is constructed), a Tree option to obtain a trace of rule logic (for an existing rule-based file), Filename to activate a file, Path to change directories, and Quit. To create a new knowledge base, move the cursor to Edit. (Note that you can move the cursor to the feature desired, type the capitalized letter on the menu, type the number corresponding to the feature desired, or press the corresponding function key.) The Edit module includes a number of options. The *Alternate, Shift,* and *Control* keys all include additional menu options.

Actions Block

In this case, we want to enter the commands for the pricing expert system. The initial line of the file will always be ACTIONS. If we want a report of the BECAUSE statements, we can create an output file with REPORT *filename*. The color of the expert system questions can be set with the COLOR statement. COLOR = *15* will give bright white printing for the system's questions to the user. DISPLAY statements can be used to introduce the system to the user. The statements displayed need to be enclosed in quotation marks. All variables that the system is to determine are identified with a FIND statement. System conclusions are also triggered by DISPLAY statements, again enclosed in quotation marks. Variable values identified are enclosed in {brackets}, preceded by a colon. The Actions section is concluded with a semicolon, the only semicolon in the section (Figure 12.1).

Rules Block

The rule base (knowledge base) is entered next. Each rule is concluded with a semicolon (Figure 12.2). A feature that needs to be kept in mind is that if variables take on numeric values, they need to be defined before they are used. This is **procedural** logic. If category variables are used, the system is **nonprocedural,** meaning that variables can be defined in any sequence. Rules should be exhaustive. One way to assure that all possible combinations of

Figure 12.1
Actions block.

```
ACTIONS
REPORT Economic
COLOR=15
DISPLAY "This is your expert economic advisor.
Speak to me."
FIND Newprice
DISPLAY "The recommended price
is:{Newprice}";
```

variable values are covered is through a decision table. In this case, the decision table would consist of three possible combinations: demand could be less than supply, equal to supply, or greater than supply. The IF AND OR clauses are used to identify situations, and THEN clauses yield conclusions. BECAUSE clauses can be used to provide explanations. Rules can be labeled (as long as the label is unique) in any manner using alphabetic or numeric characters. Each Rule section must end with a semicolon.

Note that the variables **Supply** and **Oldprice** are both defined by the

Figure 12.2
Rule base.

```
RULE 1
IF        Supply>0
AND       Oldprice>0
AND       Demand<(Supply)
THEN      Newprice=(.9*Oldprice)
BECAUSE   "Current    prices    exceed    the
equilibrium price in the short run.";
RULE 2
IF        Supply>0
AND       Oldprice>0
AND       Demand=(Supply)
THEN      Newprice=(Oldprice)
BECAUSE "The market is efficiently clearing.";
RULE 3
IF        Supply>0
AND       Oldprice>0
AND       Demand>(Supply)
THEN      Newprice=(1.1*Oldprice)
BECAUSE   "There   is   an   obvious   upside
movement in market prices.";
```

condition >0 in all three rules. This is an artificial device to trigger the system to identify these variables for evaluation. VP-EXPERT uses backward chaining, meaning that the goal variable triggers the logical sequence. The Actions section identified the variable **Newprice** as the goal variable. VP-EXPERT examines rules in order to determine rules that would lead to conclusions about **Newprice.** (Here all three rules do that.) Rule 1 would be selected first. If **Supply** and **Oldprice** were not listed in the condition statements, their value calculation would not have been triggered, and a value of 0 for both of these variables would have been assumed by the system. (Another way to accomplish this requirement to define arithmetic variables is to list them as FIND variables in the Actions section.)

A feature that is not obvious when starting with VP-EXPERT is that arithmetic variables can be used to define other variables, but any time an arithmetic variable is used on the right side of a relationship operator, that variable (or expression) must be enclosed in parentheses. If not, the error is difficult to trace. The arithmetic variable or expression will be assumed to have a zero value.

In this example, this feature is demonstrated in all three rules. In all three rules, **Supply** is enclosed in parentheses on the right side of each **Demand** condition. An arithmetic operation is used in rules 1 and 3 to conclude the value for **Newprice.**

Statements Block

The last section of the knowledge base is the Statements block. This example is very simple, consisting only of the system queries to the user for required input variable values. The keyword is ASK. In the Statements block, all lines end with semicolons (Figure 12.3).

There are three general types of input. The example includes numeric values. Another option is to give the user the specific choices available. This is accomplished by a line following the ASK statement:

CHOICES <variable name>: <option 1> <option 2> . . . <last option>;

The options would generally be qualitative labels.

The last case involves numerical values again, but limits these values within a given range, again following the ASK statement:

RANGE <variable>;i,j;

Here the variable has a lower bound of i (which must be integer) and an upper bound of j (which also must be integer). Note that whereas the limits must be integers, any continuous value between these limits is allowed.

Once the file is built, you can exit the editor. Remember that the *Alternate* key includes extra menu choices, including the choice SAVE (Alt-F6). This will

Figure 12.3
Statements block.

ASK Demand: "What is the demand for your product per month?";
ASK Supply: "What is your supply of this product per month?";
ASK Oldprice: "What are you currently charging per unit?";

save the file and allow you to name it. An automatic file extension .KBS is used unless you give a different extension.

The file can be run by using Consult from the main menu. If a trace of logic is desired, this can be activated by selecting Set from the next menu and Trace from the menu after that. Quit returns you to the Consult menu. The rule base is run by selecting Go. If there are any compiling errors, these will be flagged by the package, and you will be in the Edit mode. A common error is to forget the semicolons. Identification of logical errors can be aided by examining the trace file (filename.trc). The trace for this system is given in Figure 12.4.

The trace presents the system logic. The variable **Newprice** is the goal variable. Searching for rules leading to **Newprice** conclusions, rule 1 is tested. The conclusion for rule 1 requires knowledge of **Supply,** triggering the system to ASK the user for a **Supply** value. The user responded with a value of 400. Next, the system needs a value for **Oldprice.** The system is triggered to ASK the user, who responded with a value of 50. **Demand** is required; the value of **Demand** is ASKed of the user, who responded with a value of 350. **Supply** is greater than 0, **Oldprice** is greater than 0, and **Demand** is less than **Supply.** Therefore, all the conditions of rule 1 are met. The system concludes that **Newprice** is equal to .9 times **Oldprice.**

There are three sections to the standard output on the computer terminal.

Figure 12.4
Trace file.

```
Testing ECON.kbs
!      Newprice
!      !      Testing 1
!      !      !      Supply
!      !      !      !      (=400)
!      !      !      Oldprice
!      !      !      !      (=50)
!      !      !      Demand
!      !      !      !      (=350)
!      !      (=(.9*Oldprice))
```

What is your supply of this product per month?

What are you currently charging per unit?

What is the demand for your product per month?

The recommended price is: 45

Figure 12.5
Top window.

The top window displays system queries to the user, as well as displaying results. The lower left window displays all rules as they are examined by the system. The lower right window shows the user all variable values that have been established, along with confidence factors (CNF). In this example, CNF is always 100, as all knowledge is assumed to be deterministic. The top window in this case included the queries listed in Figure 12.5.

A MARKETING ADVISOR SYSTEM

Marketing involves a high degree of judgmental decision making. The field of marketing is concerned with the four P's (price, product, promotion, and position). Expert systems can be used to aid these decisions, including recommendation of production levels. Although a major factor in successful expert systems would be acquiring knowledge from an expert (we point out the obvious that this is *not* based on a marketing expert's rules of thumb), a general framework could be constructed as follows:

```
ACTIONS
REPORT Logic
COLOR = 7
DISPLAY "Welcome to expert product marketing advisor."
FIND price
FIND design
FIND promotion
FIND location
FIND volume
DISPLAY "The recommended pricing strategy is:{price}."
DISPLAY "The recommended design strategy is:{design}."
DISPLAY "The recommended promotion strategy is:{promotion}."
```

DISPLAY "The recommended location strategy is:{location}."
DISPLAY "The recommended production strategy is:{volume}.";
RULE 1
IF saleslastyear < = 10
THEN cycle = intro;
RULE 2
IF saleslastyear > 10
    AND saleslastmonth > 0
    AND salesnow > 0
    AND saleslastyear < (saleslastmonth)
    AND saleslastmonth < (salesnow)
THEN cycle = growth;
RULE 3
IF saleslastyear > 10
    AND saleslastmonth > 0
    AND salesnow > 0
    AND saleslastyear < (saleslastmonth)
    AND saleslastmonth > (salesnow)
THEN cycle = mature;
RULE 4
IF saleslastyear > 10
    AND saleslastmonth > 0
    AND salesnow > 0
    AND saleslastyear > (saleslastmonth)
    AND saleslastmonth < (salesnow)
THEN cycle = mature;
RULE 5
IF saleslastyear > 10
    AND saleslastmonth > 0
    AND salesnow > 0
    AND saleslastyear > (saleslastmonth)
    AND saleslastmonth > (salesnow)
THEN cycle = decline;
RULE 6
IF cycle = intro
THEN price = same
    design = same
    promotion = local
    location = local
    volume = same;
RULE 7
IF cycle = growth
    AND qual = high
THEN price = up50%
    design = same
    promotion = focused

What was your volume of sales for this product last year?   **50**

What was your volume of sales for this product last month?   **90**

What was your volume of sales for this product this month?   **200**

What is the level of quality for this product?
    avg

```
Testing PRICE.kbs
!     price
!      !       Testing 6
!      !       !      cycle
!      !       !       !       Testing 1
!      !       !       !       !       saleslastyear
!      !       !       !       !        !       (=50)
!      !       !       !       Testing 2
!      !       !       !       !       saleslastmonth
!      !       !       !       !        !       (=90)
!      !       !       !       !       salesnow
!      !       !       !       !        !       (=200)
!      !       !       !       (=growth)
!      !       Testing 7
!      !       !      qual
!      !       !       !       (=avg)
!      !       Testing 8
!      !       (=down10%)    price
!      !       (=same)       design
!      !       (=fullscale)  promotion
!      !       (=national)   location
!      !       (=up100%)     production
```

The recommended pricing strategy is: **down10%**.
The recommended design strategy is: **same**.
The recommended promotion strategy is: **fullscale**.
The recommended location strategy is: **national**.
The recommended production strategy is: **up100%**.

Figure 12.6
Price trace.

location = national
volume = up50%;

RULE 8
IF cycle = growth
    AND qual = avg
THEN price = down10%
    design = same
    promotion = fullscale
    location = national
    volume = up100%;

RULE 9
IF cycle = growth
    AND qual = cheap
THEN price = same
    design = same
    promotion = fullscale
    location = national
    volume = up100%;

RULE 10
IF cycle = mature
    AND qual = high
THEN price = up10%
    design = same
    promotion = focus
    location = local
    volume = down50%;

RULE 11
IF cycle = mature
    AND qual = avg
THEN price = down10%
    design = makecheaper
    promotion = local
    location = local
    volume = down50%;

RULE 12
IF cycle = mature
    AND qual = cheap
THEN price = down20%
    design = improve
    promotion = local
    location = local
    volume = down50%;

RULE 13
IF cycle = decline
    AND qual = high
THEN price = down10%
    design = same

What was your volume of sales for this product last year?
        2000
What was your volume of sales for this product last month?   **1800**
What was your volume of sales for this product this month?   **1700**
What is the level of quality for this product?
       high

```
Testing PRICE.kbs
!      price
!      !      Testing 6
!      !      !      cycle
!      !      !      !      Testing 1
!      !      !      !      !      saleslastyear
!      !      !      !      !      !      (=2000)
!      !      !      !      Testing 2
!      !      !      !      !      saleslastmonth
!      !      !      !      !      !      (=1800)
!      !      !      !      !      salesnow
!      !      !      !      !      !      (=1700)
!      !      !      !      Testing 3
!      !      !      !      Testing 4
!      !      !      !      Testing 5
!      !      !      !      (=decline)
!      !      Testing 7
!      !      Testing 8
!      !      Testing 9
!      !      Testing 10
!      !      Testing 11
!      !      Testing 12
!      !      Testing 13
!      !      !      qual
!      !      !      !      (=high)
!      !      (=down10%)   price
!      !      (=same)      design
!      !      (=none)      promotion
!      !      (=local)     location
!      !      (=onorder)   production
```
The recommended pricing strategy is: **down10%.**
The recommended design strategy is: **same.**
The recommended promotion strategy is: **none.**
The recommended location strategy is: **local.**
The recommended production strategy is: **onorder.**

Figure 12.7
Price trace.

```
        promotion = none
        location = local
        volume = onorder;
RULE 14
IF cycle = decline
        AND qual = avg
THEN price = down50%
        design = same
        promotion = none
        location = local
        volume = stop;
RULE 15
IF cycle = decline
        AND qual = cheap
THEN price = down80%
        design = same
        promotion = none
        location = local
        volume = stop;
ASK saleslastyear: "What was your volume of sales for this product last year?";
ASK saleslastmonth: "What was your volume of sales for this product the prior month?";
ASK salesnow: "What was your volume of sales for this product this month?";
ASK qual: "What is the level of quality of the product?";
CHOICES qual: high, avg, cheap;
```

VP-EXPERT has the ability to manipulate data from files in a variety of ways. Data can be read from databases or spreadsheets. Another feature is the ability to construct rule bases from tables created in text. The means to accomplish this is through the Create option in the Induce menu.

Assume an expert personnel administrator is often faced with the problem of applications for raises. Over the years, this administrator has developed a simple rule of thumb to make these decisions quickly. The critical factors in the expert's opinion are the employee's possession of information key to the company, as well as the potential to aid the company through computer literacy. A decision table is displayed in Figure 12.8 giving all combinations of categories of this information, with the expert's judgment for each combination. It can be created by the text editor in VP-EXPERT by accessing the Induce menu, selecting Create, giving a filename with the extension .TBL, and entering the table (including headings). This file is saved (Alt-F6 on the menu), and after typing y to confirm, you are returned to the Induce menu. To induce a text table, enter t, and respond to the system query for filename (do not enter the extension). You are asked for the name of the examples file (the .TBL file with the decision table) and the name of the rules file (add the extension .KBS to this filename). A basic knowledge-based file will be built. In this example, the rules file would be as follows.

Knowledge	Literacy	Raise and Action
Yes	None	3%_Hire_Replacement
Yes	Little	5%_Hire_Replacement
Yes	Lots	7%_Promote
No	None	0_Fire
No	Little	0_Fire
No	Lots	1%_Train

Figure 12.8
Expert personnel administrator.

```
ACTIONS
      FIND Raise_Action;
RULE 0
IF Key = Yes AND
      Computer = None
THEN Raise_Action = 3%_Hire_Replacement;
RULE 1
IF Key = Yes AND
      Computer = Little
THEN Raise_Action = 5%_Hire_Replacement;
RULE 2
IF Key = Yes AND
      Computer = Lots
THEN Raise_Action = 7%_Promote;
RULE 3
IF Key = No AND
      Computer = None
THEN Raise_Action = Fire;
RULE 4
IF Key = No AND
      Computer = Little
THEN Raise_Action = Fire;
RULE 5
IF Key = No AND
      Computer = Lots
THEN Raise_Action = 1%_Train;
ASK Key: "What is the value of Key?";
CHOICES Key: Yes, No;
ASK Computer: "What is the value of Computer?";
CHOICES Computer: None, Little, Lots;
```

```
Testing PERSONNE.kbs
(= yes CNF 0 )
!        Raise_Action
!        !        Testing 0
!        !        !        Key
!        !        !        !        (= Yes)
!        !        !        Computer
!        !        !        !        (= None)
!        !        (= 3%_Hire_Replacement)
```

Figure 12.9
Rules file—expert personnel administrator.

Note that this system does not include any more than the basics of the model. You can add output DISPLAYS to further explain the system. This example is also cryptic, because the variable **Key** represents key knowledge, the variable **Computer** represents computer literacy, and the outcomes are compound, including both raise as well as action. They are cryptic in order to define variable values in one word.

Other related VP-Expert features allow access to a database file and application of an iterative expert system rule base to search for alternatives with the proper characteristics. Knowledge bases can be chained and external programs accessed, to provide more efficient operation of larger systems. Hicks and Lee provide a great deal more information to explain the capabilities and operation of the package.

CONFIDENCE FACTORS

The last feature of VP-EXPERT that we will discuss is the use of confidence factors. These give the expert system the capability of warning the user that conclusions are less than concrete in some applications. Confidence factors look like probabilities, but they are not. They can be assigned by the user when selecting choices from a menu (triggered by ASK statements). The system will specify confidence factors for rule conclusions. Confidence factors are expressed in percentages. The system assumes a default confidence factor (CNF in VP-EXPERT) of 100 percent.

When responding to a VP-EXPERT ASK statement using the Choice menu, the system will provide a list of the available options. The user moves the cursor to the desired option and presses the ENTER key. The system will identify the user selection with a triangle next to the selected choice, but will not proceed until the END key is typed. This feature is designed to allow the user to make multiple selections from the Choice menu (sometimes appropriate), as well as to enter a confidence factor. A confidence factor other than 100 percent can be selected by pressing the HOME key instead of the ENTER key. A highlighted area will be displayed where the user can enter the confidence factor (from 0 to 100). Then the user presses the END key. If an incorrect confidence factor is entered, it can be corrected by pressing the HOME key and reentering the data. If an incorrect item was selected, the DELETE key will delete the selection, as well as the confidence factor.

VP-EXPERT uses the following conventions in dealing with confidence factors. For simple cases where an outcome is based on two variables with confidence factors, the resulting outcome is given a confidence factor equal to the product of the two confidence factors. For instance, if a characteristic is selected from the Choice menu with a confidence factor of .9 and a rule condition is assigned a confidence factor of .8 by the user, the system will give the conclusion with a confidence factor of .72. Other rules are more complex, including AND and OR connectives. If AND connectives are used in a rule, the confidence factor is calculated by using the lowest factor among the AND conditions. If two OR connectives are used (with confidence factors CNF1 and

CNF2) and both of the OR conditions are true, the formula for the condition rule confidence factor is

$$\text{Condition CNF} = \text{CNF1} + \text{CNF2} - (\text{CNF1} * \text{CNF2})$$

For instance, if the rule were

```
IF x = A (CNF = .7)
    OR y = B (CNF = .8)
THEN C;
```

and both A and B are true, C would be concluded with a confidence factor of $(.7 + .8 - (.7*.8)) = .94$. This is higher confidence than either of the two conditions, but the logic is that the conclusion is reinforced by both conditions being true.

VP-EXPERT allows the user to set a threshold confidence level for accepting a conclusion. If a confidence factor for a conclusion is less than the threshold, the condition is rejected. This threshold must be an integer percentage. The syntax for the clause is

```
TRUTHTHRESH = <value>
```

which can be used in the Actions block, as well as after the THEN portion of rules. Hicks and Lee suggest limiting TRUTHTHRESH use to the Actions block.

The values of plural variables can be sorted in descending order of confidence. This feature is activated by a SORT clause. The syntax for the SORT clause is

```
SORT <variable>
```

which must be placed after the FIND clause for the variable to be sorted and before the DISPLAY clause for this variable.

To demonstrate the use of confidence factors, we will assume a forecasting situation. Forecasting product demand is crucial to many businesses. Some product demands are highly stable, such as that for staple foods. It is relatively easy to forecast these demands by keeping score of past sales. Other demands involve more cyclical patterns, such as automobiles, which have sales patterns that are fairly predictable, although fairly complex techniques may be required. There are other products whose demand is far more challenging to forecast, such as the demand for specific toys (Cabbage Patch dolls), fads (Pet Rocks), fashion clothing, and many other products whose success depends on the reaction of the public.

Forecasting such unstable demands requires a great deal of judgment. Successful forecasters for these products well deserve the title of expert. Forecasts can consist of a variety of elements, many or all of which involve subjective assessments of varying degrees of confidence. The following expert system focuses on the preteen market for educational products. The key variables identified by the expert are the degree of redness of the product, the degree of ridiculousness, usefulness, and cost. The system will evaluate available products and suggest purchasing strategies.

```
ACTIONS
    FIND Action;
RULE 0
IF Red = Yes AND
    Ridiculous = Yes AND
    Useful = Noway AND
    Cost = cheap
THEN Action = PilotTest;
RULE 1
IF Red = Yes AND
    Ridiculous = Yes AND
    Useful = Noway AND
    Cost = high
THEN Action = BuyBulk;
RULE 2
IF Red = Yes AND
    Ridiculous = Yes AND
    Useful = Yes AND
    Cost = cheap
THEN Action = ForgetIt;
RULE 3
IF Red = Yes AND
    Ridiculous = Yes AND
    Useful = Yes AND
    Cost = high
THEN Action = Research;
RULE 4
IF Red = Yes AND
    Ridiculous = No AND
    Useful = Noway AND
    Cost = cheap
THEN Action = ForgetIt;
RULE 5
IF Red = Yes AND
    Ridiculous = No AND
    Useful = Noway AND
    Cost = high
THEN Action = Research;
```

```
Product: Maroon Mutant Samurai Slugs
    Red – maroon is sort of red (CNF=80)
    Ridiculous – sort of (CNF=70)
    Useful – no possible way
    Cost – $20 for a piece of plastic

Testing MUTANT.kbs
(= yes CNF 0 )
!     Action
!     !     Testing 0
!     !     !     Red
!     !     !     !     (= Yes CNF 80 )
!     !     !     Ridiculous
!     !     !     !     (= Yes CNF 70 )
!     !     !     Useful
!     !     !     !     (= Noway CNF 100 )
!     !     !     Cost
!     !     !     !     (= high CNF 100 )
!     !     Testing 1
!     !     (= BuyBulk CNF 70 )

Recommended Action:
Buy in Bulk with 70% confidence
```

Figure 12.10
Educational product expert system.

RULE 6
IF Red = Yes AND
    Ridiculous = No AND
    Useful = Yes AND
    Cost = cheap
THEN Action = ForgetIt;
RULE 7
IF Red = Yes AND
    Ridiculous = No AND
    Useful = Yes AND
    Cost = high
THEN Action = Research;
RULE 8
IF Red = No AND
    Ridiculous = Yes AND
    Useful = Noway AND
    Cost = cheap
THEN Action = Research;
RULE 9
IF Red = No AND
    Ridiculous = Yes AND
    Useful = Noway AND
    Cost = high
THEN Action = PilotTest;
RULE 10
IF Red = No AND
    Ridiculous = Yes AND
    Useful = Yes AND
    Cost = cheap
THEN Action = ForgetIt;
RULE 11
IF Red = No AND
    Ridiculous = Yes AND
    Useful = Yes AND
    Cost = high
THEN Action = Research;
RULE 12
IF Red = No AND
    Ridiculous = No AND
    Useful = Noway AND
    Cost = cheap
THEN Action = ForgetIt;
RULE 13
IF Red = No AND
    Ridiculous = No AND
    Useful = Noway AND
    Cost = high
THEN Action = Research;
RULE 14
IF Red = No AND

Product: Hula Hoops (any color)
    Red – can be for sure
    Ridiculousness – yes CNF=90
              plastic circles may have value
    Usefulness – not really CNF=90
              there must be some use
    Cheap – yes, definitely

Testing MUTANT.kbs
(= yes CNF 0)
!   Action
!   !   Testing 0
!   !   !   Red
!   !   !   !   (= Yes CNF 100)
!   !   !   Ridiculous
!   !   !   !   (= Yes CNF 90)
!   !   !   Useful
!   !   !   !   (= Noway CNF 90)
!   !   !   Cost
!   !   !   !   (= cheap CNF 100)
!   !   (= PilotTest CNF 90)

Recommended Action:
Pilot Test before committing full resources
with 90% confidence

Figure 12.11
Educational product expert system.

```
        Ridiculous = No AND
        Useful = Yes AND
        Cost = cheap
THEN Action = ForgetIt;
RULE 15
IF Red = No AND
        Ridiculous = No AND
        Useful = Yes AND
        Cost = high
THEN Action = ForgetIt;
ASK Red: "What is the value of Red?";
CHOICES Red: Yes, No;
ASK Ridiculous: "What is the value of Ridiculous?";
CHOICES Ridiculous: Yes, No;
ASK Useful: "What is the value of Useful?";
CHOICES Useful: Noway, Yes;
ASK Cost: "What is the value of Cost?";
CHOICES Cost: cheap, high;
```

SUMMARY

VP-EXPERT is a shell with many useful features. It includes the ability to access rules developed in a decision table, either through the VP-EXPERT editor or in spreadsheets. The ability also exists to use rules to scan databases or spreadsheets to apply an expert system search for favorable alternatives. The ability to use confidence factors is also available.

Expert systems can be used for many business applications. Most applications to date have been rule based, such as those discussed in Chapter 11 and this chapter. Shells provide a means to rapidly build systems (as you may be able to tell, those in this chapter were built in less than an hour each). Although this chapter's examples are trivial, many business applications can be usefully developed through shells.

This chapter has presented some very basic material to enable you to get started on VP-EXPERT. The examples could be used on one of the many other expert system shells on the market as well. VP-EXPERT includes a good help function. However, to use the system for more than demonstration purposes, one should obtain more complete documentation, such as Hicks and Lee (1988).

Because the technology to take an expert's opinion can be developed into a usable system rather easily, we can now focus on probably the most difficult aspect of expert systems. That is the identification and acquisition of expertise. The next chapter will discuss that issue.

REFERENCE

Hicks, R., and R. Lee. 1988. *VP-Expert for business applications*. Oakland: Holden–Day.

APPENDIX: VP-EXPERT

VP-EXPERT requires models consisting of three sections.

Actions Block	contains procedural directions one semicolon ; concludes the block
Rules Block	contains the IF/THEN rules of logic a semicolon ; concludes each rule
Statements Block	contains messages to elicit values from the user a semicolon ; concludes each line

!—comment
Actions
    DISPLAY "You can enter any heading message you desire with a DISPLAY statement."
    DISPLAY "You can also tell the user the conclusion of the session."
    COLOR #   ! sets the color for the messages to the user
    FIND <variable>   !tells the VP-EXPERT what variables are to be determined.

Rule <name>
IF   <variable> <relationship> <value or variable>   !variables right of relationship in ()
    AND <variable> <relationship> <value or variable>
    OR <variable> <relationship> <value or variable>
THEN <variable> = <outcome>   !if outcome a variable value, variable in ()
ELSE <variable> = <outcome>   !optional—dangerous to use
BECAUSE   "give reason";   !optional—rule section must end in ;

!Statements Block
ASK <variable>: "question";   !means to enter variable value
CHOICES <variable>: <option1>, <option2>,.., <optionx>; !option if specific values
RANGE <variable>;i,i;   !can restrict numeric values between integer lower and upper bounds

Arithmetic operations can be incorporated into rules. However, all arithmetic operations must have parentheses around them, and must be to the right of the relationship.
Any time a variable value is used to check a condition (right of the relationship operator), the variable must be enclosed in parentheses.
When arithmetic operations are called, the program logic reverts to procedural sequence. You need to worry about logical sequence in that case. All variables used must be defined prior to use.

The system requires all combinations of conditions be modeled. A decision table can be built outside of the system, and can be fed to VP-EXPERT to generate a set of rules. You then need to use the editor to add other statements.

Variables can take on plural values if the statement:
PLURAL: <variable>,.., <variable>;   !is placed in the Statements Block.

SEQUENCE OF COMMANDS:

VPX

	Choices—	Help	
		Induce	create a new file from outside decision tables
		Edit	edit the active file or create a new file
		Consult	run the active file
		Tree	obtain a logical trace of rules
		Filename	activate a file
		Path	change directory
		Quit	quit the system

Induce	Help	
	Create	open a new knowledge base system from a text file
	Database	call a database for decision table as basis for rule base
	Text	call a word processing file for decision table
	Worksht	call a spreadsheet file for decision table
	Quit	go back to main menu

Consult	Help	
	Go	run a knowledge base file
	WhatIf	see what happens if an answer to a question was changed
	Variable	what happens if a variable value was changed
	Rule	examine a rule or rules
	Set	allows calling for a trace, or changing screen features
	Edit	edit the active file
	Quit	return to main menu

	Go	Help	
		How?	see why a variable has a particular value
		Why?	see why a question is being asked (activate by /)
		Slow	scrolling is slowed
		Fast	scrolling is speeded
		Windows	to change window arrangement
		Quit	return to Consult menu

	Set	Help	
		Trace	generate a trace file
		Slow	scrolling is slowed
		Fast	scrolling is speeded
		Windows	to change window arrangement
		Quit	return to Consult menu

Tree	Help	
	Text	view trace file in text
	Graphics	view trace file in graphics mode
	Quit	return to main menu

See Hicks and Lee (1988) for more information.

CHAPTER THIRTEEN

Knowledge Acquisition

Expert systems can be effective tools, but an obvious determinant of effectiveness is the knowledge that is contained in the system. The power of expert systems comes from the quality of the knowledge they contain. Computers are extremely consistent and always do what they are programmed to do. Expert systems can cope with high degrees of complexity and can apply the best judgment for each case that has been considered. But a key element is selecting the action recommendations. This activity is referred to as knowledge engineering.

In this chapter we will discuss the various techniques developed to acquire knowledge for expert systems:

- Interviewing techniques
- Protocol analysis
- Repertory grid technique
- The expert-driven approach
- Induction by the system

The knowledge engineering process includes defining a problem, acquiring expert knowledge, designing an architecture, building a knowledge base, and testing and refining the program. The most crucial element is knowledge acquisition, a difficult and time-consuming activity. Knowledge acquisition is the process of gathering knowledge about a domain, usually from an expert, and incorporating it into a computer program.

Many expert systems have been developed for medical, scientific, and engineering tasks, where objectives are clear and the relationships between cause and effect have been thoroughly studied. The problem domain of management is wider and shallower than that of most expert systems. Tasks tend to be open ended and nonrepetitive. A number of knowledge acquisition techniques have been developed. Selection of a knowledge acquisition technique requires identification of the types of knowledge a specific method can elicit. Therefore, selection of a knowledge acquisition technique is dependent on the attributes of the problem domain and the types of knowledge associated with a specific type of decision.

KNOWLEDGE

Knowledge can be classified in a number of ways. One classification involves surface knowledge (combining declarative and procedural knowledge into problem-solving heuristics for quick solution of commonly occurring problems) versus deep knowledge (fundamental knowledge of a domain, including definitions, axioms, general laws, principles, and causal relationships). Surface systems are limited for the analysis of complex problems, but are the basis for most common expert systems using production rules. Heuristics involve empirical knowledge in the form of pattern action rules acquired through long experience by an expert (surface knowledge). Another dimension to knowledge in expert systems is declarative (knowledge about the problem domain) and procedural (knowledge about how experts cope with a problem). Declarative and procedural knowledge have slightly different features, requiring different kinds of knowledge acquisition techniques.

Expertise

Human knowledge has advanced a great deal over the centuries. The pace of knowledge development has grown as well. Based on the amount of data published, this growth could almost be called explosive. However, every advance in knowledge opens new doors to the unknown. The more we learn, the more we realize we do not know.

The same could be said of specific human experts. Some of us have developed the ability to cope with specific problems. Expertise involves a better understanding of a specific field, accompanied with better understanding of the need for additional knowledge. Humans do better with knowledge concerning concrete, well-defined problem environments. They do not do as well when dealing with human behavior.

The idea of expert systems is to harness the knowledge of a respected expert. Some have pointed out that experts may do better than others at a specific task, but are not necessarily perfect. Therefore, expert systems are rarely expected to be perfect at dealing with their appointed tasks, but should be based on fairly effective approaches to the particular problem and have the advantage of consistency.

Selection of an Expert

A fundamental requirement of experts is that they have a means of coping with the problem domain that is effective. Recognition of experts will have to be based on reputation. There are other necessary expert characteristics as well. The expert must be available and must be willing to cooperate in the knowledge acquisition and system testing steps of the expert system development process. In addition, experts must be capable of communicating their knowledge.

A variety of degrees of formalization can exist for a particular problem domain. As a problem domain becomes better understood, formal theories or normative models can be constructed. Before this formal structure is developed, problem solving and understanding depends on informal, intuitive, and possibly unarticulated models. Problem domains vary in size and complexity as well as degree of structure. Complexity relates to the number of interrelationships between elements.

An obvious approach to improve expertise is to obtain multiple views from more than one expert. The Mitchell case to follow provides an example where multiple experts were used. Ram et al. (1989) noted the advantage of obtaining multiple views, but also pointed out that added problems occur when different experts have conflicting approaches to a problem. Focusing on these differences of opinion should provide identification of the key issues in developing the knowledge base for the problem domain.

Another feature of human experts is that they continue to learn. Some expert systems have the capability of learning (adjusting their sets of rules based on the outcome of past decisions). However, most are rule-based systems, as presented in Chapter 12. It is important to monitor the performance of expert systems and to adjust the rules in light of new knowledge.

Expert System Development

Building an expert system requires a number of steps. The **prototyping** approach has been discussed as an appropriate procedure, because by necessity, expert system development is going to involve learning, and the entire system cannot be planned ahead of time as is traditional for more structured business computer applications.

Graham and Jones (1988) provided a sequence of expert system development, sketched in Figure 13.1. Between the steps of knowledge elicitation and modeling, there is a feedback loop representing the correction of inconsistencies due to misunderstanding between the expert and the knowledge engineer. Between the steps of internal testing and coding, faults in the code can be corrected. Between internal tests and modeling, model logic failures can be identified and corrected. In field trials, invalid system advice can be recognized, which requires returning to the expert to further develop the knowledge base.

Figure 13.1
Expert system development. (Based on Graham and Jones [1988], p. 284)

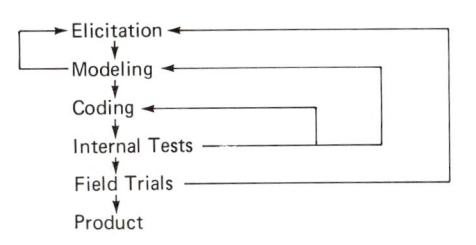

Development of an expert system requires a number of factors. There must be a suitable problem. Expert systems are appropriate for a narrow class of problems, one that is complex enough that alternative methods have less than desired performance, but where knowledge of successful means of coping with the problem domain exists. There must be a recognizable source of expert knowledge. Machine induction offers the potential for developing new expertise. However, most actual applications have involved tapping the heuristic behavior of human experts. Then expert systems need to be constructed. The technology for developing expert systems has advanced a great deal in the last decade. However, it does no good to build a system around faulty expertise.

METHODS

Interviews with Experts

The major knowledge acquisition method to date has been use of interviews with experts, and therefore knowledge has been acquired through linguistic transmission. Knowledge acquired in this way is relatively imprecise, incomplete, and inconsistent. Knowledge is often subconscious. Furthermore, the interviewing process lacks overall structure and is time consuming and tedious.

In order to obtain accurate and complete understanding of how the expert deals with the problem being modeled, interviewers need to be able to develop a rapport with the user. They need to have the ability to listen and be able to suggest solutions to clarify points skipped over by the expert. An important characteristic is that the expert, as well as the expert's boss, feel that the project is worthwhile. A useful approach is to begin with simple structuring of the problem and iteratively develop a more complex model of the expert's problem-solving process. Experts often travel heavily and are unavailable for extended periods of time. In order to develop an effective system, the expert must have sufficient time available to work with the knowledge engineer. Knowledge engineers, in turn, must be prepared when they are able to meet with experts. They should have done some background research to understand the general problem area, as well as have an agenda for the meeting. Experts may tend to go off on tangents. Knowledge engineers need to be able to diplomatically redirect thought to the problem at hand. A number of meetings are usually required. Experts may get frustrated unless some tangible results are available to exhibit at each meeting.

A valuable approach is to use a problem representation that the user understands, such as a decision tree or decision table. An iterative approach allows a prototype of the expert system to be built, which the expert can review. As the system is developed, the expert can then see missing elements and add more complex knowledge to the knowledge base.

The classical approach to knowledge acquisition is to employ a knowledge engineer to replicate the knowledge underlying expert performance by using knowledge acquisition techniques. Experts know more than facts and procedures, arranged into their body of knowledge enabling them to make informed and wise decisions. However, experts are often unaware of how they make decisions. Protocol analysis and the repertory grid method are commonly used techniques to complement the basic interviewing method.

Protocol Analysis

Protocol analysis is based on a transcripted interview, followed by attempts to structure the process and produce more meaningful results. In a decision-making setting, the expert is asked what he or she is doing, and why. The expert is usually in a natural situation, and the session takes relatively little of the expert's time.

Bouwman (1983) provided a detailed description of protocol analysis. Protocols are minute-by-minute transcripts of decision-making behavior. The intent is to identify the thought processes of a human diagnostician. Not only must various conditions be tested, but the focus is upon *how* diagnoses are formulated, intermediate decisions that are required, and any other steps used (as well as the reasons for these steps).

By having the expert verbalize his or her immediate thoughts instead of the reasoning behind decisions, comments can be more coherent and structured (Figure 13.2). Techniques include verbalization (thinking aloud), which results in minimum interference with the decision-making process. Another technique is retrospective verbalization, which increases interference by requiring subjects to recall the decision-making process, but often makes the resulting protocols easier to analyze.

Protocol analysis is particularly useful when cases have been selected in advance. It usually reveals a wealth of detail. However, the questioning can interfere with the decision task if the task is normally performed under pressure. Often, the expert will attempt to be more systematic than normal.

Related knowledge-gathering techniques include observation through videotape. The knowledge engineer can obtain a better idea of the sequence of tasks, the expert's role, and time constraints. However, this approach can be excessively time consuming.

The specific objective of the researcher's analysis should be considered in selecting a particular protocol technique. Protocol analysis requires a time-consuming search to balance elimination of irrelevant information and to avoid discarding essential information. Because only a few situations are explored in most protocol analyses, it is difficult to obtain perfect accuracy. Protocol analysis seems suitable for well-structured, homogeneous problem domains. It has been successfully applied for diagnosis problems. In diagnosis, knowledge is represented by rules or procedures. Protocol analysis is suitable for elicitation "the retained earnings have decreased somewhat...the debt equity ratio...is 0.57 which is also about the industry average...and as far as this ratio is concerned the company...has remained at approximately the same level through the years...the quick ratio...shows a figure of 0.24...which is very low with respect to other companies...and especially since it still was 2.74 last year...the current ratio...has also fallen back from 5.1 to 1.59...as the company average is 2...we see that the stock market price has declined from 40 dollars in 72 to 27 in 73...the interest rate...of additional debt has remained on 0.05...as the capital cost of additional equity has increased...there has been no dividend paid out during the last year...we see that in 1973 the demand...shows a large decline relative to 1972...the estimated demand...therefore appears to be way too high...the amount sold is equal...to the amount made and they have no lost demand...the market share is back again to the level of 1971...which makes one suspect that 1972 has been a one-time thing...which may very well have led to ...unwarranted expansions...

Figure 13.2
Example audio representation protocol analysis. (From Bouwman [1983], p. 655)

of heuristics and simple concepts often used in diagnosis. It is less effective in identification of deep knowledge or reasoning processes.

The experiment Bouwman conducted involved 15 masters students in industrial administration and three CPAs (in the Netherlands). The subjects were asked to make a quick financial evaluation of the position of various firms and to indicate any underlying problem areas. Each subject analyzed four different cases in one session. The first case was used to familiarize subjects. Subjects were asked to complete evaluations in 10 to 15 minutes (actually taking from 8 to 25 minutes).

The analysis consists of successively more detailed representations of the thought process (Figure 13.3). The audio representation is the transcription of the verbal thought process of the subject. This is split up into semantic (knowledge, operator, and indicator) elements to develop operator representation. These semantic elements are arranged into functional groups, including linking each operator element to the knowledge element it uses and the knowledge element it produces. Subjects typically were found to use a limited number of operators, but to use those operators frequently. The final step is to recode the protocol behavior in terms of the operators identified.

[1] Select next item from financial information
        success   failure – go to [5]
    Examine item
        go to [2]
[2] Test if examination is significant
    yes – integrate into existing knowledge; go to [3]
    no – go to [3]
[3] Test if significant change in knowledge
    yes – formulate/update problem hypotheses;
            formulate confirmation leads; go to [4]
    no – go to [4]
[4] Test if necessary to continue
    yes – go to [1]
    no – go to [5]
[5] Formulate final diagnosis

Figure 13.3
General diagnosis model. (Based on Bouwman [1983], p. 657)

Repertory Grid Technique

This is an approach to handle expert confusion between facts and factors
influencing decision making. The technique is generally attributed to Kelly
(1955). Experts are viewed as scientifically oriented, seeking to predict and
control events by forming theories, testing hypotheses, and weighing experimental evidence. The repertory grid is a method to identify the expert's
personal theory of the problem domain.

A common application of repertory grids involves a series of steps,
demonstrated in Figure 13.4.

Step 1 is to identify elements. This can be available decision options.
General methods for specifying elements include providing the expert a list of
situations, asking the expert for specific instances, or through general discussion.

Step 2 identifies constructs, or characteristics that elements can have.
Common means to obtain these characteristics are similar to those used in
identifying elements. By considering available alternatives, the expert can be
asked what favorable features each alternative has relative to the others as a
means of identifying constructs.

Step 3 involves rating the performance of each element on each construct.
The existence or nonexistence of favorable construct performance by each
element can be represented by a zero–one variable. Ranking would involve

---

Step 1: Identification of elements
         Identify representative set of elements
         for each knowledge category

Step 2: Identification of constructs
         Define element qualities

Step 3: Link constructs to elements
         dichotomizing
         ranking
         rating

Step 4: Analyze the grids
         Interpret relationships

Figure 13.4
Repertory grid procedure. (Based on Graham and Jones [1988])

ordering the relative advantage of each element on each construct. Rating could involve a cardinal value, or score, for each element–construct pair. A convenient way to do this would be to score each element on a 1 to 9 (or 0 to 1) scale on each construct. Ratings could also be qualitative (such as poor / average / good / excellent).

Step 4 involves inferring knowledge from the completed repertory grid. Analytic techniques such as the analytic hierarchy process (see Chapter 2) or fuzzy sets (a mathematical technique based on probabilistic assessments of membership functions) could be used as the basis of logic for the expert system.

Several successful implementations of the repertory grid approach have been developed, including ETS [Expert Transfer Systems (Boose and Bradshaw 1987)], Aquinas (an extension to ETS), and KRITON (Diederich, Ruhmann, and May 1987). ETS interviews experts and helps them construct, analyze, test, and refine knowledge bases, and is suitable for classification domains, such as problem diagnosis. Aquinas extends this capability to allow experts to structure information in hierarchies. KRITON employs several knowledge acquisition methods. For human declarative knowledge, the repertory grid technique is used. For procedural knowledge, protocol analysis is used. Frame, rule, and constraint generators are used to build up the final knowledge base.

The repertory grid technique has many features in common with the analytic hierarchy process presented in Chapter 2. The first two steps, in fact, seem exactly the same. AHP uses pairwise comparisons as a specific approach to rate the performance of each element on each construct. The inferred knowledge from AHP as originally designed is to infer knowledge through pairwise comparisons of each alternative on each construct. An expert system application involving a large database of alternatives could incorporate AHP through use of the resulting weights obtained on each construct, as well as a means of converting alternative rankings into scores. AHP does involve a specific structure, which may be improved by alternative procedures. But AHP seems the easiest framework with which to explain repertory grid analysis.

The technique can be explained through a project selection model. Assume computerization proposals from a number of different departments have been received. The decision is to select projects for funding. A common means of dealing with this problem is benefit–cost analysis. The value of each project would be calculated in dollar terms and compared with the expected development, operation, and maintenance costs, also expressed in dollar terms. The ratio of benefits to costs could then be used to rank projects by their attractiveness. If the ratio of benefits was less than 1.0, the project would be dropped. Unfortunately, there are usually more good ideas for computerization than available resources can support. Therefore, linear programming can be appropriate (see the zero–one assignment at the end of Supplemental Chapter 2). Linear programming is not always necessary, as another approach is to rank proposals by their ratio of benefits to costs and select those from the top of the list until resources run out (a heuristic, but often an effective heuristic.) A problem with benefit–cost analysis is that realistically, many of the benefits are not easily estimated in dollar terms. Therefore, multiple-objective analysis is often appropriate. AHP and repertory grid analysis both directly consider multiple objectives.

Assume a project proposal list, given in Figure 13.5. The elements to be considered might be the relative contribution of benefit to cost (construct **BEN** divided by construct **COST**), contribution to a computerized data collec-

		COST	BEN	DATA	AUTO
A	Shop floor terminals	40000	80000	yes	yes
B	Office automation	20000	22000	no	yes
C	Extra memory	50000	67000	yes	no
D	CAD work station	25000	30000	no	yes
E	LAN	30000	25000	yes	yes
F	DSS–new site select	20000	35000	no	yes

Figure 13.5
Available computerization projects.

		BEN/COST	DATA	AUTO
A	Shop floor terminals	1.0	1.0	1.0
B	Office automation	.2	.1	.9
C	Extra memory	.4	.6	.1
D	CAD work station	.3	.3	1.0
E	LAN	.1	.9	.6
F	DSS–new site select	.8	.1	.7

Figure 13.6
Project element/construct links.

tion network (construct **DATA**), and compatibility with a company long-term goal of increasing automated manufacturing (construct **AUTO**). The elements would be the available projects. This could be obtained in a real setting by collecting project proposals periodically.

Step 3 of the repertory grid procedure is to link constructs to elements. This amounts to identifying the performance of each element on each construct (Figure 13.6). This could be binary (where the link would be a 1 for the existence of the construct characteristic by the element, and 0 if not), ranking (giving each element a relative rating on each construct), or some cardinal value measuring the accomplishment of each construct by each element. AHP would provide a cardinal value. Values could also be obtained by simple judgment on whatever scale was desired (for instance, 1 is very good, 0 is very bad, other values between representing degrees along that scale). Figure 13.6 gives a sample set of cardinal ratings on a zero-to-one scale.

The last step is to analyze these grids. AHP would provide a straightforward analysis through a cardinal score for each element. Assume that the three constructs of **BEN/COST, DATA,** and **AUTO** are evaluated using AHP. Assume **BEN/COST** is considered three times as important as **DATA** and three times as important as **AUTO. DATA** and **AUTO** are considered equally important. This set of pairwise comparisons would yield the formula:

$$\text{value} = .6 \text{ BEN/COST} + .2 \text{ DATA} + .2 \text{ AUTO}$$

This formula could then be applied to the available elements, yielding scores as indicated in Figure 13.7. A sort would rank the proposals in the order A F D C E B. One use of the system would be to fund projects in this order until resources were exhausted. Another approach would be to develop a rule base, restricting selected projects to those with an overall minimum score, such as .5. Still a third approach would be to include constraints, requiring minimum benefit/cost ratios, and among those proposals with ratios at or above the

```
A  Shop floor terminals .6(1.) + .2(1.) + .2(1.)  = 1.0
B  Office automation   .6(.2) + .2(.1) + .2(.9)  = .32
C  Extra memory        .6(.4) + .2(.6) + .2(.1)  = .38
D  CAD work station    .6(.3) + .2(.3) + .2(1.)  = .44
E  LAN                 .6(.1) + .2(.9) + .2(.6)  = .36
F  DSS–new site select .6(.8) + .2(.1) + .2(.7)  = .64
```

Figure 13.7
Project scores.

minimum, select projects in the order of score (until resources were exhausted).

Grid methods are best suited for structured problems whose solutions may be enumerated prior to analysis. However, design and planning problems are not as well served by the repertory grid method. The same is true for elicitation of deep causal knowledge or strategic knowledge. Grid methods can elicit traits and build relationships, but they cannot determine how or when this information is used in the problem-solving process. Facilities for choosing or mixing reasoning processes are not provided.

Expert-Driven Knowledge Acquisition

Expert-driven knowledge acquisition involves having the expert encode his or her own knowledge. This has the advantage of focusing more on the procedure and involves less distortion. However, as noted before, the expert is likely to be vague about the nature of associations among events and may well forget to specify certain pieces of knowledge. Graham and Jones note that experts are often too close to the problem to view it objectively. Knowledge engineers can become experts by thorough study of the problem themselves. However, this approach is generally too slow for commercial benefit.

A number of systems have been developed to aid expert-driven knowledge acquisition. GISMO (Pracht 1987) is a visual modeling approach. MOLE (Eshelman et al. 1987) is an expert system shell that can help domain experts build a heuristic problem solver by working with them to generate an initial knowledge base and then detect and remedy deficiencies. INFORM (Moore and Agongino 1987) is a domain-independent, expert-directed tool using influence diagrams and graphical representations of problem structure. Student (Gale 1987) and OPAL (Musen et al. 1987) also use visual modeling approaches.

Liebowitz (1988) noted some of the biases that experts (and all other humans) have which need to be considered. Humans are poor intuitive statisticians, tending to allow small samples to overinfluence their conclusions. When statistical relationships are accepted, causality is often incorrectly assumed. Humans also tend to anchor, or start with a hypothetical model of cause and effect, and stick with this hypothesis until overwhelming evidence refutes it. This means that there is a bias toward the initial hypothetical model in the mind of the human. Furthermore, there is a bias toward the more recent experiences.

These human limitations are one reason to seek machine-driven knowledge acquisition. Another reason is that many business problem domains are overwhelmingly complex.

Machine-Driven Knowledge Acquisition

Machine-driven knowledge acquisition involves programming facts and rules. The aim is to have the machine itself learn how problems are solved, an idea related to the original aims of artificial intelligence. The four learning types are: learning by rote, learning by being told, learning from examples, and learning by analogy. Learning from examples through induction appears to be the most common approach. A number of statistical approaches are related to the expert system knowledge acquisition process. The use of statistics in general is an attempt to objectively learn about the relationships between variables. Many tools exist, although obviously there are limitations to what tools such as regression, multidimensional scaling, cluster analysis, and other techniques can accomplish. It has long been recognized that statistical models are often difficult to generalize and are limited in their ability to determine cause and effect. However, this approach provides a solid basis for automated intelligent behavior. Many possibilities for developing machine-driven learning exist. Gaines and Shaw (1986) presented a method for converting repertory grid input into a set of production rules.

Induction involves the expert describing a set of example cases including the decisions and attributes that were considered. Induction is objective, repeatable, indefatigable, consistent, and easy to understand. The problem is that verification of induced rules is difficult, because the quality of induced results will depend both on the algorithm used and the particular example set available. Induction systems have not performed well when there was contradictory data or probabilistic rules.

The following examples demonstrate some of the features of knowledge acquisition. In the first example, expert interviews were used, along with protocol analysis. This yielded a set of elements and constructs. Although the repertory grid was not used, the outcome yielded a knowledge structure very similar in content.

 ### *SMALL TELECOMMUNICATIONS COMPANY VENTURE ANALYSIS*
Ellis and Brown (1987)

The courts ordered divestiture of AT&T to take place on January 1, 1984. This changed the traditionally regulated, noncompetitive telecommunications industry into one that is largely unregulated and competitive. Small telecommunications companies (15,000 access lines or less) were especially affected.

Many of these small telecommunications companies expanded their business expertise beyond local telephone service into ventures in a wide variety of fields. Most of these companies did not have a large working-capital base. The primary source of funds for these small companies was the Rural Electrification Administration, which provided low-interest, government-insured loans. This reliance on external funding led to high degrees of risk aversion. In addition, these companies usually had small labor forces, reducing the expertise available for business decision making. The former regulated environment did not develop competitive skills in most companies.

VALUES is a venture analysis expert system designed to aid small telecommunications firms to rapidly categorize potential venture opportunities. It includes an uncertainty management scheme, attaching a likelihood to event occurrences. Domain knowledge was acquired from a single expert who had over 20 years of experience in evaluating small independent telecommunications companies.

Knowledge Acquisition

The expert was interviewed extensively and observed for over six months. A protocol analysis was also conducted. Based on these knowledge acquisition techniques, the expert's perception of the important elements of venture acquisition and his problem-solving strategies were modeled.

Seven key attributes were identified. These seven attributes (size, entry cost, payback period, technological level, return on investment, compatibility of the venture with the acquiring company, and risk–return spread) affected three criteria (risk, return, and fit). The three criteria were dimensioned into three parts each (low, medium, and high), yielding 27 categories. Risk evaluation was affected by size, entry cost, payback period, and technological level. Return evaluation was affected by size and return on investment. Fit was evaluated on the bases of size, risk–return spread, compatibility, and technological level.

Evaluation was also based on the investing company's values and objectives, current financial status, and current venture portfolio. The ventures were evaluated on their compatibility with the investing company, their technological level, and expected cash flows.

The expert system categorizes venture opportunities through a rule-based system. The heuristics used by VALUES closely match the expert's technique. The first step is to gather facts about the venture and the investing company. These facts are used to assess risk, return, and fit. These assessments are used to classify the venture into one of three outcomes: a recommended venture, a venture that requires additional investigation, or a venture that is not recommended. Backward chaining is used in the final classification (the rules assume one of the three outcomes and then seek to prove that assumption). The system was implemented in LISP. The system is very fast and includes explanations for its conclusions.

The system was validated by testing on actual data from nine venture analyses for a small company. The expert classified the venture opportunities before the expert system was run. The expert revised his first assignments. The system matched the expert's final assessment in all cases.

The system was to be used in executive training sessions and as a quick screening tool to determine ventures to explore further.

Note that the interview process with the expert took about six months, which seems to be a fairly typical investment of time for both the expert and the knowledge engineer. Collopy and Armstrong conducted a study that included a comparative use of expert interview and protocol analysis. This work reported a pilot study of a system to make accurate time-series forecasts using two experts. Supplemental Chapter 1 will review the importance of forecasting, as well as some of the complications involved.

FORECASTING
Collopy and Armstrong (1989)

In the in-depth **expert interview,** forecasting rules were elicited. This approach is less expensive than other approaches, including protocol analysis, is less likely to be subject to researcher bias, and can capture most relevant knowledge possessed by the expert. However, the method is only appropriate when the expert has a clear awareness of the problem-solving process. **Protocol analysis** was also used, primarily because it was expected to be particularly appropriate when awareness of the problem-solving process is low.

In the comparative test, six monthly time series were selected to represent different patterns. There were 24 forecasting models and combinations available to subjects. Graphics displays of time series were given to experts, who were asked to describe the methods that would produce the most accurate forecast as measured by mean absolute percentage error. Once an initial selection was made, the experts were allowed to examine the forecasts obtained by various methods, and they could then modify their choices. No time limits were imposed. Two experts were tested using both methods, with one using direct assessment first, and the other using protocol analysis first. Selections were evaluated by using benchmark forecasts (Figure 13.8).

The experiment was designed to focus on acquisition of rules used by experts in forecasting. In the protocol analysis procedure, notes were taken of the expert's verbalization of thoughts (and the session was taped). If the

SUBJECT A

Preparing the Data
  Eliminate errors and outliers
Seasonality
  Determine number of seasonal cycles in the data
  Determine seasonal factors: Apply Census X–11
  Identify changes in seasonal patterns
    based on horizon, dampen seasonal factors
  If natural growth series, apply multiplicative seasonal factors
  If bounded series, apply additive seasonal factors
Level and Trend
  Determine level and trend, apply Holt–Winters' method or Brown's method
Model Formulation
  If frequent trend reversals, apply no trend model
  If near previous limit, combine regression and no trend
  If high uncertainty, apply damped trend or no change
  When combining, models should be as different as possible

SUBJECT B
Level and Trend
  Identify presence/absence of trend
Variability
  Identify variability
Model Formulation
  Choose between simple smoothing and linear smoothing
  If great deal of variability, apply random walk model
  If annual and trend, apply damped smoothing
  For rapidly rising series, apply no trend or damped trend
  When uncertainty high, apply no change
  In absence of other information, apply no change
  As horizon gets longer, move toward no change

Figure 13.8
Direct assessment examples. (From Collopy and Armstrong [1987], p. 107). Reprinted with permission. *DSS-89 Transactions: Ninth International Conference on Decision Support Systems,* George R. Widmeyer, Editor. Published by The Institute of Management Sciences, 290 Westminster Street, Providence, Rhode Island 02903.

> expert quit talking, the interviewer prompted the expert to continue talking. After the session, the interviewer expanded notes while listening to tapes. This was followed by a coding of the heuristics and procedures used by subjects. These descriptions were then given to the subjects for validation.
>
> The direct assessment method took an average of 23 minutes, as opposed to an average of 55 minutes for protocol analysis. Summarizing direct assessments took about an hour, whereas summarizing and coding protocol analysis took about four hours.
>
> Direct assessment provided some rules that did not arise during protocol analysis sessions. This was because the protocol analysis did not cover a broad enough variety of forecasting situations. On the other hand, the protocol analysis sessions provided information about weights that each expert placed on various features, which the direct assessment technique did not. Furthermore, protocol analysis made it possible to determine the relative frequency of factors.
>
> It was expected that videotaping would provide additional information, but audio taping provided an equivalent amount of information. Furthermore, the audio tape was easier to code.

The Collopy and Armstrong study demonstrates the relative strengths of interviews and protocol analysis. Interviews allow coverage of a more complete set of circumstances, important to include in expert systems. Protocol analysis, on the other hand, provides a more complete picture of knowledge used for specific situations. The next example demonstrates the application of a variety of knowledge acquisition techniques in a marketing environment. Interviews with experts were used, along with protocol analysis. A problem-sorting technique with some of the features of grid systems aided decision makers in clarifying how they dealt with the planning problem. The knowledge engineers also conducted a significant amount of research (reading) to gain familiarity with the problem, and they enhanced the knowledge acquired by having the experts test the system. The need for a variety of knowledge acquisition techniques to acquire different types of knowledge is emphasized.

MEDIA PLANNING
Mitchell (1987)

The media planning problem is to allocate advertising budget for a product (or service) to a number of media options over a planning horizon. Media options typically include a variety of magazines (different circulations by demographic group, different ad sizes, varying features), television (time of day, varying exposure by demographic group), radio, newspapers, and other media forms. In order to compare media effectiveness, media are rated by gross rating points (GRP), the amount of advertising directed at a particular audience. The rating 100 GRP indicates sufficient advertising exposure to reach the targeted audience. Media plans involve allocating available budget across available media to reach the target audience.

The media plan is developed by groups of people. Primary groups are the advertiser with a product or service and the advertising agency, which is hired to develop and place advertisements. The advertiser has a group responsible for the marketing plan of a product. The advertising agency also has a group focusing on an account. Within the advertising agency, the media planner is responsible for developing a media plan effectively using budget resources to achieve sales objectives, through a plan consistent with the marketing strategy for the product.

A media plan includes a time-based schedule of advertising elements by type. The plan also includes a tentative budget, the target market (by demographic group), sales and market share data for the product and its competitors by market, and additional information about purchaser habits. Information is acquired on competitor media strategies and expenditures, unit costs for advertisements across media options, and the creative strategy for the product.

The problem domain involves a well-defined (but very large) solution set, but the exact procedures for selecting a specific solution and the criteria for evaluating a solution are less structured. Large amounts of data must be synthesized. Furthermore, evaluating the effectiveness of a media plan is complicated because a number of variables affect sales in addition to the media selected.

Common Media Planner Procedures

A common means of simplifying the decision is to use goals and constraints to reduce the number of alternatives considered. This parallels the linear programming approach. The constraints are the required limits on the decision, whereas the goals are the desired functional attainments. Reach is the percentage of the target audience that has the opportunity to see at least one advertisement from the campaign. Frequency is the potential number of advertisements that someone in the target audience will have the opportunity to see. Both of these measures are typically used as goals. The available budget may be included as a constraint. This approach to the problem provides a means of **structuring** the decision. Mathematical programming provides a means of supporting the analysis of the decision alternatives.

Another typical approach to the problem is to **decompose** the problem into a series of subproblems. For instance, early in the analysis each media form (television, magazines, etc.) may be allocated a specific proportion of the budget. There will be some interaction between media results, but the decomposition approach generally disregards this interaction, allowing each of the media forms to be treated independently in smaller subproblems.

Media Planning Process

Mitchell provides a series of steps used to develop a media plan.

1. Information (discussed previously) is gathered and synthesized. This provides a means of defining the problem dimensions.
2. Goals and constraints are set.
3. Rough drafts of the media plan are developed.
4. The expected performance of rough media plans are evaluated relative to goal and constraint satisfaction. If goals and constraints are not satisfied, plans are adjusted until either goals and constraints are met or it is deemed necessary to adjust them.

Mitchell noted that expert media planners tend to rely on various heuristics (procedural knowledge) and beliefs (declarative knowledge). Example heuristics would be: (1) to increase reach, add another media option and (2) to increase frequency, increase expenditures in current media options. Example beliefs would be: (1) pulse media schedules are usually more effective than continuous schedules, (2) at least three advertising exposures are needed within a purchase schedule, and (3) a budget of at least $3 million is needed for network television.

System

Researchers at the University of Toronto (including Mitchell) were developing a frame- and rule-based expert system programmed to contain information about various brands and media options. The frames were organized hierarchically, with a frame for each media planner containing his or her specific heuristics and beliefs. Modules were developed for each subproblem, such as for network television. Another module integrated the various budget allocations for each time period and checked for goal attainment and constraint satisfaction. This last module could also adjust the plan if any goal or constraint was not satisfied.

A variety of user levels were designed. At one level, the system would operate as a decision frame to structure the problem for the planner, as well as provide the required information and perform calculations. Tradeoffs with respect to different goals and constraints could be identified, aiding the user in selecting among available options. At this level, the system would perform as a DSS. The system could also act as a pure expert system by using specific problem dimensions to generate goals and constraints and develop the media plan for suggestion to the user.

Knowledge Acquisition Procedures

Three stages of knowledge acquisition were applied. The first stage had the goal of developing an understanding of the process media planners used to develop media plans and the critical factors affecting results. Textbooks and manuals were reviewed, and a number of discussions were held with numerous media planners. This provided an understanding of the critical variables in media plan development, as well as a broad understanding of the planning process. However, this did not provide sufficient detail to develop a computer program.

A number of general procedures were found to be common to all media planners. Differences (such as how audience data is used to compare media options) provided clues as to optional features to be accommodated in the computer system.

More detailed understanding of the process was developed through extensive **interviews** with media planners at major agencies. The structure of these interviews varied, sometimes involving general questions and requests for diagrams, other times providing the planner with specific problem scenarios and asking the planner to think out loud (**protocol analysis**) while developing a plan. The protocols were found the most useful in developing the decision frame system. An initial program was encoded, and knowledge gaps were identified. Return visits provided a means of filling in these gaps (**prototyping.**)

The second stage had the goals of acquiring the necessary knowledge, to gain an understanding of how media planners form goals and constraints and to understand how budget allocations are made between media. This knowledge was acquired through interviewing a number of media planners, using a variety of acquisition techniques.

The last stage was to develop standardized materials that were given to a large sample of media planners. These planners were asked if the system was consistent with their planning procedures and whether declarative and procedural knowledge was correct. They were also asked to identify differences between planners.

Elicitation Procedures

In order to better understand declarative knowledge of an individual, subjects were given a number of important concepts from the problem domain and were asked to mention everything that came to mind when they thought of these concepts. This approach seeks to tap the **neural network** of the human thought process, which involves the stream of consciousness the human applies. A particular thought can trigger a related thought, and so on, yielding a thought chain. These are typically not linearly related and often yield different thought patterns. The purpose was to determine the associations media planners have linked to various media options, target audiences, product categories, and brands used in developing media plans.

Problem Sorting

This procedure involved giving planners a series of media planning problems. These problems included various target audiences and advertising budget sizes. Planners were asked to group these problems in terms of similarity of their resulting plans. The purpose was to determine if media planners initially categorize media problems, and, if so, what these categories were. If categorization is used, this knowledge can be used to structure problem dimensions. It also would indicate that heuristic classification procedures could be applied.

Protocol Analysis

Thinking-out-loud protocols were obtained by recording planners' thoughts during planning sessions. Protocol analysis was used for setting the goals and constraints, developing the actual media plan, adjusting the plan when goals and constraints are not satisfied, and evaluating media plans. Planners were given a cross section of scenarios in order to develop procedural knowledge.

Use of the Expert System

An additional means of knowledge acquisition was to test the system with media planners. The planners would be given a cross section of problems and would be asked to use the system. The system can record each decision and decision sequence. By using the same problem scenarios used in the protocol analysis, the impact of the decision frame system can be evaluated.

Another type of knowledge acquisition procedure is to compare the results of the system with the plans developed without the system. This provides an empirical means of validating the system.

Mitchell concluded that different knowledge acquisition procedures are appropriate at different stages of the system development. This would imply the need for understanding each type of knowledge acquisition. He found a constant interchange between system development and the need for additional knowledge.

THE POTENTIAL OF INDUCTION METHODS

A tremendous wealth of organizational knowledge currently exists in computer systems. This knowledge consists of memoranda and letters, reports analyzing problems and opportunities, and information developed by the management information system. Many times the asset value of data is largely unrecognized. Sometimes computer information systems are so clogged with data that the data pertaining to a current problem that is already in the system is effectively inaccessible.

Einhorn and Hogarth (1982) emphasized that diagnosis and prediction are based on the same causal structure. Therefore, causal structure is useful both in diagnosis and in planning. In describing the relationships between causes and effects, different types of cues were used to determine whether or not a causal relationship existed. These cues can include temporal order (time sequence) and location of variables close to each other in space or time. The number of alternative explanations would be expected to be inversely related to the strength of confidence in a hypothesized cause-and-effect relationship. The degree of evidence confirming a hypothesized relationship can be used as the basis for assuming relationships.

A number of expert systems outside of the business domain that deal with diagnosis have been constructed, including MYCIN, PROSPECTOR, and DIPMETER ADVISOR. These systems are unique in that they (1) separate knowledge about the problem domain into a knowledge base that can be manipulated as a separate entity, (2) provide an inference engine operating on the knowledge base to extract knowledge and make inferences, (3) make use of probabilistic or certainty factors concerning relationships, and (4) include explanation facilities.

Expert systems based on inference engines reasoning from "first principles" have recently been developed for deep and narrow problem domains, where existing experts can be consulted, and the problem domain is well formulated and usually static. Deep models have the capability of deducing behavior from structure and may be capable of extension to predictive models. Production rule models, on the other hand, are infeasible for problem domains of significant size.

Managerial problems are usually wide and shallow, with few accepted generalities. Managerial problem diagnosis was studied by Bouwman, who used protocol analysis to study how financial analysts diagnosed accounting statements. Problem detection was the first step in their diagnostic process. To detect problems, financial analysts used trend computations, comparison with other information as well as with norms, and heuristics. Insignificant problems were screened out, followed by actual diagnostic reasoning, involving integration of new findings with existing knowledge and forming of hypotheses to attempt explanation of the situations encountered. Existing causal theories were searched for potential explanations of problem causes.

Courtney, Paradice, and Ata Mohammed (1987) proposed a system including (1) a user interface, (2) a monitor to search for problem situations, (3) a problem processor to search for problem causes, (4) a knowledge manager to maintain causal relationships and historical information about successful diagnosis, (5) a data manager supplying data to the rest of the system, (6) a dictionary manager maintaining information on all data items and variables in the system, and (7) a process control subsystem linking various system elements together and controlling information flow (Figure 13.9).

It was assumed that users would select monitored variables and standards for these variables. This would allow the system to monitor results and identify situations where performance on key variables was unsatisfactory relative to standards. Variables violating its standards are problem symptoms. A list of problem symptoms is delivered to the problem processor.

Problem diagnosis involves using Bouwman's approach with information in the knowledge base to construct clusters of related symptoms. Bouwman's

USER INTERFACE

MONITOR for problem identification

PROBLEM PROCESSOR to identify cause

KNOWLEDGE MANAGER to maintain causal relationships and historical information

DATA MANAGER

DICTIONARY MANAGER information on data and variables

PROCESS CONTROL SUBSYSTEM

Figure 13.9
Causal inductive model. (From Courtney, Paradice, and Ata Mohammed [1987], published by the Decision Sciences Institute.)

approach was also used to construct a causation tree for each cluster. Explanatory models based on the causation tree are tested with data extracted from the database. Results are presented to the user.

The knowledge manager provides organizational memory for past successfully diagnosed problems, along with the diagnoses. This knowledge is represented in a hierarchical database, along with a count of occurrences for each cluster. Alternative diagnoses for each cluster are also maintained. This module can be viewed as simulating experiential human learning.

Whenever a cluster of problem variables is identified, the knowledge manager is searched to determine if a previous diagnosis has occurred. The results of the diagnosis are presented to the user, along with current data values for variables constituting the diagnosis. If the user believes a previous diagnosis explains the current problem, it is used for the current problem. If no previous diagnosis is acceptable, a formal diagnosis is undertaken using the problem diagnosis module.

SUMMARY

Expert knowledge has a number of dimensions. It is important for expert systems to contain accurate expertise (declarative knowledge), as well as apply sound procedures (procedural knowledge). Most problem domains where expert systems have been applied in physical sciences such as medicine and geology have captured deep knowledge. These systems support human decision makers by encoding complex relationships. Most business applications involve less structure, with dynamic environments where complexity is due to relationships that are less well understood. Surface knowledge is often used as the basis for decision making, because deep knowledge is not available. Expert system methodology has great promise in business applications in two ways. Surface knowledge (in the form of heuristics) has been the predominant basis of business expert systems to date. Another avenue of promising research is to use computer systems to identify deeper knowledge, providing tools for humans to learn more about the fundamental relationships between decisions and their expected consequences in a quicker manner.

There are a number of knowledge acquisition techniques available. This chapter has reviewed the basic categories, including interviews with experts, protocol analysis, grid techniques, expert-driven learning, and machine induction. Each has positive features, making them appropriate in some context, as well as limitations. Interviews with experts are potentially the fastest, but may be the least systematic, resulting in more gaps in knowledge acquired. Protocol analysis provides a useful means of identifying processes, but it is only accurate for the types of cases that were examined. Grid techniques provide a useful means of identifying factors of importance. Converting grid technique results into quantitative rules can be difficult, although AHP is one means of converting qualitative concepts into numerical scores. Knowledge engineers could take it upon themselves to become expert, but this is the least efficient means of knowledge acquisition, as well as the most time consuming. The future undoubtedly will see more work on automated knowledge acquisition. However, this approach is currently limited because of the fundamental limits of statistical approaches in general, which require a great deal of human interpretation if sound results are expected. But the future potential of this approach is very promising.

The Mitchell case demonstrates the value of using a variety of knowledge acquisition procedures. It also demonstrates that knowledge acquisition is a time-consuming and iterative procedure. The need to validate acquired knowledge must be emphasized. As in all computer applications, the output of the system will only be as good as the knowledge on which it is based.

REFERENCES

Boose, J. H., and J. M. Bradshaw. 1987. A knowledge acquisition workbench for eliciting decision knowledge. *Proceedings of the Twentieth Hawaii International Conference on Systems Science* 1:450–57.

Bouwman, M. J. 1983. Human diagnostic reasoning by computer: An illustration from financial analysis. *Management Sci.* 29:653–72.

Collopy, F., and J. S. Armstrong. 1989. Toward computer-aided forecasting systems: Gathering, coding, and validating the knowledge. In *DSS-89: Transactions of the Ninth International Conference on Decision Support Systems,* ed. G. R. Widmeyer, 103–19. Providence, RI: The Institute of Management Sciences.

Courtney, J. F., Jr., D. B. Paradice, and N. H. Ata Mohammed. 1987. A knowledge-based DSS for managerial problem diagnosis. *Decision Sci.* 18 (3):373–99.

Diederich, J., I. Ruhmann, and M. May. 1987. KRITON: A knowledge-acquisition tool for expert systems. *Internat. J. Man-Machine Studies* 26 (1):29–40.

Einhorn, H. J., and R. M. Hogarth. 1982. Prediction, diagnosis and causal thinking in forecasting. *J. Forecasting* 1 (1):23–36.

Ellis, Q., and D. E. Brown. 1987. Values: A venture analysis expert system for small telecommunications companies. In *Proceedings of the First Annual Conference on Expert Systems in Business,* ed. J. Feinstein, J. Liebowitz, H. Look, and B. Silverman, 63–70. New York: Learned Information, Inc.

Eshelman, L., D. Ehret, J. McDermott, and M. Tan. 1987. MOLE: A tenacious knowledge acquisition tool. *Internat. J. Man-Machine Studies* 26 (1):41–54.

Gaines, B. R., and M. L. G. Shaw. 1986. Induction of inference rules for expert systems. *Fuzzy Sets and Systems* 18 (3):315–28.

Gale, W. 1987. Knowledge-based knowledge acquisition for a statistical consulting system. *Internat. J. of Man-Machine Studies* 26 (1):55–64.

Graham, I., and P. L. Jones. 1988. *Expert systems: Knowledge, uncertainty and decision.* London: Chapman & Hall.

Kelly, G. A. 1955. *The psychology of personal constructs.* New York: Norton.

Liebowitz, J. 1988. *Introduction to expert systems.* Santa Cruz, CA: Mitchell.

Mitchell, A. A. 1987. The use of alternative knowledge-acquisition procedures in the development of a knowledge-based media planning system. *Internat. J. Man-Machine Studies* **26** (2):213–30.

Moore, E. A., and A. M. Agongino. 1987. INFORM: An architecture for expert-directed knowledge acquisition. *Internat. J. Man-Machine Studies* 26 (2):213–30.

Musen, M. A., L. M. Fagan, D. M. Combs, and E. H. Shortliffe. 1987. Use of a domain model to drive an interactive knowledge-editing tool. *Internat. J. Man-Machine Studies* 26 (1):105–21.

Pracht, W. E. 1987. A visual modeling approach for DSS knowledge acquisition and organization. *Proceedings of the Twentieth Hawaii International Conference on Systems Sciences* 1:478–86.

Ram, S., J. F. Nunamaker, Jr., Y. I. Liou, D. Carlson, and S. Hayne. 1989. Using group decision support systems for knowledge acquisition: An information center application. In *DSS-89: Transactions of the Ninth International Conference on Decision Support Systems,* ed. G. R. Widmeyer, 87–102. Providence, RI: The Institute of Management Sciences.

PROJECT IDEAS

Students can apply alternative knowledge acquisition techniques, such as interviewing and protocol analysis, to available experts for a focused problem domain. One approach would be to develop a decision table, exhausting all possible situations. Another would be to interview the expert to try to develop the system to work in the same manner the expert does, using a "special case" category without recommendation for rare situations. Protocol analysis can be used to try to more thoroughly identify how the expert deals with problem domain situations.

Neural networks are computer systems that are not limited to linear sequences of logic. Neural networks are based on the logical sequence identified in the human brain, where one thought may trigger a variety of other thoughts, through nerve impulses. This bears on human expertise. To see how human neural networks work, start with a seed thought. Write down your thoughts for the next five minutes. Wait at least an hour. Repeat the experiment with the same seed thought. Are the results the same? If they are different (they almost surely will be), why?

Why do traditional computer systems (based on von Neumann logic) always reach the same conclusions?

List the benefits of each of these two logic systems.

CHAPTER FOURTEEN

Knowledge Representation

Knowledge representation is the means expert systems use to store facts and rules. A simplistic expert system could be imagined where all possible states are enumerated, along with all possible alternatives. An example might be a computer chess game. However, this approach is not very efficient, because in most situations, the combination of possible states and alternatives is so large that even a computer cannot cope with it. Therefore, more efficient means of conducting state–space searches have been developed. Heuristics are rules of thumb, which are not guaranteed to obtain the optimal solution, but which seem to work fairly effectively. Computer chess games use various heuristics in order to complete games within the lifetime of a human. Some of these heuristics have proven very effective, with computer chess games currently having attained the capability of competing successfully with very strong human players (although not yet world-championship caliber).

This chapter will review alternative means of representing knowledge in expert systems. These alternatives have yielded varying degrees of effectiveness in business applications, due in part to the nature of business decision environments, which involve relatively shallow knowledge. After presenting the different available alternatives, these will be demonstrated in part using an inventory decision problem.

In this chapter we will:

- ▢ Discuss the available means of representing knowledge
- ▢ Compare the relative advantages of each method
- ▢ Provide simple examples of each method

MEANS OF REPRESENTING KNOWLEDGE

Four basic means of representing knowledge will be discussed here. Some of these methods have variations. These methods are not the only means of representing knowledge, but have been important in expert systems and/or broader artificial intelligence applications.

Formal Logic

An initial means of representing knowledge would be to rely on formal rules of logic (**propositional logic**). This approach would rely upon established truths, followed by logical extension to develop new knowledge. This follows the same procedure as formal mathematical development. This approach has been applied in currently available computer form. MACSYMA is one artificial intelligence package which can develop mathematical proofs. Formal logic systems can be deterministic, but they can also be probabilistic, such as systems based on fuzzy-set logic.

An example application of this approach can be imagined in the area of production/operations management. Consider a firm producing a wide variety of human-powered vehicles (various types of bicycles, unicycles, and skateboards). All bicycles have two primary wheels. A 10-speed bike is a bicycle. Given these two truths, it can be inferred that a 10-speed bike must have two primary wheels. However, care must be taken to be mathematically precise. *Most* firms producing computers employ very laid back employees. IBM is definitely a computer firm. Propositional logic, accepting both of these contentions as truths, would conclude that IBM employees tend to be laid back. However, that does not seem to be generally true.

The advantage of propositional logic is that rules can be inferred that must be true (given sound enough relationships and facts). New contentions can be checked for logical consistency. Problems in applying propositional logic systems to business decisions are that exceptions to the rule are difficult to deal with. Most business decision environments are loaded with exceptions.

Predicate calculus is also formal reasoning with mathematical properties. The components of predicate calculus include constants, predicates, functions, and logical connectives (AND, OR, IMPLIES, NOT). The system involves making statements that can be either true or false. General rules are programmed instead of specific values. Predicate calculus is the basis of PROLOG, a popular artificial intelligence language valuable for building an expert system from the ground up.

Predicate calculus is useful in business expert systems for categorical situations, with little context dependence. This means that few possible states or conditions can exist. MRP (materials requirements planning) systems, for instance, involve highly structured materials requisition situations. If 25 skateboards are required to be produced at the end of the week, and it takes three days to order parts and one day to assemble the parts, MRP systems can identify how many parts of what type need to be ordered at what times (after considering current inventory and safety stock requirements). A skateboard consists of one board and (assume) four wheel assemblies. Predicate calculus could deal with this problem, given a current inventory of ten boards and zero wheel assemblies and no safety stock requirements. Assuming Friday is required for assembly and Tuesday, Wednesday, and Thursday are required for delivery, 15 boards should be ordered early Tuesday, along with 100 wheel assemblies.

Note in this case that there is little context dependence. All skateboards consist of one board and, at least for this model, four wheel assemblies. This is true regardless of who ordered the skateboards, the day of the week or time of day the skateboard is built, or where it is built. Context dependence could exist, however, in cases where a particularly inept skateboard assembler was assigned, who has the habit of ruining one wheel assembly on average per skateboard. In that context, the system would need to know who was assigned the assembly and order an extra wheel assembly per final product.

Predicate calculus systems of representing knowledge have advantages in that there are clear rules, well-defined syntax, and a formal interpretation of each situation. They are also modular, in that additional information can be added to the knowledge base without complications, as long as the rules are consistent. There are some negative features, in that the knowledge typically used for business decision making does not often lend itself to this formal treatment.

Object-Oriented Knowledge Representation

The "object-oriented" approach to knowledge representation provides ways to represent both declarative and procedural knowledge about objects or entities. Declarative knowledge about objects, object classes, and relationships between classes are represented as semantic networks. Objects are grouped into classes, subclasses, sub-subclasses, and so forth, thus forming a *hierarchy* of object classes. The unique attributes or characteristics of objects at each level in the hierarchy are specified in the knowledge base definition. A subclass *inherits* the properties of its parent classes and all classes above it. Inheritance of properties is automatic, but may be overridden in special instances in which the subclass does not exhibit certain properties of the parent class. The last level in the hierarchy corresponds to "object instances," or the actual objects themselves.

To illustrate, in an accounting system, we might have the highest level of objects as accounts. All accounts would have a name and a balance. The first level subclasses could be asset and liability accounts. Assets could be divided into current and fixed subclasses. Fixed assets could have the attribute's original value and depreciated value, and so forth. When we reach the bottom of the hierarchy, we might have an object called hand-drill number M190-32, which is a specific instance of an object in the class of hand-drill machines.

The most distinctive feature of the object-oriented approach is the ability to represent procedural knowledge concerning the behavior of objects. One way of representing procedural knowledge is *"message-passing,"* which permits objects to communicate with each other and cause action to be taken through special attributes that are actually procedures or algorithms.

To continue the accounting example, we could have a class of objects called "depreciation methods," with specific instances including "straight-line," double-declining balance," etc. Attributes of each of these would consist of procedures for computing depreciation for that particular method. A given fixed asset, say machine number M190-32, could send a message to the straight-line depreciation object telling it to compute its depreciated value. The straight-line depreciation object would respond by computing the depreciated value and sending it back to machine M190-32.

Another way of simulating behavior is via "demons" or "triggers." A demon monitors the values of an attribute and takes (triggers) action under certain conditions. For example, we could set up a demon to monitor the actual value of an account balance attribute. If the account balance approached zero, the demon could send a message to "Daddy" object saying "Send money."

Semantic Networks

This form represents knowledge through graphs consisting of nodes and arcs (links) representing the relationships between word concepts (semantics). Nodes represent fact descriptions (objects, concepts, situations), whereas links represent relationships between nodes. This approach is appropriate for declarative knowledge organized around objects (nodes) and relationships between objects (links).

An example application is given in Figure 14.1. Here, there are three objects (10 speed, bicycle, 2 primary wheels), represented by nodes. These objects are linked by relationships (is a, has). Other objects and relationships would exist in this case as well. Note that characteristics can be inherited with this system. If all 10 speeds are bicycles, they inherit all of the characteristics common to bicycles.

Semantic networks are useful for a variety of operations. They support reasoning because patterns can be matched to retrieve information, such as the number of parts required for types of products. They can also support inference through derivation of general properties by examining a set of nodes for common features and relationships. They can support deductions by providing a network of relationships leading to a derived conclusion. However, semantic networks have not been commonly used for business applications, because exception handling is difficult, control is more involved, and explanation of logic is more difficult than is the case with production rules.

Semantic networks allow recording knowledge about structure, form, and properties, capabilities often very useful when recording knowledge about

Figure 14.1
A semantic network.

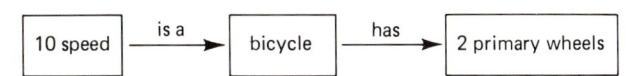

physical objects. Although useful, their application in business has not been typical; however, there is potential for future use. Semantic networks are often used in conjunction with frame systems. The primary advantages are in data access, as related knowledge can be stored together and data retrieval should be more efficient. There is a relative weakness in the ability to express complex knowledge.

Frames

The idea of frame systems is to catalog the requirements for membership of elements of a representational scheme. All knowledge about a particular object is organized by some data structure, consisting of fields for declarative knowledge. Frames allow building on prior knowledge developed about the domain, in that the characteristics or procedures appropriate to similar cases can be used as the starting assumptions for new cases. This form of knowledge representation is closely related to database systems.

Fields can contain information about many aspects of objects or situations. They can identify attributes that must be true (invariant knowledge, such as bicycles must have two primary wheels), as well as describe typical instances or concepts (specific knowledge, such as the features of a specific model of 10-speed bicycle), and they can deal with a large amount of context dependence through creation of different frames for each possible case. An example frame for a 10-speed bicycle is given in Figure 14.2. Note that frames can also contain procedures or rules.

Inheritance can be used, as in semantic networks. The system can also be used to aid in the development of new knowledge. For new products, the system can assume default entries for characteristics, which can be replaced as more complete information is received. Confidence factors would be useful in this context.

Frame systems are especially appropriate for object-oriented and access-oriented systems. Object orientation focuses on knowledge related to objects, such as products being produced. A number of computer languages and packages have been (and are) being developed around object-oriented approaches, such as the software packages KEE and KRL and the languages LOOPS (Stefik, Bobrow, and Kahn 1986) and SMALLTALK. Sometimes, gauges can

Figure 14.2
A frame.

Object	10 speed bicycle
Characteristic	Entries
Primary wheels	2
Training wheels	0
Pedals	2
Gear assemblies	1

be used to display object characteristics, and icons can be used to represent other characteristics. Access orientation focuses on gathering or sorting data-activated procedures. In object-oriented systems, when messages are sent, the knowledge about the object may be changed. In access-oriented systems, when knowledge about an object changes, a message is sent to trigger a procedure. Access orientation is appropriate for monitoring computations.

Scripts

The **script** form of knowledge representation is related to frames. Scripts are structures describing a sequence of events found in a specific context. Stereotypical sequences of actions or events can be stored, as opposed to objects or procedures represented by frames. (Frames are more general and can be used for more knowledge types than can scripts.) Scripts are clusters of facts. An example might include entry conditions, results (conditions which generally will be true), objects and/or people, tracks representing variation from general patterns, and scenes representing actual sequences of events. This form can be useful in analyzing and evaluating performances.

An example script system might include monitoring the impact of credit card acceptance on sales of products, seeking to identify situations where successful sales are made as opposed to browsing without sales. Assume a potential customer enters a shop with spare cash and credit cards.

Expert systems can gather statistics of operations under various policies, and they can identify the impact of acceptance of various credit cards on sales (Figure 14.3). New knowledge can be developed by adding new scripts. For instance, a different script could be developed for each type of credit card. In addition, a new scenario might arise if a credit card authorization check identifies a card that has been fraudulently used. This would involve a new category of outcome, where a positive outcome would be that the integrity of the credit system is improved.

Although this example is fairly straightforward, it does represent an example of how scripts operate, as well as a simplistic picture of what can be done with them. Note that scripts seem to represent knowledge in a manner similar to protocols in knowledge acquisition.

Production Rules

Production rules are the most common type of knowledge representation used in business expert systems. They consist of if-then rules and were demonstrated in Chapters 11 and 12. This approach is good for representing procedural and/or factual knowledge. Systems using this form of knowledge representation operate by an inference engine checking rules. When all required rules are true, conclusions are inferred.

To apply production rules to our skateboard example, assume the erratic wheel assembler's name is Fred. All other wheel assemblers manage to consis-

Track: Impact of credit card policy   **Roles:** Customer   **Props:** Merchandise
                                                  Sales Clerk   Cash
                                                                       Credit Cards

Entry Conditions: **Scene 1:** Customer entry
Customer interested   Customer views merchandise
          in merchandise   (interested in buying) (sees nothing of interest)
Customer has credit   (go to Scene 2)   (go to Scene 5)
          card
                               Scene 2: Customer requests use of credit card
Results: (it is)   (it is not)
Customer purchases with   (go to Scene 3)   (go to Scene 4)
          credit card
Customer purchases with   **Scene 3:** Credit card check
          cash   Card authorization is checked
Customer does not purchase   (purchase approved)   (not approved)
                               (go to Scene 6)   (go to Scene 5)
Expected Outcomes:
Net sales from cash highest   **Scene 4:** Customer response to card rejection
More sales due to credit   (purchase with cash)   (sale lost)
          card acceptance   (go to Scene 7)   (go to Scene 5)

                               Scene 5: Lost sales

                               Scene 6: Credit card purchases

                               Scene 7: Cash purchases

Figure 14.3
Script of shop.

tently assemble skateboards without damaging wheel assemblies. Two rules, the second being the most appropriate, are given in Figures 14.4 and 14.5.

Rule types include knowledge rules (relating to facts and relationships) and inference rules (relating to outcomes or solutions). Another type of rule is metarules—rules about rules. These include treatments when AND or OR

Figure 14.4
A production rule.

```
Rule 1
IF type=skateboard
AND assember=Fred
THEN order=5*skateboards
ELSE order=4*skateboards
```

Figure 14.5
Another production rule.

```
Rule 2
IF type=skateboard
THEN assembler=NOT Fred
```

clauses are used. If no AND or OR clauses are present, the inference engine checks all conditions, and if they are all true, the inference engine triggers the appropriate conclusion. If an AND condition is present and all of the AND clauses are true, the condition is accepted. If an OR condition is present and any of the OR clauses are true, the condition is accepted. Other metarules deal with the treatment of complex combinations of AND and OR conditions.

INVENTORY EXAMPLE

Inventory management is of major concern to many businesses, because inventory policies can affect costs a great deal when large quantities of capital are tied up. Although holding costs are generally quite low relative to purchase costs, firms can get into a great deal of difficulty controlling costs, as well as maintaining adequate cash on hand, when assets are tied up in inventory. There have been a number of inventory management tools developed, including economic order quantity (EOQ), reorder point (ROP) policy, and other approaches. EOQ minimizes the cost of ordering and holding inventory, but considers no other factors that may be important. ROP is a very simple policy, providing for a safety stock (which ties up additional capital), but otherwise minimizing holding costs. Contracts specifying delivery terms and allowing negotiation of more favorable prices are more efficient for large-volume items. Considerations needing attention are that demand for inventories is often uncertain, there are often price discounts involved for ordering larger quantities, and the material being inventoried may involve different storage and security requirements.

Assume a situation where inventory management policies have been developed over the years to consider a variety of these features. Past experience has been incorporated into these policies, and performance has been considered quite good, providing these policies with the credentials of expertise in the minds of management. Inventory material is classified into three groups: critical items that need to be available even though other policies might have lower inventory costs, items with intermediate criticality, and noncritical items, where effective inventory cost management is considered appropriate. Not every item the company stocks is considered worth closely managing. If only one department in the company uses a particular material, centralized inventory management is not considered worthwhile unless high dollar volumes per year are involved. Some items need special treatment, such as refrigeration, requiring that they be stored in available facilities which have limited capacities.

Other items are susceptible to theft or involve safety hazards. These items need to be guarded in some way.

Each item inventoried has certain characteristics. These include annual demand, unit cost, criticality, need for security, need for temperature control, lead time for acquisition, number of users within the company, and demand predictability. Available options include local management, contract bidding, or centralized management applying either EOQ or ROP policies, as well as the special categories of temperature control and security. EOQ will generally yield lower total costs, but involves a higher risk of running out of stock. ROP policies can involve variable safety stocks. Three levels of criticality are considered. More critical items are given higher relative safety stocks. A key determinant of safety stock is the lead time required to receive an item after it is ordered. Cost-effective inventory management is emphasized for items with low criticality.

Production Rule System

The first characteristic considered is the need for temperature control. If this feature is required, the item is stored in the facility with this feature. The second special characteristic is the need for security. If this is necessary, the policy is to hire guards.

The next characteristic considered is the number of company subunits that purchase this item. If there is only one subunit that purchases the item, the policy is to have that subunit do its own purchasing if total expected annual expenditure is less than $10,000. If the annual purchasing expense exceeds $10,000, the policy is to centrally manage the inventory of this item.

The next characteristic considered is criticality. For items with *low* criticality, items involving low annual expenditures and quick delivery times are to be purchased on demand. Items with high annual expenditures are to be purchased in a formal manner, with bids collected from alternate suppliers and terms of delivery specified. Items with intermediate annual expenditures are centrally ordered with sufficient lead time to be received on the day they are expected to be needed, with no safety stock.

Items with *moderate* criticality that involve annual expenditures below $10,000 are dealt with through EOQ, with a safety stock. The safety stock policy for items with a lead time greater than one month is to be expected demand during lead time. Items whose lead time is less than or equal to one month are to have safety stocks equal to 10 percent of annual demand. Those items with annual expenditures of $10,000 or more are to be managed by EOQ, with a safety stock equal to demand during lead time.

Items with *high* criticality are to be managed by ROP. If annual expenditures are over $5,000, the reorder point is to be demand during lead time. Items with annual expenditures of $5,000 or less are to have a reorder point equal to twice the demand during lead time.

The production rule expert system for this decision is given in the Appendix.

Figure 14.6
Inventory item frame.

ITEM:	keypart	
Annual Demand:	500	units
Number of Users:	20	
Unit Cost:	800	$
Criticality:	high	
Require Security?	no	
Temp Control?	no	
Lead Time:	3	days

Frames

There can be a very large number of items inventoried by a company (Figure 14.6). The use of frames is a highly appropriate means of storing facts about these items. This amounts to developing a database. Production rules can then be applied by having the rule-based system scan the database. This feature is available on VP-EXPERT. Although frame systems are not limited to this specific type of application, the efficiency of the production rule system can be enhanced by including them, as data access is much easier. This is one example of a hybrid system.

COMPARATIVE ADVANTAGES

Formal logic is appropriate when systems involve highly structured decisions. These systems can amount to a computer program capturing the knowledge accepted by the decision maker. Production rules are very appropriate for shallow systems applying heuristic rules. A major difficulty is that when many possible combinations of characteristics are required, a large number of rules are needed. For deep knowledge systems, semantic networks and frames have relative advantages. Frames provide the power of databases to catalog object characteristics. Semantic networks provide a flexible means to display deep knowledge. However, implementation of this approach is more involved. Table 14.1 provides a comparison of the relative advantages and disadvantages of various knowledge representation types. More information about knowledge representation can be found in sources cited in the refenences. Rich (1983) and Kobsa (1984) present early artificial intelligence aspects of the topic. Liebowitz (1988) Chapter 4 and Turban (1990) Chapter 14 discuss additional aspects of knowledge representation.

SUMMARY

Business decision making often involves high degrees of unstructured complexity. This makes the use of shallow knowledge about the only workable means of

Table 14.1

Type	Advantages	Disadvantages
Formal logic	Can be very complete and precise	Inefficient for large applications
	Modular knowledge base	Cannot express complex knowledge common to business decisions
	Clear rules	Information not grouped
Semantic networks	Easy to follow hierarchy	Node meaning may be ambiguous
	Flexible	Exception handling difficult
	Information grouped for improved data access	Control more involved
		Explanation difficult
Frames and scripts	Easy to detect missing values	Hard to program and control
	Information grouped	Inference difficult
	Build on previously developed knowledge	Package support not as well developed
		Explanation more difficult
Production rules	Natural	Limited knowledge per rule
	Highly modular and flexible	Inefficient for large applications

incorporating an expert system. Although it would be better to formally develop the body of knowledge about a business's operations, it is not certain that this is possible, because most business operations involve human behavior. In addition, many business problem domains are dynamic, making inferences of cause and effect difficult. Therefore, rules of thumb are often used, and production rules are usually the most appropriate means of representing expert knowledge.

This is not to say that there is no future for the other types of knowledge representation. Future developments in artificial intelligence may enable higher degrees of structuring business operations. In addition, there may be specific business decisions where sufficient structure exists to take advantage of the alternative means of knowledge representation. More information about knowledge representation can be found in sources cited in the references. Rich (1983) and Kobsa (1984) present early artificial intelligence aspects of the topic. Liebowitz (1988) Chapter 4 and Turban (1990) Chapter 14 discuss additional aspects of knowledge representation.

REFERENCES

Kobsa, A. 1984. Knowledge representation: A survey of its mechanisms, a sketch of its semantics. *Cybernetics and Systems: An International Journal* **15:**41–89.
Liebowitz, J. 1988. *Introduction to expert systems*. Santa Cruz, CA: Mitchell.

Rich, E. 1983. *Artificial intelligence.* New York: McGraw-Hill.

Stefik, M. J., D. G. Bobrow, and K. M. Kahn. 1986. Integrating access-oriented programming into a multiparadigm environment. *IEEE Software* (January): 10–18.

Turban, E. 1990. *Decision support and expert systems: Management Support Systems.* 2nd. ed. New York: Macmillan.

```
ACTIONS
COLOR = 15
FIND item
FIND policy
FIND guard
FIND safetystock
FIND rop
DISPLAY "The recommended policy for: {item} is: {policy}."
DISPLAY "The recommended safety stock is: {safetystock}."
DISPLAY "The recommended reorder point is: {rop}."
DISPLAY "The guard policy is: {guard}.";

RULE 1
IF tempcontrol = yes
THEN policy = TempControl;

RULE 2
IF security = yes
THEN guard = yes
ELSE guard = no;

RULE 3
IF demand > 0
AND cost > 0
THEN annual$ = (demand*cost);

RULE 4
IF users = 1
AND annual$ < 10000
THEN policy = local;

RULE 5
IF criticality = low
AND annual$ < 10000
AND leadtime < 5
THEN policy = OrderOnDemand;

RULE 6
IF criticality = low
AND annual$ < 10000
AND leadtime < 5
THEN rop = 0;
```

ITEM:	keypart	
Annual Demand:	500	units
Number of Users:	20	
Unit Cost:	800	$
Criticality:	high	
Require Security?	no	
Temp Control?	no	
Lead Time:	3	days

Figure 14.7
Inventory item frame.

ITEM:	normal item	
Annual Demand:	10	units
Number of Users:	1	
Unit Cost:	50	$
Criticality:	moderate	
Require Security?	no	
Temp Control?	no	
Lead Time:	40	days

Figure 14.8
Inventory item frame.

ITEM:	mass item	
Annual Demand:	9000	units
Number of Users:	3	
Unit Cost:	10	$
Criticality:	low	
Require Security?	no	
Temp Control?	no	
Lead Time:	5	days

Figure 14.9
Inventory item frame.

RULE 7
IF criticality = low
AND annual\$ < 10000
AND leadtime < 5
THEN safetystock = 0;

RULE 8
IF criticality = low
AND annual\$ > 10000
THEN policy = CollectBids;

RULE 9
IF criticality = low
AND annual\$ > 10000
THEN rop = 0;

RULE 10
IF criticality = low
AND annual\$ > 10000
THEN safetystock = 0;

RULE 11
IF criticality = moderate
AND annual\$ < = 10000
AND leadtime < = 30
THEN policy = EOQ;

RULE 12
IF criticality = moderate
AND annual\$ < = 10000
AND leadtime < = 30
THEN rop = 0;

RULE 13
IF criticality = moderate
AND annual\$ < = 10000
AND leadtime < = 30
AND demand > 0
THEN safetystock =
(demand*.1);

RULE 14
IF criticality = moderate
AND annual\$ < = 10000
AND leadtime > 30
THEN policy = EOQ;

RULE 15
IF criticality = moderate
AND annual\$ < = 10000
AND leadtime > 30
THEN rop = 0;

```
Testing INVENTOR.kbs
!  item
!  !  (= keypart)
!  policy
!  !  Testing 1
!  !  !  tempcontrol
!  !  !  !  (= no)
!  !  Testing 4
!  !  !  users
!  !  !  !  (= 20 CNF)
!  !  Testing 5
!  !  !  criticality
!  !  !  !  (= high CNF)
!  !  Testing 8 11 14 17
!  !  Testing 20
!  !  !  annual$
!  !  !  !  Testing 3
!  !  !  !  !  demand
!  !  !  !  !  !  (= 500)
!  !  !  !  !  cost
!  !  !  !  !  !  (= 800)
!  !  !  !  (= (demand*cost))
!  !  Testing 23
!  !  (= ROP)
!  guard
!  !  Testing 2
!  !  !  security
!  !  !  !  (= no)
!  !  (= no)
!  safetystock
!  !  Testing 7 10 13 16 19 22
!  !  Testing 25
!  !  (= 0)
!  rop
!  !  Testing 6 9 12 15 18 21
!  !  Testing 24
!  !  !  leadtime
!  !  !  !  (= 3)
!  !  (= (leadtime*demand/360)) = 4.167 (5)
```

Figure 14.10
Inventory expert system run.

Policy:	ROP
ROP:	5 units
Security:	No
Temp. Control:	No

RULE 16
IF criticality = moderate
AND annual\$ < = 10000
AND leadtime > 30
THEN safetystock = (leadtime*demand/365);

RULE 17
IF criticality = moderate
AND annual\$ > 10000
THEN policy = EOQ;

RULE 18
IF criticality = moderate
AND annual\$ > 10000
THEN rop = 0;

RULE 19
IF criticality = moderate
AND annual\$ > 10000
AND leadtime > 0
THEN safetystock = (leadtime*demand/365);

RULE 20
IF criticality = high
AND annual\$ < = 5000
THEN policy = ROP;

RULE 21
IF criticality = high
AND annual\$ < = 5000
AND leadtime > 0
THEN rop = (leadtime*demand/182.5);

RULE 22
IF criticality = high
AND annual\$ < = 5000
THEN safetystock = (leadtime*demand/365);

RULE 23
IF criticality = high
AND annual\$ > 5000
THEN policy = ROP;

RULE 24
IF criticality = high
AND annual\$ > 5000
AND leadtime > 0
THEN rop = (leadtime*demand/360);

RULE 25
IF criticality = high

```
Testing INVENTOR.kbs
(= yes CNF 0 )
!  item
!  !  (= normal item)
!  policy
!  !  Testing 1
!  !  !  tempcontrol
!  !  !  !  (= no)
!  !  Testing 4
!  !  !  users
!  !  !  !  (= 1)
!  !  !  annual$
!  !  !  !  Testing 3
!  !  !  !  !  demand
!  !  !  !  !  !  (= 10)
!  !  !  !  !  cost
!  !  !  !  !  !  (= 50)
!  !  !  !  (= (demand*cost))
!  !  (= local)
!  guard
!  !  Testing 2
!  !  !  security
!  !  !  !  (= no)
!  !  (= no)
!  safetystock
!  !  Testing 7
!  !  !  criticality
!  !  !  !  (= moderate)
!  !  Testing 10
!  !  Testing 13
!  !  !  leadtime
!  !  !  !  (= 40)
!  !  Testing 16
!  !  (= (leadtime*demand/365)) = 1.1 (2)
!  rop
!  !  Testing 6 9 12
!  !  Testing 15
!  !  (= 0)
```

Figure 14.11
Inventory expert system run.

Policy:	Local
Security:	No
Temp Control:	No

AND annual\$ > 5000
THEN safetystock = 0;

ASK item: "What is the name of this item?";
ASK demand: "What do you expect your annual demand to be in item units?";
ASK users: "How many subunits of the organization use this item?";
ASK cost: "What is the unit cost of this item?";
ASK criticality: "What is the criticality level of this item?";
CHOICES criticality: low, moderate, high;
ASK security: "Does this item require security?";
CHOICES security: yes, no;
ASK tempcontrol: "Does this item require temperature control?";
CHOICES tempcontrol: yes, no;
ASK leadtime: "What is the lead time for this item in days?";

```
Testing INVENTOR.kbs
(= yes CNF 0 )
!  item
!  !  (= massitem)
!  policy
!  !  Testing 1
!  !  !  tempcontrol
!  !  !  !  (= no)
!  !  Testing 4
!  !  !  users
!  !  !  !  (= 3)
!  !  Testing 5
!  !  !  criticality
!  !  !  !  (= low)
!  !  !  annual$
!  !  !  !  Testing 3
!  !  !  !  !  demand
!  !  !  !  !  !  (= 9000)
!  !  !  !  !  cost
!  !  !  !  !  !  (= 10)
!  !  !  !  (= (demand*cost))
!  !  Testing 8
!  !  (= CollectBids)
!  guard
!  !  Testing 2
!  !  !  security
!  !  !  !  (= no)
!  !  (= no)
!  safetystock
!  !  Testing 7
!  !  Testing 10
!  !  (= 0)
!  rop
!  !  Testing 6
!  !  Testing 9
!  !  (= 0)
```

Figure 14.12
Inventory expert system run.

Policy:	Collect bids
Security:	No
Temp Control:	No

CHAPTER FIFTEEN

Current Developments and Future Trends

The application of computers to business has seen dramatic growth and development. In the 1950s, computers were first applied to business, primarily in the area of very structured problem areas, such as payroll and accounting automation. Following explosive growth in computer hardware (and later software) development, the 1960s saw the application of computer resources to more comprehensive systems providing management information. The 1970s saw the development of decision support systems, harnessing computers to focus directly on aiding decision making. The 1980s have seen the application of expert systems in business. Note that these developments are supplementary. Improvements continue in data processing, MIS, and DSS, while expert systems use is growing. Each of these categories of computer support to business add to the support of the others. In the 1990s, we expect to see broader use of DSS, applying more models. We expect to see broader use of executive information systems, with the successful features of such systems being applied at lower levels of the organization. Expert system growth is phenomenal. In addition to the many production rule systems being developed, new advances may come in systems capable of developing knowledge important to a firm's decisions. Neural networks can already do this, for specific kinds of applications. The concept of institutionalization of computer systems will become a growing reality. The use of DSS, along with institutionalization of systems, should lead to better communications within organizations, which, in turn, may lead to wider organizational control. A major change is that group decision making is expected to become more important in the design of systems. This is because the role of groups in decision making seems to be growing in importance.

This chapter discusses:

- Application of computer systems to securities markets
- Application of computer systems to real estate
- Neural networks

□ The impact of decision support systems on organizational communication

□ The concept of intelligent organizations

Continued growth in computer support to decision making is expected because these systems give competitive advantage to those who use them. In the future, they will become necessities. The example DSSs cited from *Interfaces* list the savings with which those systems have been credited. The other types of systems are value effective as well.

Expert systems have been a major growth area. Liebowitz (1988) cited the following characteristics of contemporary business:

There are too few skilled specialists.

Increasing job complexity is overwhelming human processing capability.

Labor and training costs are rising.

The glut of information has created a decision-making bottleneck.

Institutional memories are required to protect against brain drain.

Although expert systems offer great potential in improving an organization's ability to cope with these problems, their limitations need to be understood as well. Expert systems will only be as sound as the knowledge with which they are programmed. If they make mistakes, current systems will continue to make the same mistakes, as opposed to humans, who have the ability to learn. Expert systems can take substantial investment in time and money to build. The systems that are currently available are suitable for limited domains.

This book has sought to emphasize the actual implementation of computer systems in decision support and expert systems. We have seen many interesting applications, varying in complexity as well as purity of compliance with theory. Companies are free to develop systems without referring to theory. Therefore, the differences important for concepts and definitions are often disregarded in practice. This is not at all bad. One of the strengths of the U.S. system of business is that people willing to pay the consequences are welcome to apply systems in any way they choose. If they wish to apply computers to aid decision makers, they can. If they wish to develop expert systems, they can. They do not have to follow rules about how these systems are developed. The marketplace has proven to be extremely efficient in that effective techniques will be used more and more, while ineffective techniques are discarded. The market provides a very valuable validation tool for the systems discussed in this book. That is why we have sought to emphasize actual applications and have reported them as accurately as we could. You should note that what is reported is not always what is true, as some marketing is necessary in business. Therefore, if at all possible, readers are encouraged to follow up on the examples used in this book, to acquire their own expert knowledge about the capabilities and potential of computer systems to support decision making.

We would like to present two areas where computer systems have proven very useful. These examples represent recent developments in computer program trading and real estate evaluation, two markets where dramatic changes have occurred.

Program trading has been a highly visible application of computer technology to securities trading. In April 1982, a futures contract linked to Standard & Poor's 500 stock index was introduced, providing an opportunity for index arbitrage, allowing traders to exploit differences between futures prices and the price of the underlying stocks. Index arbitrageurs use individual formulas to determine the appropriate spread, or fair value of futures prices above or below the cash value, of a stock portfolio. In April 1984, a brokerage and arbitrage firm unloaded $100 million worth of stocks, beginning widespread use of program trading on a wide scale. Although index arbitrage is the most common form of program trading, other forms, including asset allocation formulas, and portfolio insurance, also exist.

The Dow-Jones average dropped 87 points on September 11, 1986. On October 19, 1987, the Dow-Jones dropped 508 points. On October 13, 1989, the Dow-Jones dropped 190 points in 75 minutes, followed by a 65-point drop on October 16, 1989. Although the market eventually recovered from all of these drops, the volatility of the market is more extreme. A number of sources credit computer trading with at least some of the blame (Palmer 1989; Stoll and Whaley 1990; Wohlstetter 1990), although others note that the technology itself is not the problem (Wyatt 1989; Savitz 1990).

Arbitrageurs using program trading have been cited as the trigger for abnormal price changes during the "triple witching hour," the last hour of trading on days when index futures, index options, and options on index futures simultaneously expire. Triple witching hour occurs four times a year. Computerized trading adds force to the impact of triple witching hour. Stoll and Whaley found substantially heavier trading in the last half hour of index expiration days. Stocks included in the Standard & Poor's 500 index were found to have an average swing about four times that of other stocks. However, it should also be noted that recovery seems about the same for both types of stock—S&P 500 stocks just have faster swings and recoveries.

PROGRAM TRADING
Liang and Chen (1987) and Chen and Liang (1989)

Two markets are relevant to the exchange of stocks. The stock market involves trades between investors. The futures market involves stock indexes, such as the Standard & Poor's 500 and the Major Market Index (MMI). The difference between the cash index price and the index futures price is the premium, or spread. The premium theoretically equals the costs for holding stocks (interest less dividends received). But different demand and supply forces in two different markets sometimes drive the index futures far above or far below their theoretical value. This provides the opportunity to convert premiums into risk-free profit. If the premium is higher than its fair value, program traders buy stocks matching an index, and at the same time they hedge those stocks by selling the overpriced stock index futures (**buy program**). If the premium is considerably below its fair value, program traders sell stocks in the stock market, and at the same time they buy an equivalent amount of futures contracts (**sell program**). Stock index futures require cash settlement on the expiration day. Therefore, program traders must unwind their positions (reverse the position) before the expiration day.

Program trading requires keeping track of rapid changes in stock indexes, usually several times in a minute. The computer calculates return on investment based on the recorded indexes. Intelligent systems adapting to dynamic markets would be very useful in aiding program traders. PRO-TRADER (developed by Liang and Chen) is an expert system that has been developed (in prototype) based on an M.1 shell that monitors changes in stock indexes and identifies signals for trading.

The return on investment in program trading is determined by the premium and the period a program is held. The premium varies over time. Expert system support monitors premium changes in the market, determines the optimum trading strategy (including when to execute a buy or sell program and when to unwind a buy or sell program), executes transactions, and modifies the knowledge base through a learning mechanism. The problem domain involves few rules relative to other expert systems, but these rules are relatively high in volatility.

Knowledge Base

The system's knowledge base includes three types of rules. The first type of rule determines the best trading strategy. Sometimes settlement before expiration involves higher profits than unwinding upon expiration. A database keeps track of the resources on hand, including money, executed buy programs, and executed sell programs. Another type of rule calculates the return on investment based on the recorded premium. The last type of rule provides suggestions and command transactions. These rules interpret signals for trading and execute transactions when appropriate, based on the system's deductive reasoning (production rules).

The inductive learning mechanism examines the variance between the real outcome and the forecasted outcome for each transaction and adjusts the certainty factor associated with each rule, allowing the system to adapt to volatile markets. The system first examines the decision environment, then checks available resources, examines information such as general market outlook, and builds a theoretical market model based on knowledge-based rules. Changes in premium are monitored to identify signals for program trading. When a signal satisfying the rules is encountered, a command for the transaction is released. The outcome may be higher or lower than the forecasted value. In either case, the variance will activate the inductive learning mechanism adjusting the knowledge-based rules.

Decision Rules

The most crucial knowledge in the system is identifying transaction signals. There are three general strategies. A conservative strategy is to execute and hold programs, which may overlook opportunities to settle when it is most profitable. A dynamic strategy would involve executing programs when signals are encountered, and continue to buy and sell when premiums reverse course sufficiently. The variance-based strategy is more aggressive, not guaranteeing a target return, but sometimes yielding better performance. In this strategy, the system identifies trading and unwinding signals based on the mean and variance of the premium in a particular period. Decision rules are to buy or sell if the premium is higher than the mean plus standard deviation and unwind the buy or sell program if the premium is lower than the mean minus the standard deviation. Some multiple of the standard deviation can be used, allowing system adjustment to user risk preference.

System Learning

The key variable for the system is the probability that the premium may exceed a particular value (learning by observation). The major factor in premium probability is the market trend, provided by the user (learning by instruction). The system analyzes historical premiums and then determines the probability that the premium will exceed a certain value. Based on this input and the certainty factor determination, the system formulates a theoretical market model as the basis for its suggestions.

Three standard patterns of the market are maintained. These patterns represent the probability of the premium performance in bull, neutral, or bear markets. Humans can input the probability of each of these standard patterns. PROTRADER assumes that the premium distribution for each of the three patterns is normally distributed. The judgment obtained from humans is modified by observing actual market performance with the system's theoretical model.

Program trading has been around for a number of years. It has apparently had a strong influence on the stock market, some of which may have been good (theoretically providing a more efficient market). It remains to be seen if these systems will ultimately prove beneficial. One potential problem is that the market has been fundamentally altered. Some of this is due to organizational changes, as many new markets have opened throughout the world. But the speed with which computer systems can influence markets makes concern over control a pertinent area of study.

Another factor of interest is the quality of the logic (knowledge) that is included in computer trading systems. An expert system will provide a much higher degree of consistency than humans can. But expert systems are not guaranteed to be more correct. They can only do what they are programmed to do, and the most important focus should be on the quality of the rules included in expert systems. The dynamic nature of the stock market makes continued validation of expert systems important. Systems tend to do well over the period they are developed in, but may not do as well later.

As if the economy were not in enough trouble, another example of computer support is in the changing market of real estate.

COMMERCIAL REAL ESTATE
Trippi (1989, 1990)

Commercial income-producing properties include office buildings, industrial parks, shopping centers, hotel/motel developments, and specialized projects servicing recreational markets. Unlike many other assets, such as stocks and bonds, acquisition and divestment are discrete, rather than incremental, assets are relatively nonliquid (making it difficult to correct mistakes), and transaction costs are high. Investment performance is sensitive to external environmental factors, such as general business conditions, interest rates, inflation, taxation, and changes in neighborhood quality. There is no centralized market where information about available markets is presented in a timely and consistent manner.

Commercial real estate operations require intelligence for new acquisition or development opportunities, as well as monitoring of existing assets for potential problems. Analytic complexity in real estate decisions involves different rent and escalation formulas due to varying lease ages, unpredictable vacancies, and irregular improvement costs.

Most existing DSSs supporting commercial real estate investment analysis focus on the evaluation of alternatives. An early DSS was the DECISIONEX system introduced in the mid-1970s. This system was only available through time-share service and had a high cost, reportedly in the $10,000 to $50,000 per month range. The system's primary function was to provide "what-if" analysis for proposed projects. Key cost and income parameters were entered on per square foot and total amount bases. Detailed projections of tenant space income and expenses, return on investment, and other investment criteria were generated. Alternative projects could be compared with each other if capital was constrained. A more detailed system could be used to analyze operating the investment project (such as a hotel) as a business.

In the late 1970s and early 1980s, simpler and less expensive systems were available. At that time, computerized property listing services were widely available, and most real estate offices had a computer terminal. The DSSs were primarily intended as marketing tools, allowing prospective investors to evaluate listed properties. But these systems could also be used for in-house investment analysis.

In the late 1980s, a number of software packages were available for purchase, supplementing the on-line DSSs available. Their capabilities included lease-by-lease analysis of income and expenses, projection of financial performance, and valuation analysis of specific properties. PLANEASE is a system oriented toward office and shopping center analysis. Variables can be automatically ranged through sensitivity analysis, as well as a sophisticated risk analysis based on Monte Carlo simulation. REALPLAN is a system designed for use by chief financial officers with real estate portfolio management responsibilities. REALPLAN includes optimization capabilities and a comprehensive database.

There is potential for expert system assistance. Expert systems could be applied to broaden and simplify the search effort to identify investment opportunities, identify goals and constraints, formulate and select alternative action strategies, and explain results.

Many of the project acceptance rules used by investment professionals are heuristic. These can include capitalization rates, leverage, and below-market price indicators. RESRA (Review Expert System for Residential Appraisals) supports appraisal. Real estate appraisal is a useful application area, because appraisals are notably variable. The system was developed in PROLOG in four months, based on the expertise of two highly skilled appraisers. Another promising application area is prescreening of acquisition candidates in order to reduce the number of serious alternative investments to be evaluated.

Eliot (1988) presents a case study of the implementation of RESRA. Expert systems have become a major growth area of computer support to business. Rule-based systems allow rapid application of consistent rules which can be evaluated for accuracy and soundness in many contexts where standard procedures are appropriate. Expert system products can be complex packages focusing on a specific company's particular problem. There are also more general mass-marketed products appearing, providing support for income tax preparation, personnel policy guidance, sales advice, and many other fields.

Rule-based systems rely upon knowledge developed in the conventional manner. Situations are identified, and the best procedure determined in the knowledge acquisition phase of expert system development. A goal of expert system development is to harness computers to generate knowledge automatically. Neural networks provide a tool which seems capable of aiding this knowledge acquisition goal.

NEURAL NETWORKS

Neural networks are computer systems linking inputs with outputs in a network structure of nodes and arcs (connections). They are inspired by replicating portions of what is known about the way human brains function. In the human brain, neurons are connected in a complex network, with activity generated by impulses from one neuron to another. Neural networks have proven to be very good at identifying patterns, with some ability to generalize. These systems are not strictly programmed, but are given many cases of sets of inputs along with results. The systems "learn" by adjusting the weights of relative impact of inputs upon output, trying many combinations of weights until a good fit to the training cases is obtained. Then the resulting network can be used to evaluate future cases.

An early approach was to develop a computer system where a set of input values was linked to an output variable by a network. Each input variable and the output possibilities were represented by nodes. A network of arcs connected the nodes. Each arc had a weight associated with it. The weighted sum of input values leading into an output node determined whether the output node fired or not. If this value was above a threshold value, the conclusion associated with this node was assumed. The weights on the arcs connecting nodes were adjusted during a training period, where the computer tried many combinations of weights, retaining those weights where improved accuracy was obtained and rejecting changed weights otherwise.

This system can be viewed as being similar to a regression analysis. The input variables in fact are selected in much the same manner as independent variables in a regression model. Input variables are those characteristics that have explanatory power in selecting among alternative outcomes. Like regression models, the weights yielding the best fit in explaining the outcomes of the training sample are sought. Neural networks have proven quite effective at tasks humans do better than computers, such as recognizing faces, aircraft, fingerprints, voices, and handwriting. They are usually relatively poor at doing things traditional computers do better than humans, such as accurate arithmetical computation, transaction processing, or anything requiring numerical precision.

This is not to say that neural networks have no application involving numerical analysis. A hybrid neural network has been applied by the Chase Manhattan Bank (Marose 1990) to aid in reducing losses on loans to corporations. Neural network technology is used to identify patterns in financial statement ratios against loans of three categories: good loans (those that are paid off), criticized loans (those causing bankers concern), and loans that were charged off (those that were not repaid). This element of the system is combined with other expert system features which provide a listing of significant items to the human loan evaluator. The neural network component runs on a mainframe computer, which is linked to the personal computers of analysts. Data is available from COMPUSTAT, a major commercial database source.

The neural network system develops a model for each company analyzed by training on up to six years of financial data, which is compared to the particular industry norms generated from COMPUSTAT. A separate report module takes analysis from the neural network and presents results to analysts, along with a list of significant items explaining the results. Analysts also have a financial spreadsheet system available, enabling them to conduct more detailed analysis. Therefore, a fairly complete analysis system is available. Unlike most neural network applications, this system is capable of explaining how conclusions were reached.

There are many technical developments in artificial intelligence which have yielded more efficient neural networks. Intermediate, or "hidden," layers of nodes are usually placed between the input nodes and the output nodes. A number of improvements in learning algorithms have been applied, using dynamic feedback and faster, more efficient learning. There are many packages currently on the market, many at popular prices (see *AI Expert,* December 1989, pages 60 to 61 for one listing). A number of articles and books have recently been published which explain neural networks. *AI Expert* contains a number of applications, some in business, to include loan approval and financial market analysis. Wasserman (1989) reviews much of the historical development of technical features. General overviews of neural networks are provided by two series of articles by Caudill (1987, 1989), a primer in eight parts beginning in 1987 and a series on using neural networks beginning in 1989. Two other overviews of the topic are given by Obermeier and Barron (1989) and Storrie-Lombardi (1990).

The impact of the dramatic changes in technology available to aid decision making is expected to change the way in which organizations operate. The next section presents a view of some of the impacts of computer decision support.

FUTURE IMPACT ON ORGANIZATIONS

We expect continued development in all areas of computer support to decision making. Alter (1989) reviewed past DSS development and gave his views of what the next decade holds in store. He expected more systems of each type, focusing on helping people work better together. Alter saw the need to integrate systems, similar to the institutionalization concept presented in Chapter 9. Without linking systems, the full potential of decision support, to include communication, will not be attained.

Alter saw three streams of DSS practice, including executive information systems, traditional DSS, and expert systems. Although each of these types of systems serves a role and use of each system is expected to expand, electronic communication provides a means to enhance the use of each, to help people work together. This should lead to the crossover of effective techniques developed in one system to the others. If an effective model is developed in a DSS, once it is refined it could easily be added to an executive information system. Effective interfaces developed for EIS may well be incorporated into DSSs and expert systems. If a decision problem analysis developed on a DSS is found to be particularly effective, it can be incorporated into an expert system. Overall, the categories useful to describe what can be done do not require independence, nor should they. Companies will do what is most effective.

The impact of computer systems in program trading has already been observed. Support to the real estate market has been more subtle, but serves as an example of how computers can change the way business is conducted. There may well be changes in the way businesses will be organized, as well as how they will operate. A major expected change is in the number of middle managers within organizations. Middle managers formerly served the role of directing activities, whereas top management focused upon strategic issues. Computer communication can be expected to make direction of operations much easier, reducing the need for many middle managers. Much flatter organizations involving a greater degree of participative decision making may develop, with computers providing the means to more effectively control more people than was possible in the past. Many administrative tasks can be eliminated.

Impact of Systems on Communications

The proliferation of computers can be expected to enhance organizational communication. Sanders, Courtney, and Loy (1984) examined the impact of DSS on organizational communication. In MIS, one of the important problems is obtaining adequate communication between users and system designers. Without adequate communication, efficient systems that do not provide effective information support often result. Satisfaction with computer systems has been shown to rely upon top management support, user involvement, and the technical quality of the computer system. This is also important in construction of DSSs. Huff et al. (1984) noted that over 28 percent of the DSSs developed and over 24 percent of the implemented DSSs they surveyed had central information support in designing and building DSSs. Hogue and Watson (1983) also found significant central system support in these phases of DSS development.

Interpersonal communication may be even more important with DSSs than central MISs, because DSS development is often interactive and adaptive. Analysts familiar with modeling techniques may be involved, which adds to the need for communications. Group decisions are often involved, and the nature of decision making requires more focus on information processing and communication.

Naylor (1982) argued that DSSs could hamper communication between users and the central information system, because managers could become more isolated. According to this view, managers would end up spending most of their time at a terminal, thus actually reducing communication. Mintzberg (1979) warned that MISs create a structure within organizations deemphasizing the verbal networks that were developed prior to computerization for informal information gathering.

These views contradict the expectations of Wagner (1982) and Huber (1982), who expected DSS usage to lead to more effective managerial communication. Sanders, Courtney, and Loy argued that DSSs encourage communication for a number of reasons: Adaptive DSS development requires continued interaction between manager and analyst, decisions supported by DSSs often involve group decisions, and there is a greater need for human information processing in a DSS environment.

Sanders, Courtney, and Loy examined DSS usage versus organizational communications. A field survey of DSS users was conducted, examining users of IFPS (Interactive Financial Planning System). A total of 378 IFPS users from 124 organizations responded to the survey. Subjects were categorized as managers (132), financial and planning analysts—for whom IFPS was originally designed—(156), MS/OR analysts (20), and data processing personnel (33), and "others" (37).

Measures of profitability, application to major organizational problems, decision quality, user satisfaction, and degree of use were developed. DSS success was evaluated on decision-making satisfaction, as well as overall satisfaction. Decision maker satisfaction was found in the following areas:

Utilization of the DSS enabled better decisions.

Priorities were easier to set because of the DSS.

The quality of decisions improved.

More relevant information was obtained through the DSS.

Greater use of analytical aids resulted from the DSS.

Overall satisfaction consisted of:

The user became dependent on the DSS.

The user became more valuable to the organization.

The user personally benefitted from the DSS.

The user relied upon the DSS in performing his or her job.

DSS was important for the organization.

Overall satisfaction with DSSs and the decisions resulting from use of these systems were found to increase for managers and financial planning analysts.

To measure the impact of DSS upon communications within the organization, the following question was asked: Does IFPS encourage communication with others in the organization?

IFPS encourages communication with others:

Managers	42% agree	45% uncertain	13% disagree
Analysts	48% agree	38% uncertain	14% disagree
Others	55% agree	31.5% uncertain	13.5% disagree

These results indicate a tendency (which was statistically significant) for IFPS use to encourage communication. A strong majority of the managers indicated that they worked with others to develop IFPS models. The assessment that IFPS encouraged communication with others was significant for managers (as well as some other groups). A moderate relationship was found between the length of time managers had been using the DSS and the level to which they perceived that the system encouraged communications. This contradicts other conjectures that use of DSS would decrease communications in the long run.

Better computer hardware itself might be enough to motivate better communications. But the need for improved communications also increases as decision making becomes more participative and as organizational structure becomes broader.

Support to Enhance Organizational Intelligence

In addition to enhancing organizational communication, computers provide a means to more effectively use organizational intelligence. Organizational knowledge currently exists in the minds of management and in various organizational documents. Computer facilities offer the opportunity to more effectively manage and use this knowledge.

A tremendous wealth of organizational knowledge currently exists in computer systems today. These documents include memoranda and letters, as well as reports analyzing various problems and opportunities faced by the organization. This knowledge represents the thinking of the most knowledgeable people in the organization, and it represents the most valuable organizational asset other than people themselves. Organizational policies and actions expected to lead to organizational success are based on this knowledge.

Many times the asset value of data is largely unrecognized. Sometimes computer information systems are so clogged with data that particular data is operationally inaccessible. It is often frustrating to realize that an important bit of information is stored somewhere on the system, without the slightest clue as to how it can be found. However, integration, shared databases, and more open accessibility policies can lead to more efficient utilization of this data. Furthermore, artificial intelligence approaches can aid in the capture, management, and sharing of knowledge in the organization.

Data by itself is not terribly useful. Means of interpretation are necessary in order to obtain useful information. Real power in information management lies in the diagnostic knowledge leading to the source of problem identification and the generation and evaluation of solutions.

Potential

Systems capable of scanning organizational documents and automatically extracting organizational knowledge are within the realm of possibility. The technology to encode standard operating procedures automatically already exists (through production rule systems). Research is currently being pursued to aid in identification of less obvious relationships. Systems capable of constructing models of the relationships between significant components of the organization's environment are being considered. Such systems would be able to scan a document and deduce relationships between sales volume, price, and advertising expenses. Once the system has developed a model, this model can be used for future applications in an advisory mode or to train new managers in various aspects of the organization's operations. The model also might be able to predict the impact of alternative strategies.

Knowledge processing is a new frontier. There is a great deal of potential value in applications of knowledge-based systems in many business fields. However, there are hurdles between the conceived ideal and reality. Effective procedures for acquiring knowledge are still to be developed. Efficient ways to represent this knowledge still need to be designed. Appropriate applications utilizing this knowledge are not completely identified. However, there is a great deal of research underway in these areas. Certainly, the potential payoff of this field of study is very great.

SUMMARY

Automated systems have appeared in business and have had a significant impact. Business operations are arguably more efficient now than they were before computers. This impact has been very noticeable in the stock market, but also exists in other areas of business, such as real estate. Not only do computer systems allow very rapid transactions (expert systems) and more thorough analyses (decision support systems), they can have other benefits as well. The use of decision support systems has had a noticeable impact on improving the effectiveness of organizational communication. New opportunities exist, with the development of systems capable of learning about the relationships between decisions and impacts a possibility in the near future.

Knowledge utilization should recognize that most relationships in business involve high levels of uncertainty. An issue of importance is that the system should be able to operate despite this uncertainty, while informing the user of the degree of uncertainty.

There are issues involved with the utilization of expert knowledge. If an employee who has developed valuable expertise allows this knowledge to be acquired in an expert system, a potential problem of ethics arises. The value of incorporating this knowledge into an expert system is that the knowledge can be preserved and multiplied. The employee may be forfeiting personal competitive advantage, however. Although this potential problem has long been recognized, there is little evidence of its being a problem in practice. There are other potential problems concerning the use of expert system knowledge. Two legal problems involve treating expertise as an asset, as well as a liability if the expert system leads to an erroneous conclusion.

The 1980s saw dramatic new opportunities to apply computers to aid decision making. As computer hardware and software development continues to explode, we expect that future growth will be at least as rapid as it has been in the 1980s. As Alter expected, the use of the systems discussed in this book should continue. But we also expect dramatic new systems. Ten years ago, there was little discussion of executive information systems. The idea of expert systems was still within a narrow artificial intelligence domain, with some early systems appearing, but with little application to business. The idea of supporting group aspects of decision making was not a developed topic. Most of the discussion in the field focused on arguments about definitions of what decision support systems were, and whether or not they were really MIS (in MIS faculties) or just solid operations research analysis (in operations research/ management science faculties). People like Alter were not sidetracked by these arguments, but went out and developed commercially viable systems, polishing theory through experience.

We expect the same progress to continue. Real progress will be made in the field by the users of systems in business. Academics can serve the most by observing what has successfully been done and seeking out unsuccessful attempts, to try to make sense and order out of the exploding field of computer support to decision making. Meanwhile, students have the option of entering the exciting world of business, hopefully with fresh ideas of applying concepts, or of entering academics and joining the sometimes argumentative effort to make sense out of how decision making can be better served by computers.

REFERENCES

Alter, S. 1989. Shaping the systems of the 1990s. In *DSS-89: Transactions of the Ninth International Conference on Decision Support Systems,* ed. G. R. Widmeyer, i–iii. Providence, RI: The Institute of Management Sciences.

Caudill, M. 1987. Neural networks primer. I. *AI Expert* 2 (12):46–50, 52.

Caudill, M. 1989. Using neural nets. I. Representing knowledge. *AI Expert* 4 (12): 34–41.

Chen, K. C., and T.-P. Liang. 1989. PROTRADER: An expert system for program trading. *Managerial Finance* 15 (5):1–6.

Eliot, L. E. 1988. Security Pacific's RESRA: A case study. *AI Expert* 3 (4):48–54, 57–59.

Hogue, J. T., and H. J. Watson. 1983. Management's role in the approval and administration of decision support systems. *MIS Quarterly* 7 (2).

Huber, G. P. 1982. Group decision support systems as aids in the use of unstructured group management techniques. In *DSS-82: Transactions,* ed. G. W. Dickson, 96–108. Providence, RI: The Institute of Management Sciences.

Huff, S. L., S. Rivard, A. Grindlay, and I. P. Suttie. 1984. An empirical study of decision support systems. *INFOR* (February):21–39.

Liang, T.-P., and K. C. Chen. 1987. Issues in developing expert systems for program trading. In *Proceedings of the First Annual Conference on Expert Systems in Business,* ed. J. Feinstein, J. Liebowitz, H. Look, and B. Silverman, 145–59.

Liebowitz, J. 1988. *Introduction to expert systems,* 131. Santa Cruz, CA; Mitchell.

Marose, R. A. 1990. A financial neural-network application. *AI Expert* 5 (5):50–53.

Mintzberg, H. 1979. *The structuring of organizations.* Englewood Cliffs, NJ: Prentice-Hall.

Naylor, T. H. 1982. Decision support systems or whatever happened to M.I.S? *Interfaces* 12:92–94.

Obermeier, K. K., and J. J. Barron. 1989. Time to get fired up. *BYTE* 14 (8):214–24.

Palmer, J. 1989. A pox on program trading: Two seasoned pros make the case against index arbitrage. *Barron's* 69 (44):6–7, 18–24, 30.

Sanders, G. L., J. F. Courtney, Jr., and S. L. Loy. 1984. The impact of DSS on organizational communication. *Information & Management* 7:141–48.

Savitz, E. J. 1990. More margin: Critics propose it for program traders. *Barron's* 70 (2):33, 35.

Stoll, H. R., and R. E. Whaley. 1990. Program trading and individual stock returns: Ingredients of the triple-witching brew. *J. Business* 83 (1):S165–S192.

Storrie-Lombardi, M. C. 1990. Advances in neural network technology. *MacTech Quarterly* 2 (2):102–11.

Trippi, R. R. 1989. Management support systems for commercial real estate investment decisions: DSS and expert systems. In *DSS-89: Transactions of the Ninth International Conference on Decision Support Systems,* ed. G. R. Widmeyer, 137–145. Providence, RI: The Institute of Management Sciences.

Trippi, R. R. 1990. Decision support and expert systems for real estate investment decisions: A review. *Interfaces* 20 (5):50–60.

Wagner, G. R. 1982. Beyond theory Z with DSS. *DSS-82: Transactions,* ed. G. W. Dickson, 149–55. Providence, RI: The Institute of Management Sciences.

Wasserman, P. 1989. *Neural computing: Theory and practice.* Belmont, CA: Van Nostrand–Reinhold.

Wohlstetter, C. 1990. Market madness. *Chief Executive* 56 (March):22–24.

Wyatt, E. A. 1989. Program trading. *Barron's* 69 (18):58.

Forecasting

This chapter discusses forecasting techniques. These techniques are extremely important in DSS, because forecasting is necessary in the initial phase of problem identification, and it is critical in the evaluation of alternatives as well. Most of the original DSSs were concerned with forecasting the results of alternative actions.

A wide variety of forecasting techniques is available. Statistical approaches provide some capabilities, which we will discuss in this chapter. But forecasting economic activity has always required strong subjective human activity. The Delphi technique, described in the example to follow, is one means to structure subjective estimates of multiple experts in order to develop a refined forecast. Regression analysis is an obvious approach if objective statistical data is available. Some of the many statistical considerations of using regression for forecasting are presented. The Box–Jenkins technique can often be very useful when cyclical data (often encountered in economic activities) is present. The last section of this chapter will discuss the *Business Conditions Digest* and the *Survey of Current Business,* Department of Commerce publications focusing on U.S. business performance. Included is the index of leading indicators, a valuable means of predicting short-term general economic conditions. Because the performance of the overall economy is often highly correlated with the performance of each business, this can be a major source of input for forecasting, either as general background information to the decision maker or as data on general economic conditions.

This chapter will provide you:

- □ A general overview of alternative means of forecasting
- □ An example of a Delphi forecast in a real application
- □ A review of categories of forecasting methods
- □ A discussion of factors involved in using regression for forecasting
- □ A presentation of the Box–Jenkins forecasting method
- □ A discussion of the index of leading indicators

One of the major problems in decision making is anticipating future events. Life is interesting because nobody knows what will happen. We need only remember the price of oil before 1973 or the stock market conditions in early 1929 or before October 1987 to realize that our perceptions of the world are subject to change. One of the most valuable gifts one could have in business would be to be able to predict future market events. Those who have been successful in the past have often achieved success because of their ability (luck) in anticipating events, or at least the flexibility to prepare for the unexpected. No one has been able to completely understand the economic activity of the United States, let alone a particular company. So consideration of forecasting is a very important element in business.

FORECASTING THE ALASKAN ECONOMY
Eschenbach and Geistauts (1985)

Alaska has undergone dramatic economic change. The North Slope oil find resulted in a tremendous amount of revenue relative to pre-oil times. Over 90 percent of the state government's budget came from oil in the early 1980s. The state government sought to develop a broader economy.

In 1982, the Alaska Department of Commerce and Economic Development funded a study to examine the Alaskan economy, energy, and resource development future. Because of its location, climate, terrain, and small population, resource development, rather than manufacturing or services, seems to be the primary basis for the Alaskan economy. There are enormous resources in Alaska, including over 19 billion barrels of oil, 2.9 trillion cubic meters of natural gas, half of the U.S. coal reserves, and deposits of a number of minerals. Furthermore, there are significant fishing, timber, and agricultural resources. Major tourist attractions exist as well.

A major obstacle to development was the lack of infrastructure, both physical and institutional. Transportation facilities, energy development, and public facilities were required. Many development projects had been proposed. A major policy question was which projects to fund. Alaska had a Permanent Fund, which could be used to promote diversification. In 1985, the interest on this fund was used to pay each citizen a dividend, favoring consumption and security rather than economic diversification.

Other goals of the state included developing jobs for Alaskans, improving public services, and promoting health and safety. Resource development threatened the culture of native Alaskans and conflicted with environmental values. Some Alaskan industries, such as the fishing industry, had conflicts with development.

Forecasting the impact of alternative proposals is a crucial factor in long-range planning. When a development project is adopted, the impact on resource prices can be significant, modifying the economy substantially, leading to boom and bust cycles. Econometric forecasting is often ill-suited to these situations, because of its heavy reliance on historical data and trends. However, this historical data was not available for Alaska.

The political process often emphasizes noneconomic criteria. Although economic factors may determine the choices available, the decision was made politically. An effective forecasting methodology must be sensitive to potential shifts in the focus of government policy and must help evaluate feasibility and desirability. The main objective was to predict future developments. But believability and value implications became important as well.

Objective

The objective of the study was to forecast at least 40 years of the Alaskan economy. Shifts in trends and policies to be adopted were to be included.

Technique

Econometric and time-series analyses assume critical development events, but these critical events are what need to be forecast. Critical events can only be forecast by human judgment. This judgment must appear to be objective and credible.

A Delphi approach was selected for forecasting the long-range Alaskan economy. The Delphi approach involves repeated iterations of forecasts by experts, isolated from each other. After each iteration, results (without attribution of forecaster) are shared among the experts. Experts respond to a series of questionnaires. After each round, answers to each questionnaire are summarized and incorporated in the next round's questionnaire.

Research Design

Three criteria for successful outcome were determined. These were validity, credibility, and logistical feasibility. Validity is inherent in the Delphi technique, which has been used in many qualitative studies. Funding limits constrained the study to three rounds of questionnaires and led to limiting participants to Alaska residents. In order to obtain credibility, care was taken in selecting the panel. As many recognized Alaskan leaders and experts as possible were sought. There were also efforts to balance expertise, responsibility, geographic affiliation, and advocacy orientations. Opposing viewpoints were sought. The objectivity of responses was improved by separating forecasts of events from evaluations of their desirability.

Because there were no face-to-face meetings, travel expenses were minimal and participation increased. Sixty percent of those asked participated, yielding 91 panel members for the initial iteration. Over 60 pages of questions and feedback were used. Eighty-five percent of those who began the study participated in all three iterations. Native Alaskans are a major political force in Alaska, requiring oral non-English questionnaire completion in some cases.

In the final round, each panelist was asked to explicitly consider interactions among factors, thus accomplishing an implicit cross-impact analysis. Each panelist also generated a scenario of what he or she expected to happen. These scenarios were sorted into high-, medium-, and low-growth categories, used as the basis for group scenarios.

Results

Logically consistent low-, medium-, and high-growth scenarios were developed with cross-impact results. Because the forecast was long range, it was difficult to validate. An Arthur D. Little econometric study, published in 1983, was available. Where there was common ground, the Delphi study yielded consistent approaches with the Little study. Population predictions in the short run proved to be grossly inaccurate, although they did match a longer-range prediction by the U.S. Census Bureau.

A year later, a short follow-up fourth round was conducted in order to test prediction stability. Almost all of those who completed the initial study participated in this fourth round. Predictions proved to be very stable.

Feedback

The study has been frequently cited by officials, and study predictions helped lead to the establishment of a Division of Mining in the state government. There was a strong interest in copies of the study, and a number of similar studies were undertaken. There were at least four printings of the study.

One of the benefits of the study was that panelists studied the topic in greater depth, with more diversity of opinion than they otherwise would have had. Because many panelists were key citizens of Alaska, the study had many educational benefits as well.

This example demonstrates a long-range strategic forecast. Forecasting this class of activity requires subjective opinion, because too many assumptions would be required to develop a more quantitative prediction. There are, however, many other forecasting problems where other techniques have proven appropriate.

CLASSES OF FORECASTING TECHNIQUES

Economic data often includes cycles, whether you are measuring things relating to the national economy or to the sales of a particular business (Figure S1.1). Many economic activities are seasonal. There are also changes in economic conditions, such as unemployment and inflation. Sometimes there are detectable trends or relationships.

Figure S1.1
Forecasting techniques. (Based on Chambers, Mullick, and Smith [1971])

QUALITATIVE METHODS
   Delphi method
   Panel consensus
   Market research
   Historical analogy

TIME SERIES AND PROJECTION
   Moving average
   Exponential smoothing
   ARIMA models
   advanced models

CAUSAL METHODS
   Regression models
   Econometric models
   Life–cycle analysis
   Indexes
   Surveys

A broad range of forecasting tools are available. These can vary substantially, depending on the characteristics of the forecasting problem, as well as the available information on which the forecast can be based.

Three broad categories are qualitative, time-series, and causal methods.

Qualitative Methods

These methods (such as the Delphi method in the example just reviewed) are valuable for situations calling for human judgment. Although we all realize that nobody knows what will really happen, qualitative approaches are most valuable for forecasting changes in underlying conditions. They are also valuable for identifying expected behavior of humans, such as market response. **Delphi methods** use a panel of experts in a sequence of questionnaires. These experts are kept separated. Their individual opinions are shared after each iteration, allowing them to see what other experts think. The method, as in the Alaskan example, usually results in some convergence of opinion. This procedure is one of the better approaches to forecast long-range impact.

Panel consensus involves combining the opinions of a group of experts. The difference between this approach and the Delphi method is that anonymity is not required. A possible deficiency relative to the Delphi method is that social factors may lead to some experts being swayed, and true consensus may not be obtained.

Market research is a systematic and formal procedure of developing and testing hypotheses about market response. Usually, a significant effort is required to gather market data from questionnaires and surveys, as well as to analyze the data, generally through statistical analysis such as time-series or causal regression models.

A comparative analysis of new situations to old conditions can be forecast through **historical analogy.** If a new product is being marketed, the response of old products to marketing campaigns can be used as a basis to predict how a similar marketing campaign might work. There are dangers because each new situation is different, but a great deal of insight can be gained by remembering past experience.

Time-Series Forecasts

In this class of model, only historical data on the variable to be predicted is required. A wide range of time-series forecasting techniques exist, from simple moving average calculations through very advanced models incorporating seasonality, trend cycles, and other elements. The simplest approach is to fit a straight line through the past few observations in order to identify a trend. This is what an ordinary least squares regression of the dependent (predicted) variable versus time provides. However, there are usually other complications involved with time-series data. Each of the time-series methods requires data in the form of a measured response of the variable being forecast over time. A fundamental assumption is that the passage of time and the other components included (such as seasonality and trend) explain all of the future change in the variable to be predicted. An advantage of strict time-series forecasting is that it does not require a theory of causation.

Another simple approach is the **moving average** method. The concept is that the next period's predicted value will be the average of the last n observations. This can be modified by weighting these n observations in any way the analyst or user wants. Although this method is very simple, it has proven to be useful in stable environments, such as inventory management.

Another relatively simple approach that has proven highly useful is **exponential smoothing.** With exponential smoothing, the forecast for the next period equals the forecast for the last period, plus a portion ($0 \leq \alpha \leq 1$) of last period's forecast error. The parameter α can be manipulated to change the model's response to changes. An α of 0 would simply repeat last period's forecast. An α of 1 would forecast last period's actual demand. The closer α is to 1, the more the model responds to changes. The closer α is to 0, the less it is affected by changes.

There are many variations to exponential smoothing, allowing more complex adaptation to trend changes or seasonal factors. Because of its very simple computational requirements, exponential smoothing is popular when many forecasts need to be computed regularly.

Trends can be identified through regression of the variable to be predicted versus time. But the degree of fit of this model is often not very good, and more accurate information is usually available.

ARIMA (AutoRegressive Integrated Moving Average) models provide a means to fit a time-series model incorporating cycles and seasonality in addition to trend. Box–Jenkins models are of this class. ARIMA models have up to three parameters: autocorrelation terms, differencing terms, and moving average terms. These will be discussed later in this chapter. Exponential smoothing is a special case of the Box–Jenkins technique. However, whereas exponential smoothing is very computationally efficient, ARIMA models require large amounts of computation time. Furthermore, because so many parameters are used, larger amounts of data are required for reliable results. ARIMA models work very well when the time-series data has high degrees of autocorrelation, but they perform rather poorly when this condition does not exist. It usually is a good idea to test for autocorrelation and compare the fit of the ARIMA model with linear regression against time, or some other forecasting model. A regression of the variable to be forecasted versus time is a special case of ARIMA (zero autocorrelation terms, zero moving average terms).

Other more advanced techniques to forecast time series exist. One of these is X-11, developed by the Census Bureau. That technique decomposes a time series into seasonal, trend, cycles, and irregular components. As a rule, the more sophisticated the technique, the more skill is required to use it to obtain reliable results.

Causal Methods

Causal methods go beyond accepting the time-series assumption that underlying conditions will continue. Causal models allow the forecaster to include a variety of explanatory variables. **Regression** of the dependent variable against variables other than (or in addition to) time is the simplest approach. Sales can be related to gross national product, for instance.

More advanced techniques include **econometric** models. These are systems of interdependent regression equations describing some sector of economic activity. Because of the simultaneous nature of the system of regressions, more complex analytic support is required. These models tend to be relatively expensive to develop, requiring additional data as well as intensive identification of relationships. A number of well-published, commercially available econometric models exist, such as those of Chase Econometrics and the Data Resource Institute.

Life-cycle analysis is based on the concept of the product life cycle. This idea proposes that products go through a demand cycle. New products start off with relatively low demand. If they catch on and gain in popularity, demand for the products will increase at a higher rate of growth. When demand for the products matures, the rate of growth will slow down and ultimately decline. This curve has an S shape (and is often referred to as an S-curve). Note that this approach combines the features of historical analogy (qualitative) and time-series regression.

Indexes provide a simpler way to forecast. With this approach, a group of indicators, covering a variety of aspects expected to influence the predicted variable's behavior, is monitored to get an idea of future behavior. An example is the Department of Commerce's Index of Leading Indicators (described in the following discussion). The economic performance of leading indicators in a variety of sectors of the economy is monitored. At any one time, some of these are usually improving, while others are declining. The direction of movement of all the selected indicators are weighted and combined, providing an index of overall expectation. Another such index is often used by technical analysts in trying to predict the Dow-Jones average or general stock market performance. The intent of indexes is not to provide precise degrees of change, but rather to provide a better picture of the direction of change.

Surveys are highly useful in predicting the response of the public to new products, political activity, and many other behavioral responses. The idea is, if you want to know how people will react to something, ask them. This of course involves some complications, as discussed in Chapter 5. People tend to be biased in responding to questions from strangers, and they change their minds over time anyway (for those of you who remember 1948, recall that Dewey was predicted to defeat Truman on the basis of surveys).

Indirect forecasting is a way to combine some of these methods. Regression can be used to obtain a strong relationship between the variable to be predicted and some other more general variable. This other variable may also be difficult to predict. Qualitative forecasting, such as expert opinion, can be used to obtain a prediction of this other variable. This approach fits the idea of a decision support system very well. The regression model is the forecast generator. The expert (or decision maker directly) is a source of the future independent variable value.

Because of the basic role regression plays in many forecasting techniques, regression will be presented in more detail in Appendix D. The next discussion on forecasting will be followed by discussions of the Box–Jenkins method and the *Business Conditions Digest*.

FORECASTING MODELS

Regression (see Appendix D) is one source of forecasting models. Regression can be used to obtain the relationship:

$$Y = \beta_0 + \beta_1 X_1 + \beta_2 X_2$$

This can then be used as a formula for prediction. Because you know (or have estimates for) X_1 and X_2, your regression model gives you a formula to estimate Y.

Coincident Observations

Note that establishing relationships is one thing—forecasting is another. In order for a model to do you any good for forecasting, you have to know the future values of the independent variables. Measures such as r^2 assume absolutely no error in the values of the independent variables you use. The ideal way to overcome this limitation is to use independent variables whose future values are known.

Time

Time is a very attractive independent variable, because you will not introduce additional error in estimating future values of time. About all we know for sure about next year's economic performance is that it will be next year. In addition, models using time as the only independent variable have a different philosophical basis than causal models. With time, you do not try to explain the changes in the dependent variable. You assume that whatever has been causing changes in the past will continue to do so at the same rate in the future.

Lags

Another way to obtain known independent variable values is to lag them. Instead of regressing a dependent variable value for 1963 against the independent variable observation for 1963, regress the dependent variable value for 1963 against the *1962* independent variable observation. This would give you one year of known independent variable values with which to forecast. If the independent variable is a leading indicator of the dependent variable, r^2 of your model might actually go up. However, usually lagging an independent variable will lower r^2. Additionally, you will probably lose an observation, which in economic data sets may be a high price to pay. But at least you will have perfect knowledge of a future independent variable value for your forecast.

That is not to say that you cannot utilize coincident models. (Coincident models include variables that tend to change direction at the same time.) These models in fact give decision makers the opportunity to play "what-if" games. Various assumptions can be made concerning the value of the independent variables. The model will quickly churn out the predicted value of the dependent variable. Do not, however, believe that the r^2 of the forecast reflects all of the accuracy of the model. Additional errors in the estimates of the independent variables are not reflected in r^2.

Nonlinear Data

So far we have only discussed linear relationships. Life is usually nonlinear. Straight lines do not perform well in fitting curves. There is one trick to try when forecasting obviously nonlinear data. Logarithmic transforms of certain types of curves fall back into straight lines. When you make a log transform of the dependent variable, however, you will need to retransform the resulting forecasts to obtain useful information.

Cycles

In Chapter 5 we commented that most economic data is cyclical. We noted previously that models with the single independent variable of time have some positive features. There is a statistical problem involved with OLS regressions on cyclical data. The error terms should be random, with no pattern. A straight-line fit of cyclical data will have very predictable patterns of error (autocorrelation). This is a serious problem for OLS regression, warping all the statistical inferences.

Autocorrelation can occur in causal models, although not as often as in regressions versus time. When autocorrelation occurs in causal models, more advanced statistical techniques are called for, such as second-stage least squares. However, when autocorrelation occurs in regressions where time is the only independent variable, Box–Jenkins models are often very effective. Box–Jenkins forecasting takes advantage of the additional information of the pattern in error terms to give better forecasts.

Box–Jenkins Models

Box–Jenkins models were designed for time series with:

> No trend
>
> Constant variability
>
> Stable correlations over time

Box–Jenkins models have a great deal of flexibility. You must specify three terms:

1. **P**—the number of autocorrelation terms (see Appendix D)
2. **D**—the number of differencing elements
3. **Q**—the number of moving average terms

The **P** term is what makes a Box–Jenkins model work, taking advantage of the existence of strong autocorrelation in the regression model $Y = f(\text{time})$.

The **D** term can sometimes be used to eliminate trends. A **D** value of 1 will work well if your data has a constant trend (it is linear). A **D** value of 2 or 3 might help if you have more complex trends. Exceeding a **D** value of 3 is beyond the scope of this book. If there is no trend to begin with, a **D** value of 0 works well.

The model should also have constant variability. If there are regular cycles in the data, moving average terms equal to the number of observations in the cycle can eliminate these. Looking at a plot of the data is the best way to detect cyclical data. One easily recognized cycle is seasonal data. If you have monthly data, a moving average term **Q** of 12 would be in order. If you have quarterly data, a **Q** value of 4 should help. If there is no regular pattern, a **Q** value of 0 will probably be as good as any.

The **D** and **Q** terms are used primarily to stabilize the data. The **P** term is the one that takes advantage of autocorrelation. The precise number of appropriate autocorrelation terms (**P**) to use can be obtained from the computer package. For IDA, the command PACF for the dependent variable will give you the desired information. IDA will give you a correlogram with autocorrelation coefficients. These autocorrelation coefficients give you an idea of the correlation of your dependent variable with lags of the same data. This correlogram will settle down to 0 (hopefully). The **P** term is the number of terms significantly different from 0. Significance is a matter of judgment. Because Box–Jenkins models are often exploratory, you will want to try more than one model anyway, to seek the best fit (lowest mean square forecasting error).

Box–Jenkins models tend to be volatile. They are designed for data sets of at least 100 observations. You will not always have that many observations. We are looking at them as an alternative to time series, especially when autocorrelation is present in a regression versus time. So the idea is to compare different models and select the best one.

Box–Jenkins models require a computer package for support. There are a number available. IDA has been mentioned, and quick and dirty commands for using IDA are given at the end of the chapter. Minitab and SAS are other sources. Specific operating instructions require a review of the corresponding manuals. In general, IDA is very good for diagnosing a data series before running Box–Jenkins models. SAS requires less parameter settings, but is a little more rigid. Minitab commands for Box–Jenkins are very easy and are also given at the end of the chapter. Cryer (1986) provides additional information on ARIMA models, and Ling and Roberts (1982) give more complete information about IDA.

Now that we have seen some of the techniques available for forecasting, we will review the index of leading indicators, a governmental measure of short-term future economic performance.

Index of Leading Indicators

Gross national product (GNP) is a measure of the value of all goods and services produced in the United States. This is a fundamental economic measure of productivity. Although it has been criticized for not measuring all economic goods and costs (unpaid work is not measured, such as housekeeping and family child rearing; pollution resulting from a production process inflates the measure, as added costs are incurred in cleaning it up; etc.), it is a practical and useful measure of economic performance.

The *Business Conditions Digest* included over 100 time series in seven economic areas. This publication was discontinued in March 1990, but much of the information is continued in the *Survey of Current Business*. Economic time series tend to have noticeable cycles. The series other than GNP are classified by their relationship to GNP. Leading indicators are series that tend to peak and trough some predictable length of time prior to the peaks and troughs of

GNP. Leading indicators, such as formation of business enterprises, can be useful in predicting future trends in GNP. Lagging indicators, such as business investment expenditures or inventories on hand, tend to have peaks and troughs following GNP. GNP can be used to predict future trends in lagging indicators. Other series tend to be coincident with GNP. Appendix B provides classification of some series at business cycle peaks.

The Department of Commerce maintains these series, sometimes adding new series and deleting old series. The cyclical relationship of each series to GNP is not constant. Occasionally, the classification of the other series will change. Data is also updated periodically.

The *Business Conditions Digest* included a number of sections. A current classification of cyclical indicators was located near the front of the book. A recap of current statistics, including the last two available annual figures and the last few monthly and quarterly observations, was given for each series. This was followed by a graphical section, providing a picture of the recent performance of each series. This was followed by more detailed tabular data. Near the end of each issue, a selected number of historical data series were updated. An index provided information identifying where data for each series could be found in the current issue, as well as references to definitions (in the *Handbook of Cyclical Indicators*) and the last historical update. The index was organized in alphabetical order by series name. The *Survey of Current Business* continues monthly and annual updates for many of the data series, including a complete description of the index of leading indicators. Historical sources are given, although future publication plans were not given in the last available issue.

The *Handbook of Cyclical Indicators* is a separate publication, published about every seven years. It contains definitions of each series, as well as historical data for each series. It is the safest place to find old information, as series are fully revised. Indexes are often recalculated on a new base year if the rate of change becomes too large.

SUMMARY

Forecasting is a crucial element in decision making. Identification of a problem or an opportunity requires forecasting. Furthermore, the step of alternative evaluation requires decision makers to predict expected organizational response and performance to implemented decisions.

There are a variety of forecasting techniques available. Qualitative methods provide some structure to enhance judgment. Time-series methods provide a means to extend past trends into the future. The Box–Jenkins method is an example of this type of forecasting model. Causal models, based on theories of what makes the forecast variable change, provide an additional means of predicting future variable values.

Although forecasting has long been recognized as being important (the Delphi method gets its name from the oracle in ancient Greece), nobody has developed the ideal means of forecasting. Crystal balls do not seem to work and neither do Ouija boards. Expert opinion and the most sophisticated models in the world are not perfect either. President Reagan used to refer to professional economists having predicted nine of the last two recessions.

Although forecasting is challenging, some means of aiding human prediction exist. We have reviewed the broad categories that exist. As you have seen, results are still a human responsibility, calling for judgment. Because that is what decision support systems are all about, it seems appropriate to consider forecasting methods as decision support system tools.

This chapter includes a number of appendixes. Appendixes A and B provide some added information on the *Business Conditions Digest* and the *Survey of Current Business*. Appendix C gives a Durbin–Watson table, which is necessary for interpreting the presence of autocorrelation in regression models. Appendix D gives an introduction to regression analysis. These appendixes are followed by quick and dirty introductions to enable students to use SAS, Minitab, or IDA in conducting regression or Box–Jenkins analyses.

REFERENCES

Chambers, J. C., S. K. Mullick, and D. D. Smith. 1971. How to choose the right forecasting technique. *Harvard Business Rev.* (July–August):45–74.

Cryer, J. D. 1986. *Time series analysis.* Boston: PWS Publishers.

Eschenbach, T. G., and G. A. Geistauts. 1985. A Delphi forecast for Alaska. *Interfaces* 15:100–109.

Ling, R. F., and H. V. Roberts. 1982. *IDA: A user's guide to the Ida interactive data analysis and forecasting system.* New York: Scientific Press.

PROJECT IDEAS

An excellent data set is available from the *Business Conditions Digest* and the *Survey of Current Business*. There are over 100 series of data reported on a monthly and annual basis, dating back to before World War II. The data set includes:

Series	43	Unemployment rate
	47	Industrial productivity index
	50	Gross national product
	59	Retail sales volume
	85	Rate of change in money supply M1
	109	Prime rate of interest
	112	Net business loans
	293	Personal savings rate
	310	Implicit price deflator (inflation)
	910	Index of leading indicators

Any one of these series could be assigned with the intent of forecasting into the near future. This can be tied to assigning readings related to the series in current news publications.

If just one series is obtained, regressions against time, as well as Box–Jenkins models, are useful, although the relationships with time for cyclical data are generally poor. Leading indicators can be used to forecast gross national product as an alternative to time regression or Box–Jenkins models.

If a data set is maintained, this series provides an excellent laboratory for looking at correlation analysis and developing causal models. Causal models can also be compared with Box–Jenkins models. There is great variety in relative fit. Other sources of data are readily available in *Employment and Earnings* or in the *Monthly Labor Review*.

Indirect Forecasting Assignment

Assume you have the responsibility of forecasting quarterly sales (the next three quarters) for your company, which produces computer disks. You have information on the past 18 quarters on company sales, total market sales, and your company's percentage of the market.

Quarter	Company Sales	Percentage of Market	Total Market Sales
I 1	18	9	200
II 1	16.1	7	230
III 1	20	8	250
IV 1	20.8	8	260
I 2	22.8	8	280
II 2	27	9	300
III 2	29.7	9	330
IV 2	32.4	9	360
I 3	40	10	400
II 3	35.2	8	440
III 3	43.2	9	480
IV 3	53	10	530
I 4	63.8	11	580
II 4	58.6	9	640
III 4	70	10	700
IV 4	84.7	11	770
I 5	106.6	13	820
II 5	87	10	870

Assume you have obtained an expert opinion of the Total Market Sales for the next three quarters to be

III 5	930
IV 5	960
I 6	950

Develop a forecast using a regression to obtain the relationship of Company Sales to Total Market Sales and then use the expert forecast as a source of Total Market Sales.

Compare this forecast with time-series forecasts, such as moving average and regression of Company Sales against time.

Discuss the relative benefits of both approaches.

APPENDIX A: Components of the Index of Leading Indicators

Series

1 Average weekly hours of production of nonsupervisory workers, manufacturing

5 Average weekly initial claims for unemployment insurance, state programs

8 Manufacturers' new orders in 1982 dollars, consumer goods, and materials

19 Index of stock prices, 500 common stocks

20 Contracts and orders for plant and equipment in 1982 dollars

29 Index of new private housing units authorized by land building permits

32 Vendor performance, percentage of companies receiving slower deliveries

83 Index of consumer expectations

92 Change in unfilled orders in 1982 dollars of durable goods

99 Change in sensitive materials prices

106 Money supply M2 in 1982 dollars

From *Survey of Current Business,* June 1990, p. C1, Series 910, Index of leading indicators.

APPENDIX B: Selected Classification of Cyclical Indicators

Economic Process

	Employment and Unemployment	Fixed Capital Investment	Prices, Costs, and Profits	Money and Credit
Leading Indicators	Job vacancies Comprehensive unemployment (one series)	Formation of business enterprises	Stock prices	Interest rates (one series)
Roughly **Coincident** Indicators	Comprehensive employment (one series)	Business investment		Money velocity
Lagging Indicators	Comprehensive unemployment (two series)	Business investment expenditures (one series)	Unit labor costs	Outstanding debt

Note that there are a number of series in many of these classifications, and each particular series may be identified as being a leading indicator (L), a roughly coincident indicator (C), a lagging indicator (Lg), or timing unclassified (U). The identification can also differ at business cycle peaks and business cycle troughs.

From *Business Conditions Digest.*

Significance points of d_L and d_U at the .05 level:

	k' = 1		k' = 2		k' = 3		k' = 4	
n	d_L	d_U	d_L	d_U	d_L	d_U	d_L	d_U
15	1.08	1.36	.95	1.54	.82	1.75	.69	1.97
20	1.20	1.41	1.10	1.54	1.00	1.68	.90	1.83
25	1.29	1.45	1.21	1.55	1.12	1.66	1.04	1.77
26	1.30	1.46	1.22	1.55	1.14	1.65	1.06	1.76
27	1.32	1.47	1.24	1.56	1.16	1.65	1.08	1.76
28	1.33	1.48	1.26	1.56	1.18	1.65	1.10	1.75
29	1.34	1.48	1.27	1.56	1.20	1.65	1.12	1.74
30	1.35	1.49	1.28	1.57	1.21	1.65	1.14	1.74
31	1.36	1.50	1.30	1.57	1.23	1.65	1.16	1.74
32	1.37	1.50	1.31	1.57	1.24	1.65	1.18	1.73
33	1.38	1.51	1.32	1.58	1.26	1.65	1.19	1.73
34	1.39	1.51	1.33	1.58	1.27	1.65	1.21	1.73
35	1.40	1.52	1.34	1.58	1.28	1.65	1.22	1.73
36	1.41	1.52	1.35	1.59	1.29	1.65	1.24	1.73
37	1.42	1.53	1.36	1.59	1.31	1.66	1.25	1.72
38	1.43	1.54	1.37	1.59	1.32	1.66	1.26	1.72
39	1.43	1.54	1.38	1.60	1.33	1.66	1.27	1.72
40	1.44	1.54	1.39	1.60	1.34	1.66	1.29	1.72
45	1.48	1.57	1.43	1.62	1.38	1.67	1.34	1.72
50	1.50	1.59	1.46	1.63	1.42	1.67	1.38	1.72
55	1.53	1.60	1.49	1.64	1.45	1.68	1.41	1.72
60	1.55	1.62	1.51	1.65	1.48	1.69	1.44	1.73
65	1.57	1.63	1.54	1.66	1.50	1.70	1.47	1.73
70	1.58	1.64	1.55	1.67	1.52	1.70	1.49	1.74
75	1.60	1.65	1.57	1.68	1.54	1.71	1.51	1.74
80	1.61	1.66	1.59	1.69	1.56	1.72	1.53	1.74
85	1.62	1.67	1.60	1.70	1.57	1.72	1.55	1.75
90	1.63	1.68	1.61	1.70	1.59	1.73	1.57	1.75
95	1.64	1.69	1.62	1.71	1.60	1.73	1.58	1.75
100	1.65	1.69	1.63	1.72	1.61	1.74	1.59	1.76

k' is the number of independent variables excluding the intercept.

APPENDIX D: OLS Regression

Ordinary least squares regression (OLS) is a model of the form:

$$Y = \beta_0 + \beta_1 X_1 + \beta_2 X_2 + \cdots + \beta_n X_n + \epsilon$$

where Y is the dependent variable (the one being forecast),
X_n are the n independent (explanatory) variables,
β_0 is the intercept term,
β_n are the n coefficients for the independent variables,
and ϵ is the error term.

OLS regression is nothing more than the straight line (with intercept and slope coefficients β_n) that minimizes the error terms ϵ_i over all i observations. The idea is that you look at past data to determine the β coefficients which worked best, and given knowledge of the X_n for future observations, the most likely future value of the dependent variable will be what the model gives you. This approach assumes a linear relationship and error terms that are normally distributed around 0 without patterns. Although these assumptions are often unrealistic, regression is highly attractive because of the existence of well-developed computer packages, as well as highly developed statistical theory. Statistical packages provide the probability that estimated parameters differ from 0.

Tests of the Regression Model

SSR

The accuracy of any forecasting model can be assessed by calculating the sum of squared residuals (SSR). All that means is that you obtain a model that gives you a forecasting formula, then go back to the past observations and see what the model would have given you for the dependent variable for each past observation. Each observation's residual (error) is the difference between actual and predicted. The sign does not matter, because the next step is to square each of these residuals. The more accurate the model is, the lower its SSR. An SSR does not mean much by itself. But it is a very good way of comparing alternative models, if there are equal opportunities for each model to have error.

r^2

SSR can be used to generate more information for a particular model. r^2 is the ratio of explained squared dependent variable values over total squared values. Total squared values are defined as explained squared dependent variable values plus SSR. To obtain r^2, square the forecast values of the dependent variable values, add them up (yielding MSR), and divide MSR by (MSR + SSR). This gives the ratio of change in the dependent variable explained by the model. r^2 can range from a minimum of 0 (the model tells you absolutely nothing about the dependent variable) to 1.0 (the model is perfect).

Adjusted r^2:

Note that in the previous model, you were allowed an unlimited number of independent variables. The fact is that adding an independent variable to the model will always result in r^2 equal to or greater than r^2 without the last independent variable. This is true despite the probability that one or more of the independent variables have very little true relationship with the dependent variable. To get a truer picture of the worth of adding independent variables to the model, adjusted r^2 penalizes the r^2 calculation for having extra independent variables:

$$\text{Adjusted}(r^2) = 1 - \frac{\text{SSR } (i - 1)}{\text{TSS } (i - n)}$$

where SSR is the sum of squared residuals, MSR is the sum of squared predicted values, TSS = SSR + MSR, i is the number of observations, and n is the number of independent variables.

Although these measures provide some idea of how well a model fit past data, it is more important to know how well the model fits data to be forecast. A widely used approach to measure how well a model accomplishes this is to divide the data set into two parts (for instance, the first two-thirds of the data used to develop the model, and then test this model on the last one-third of the data set). An idea of model accuracy can be obtained by developing a prediction interval. The upper bound of this prediction interval can be obtained by

$$\text{Forecast } + 2(\sqrt{\text{mean square forecast error}})$$

and the lower bound can be obtained by

$$\text{Forecast } - 2(\sqrt{\text{mean square forecast error}})$$

If the forecast errors are independent and identically normally distributed with a mean of 0, then the future observation should fall within these bounds about 95 percent of the time.

Causal Models

So far we have referred to a general regression model, with any number of independent variables. This type of model seeks to explain changes in the dependent variable by changes in the independent variables.

It must be recognized that a good fit in a model says nothing about causation. The real relationship may be due to the dependent variable causing changes in the independent variable(s). Regression models would not know any better.

Models with more than one independent variable introduce added complications. In general, from a statistical viewpoint, it is better to have as simple a model as possible.

One rational way to begin constructing a multivariate causal model is to collect data on as many candidate independent variables (plus of course the dependent variable) as possible. Independent variables should make some sense in explaining the dependent variable (you should have some reason to think changes in the independent variable cause changes in the dependent variable). Then run a correlation analysis. *Correlation between the dependent variable and a candidate independent variable should be high.*

Multicollinearity

The primary complication arising from the use of multiple independent variables is the potential for multicollinearity. What that means is that two or more independent variables are likely to contain overlapping information. The effect of multicollinearity is that the *t* tests are drastically warped, and bias creeps into the model. This has the implication that as future information is obtained, the estimates of the β coefficients will likely change drastically, because the model is unstable. Multicollinearity can be avoided by *not* including independent variables that are highly correlated with each other. How much correlation is too much is a matter of judgment. Note that the sign of correlation simply identifies if the relationship is positive or negative. In a positive relationship, if one variable goes up, the other variable tends to go up. A negative correlation indicates that as one variable goes up, the other variable tends to go down.

To demonstrate this concept, assume you have a correlation matrix, giving you the correlations between the dependent variable *Y* and candidate independent variables *A, B, C,* and *D.*

	Y	A	B	C	D
Y	1.0	$-.1$	$-.8$	$-.6$	.9
A	$-.1$	1.0	.2	.2	$-.2$
B	$-.8$	.2	1.0	.2	$-.8$
C	$-.6$	.2	.2	1.0	$-.7$
D	.9	$-.2$	$-.8$	$-.7$	1.0

Note that a first priority should be the existence of a theoretical relationship between independent variables and the dependent variable. You should have a reason for expecting *A, B, C,* and *D* to have some impact upon *Y.* Correlations can be used to verify the relationship among a pair of variables. In this matrix, variables *D, B,* and *C* have some identifiable relationship with *Y. D* has a direct relationship (as one goes up, the other tends to go up). B and C have inverse relationships with Y (as one goes up, the other tends to go down). The regression model $Y = f(B, D)$ is likely to be multicollinear, because B and D contain much of the same information.

Test for Multicollinearity

A variance inflation measure provides some measure of multicollinearity in a regression. In SAS, the option VIF can be included in the model line. If the variance inflation measure is below 10, the rule of thumb is that you do not reject. However, this is a very easy test limit to pass. The first priority would be to select variables that would make sense. Second, it is best to design models without overlapping information.

Regression Model Assumptions

The basic simple regression model is

$$Y_i = \beta_0 + \beta_1 X_i + \epsilon_i$$

where Y_i is the ith observed value of the dependent variable, X_i is the ith observed value of the independent variable, and ϵ is a normally distributed random variable with a mean of 0 and a standard deviation of s_ϵ. The error term is assumed to be statistically independent over observations.

Autocorrelation

Autocorrelation exists in a regression model if there is correlation between error ϵ_i and some prior error of a given lag ϵ_{i-j}. For j of 1 (first-degree autocorrelation) to be significant, an apparent influence of the immediately preceding error on the current error would exist. Second-degree autocorrelation is the correlation between error in a given time period and the error two time periods prior. Autocorrelation can be of any degree up to 1 less than the number of observations, although larger degrees of autocorrelation are less likely to exist, and estimating them is more difficult because there are fewer instances to observe.

Autocorrelation can often occur in time-series data involving cycles. OLS regression seeks to force a straight line through wavy data. Therefore, there may well be a relationship between error in a given time period and the error one period prior. If you are at the high side of a cycle, and the cycle is longer than the period between observations, you are more likely to be on the high side of the regression line the next observation. This would be positive autocorrelation, as the sign of the error is likely to be the same. Negative autocorrelation exists when there is a significant tendency for error in the following period to have an opposite sign.

Over the long run, autocorrelation does not affect the bias of model estimates (in the short run, it can make it erratic). However, autocorrelation in a model results in underestimation of the standard errors of the β coefficients (you get misleading t scores, biased the wrong way).

Test for Autocorrelation

The Durbin–Watson test provides an estimate of autocorrelation in a regression model. The null hypothesis of this test is that there is no autocorrelation in a regression model. Durbin–Watson statistics can range between 0 and 4. The ideal measure indicating no autocorrelation is 2. Appendix C includes a table of values for lower and upper Durbin–Watson limits at the .95 confidence level. d_L is the lower limit, and d_U is the upper limit. You need a computer regression package to obtain d, the estimate of first-order autocorrelation. Then obtain d_L and d_U from the table (k' is the number of nonintercept independent variables, and n is the number of observations).

To test for positive autocorrelation (ϵ_i is directly related to ϵ_j):

If d is less than d_L, reject the null (conclude there is positive autocorrelation).

If d is greater than d_L but less than d_U, there is no conclusion relative to positive autocorrelation.

If d is greater than d_U, accept the null (conclude no positive autocorrelation exists).

To test for negative autocorrelation (ϵ_i is inversely related to ϵ_j):

If d is less than $4 - d_U$, accept the null (conclude no negative autocorrelation exists).

If d is greater than $4 - d_U$ and less than $4 - d_L$, there is no conclusion relative to negative autocorrelation.

If d is greater than $4 - d_L$, reject the null (conclude the existence of negative autocorrelation).

There is a continuum for the evaluation of d:

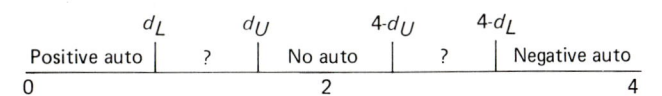

If autocorrelation exists in a regression against *time* ($Y = f\{\text{time}\}$), this feature can be utilized to improve the forecast through a Box–Jenkins model. Second-stage least squares is an alternative approach, which runs the OLS regression, identifies autocorrelation, then adjusts the data to eliminate the autocorrelation, reregresses on the data, and replaces the autocorrelation. As you can see, second-stage least squares is rather involved. (The SAS syntax for second-stage least squares regression is given at the end of the chapter.)

To summarize autocorrelation, the error terms are no longer independent. One approach (Box–Jenkins) is to utilize this error dependence to develop a better forecast. The other approach (second-stage least squares) is to wash the error dependence away.

Heteroscedasticity

The regression model statistics and associated probabilities assume that the errors of the model are unbiased (the expected mean of the errors is 0), the error terms are normally distributed, and that the variance of the errors is constant. Heteroscedasticity is the condition that exists when error terms do *not* have constant (or relatively constant) variance over time. If errors are homoscedastic (the opposite of heteroscedastic), they would look something like the following:

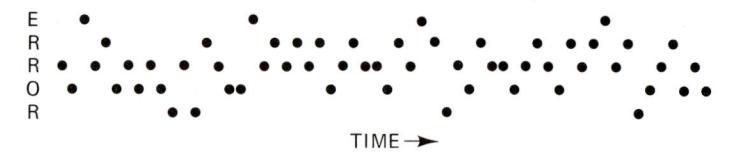

Heteroscedasticity would look like:

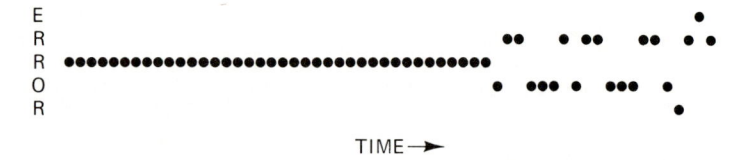

This plot of heteroscedastic error implies that the variance of the errors is a function of a model-independent variable. If we were dealing with a time series and the errors became worse with time, this should lead us to discount the goodness of fit of the model, because if we were going to use the model to forecast, it would be more and more inaccurate when it was needed most.

Of course, if the opposite occurred and the errors became smaller with time, that should lead us to be more confident of the model than the goodness-of-fit statistics would indicate. This situation is also heteroscedastic, but would provide improving predictors.

There is no easy to use test for heteroscedasticity. About the best quick test is to plot the errors versus time and apply the eyeball test.

You need to have a data file (or files). Assume you have data files created named DAT1 DATA and DAT2 DATA.

SAS MODEL FILE

CMS FILEDEF DISK1 DISK dat1 data;	these two lines link the data files
CMS FILEDEF DISK2 DISK dat2 data	
DATA label;	all SAS commands end in;
INFILE DISK1;	
INPUT v1 v2 v3 . . . vm;	vm variable names in data set
INFILE DISK2;	must be in the order of variable
INPUT vn . . . vz;	entry in data files
PROC PRINT;	prints all active data unless VAR line used
VAR vx vy;	specifies which variables to print
PROC CORR;	prints correlation matrix (all unless VAR line)
VAR vx vy;	specifies which variables to correlate
PROC PLOT;	plots graph
PLOT dv*YEAR;	dv—vertical axis YEAR—horizontal axis
PROC REG;	runs ordinary least squares regression
MODEL dv = vx vy/DW VIF;	of dv as dependent upon variables following =
OUTPUT OUT = x P = y R = z;	creates data file x with prediction y and residual z
	initially you should use TIME as the independent variable
	DW gives you the Durbin–Watson statistic
	VIF gives you the variance inflation measure

Based upon *SAS User's Guide: Basics* (1982). SAS Institute.

```
PROC PLOT;
   PLOT dv*YEAR y*YEAR = 'P'        /OVERLAY; plots actual and
                                     prediction together
   PLOT z*YEAR/VREF = 0;            plots residual with centerline at
                                     0
PROC PRINT;
   VAR YEAR dv y z;                 prints actual, predicted, and
                                     error if you include future
                                     estimates of all independent
                                     variables in the data set
                                     (data file), SAS will calculate
                                     forecast
```

Syntax to generate lagged variable LIND:
```
L1Q = LAG1(LIND);
L2Q = LAG2(LIND);
L3Q = LAG3(LIND);
```

Second-stage least squares syntax:
```
PROC AUTOREG PARTIAL;
   MODEL GNP = PROD IPD L1Q L3Q TIME/METHOD = ML;
   LAGLIST 1 2 3;
   OUTPUT OUT = X P = PR R = E2;
```

Minitab provides a very accessible means of analyzing statistical data, with very English-oriented commands.

The package is also capable of supporting Box–Jenkins analysis.

An example batch set of commands is given, reading 16 columns of data with 117 observations (rows), and naming these variables (columns).

Two variables are plotted against each other, followed by a correlation matrix. A regression model, with a Durbin–Watson statistic, is obtained, and three future values predicted.

An ARIMA (Box–Jenkins) model is obtained by giving P, D, and Q, followed by the variable to be analyzed.

The forecast line tells Minitab how many forecasts you want.

```
read data from 'a:mtqtr' into c1-c16
name c1 'obs' c2 'date' c3 'unemp' c4 'prod' c5 'gnp' c6 'm1' c7 'prime'
name c8 'psave' c9 'ipd' c10 'deficit' c11 'trabal' c12 'lind'
name c13 'netbl' c14 'invent' c15 'retail' c16 '12q'
plot 'obs' 'gnp'
correlate c5 c1 c3 c4 c5 c6 c7 c8 c9 c10 c11 c12 c13 c14 c15 c16
regress 'gnp' on 1 predictor in 'obs';
dw;
predict for 118;
predict for 119;
predict for 120.
regress 'gnp' on 1 predictor in '12q';
dw;
predict for -1;
predict for 1;
predict for 2.
end
```

Syntax for Box–Jenkins:
```
pacf 5 'gnp'; to determine the number of autocorrelation (P) terms
arima 2 0 0 'gnp'; arima P D Q
forecast 3. to obtain forecasts
```

The IDA package provides a very user-friendly means of diagnosing data, necessary for Box–Jenkins analysis. Data files for IDA can be built within the package (you have to enter the data at the terminal) or read. IDA stores files with command FSAV in binary form. IDA is highly interactive. You get what you ask for. The help routines are excellent, although pretty wordy. It always asks if you want an explanation. You usually learn to respond no.

IDA   accesses the IDA package
BOUT   creates an output file for printing. You print this file for output.
HELP   gives you a help menu

DATA AND EDITING
ENTE   to enter data you can select TERMinal or FILE
  (for FILE, if built by FSAV say yes;
  if not (like SAS data file) use free format)
PRTS   print some of the data—it asks for rows, columns
CHGO   to change one observation—it asks for row, column
FSAV   saves data file in binary form

DIAGNOSIS
PLTS   plots data on a normalized scale to detect trend, cycles
PACF   provides partial autocorrelation factors for P terms (lag about 12)

ANALYSIS
BOXJ   runs Box–Jenkins—you need to specify P, D, Q

(use all observations	P—from PACF
nonseasonal data	D—trend difference term
	(0—no trend
ask for constant	1—linear trend
standard options	2—quadratic trend)
maximum of 50 iterations)	Q—moving average terms

When you have finished all your models,
RECO   unsuppresses predictions
PRTS   print rows for future values (the BOXJ predictions)

Based upon Ling and Roberts (1982).

INTERPRETATION

MPLS   multiple plot of actual versus predicted indicates fit
                (enter type and date, narrow option, standard options)

QUIT   PRINT output file named in BOUT above

You can use BOUT to create a new output file any time. Everything that happens on the screen (except questions) is stored.

IDA's strength is Box–Jenkins diagnosis. You can use it for regression, but SAS is better. For Box–Jenkins, you only need the dependent variable entered. You can use DIFF to analyze trend, and try to predict which D parameter will work best, but with less than 100 observations, the gain from detrending will often be overwhelmed by the cost of losing the observation. If there are regular cycles to the data, Q terms can be used. With small, annual data sets, Q of 0 is usually best.

Linear Programming

Linear programming is a technique that has proven extremely useful in business decision making. The essential concept underlying linear programming models is optimization. If a decision-making problem can be modeled in linear programming form (and a rather rigid set of assumptions are met), a mathematical solution to this system yields the best possible decision. This usually involves allocation of limited resources to alternative uses. The biggest drawbacks to this very promising technique are that the decision problem must be expressed in linear functions, and because the very best possible solution is sought, minor changes in assumed coefficient values can have a drastic impact upon the resulting solution.

This chapter will present:

- How linear programming models can optimize a system
- What kinds of business problems can be modeled with linear programming
- What assumptions are required in a linear programming model
- What complications can arise in the solution of linear programming models
- What sensitivity analysis can provide, as well as its limitations
- How solutions requiring integer values for specific variables can be obtained

APPLICATIONS OF LINEAR PROGRAMMING

Linear programming models are useful in a variety of applications (Figure S2.1). The petroleum industry has long relied upon linear programming models to aid in production scheduling. This industry faces a wide variety of refining

Diet Models – How much of each ingredient to include
>   Minimize cost of ingredients such that nutritional requirements met

Capital Budgeting – What to invest in at what time
>   Maximize return subject to budget limits, cash flow requirements

Product Mix – What to produce
>   Maximize profit subject to budget and resource limits

Blending Models – What to produce with what ingredients
>   Maximize profit subject to resource limits and contract requirements

Work Scheduling – How many people work what times
>   Minimize cost subject to adequate staffing

Inventory Models – What to produce to stock or purchase at what time
>   Minimize cost subject to having sufficient stock available by time

Crop Planning – What to plant at what time
>   Maximize profit subject to restrictions by location

Media Planning – What to advertise where and when
>   Maximize exposure subject to budget limitations

Input/Output Models – "optimal" assignment of production responsibilities

Least Absolute Value Regression – Minimize first–order error metric

Figure S2.1
Example linear programming applications.

options, well-defined limits to production, and a highly dynamic decision environment. Other classes of problems can be modeled with linear programming. Transportation models, assignment models, and critical path scheduling models could all be solved with linear programming. There are, however, more efficient means of solving these special classes of problems than the conventional linear programming solution technique (simplex). The types of decisions that can be analyzed are limited by imagination, as well as by the need to assure that the required assumptions for linear programming are valid in the situation being modeled.

Linear programming is highly effective for product mix decisions, as demonstrated in the following application. This decision involves determining the quantity of each of a variety of possible products to produce each day. Through a linear programming model, this complex decision can be made not only much more rapidly, but also much more effectively.

DAIRYMAN'S COOPERATIVE CREAMERY ASSOCIATION
Sullivan and Secrest (1985)

Dairyman's Cooperative Creamery Association (DCCA) implemented a microcomputer system to aid its daily production planning and inventory forecasting of operations. Before the DSS, these activities required four hours per day of intensive hand calculations. This decision had to consider uncertainties in both the amount of raw material available each day, as well as the demand for DCCA's products. Sales demand was less a problem, because the government had a program to purchase surplus milk, in the form of butter, cheese, or powder. But DDCA felt it was very important to meet customer demand.

DCCA was the largest single milk-processing plant at one location in the United States. It received about five million pounds of raw milk per day, which was stored in silos and transferred to different production stations.

About 50 dairy products were produced. However, there was some degree of relationship between the amounts of various products. If cheese was processed, there were also whey, salty whey, fines, and scrap cheese. Some of these products were inputs for other products. Whey was transformed into whey protein slurry, whey protein powder, whey cream, and lactose. Whey cream, in turn, went to the cream process department. The output from the cream process department was input for the butter department, affecting buttermilk quantity, and other departments down the line.

Plant supervisors were responsible for allocating and estimating milk flow demand and supply. Total storage, available storage, equipment capacities, personnel limitations, maintenance requirements, customer demands, and quality levels had to be considered in this allocation decision. All of these factors varied on a daily basis.

Problem

DCCA experienced rapid growth, resulting in a larger organization and the need for closer, timely communication between supervisors and production managers. It was difficult to accurately estimate expected levels of various milk by-products, due to the complex interrelationships between products. Operations were scheduled in an ad hoc manner.

Daily decisions included production levels by product, equipment allocations, personnel assignments, transportation arrangements, and other decisions.

Data Collection

At 4:00 a.m. each day, information was available including:

Accurate estimates of milk to be received that day

The exact quantity of milk to be pumped to the cheese plant

Rough estimates of milk, skim milk, condensed milk, and cream to be shipped to outlets

Accurate estimates of required production for cottage cheese, cream cheese, sour cream, yogurt, whipping cream, half-and-half, whey products, butter, and buttermilk

Exact levels of current inventory

A microcomputer preprocessing system was developed to elicit this daily information. Once entered, the user could review these values and make changes.

Alternative Generation

The system converted the daily input information into coefficients in a 36-constraint linear programming model. Constraints included product flow input/output balancing requirements, product conversion constraints, and equipment and inventory capacity limitations. The objective function of this model was to maximize the evaporator utilization capacity, because most products pass through this bottleneck operation. This had the affect of pulling milk flow through the various operations. One reason that profit was not used was that the government surplus purchase program made that function less important.

The solution to this linear programming model provided a suggested production schedule. Linear programming is the most common means for a decision support system to generate an alternative. For most other techniques, human generation of alternatives is necessary.

Alternative Evaluation

Sensitivity analysis could be provided, but it was found that it was more effective to allow decision makers to rerun the model with what-if assumptions. One difficulty with sensitivity analysis was that supervisors found it too complicated.

Decision

Plant supervisors made the decision when they were satisfied with their analysis. The time required was about 15 minutes to enter daily data, about 10 minutes for the linear programming model to be solved, and some time for what-if analysis. The four-hour manual decision was reduced to less than one-half hour.

Implementation

The DSS was designed with the cooperation of DCCA personnel. They defined specifications for the system and feedback on the user interface, as well as the model structure. This gave the supervisors a sense of ownership of the system.

Monitoring

Plant supervisors could adjust the daily plan to account for unforeseen changes. It was found that the system forced supervisors to be explicit about objectives and to quantify and record data in a systematic manner.

The system was critiqued by plant supervisors, some of whom had been involved in production planning for over 20 years. The system was judged to be sound and intuitively pleasing.

Use of the system resulted in increased daily plant throughput by an estimated 150,000 pounds per day. Conservatively, this yielded an estimated $200 per day increased profit, for 240 days per year. Additional benefits were that supervisors had more time for other responsibilities, which improved operations in many other ways. Overall, these benefits were judged to increase DCCA profits by about $100,000 per year. The system cost very little to build, as an available microcomputer system was used.

Comments

This system is what we view as an excellent demonstration of the ability to develop decision support systems. The model was basically a standard linear programming model. In fact, the project was built by an MBA student, as part of his course project requirements. Many organizations face situations where complex decisions have been made for decades without the aid of a readily available means of analysis. Linear programming is especially attractive, in that solutions optimizing an objective function can be developed in total detail very quickly. This makes it an **optimization** DSS in Alter's taxonomy.

The features that made this system more than just a linear programming application included the interactive elements, allowing supervisors to input daily data very quickly, as well as the ability to conduct what-if analysis. Because the model ran very quickly, the simple approach of changing model parameters and rerunning the model was highly appropriate. Another feature was that users played a major part in developing the system. This not only provided a more accurate system, but made it easier to implement.

Decision support systems presented in the literature tend to be involved operations, requiring substantial coordination and development time. We would propose there is probably more benefit in millions of small systems, dealing with relatively small problems, each improving operations a little bit. The combined impact of many small systems will probably outweigh the sum total of major systems.

MODEL COMPONENTS AND ASSUMPTIONS

To demonstrate what a linear programming model consists of, assume an automobile manufacturer needs to schedule the number of automobiles to produce for each style it manufactures. The model and its solution are given in the Appendix and can be referred to in order to follow the explanation throughout the chapter. There are a number of decisions (nearly infinite) that could be made. But the decision is limited by the available resources, the maximum expected demands, and the requirements to produce minimum quantities to meet contracted commitments. The objective of the decision is to produce the combination of vehicles that would yield the greatest profit to the firm.

Components

Linear programming models consist of variables, functions in terms of these variables, and limits to the functions. To build a linear programming model of a decision problem, it is usually easiest to concentrate upon the decision to be made. Those things that are within decision maker control are usually the appropriate decision variables. In the automobile case, the decision is how many vehicles by style. Another element that often helps the modeler is to identify the objective of the decision. Usually, this will be profit. The objective, in order to be useful, needs to be expressed as a linear function. The variables are those problem elements within decision maker control that contribute to profit. If there is difficulty identifying decision variables, sometimes thinking about how profit can be measured helps that identification. The last element of the model is the set of limits to the decision. Linear programming is very flexible in allowing the modeler to impose any limits to the decision, as long as each limit is expressed in linear form. It is possible to limit the decision so much that there is no possible way to satisfy all the limits (infeasibility). If that happens, the crux of the decision will be what limits have to be released. The reverse occurs when important limits are omitted. If the resulting model solution seems impractical, the outrageous features of the solution provide clues as to the missing limits.

Variables

The variables are very often the levels of entities within the control of the decision maker. Other variables can be function levels, such as the variable SUM in the demonstration model. Variables, as the name implies, are allowed to take on different values. Some LP models require specific variables to take on specified values, either general integer or 0–1. As far as modeling is concerned, this is no problem; simply specify which variables have which restrictions. Requirements for integer or zero–one variables cause significant problems for solution, but this can be left to the computer. In the example, there are eight types of cars (Figure S2.2).

Functions

Functions are mathematical statements measuring something in terms of the variables. Profit is an example of a function. In order to measure a functional value, we must know the rate of contribution of each variable unit to the function. In the case of profit [function 1], we need to know how much profit the automobile company can expect from each car, by style. Functions can be

Variable		Class	Minimum	Maximum	Profit Rate
MINI	Small car	Small	300	1500	500
CPE	Coupe	Small	200	3000	550
HB	Hatchback	Medium	500	2000	550
MID	Midsized car	Medium	300	5000	600
SW	Station wagon	Medium	100	1000	800
VAN	Van	Large	100	2000	900
LUX	Luxury	Large	50	1200	1000
PIG	Super luxury	Large	10	500	2000

Figure S2.2
Automobile model variables.

limited to form constraints. Constraints can be equalities ($=$), less than or equal relationships ($\leq$), or greater than or equal relationships ($\geq$). If contracts had been signed to provide a minimum number of cars by style, the linear programming model could be constrained to force those minimum levels to be met by the solution [constraints 2) through 9)]. One constraint would be required for each variable with a minimum level of attainment. The function in this case would simply be the limited variable. The same can be done to limit the decision to stay at or below maximum demand levels [constraints 10) through 17)].

Resource limitations can be included, such as the number of engines by size [constraints 18) through 20)], the amount of chrome [constraint 21)], plastic [constraint 22)], or labor available [constraint 23)] (Figure S2.3). A

Resource	Limit	Units
Small engines	1000	
Medium engines	2000	
Large engines	500	
Chrome	10000	Tons
Plastic	25000	Cubic feet
Labor	120000	Labor–hours

Figure S2.3
Resource limitations—car model.

major benefit of linear programming is the ability to impose any limit on the model, as long as the limits include only linear functions. The auto company may have a policy that no more than 40 percent of its production be small cars (variables MINI, CPE, and HB). The function representing small cars can be constrained to be less than or equal to 40 percent of another function, representing the total number of cars. Constraint 24) defines the variable SUM, whereas constraint 25) limits the decision to include at most 40 percent small cars.

Assumptions

A key element of linear programming models is the set of assumptions required. These assumptions are **linearity, certainty,** and **continuity.** It is not necessary to assume a single objective, although it must be realized that the optimal solution obtained is only optimal with respect to the function used as the objective.

Linearity: All functions must be linear. Often, this is no problem. It seems reasonable to assume that each hatchback car will use the same quantities of resources. Each car will also be expected to use approximately the same number of labor-hours. The function would not truly be linear, however, if there were economies of scale available. This could happen with labor-hours, although if the decision produced by the model is not significantly different from current operations, the resulting nonlinearity should not be important. One function where nonlinearity may be a problem is the objective function of profit. If the company is large enough to be able to influence the sales price with large increases in volume, diminishing returns to scale could result. This would lead to a nonlinear profit function. Here, again, this will not be a problem if the quantity in the solution is not too large relative to current production.

Certainty: The resulting LP solution will be optimal *if* the coefficients used are correct. A general linear programming model can be expressed as

$$\text{Maximize} \quad \sum_{j=1}^{n} c_j x_j$$

$$\sum_{j=1}^{n} a_{ij} x_j \leq b_i \quad \text{for } i=1 \text{ to } m$$

$$x_j \geq 0 \quad \text{for } j=1 \text{ to } n$$

There are three classes of coefficients in this model. If the contribution coefficients c_j are estimates, or are random variables, you will get a feasible solution, but you are not guaranteed the best possible solution. If the coefficients b_i (right-hand-side values) or the technological coefficients a_{ij} are estimates with some variance, the solution may not be feasible when implemented. There is a certain degree of sensitivity analysis which can be conducted to determine how much the c_j or b_i coefficients can vary before it makes any difference. We will examine sensitivity analysis in the next section. There is also a limited amount of sensitivity analysis that can be accomplished if the a_{ij} coefficients vary. This is beyond the scope of this book. The important thing to remember about certainty is that *the validity of the resulting solution depends on the accuracy of the model coefficients*. Even if a coefficient varies a bit, the resulting solution may be useful.

Continuity: Linear programming solutions are generally obtained with the simplex technique. This technique converts all constraints to equalities by adding slack or surplus variables. The resulting solution will be a set of variable values which simultaneously solve the entire set of equations that have the greatest (or if minimizing, the least) objective function value. Because the variable values are the result of simultaneously solving equations, the optimal solution may well contain fractional values. In the demonstration model, for instance, a solution of 413.5 minicars may result. Such a solution may not be possible. A feasible solution can usually be obtained by rounding, to either 413 or 414 minicars. However, the best solution containing only integer decision variable values is not necessarily a solution with these values. This is especially a problem for variables that have to be either 0 or 1 (for instance, do a project or do not). Sometimes, the existence of noninteger solution values does not matter. One week you could schedule 413 cars, and the next week you could schedule 414 cars. If it does make a difference, there are solution techniques that guarantee integer or zero–one decision variable values.

Complications

Solution of a linear programming model can yield a number of results. The possible results can be viewed as a tree (Figure S2.4). The first branch is for **feasibility.** If all goes well, the model is feasible. If the constraint set includes conflicting constraints, there is no possible solution to the model. This is hopefully because one or more constraints were included that were too tight. In the automobile model, if at least 3,000 small cars (mini) were specified, this would be infeasible, because there are only 1,000 small engines available [constraint 18)]. Something would have to give. Either fewer minis or more small engines would be necessary. As it is, there is no problem. The model is feasible, with the result given.

The next branch of possible model outcomes is **boundedness.** If you have a simple model with the objective of maximizing $A + B$ subject to $A \leq 10$, there is an unlimited objective function value. B could increase infinitely. An **unbounded** solution is usually due to a missing constraint, and if the computer solution indicates an unbounded solution, this is a clue to the modeler to add some missing limit to the model. The automobile example is bounded, and no problem exists. In fact, all eight decision variables are individually limited. The variable SUM (used to measure the total number of vehicles) is not directly limited, but constraint 24) effectively limits that variable as well.

Figure S2.4
Possible linear programming results.

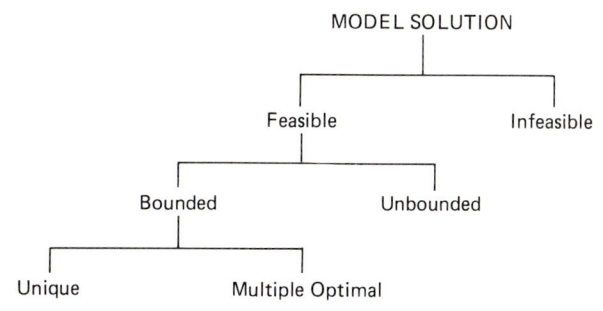

The final branch of possible outcomes is the number of optimal solutions. We would normally expect one best (**unique optimal**) solution. Linear programming guarantees us the best objective function value to a model. There may, however, be more than one solution yielding that optimal value (**multiple optimal solutions**). In the automobile model solution, we are given the value of each model variable, telling us that if we accept the model assumptions, we can expect a profit of $2,607,470 if we schedule production to make the given levels of automobiles. The variables MINI, VAN, and LUX are set at the minimum required. Variable SW (station wagons) is set at its maximum. All other vehicles are somewhere between those limits.

Detection of multiple optimal solutions: The solution includes reduced costs for decision variables, indicating how much the objective function coefficient for each decision variable must increase before another solution would be superior to this one. In addition, the output includes values for slack and surplus variables, which tell us how much each $\leq$ constraint is below the limit (slack), and how much each $\geq$ constraint is above its limit (surplus). The slack for the maximum demand for station wagons (SW) is 0, because the suggested solution is at the maximum limit [constraint 14)]. The equivalent of a reduced cost is the **dual price** (also called shadow price or marginal value). The dual price also represents how much the objective function coefficient for the slack/ surplus variable would have had to increase before the optimal solution (the decision) would change. Of course, slack and surplus variables do not have objective function coefficients. But the dual price can be interpreted as the marginal value of resources for $\leq$ constraints, and the marginal cost of $\geq$ constraints. Note that in the example, the dual prices for $\geq$ constraints are either 0 or negative, and the dual prices for $\leq$ constraints are either 0 or positive. The dual price indicates the rate of change in the objective function per unit change in the constraint right-hand side.

There is a great deal of valuable interpretation available from dual prices, which we will cover in the next section. At this stage, we need the dual price to indicate whether or not there are multiple optimal solutions to the model. All variables that are included in the solution have reduced costs/dual prices of 0, because they *are* part of the solution. Note that this is true in the automobile model solution. We had 8 decision variables in our model and 24 constraints (inequalities plus one equation). The solution technique would create 24 new variables to convert these constraints to equalities [including constraint 24), which already was an equality]. Thus there would now be a system of 24 equations in 32 variables. Mathematically, this set of equalities can be solved by taking any 24 of the 32 variables, and there will be one solution (m equations in m unknowns). The other 8 variables would have values of 0. If the solution values included any negative values, the model would be infeasible. However, the solution could include variable values of 0, even though those variables were part of the solution set. The set of 24 variables that are part of the simultaneous solution are called **basic** variables. The other eight variables are **nonbasic.** Multiple optimal solutions occur when nonbasic variables have reduced costs/ dual prices of 0. To determine if there are multiple optimal solutions, first look for variable values (decision and slack/surplus) of 0 along with corresponding reduced costs/dual prices of 0. If there are no such cases, there is a unique optimal solution. If there are zeros in both columns for a variable, you need to count the number of nonzero variable values (decision and slack/surplus) and compare it with the number of constraints. If there are fewer nonzero variable values than constraints, there would have to be a basic variable with zero solution value. Because it would be a basic variable, its reduced cost/dual price would be 0. In this case, there would still be a unique optimal solution. Multiple optimal solutions exist when a **nonbasic** variable has a zero reduced cost/dual price. It should be noted that detection of multiple optimal solutions is much more straightforward if you have the final simplex tableau available. For large problems, this can be extremely bulky, however, and very often you do not have that information.

Actually, multiple optimal solutions are opportunities rather than problems, because their existence would indicate more than one way to obtain the best possible outcome (as measured by the objective function). The decision maker would have added flexibility.

Additional complications: Linear programming solution codes take care of inserting the slack and surplus variables and obtaining the optimal solution. They work very efficiently in general, although most codes have difficulty with very large models (tens of thousands of variables and thousands of constraints). In general, the larger the model, the longer it takes on the computer. In addition, because computers work in binary terms, rounding becomes a problem for large models. There is one potential source of severe problems, however. **Degeneracy** can occur when more than two constraints intersect at the same point. What happens is that the reduced costs/dual prices are not dependable, and the solution method could actually cycle. Most codes have been written to minimize the risk of cycling. But care must still be taken with interpretation of reduced costs/dual prices. Potential degeneracy occurs when basic variable values of 0 exist.

SENSITIVITY ANALYSIS

Sensitivity analysis refers to determining how much any one coefficient could change before model results would change. We will review the major elements of sensitivity analysis, which should indicate to you how little change would be necessary to have an impact on a linear programming solution. This is because optimization by nature yields extreme solutions. Any change in assumed model coefficients is liable to have dramatic impact.

There are some important limits to sensitivity analysis. You can tell what will happen to the optimal solution if any model coefficient changes with the important limitation that *all* other model coefficients remain the same. If more than one coefficient were to change, more thorough techniques, such as parametric programming, would need to be applied. But that implies an enormous number of linear programming solutions, covering all expected coefficient value combinations. The sensitivity analysis we will discuss assumes only one coefficient change at a time. We will discuss changes in contribution rates c_j and right-hand-side values b_i. More advanced techniques are required to analyze the impact of changes in technological coefficients a_{ij}.

Reduced Costs

Reduced costs are by definition the amount that a decision variable contribution coefficient must improve before that decision variable would be introduced into the solution. In effect, a reduced cost is how much a product is underpriced. For minimizations, it is how much a variable is overpriced. In the automobile example, all reduced costs for decision variables are 0, because each of the eight models is included in the solution. Nonzero reduced costs are only possible for nonbasic variables.

The ranges of reduced costs include information concerning how much the c_j could change before the optimal solution (decision variable values) would change. Note that the objective function would change with any change in c_j of a variable with a solution value greater than 0. If the contribution of MINIs increased from its current value of $500 per car to $510 per car, the contribution coefficient would still be within the indicated allowable range of an increase of $16.28. The change in c_{mini} would be $+10$, which is less than 16.28. This implies that the optimal decision would remain the same. However, the objective function would increase by $3,000 to $2,610,470, because the optimal decision still would include 300 MINIs. The important point is that you should continue to produce exactly the same schedule of cars, because there is no other schedule that will yield more profit. All other solution elements, however, are likely to change, such as the objective function value, the reduced costs, and possibly the dual prices for constraints.

Each c_j for each decision variable has an allowable increase and an allowable decrease. Within this range, the optimal solution (not necessarily the optimal objective function value) will remain the same. For VANs, the current

c_j of \$900/VAN could increase by over \$965 (to \$1,865+) or decrease to negative infinity, before a new solution would be optimal. What this implies is that the profit rate for vans could be a loss of \$8,000 per vehicle, and the optimal solution would remain the same. This is because the optimal decision is to produce the minimum required number of vans (100). You would make a great deal less profit, of course, if vans incurred a loss of \$8,000 each, but this solution would still have more profit than any other solution which could satisfy the model constraint set. On the other hand, if the c_j for VANs increased to \$1,900, there would be a different solution that would be superior to this production schedule. The current schedule would be much better (\$2,707,470) than it is now, but a changed production schedule would be even better. You would need to change the input data and rerun the model to find out what that superior schedule would be. But you can save the effort if the expected change is less than the allowable range.

Objective functions are functions, not constraints. Therefore, the important feature is the relative value of contribution rates. You will get precisely the same result (decision) if you used contribution rates of thousand dollars/car as you would with dollars per car, as long as all of the contribution rates are in common terms. What matters is the relative weights, not the magnitude. Of course, the ranges and dual price information would then be in thousand dollars rather than dollars. Another implication is that if all contribution coefficients were to increase by 5 percent across the board, there would be no change in the optimal decision. Therefore, sensitivity analysis of contribution coefficients is only useful for change in one contribution coefficient, with the exception of the 100 percent rule.

The 100 percent rule provides a small bit of added power to determine if an optimal solution would change under conditions of **multiple** changes in contribution coefficients:

$$\sum_{j=1}^{n} \frac{\text{change } (c_j)}{\text{allowable change}}$$

If the sum of changes in contribution coefficients divided by their allowable changes total no more than 1.0, the 100 percent rule establishes that the current optimal solution would still be optimal given the changes. A tricky part is that if the sum of changes is greater than 1.0, nothing is proven. In that case, you would not know if the current solution would be the same or not.

In the example, if the profit rates for all cars were all dropped \$1, the calculation would be as shown in Table S2.1. In this example, the sum of the ratios is less than 1.0, and we can conclude that the optimal solution would remain the same.

Dual Prices

The dual prices for constraints contain a great deal of information that is highly useful (Figure S2.5). Each constraint limits the model solution. If it were not for

Table S2.1

Variable	Change	Allowable	Ratio
MINI	−1	∞	0
CPE	−1	17.284	.0579
HB	−1	17.160	.0583
MID	−1	966.666	.0010
SW	−1	115.698	.0086
VAN	−1	∞	0
LUX	−1	∞	0
PIG	−1	915.698	.0011
Total			.1269

a particular constraint, it is possible that the objective function would be better. There are two possibilities: The constraint is at its limit (**binding**), or the constraint is not at its limit (**nonbinding**). A nonbinding constraint has slack (for ≤ constraints) or surplus (for ≥ constraints). A nonbinding constraint implies that the slack/surplus variable associated with that constraint is basic. The dual price for a nonbinding constraint is by necessity 0. Because the constraint is not at its limit for the current solution, changing the right-hand side a small amount would have no impact upon the optimal solution. Therefore, the rate of change in the objective function per unit change in the right-hand side would be 0. An example of a nonbinding constraint is constraint 3). This constraint forces the number of coupes to be at least 200. The optimal solution includes 445 coupes. The constraint has a surplus of 245, as indicated in the variable value column for constraint 3). If the contracted minimum were to be increased to 201, there would be no change in the solution. The surplus variable for constraint 3) would decrease to 1, but the decision variables (and the objective function value) would remain the same. Therefore, the rate of change in the objective would be 0 for constraint 3). This is indicated in the dual price column.

    If a slack/surplus constraint is binding, such as labor [constraint 23)], the dual price gives the marginal value of that resource. If 120,001 labor-hours were available instead of 120,000, the objective function would increase by $16.86, the dual price for labor. This implies that at the margin, an extra labor-hour is worth $16.86 more than the current cost of $12/hour. (The profit function is already paying $12/hour.) If the firm could hire extra labor or pay overtime to

---

The definition of a dual price is **the rate of change in the objective function per unit change in right–hand–side coefficient** for a particular constraint.

Figure S2.5

its present employees, at a cost of less than $28.86 per hour, it would increase profit. On the other hand, if the last labor-hour costs more than $28.86, the firm would be better off saving what it pays labor and manufacturing less product. The dual price of $16.86 is marginal and not average. On average, the firm is making $2,607,470 profit (paying $12/hour for labor) per 120,000 hours, or an average profit of $21.73/hour (above the $12 paid for). This is because the first hours are used for required products. Then hours are used for the most profitable product, until that most profitable product is constrained. This goes on, with ever decreasing profit/hour, until the marginal rate of $16.86/hour (above the $12 paid for) applies. The range analysis gives the limits in constraint right-hand sides for which the current dual price applies. The current right-hand side of 120,000 could increase by 3,016, or decrease by 8,450, before the dual price would change. This implies that between 111,550 and 123,016 labor-hours, each labor-hour contributes $16.86 to profit. Below 111,550 labor-hours, the marginal value would be higher. Above 123,016 labor-hours, the marginal value will be lower. The reason is that new combinations of constraints would limit the optimal solution at these labor-hour levels. It should be noted that whereas the dual price is constant over its allowable range, the optimal solution and profit will change with each change in labor-hour levels.

Negative dual prices occur with $\geq$ constraints and possibly with strict equalities. This is because these constraints force variables into the solution, which reduces the more attractive alternatives available in the model. If the dual price is 0, such as constraints 3) through 6), forcing minimum quantities of these cars does not detract from profit, because they were profitable enough to be attractive. However, if it were not for the requirement of 300 minicars, less than that number would have been selected for production. The impact upon the objective function is a loss of $16.28 per minicar. The resources to produce this vehicle could have been used for more profitable alternatives. The dual price of -16.28 applies from 0 to 560.8 minicars. Above 560.8, the rate of change in the objective function can be expected to be worse. The firm would be able to increase profit if it could subcontract work on minicars, even though the production cost was up to $16 higher than the firm's production cost of $1,660/car. Vans and luxury sedans would be even better candidates for subcontracting.

There are two fundamental rules on which all sensitivity analysis is based. Given these, you should be able to deal with a variety of questions for any kind of linear programming solution.

1. **Reduced costs** are the amount that a c_j must improve before it is attractive enough to be part of the basic solution (take on a nonzero value). The optimal **decision** will remain the same as long as any one c_j stays within its allowable range, **and no other model coefficients change.**

2. **Dual prices** are the rate of change in the objective function per unit change in the right-hand-side coefficient. The **dual price** will remain constant as long as the associated b_i stays within its allowable range, **and no other model coefficients change.**

INTEGER AND ZERO–ONE MODELS

In the discussion about the assumption of continuity, we said that simplex was liable to give fractional decision variable values in the optimal solution. For some models, this is unacceptable. For instance, you cannot physically have .48 of a building or buy .85 automobiles.

There is absolutely no problem modeling those cases where integer or zero–one restrictions on the variables are required. Simply specify variables by the appropriate class and add these specifications to the model. There is a problem **solving** these classes of models. Development of generally useful algorithms for either integer or zero–one programming is an area where improvement in algorithms would be extremely useful. We will present two approaches.

Branch and Bound Algorithm

The branch and bound algorithm is a means to logically apply simplex in a chain of models to establish the optimality of an integer (including zero–one) solution. The algorithm begins with identification of the optimal solution to the model where the requirements for integer variable values are relaxed.

Given the model:

$$\begin{array}{llll} \text{Maximize} & 1.2X & + 1.1Y \\ \text{s.t.} & 5X & + 6Y \leq 13 \\ & 4X & + 3Y \leq 9 \\ & X, \ Y \ \{\text{integer}\} \end{array}$$

The initial solution is $X = 5/3$, $Y = 7/9$, with an objective function value of 2.856. This solution is not satisfactory, because it does not give all integer values for the decision variables. It does, however, provide an upper bound on the integer solution. When we add further restrictions, we cannot possibly exceed an objective function value of 2.856.

The next step is to branch on a noninteger decision variable. We arbitrarily select X and create two new models. On branch {A}, the constraint that $X \leq 1$ (the next integer below its current value) is **added** to the original model. On branch {B}, the constraint that $X \geq 2$ (the next integer above its current value) is added to the original model.

For the model on branch {A}, adding the restriction that $X \leq 1$, the optimal solution is $X = 1$, $Y = 4/3$, with an objective function value of 2.667. This is not all integer, so additional branching will be required. We will **add** the constraint that $Y \leq 1$ (retaining the constraint that $X \leq 1$) on branch {A1}, and we will add the constraint that $Y \geq 2$ on branch {A2}.

On branch {A1}, when $X \leq 1$ and $Y \leq 1$ are added to the original model, the result is $X = 1$, $Y = 1$, with an objective function value of 2.3. This is our first **feasible** solution to the original model and provides a **lower bound** to the solution. But it does not prove that this solution is **optimal,** because there may be other branches where the objective function value of 2.3 can be exceeded.

On branch {A2}, with constraints $X \leq 1$ and $Y \geq 2$, the solution is $X = 1/5$, $Y = 2$, and the objective function value is 2.44. Because the objective function value is greater than the current lower bound of 2.3, we must pursue this branch further. Additional branching is required, constraining $X \leq 0$ on branch {A2a} and constraining $X \geq 1$ on branch {A2b}. For branch {A2a}, with $X \leq 0$, the optimal solution is $X = 0$, $Y = 13/6$, requiring additional subbranching. On branch {A2a1}, $Y \leq 2$, whereas $Y \geq 2$ and $X \leq 0$, the solution is integer, with $X = 0, Y = 2$, and the objective function value is 2.2. This is below the lower bound of 2.3, and this subbranch can be abandoned, as nothing better could possibly be encountered. Branch {A2a2} constrained $X \leq 0$ and $Y \geq 3$, which is **infeasible.** This subbranch can also be abandoned, as adding further constraints cannot possibly lead to a feasible solution. Therefore, we have **fathomed** the subbranch where $X \leq 0$.

Branch {A2b} had added constraints $X \leq 1$, $Y \geq 2$, and $X \geq 1$. This is infeasible, fathoming all branches where $X \leq 1$ after the original model.

Branch {B} added the constraint that $X \geq 2$, yielding the solution $X = 2$, $Y = 1/3$, with an objective function value of 2.767. Subbranches of $Y \leq 0$ and $Y \geq 1$ are added. On branch {B1}, $Y \leq 0$, the optimal solution is $X = 2.25$, $Y = 0$, and the objective function is 2.70. Further subbranching is required. When $X \leq 2$ is added to the constraint set on branch {B1a}, the optimal solution is $X = 2$, $Y = 0$, and the objective function value is 2.4, which is not only integer, but has a higher objective function value than the current lower bound of 2.3. Therefore, this solution becomes the current solution, with a new lower bound of 2.4. Branch {B1b} forces $X \geq 3$, which is infeasible.

The last branch, {B2}, forces $Y \geq 1$ whereas $X \geq 2$. This is infeasible, exhausting all possibilities. The optimal solution to the model is the current solution, with $X = 2$ and $Y = 0$ with an objective function value of 2.4. A sketch of the branches, using the notation $[X, Y]$ objective function value, is given in Table S2.2.

An alternative means of solving integer problems is **enumeration.** This is not very practical for most integer models, because although there is a finite number of solutions, this number is liable to be extremely large. But for relatively small zero–one models, enumeration can be quite effective and is the basis for implicit enumeration methods. In this model, enumeration would systematically seek to identify all feasible solutions and select the feasible solution with the best objective function value. One approach would be to count off all possible X and Y values until infeasibility was encountered. As you can see, from Table S2.3, there were six feasible solutions to the model, and both algorithms identified the optimal solution.

Table S2.2

Original Model		
[5/3, 7/9] 2.856		
Branches		

{A}	$X \leq 1$ [1, 4/3] 2.667	
{A1}	$Y \leq 1$ **[1, 1] 2.3**	Lower bound
{A2}	$Y \geq 2$ [1/5, 2] 2.44	
{A2a}	$X \leq 0$ [0, 13/6] 2.383	
{A2a1}	$Y \leq 2$ **[0, 2]** 2.2	Fathomed, below lower bound
{A2a2}	$Y \geq 3$ [infeasible]	Fathoming branch where $X \leq 0$
{A2b}	$X \geq 1$ [infeasible]	Fathoming branch where $Y \geq 2$, and thus branch where $X \leq 1$
{B}	$X \geq 2$ [2, 1/3] 2.767	
{B1}	$Y \leq 0$ [2.25, 0] 2.70	
{B1a}	$X \leq 2$ **[2, 0]** 2.4	
{B1b}	$X \geq 3$ [infeasible]	Fathoming branch where $Y \leq 0$
{B2}	$Y \geq 1$ [infeasible]	Fathoming everything

Table S2.3

X	Y	Feasible?	Objective Function
0	0	Yes	0
0	1	Yes	1.1
0	2	Yes	2.2
0	3	No	
1	0	Yes	1.2
1	1	Yes	2.3
1	2	No	
2	0	Yes	**2.4**
2	1	No	
3	0	No	

SUMMARY

Linear programming is one of the most powerful analytic tools available for decision support systems. LP provides a means to generate solutions with the model that are optimal for the given objective function. Not only is the best possible decision (relative to the objective function) promised, but a great deal of economic interpretation of the limits to the decision is available. However, the conclusions to be drawn from linear programming are highly sensitive to the accuracy of the model. Errors in data, or changes in demands, costs, or resource usage, can make major differences. This is because, by definition, linear programming seeks the very best possible solution, squeezing the last bit of objective function value from the constraint set. Thus, although LP is extremely attractive, it is extremely dangerous. In addition, the assumptions required are more difficult to satisfy.

The objective function used is another source of difficulty. Profit is generally accepted as the paramount concern of business. However, as society becomes more complex, and as we need to think in terms of longer-range impacts of decisions, factors other than profit need to be considered as well. Individual decision makers have always had to balance tradeoffs in objectives, such as profit, satisfaction, living conditions, and so on. Companies are having to consider more complicated combinations of objectives, such as public opinion, reliance upon suppliers, labor relations, and many other elements that do not easily translate to functions compatible with profit.

This chapter did not cover how linear programming models are solved. Computer software is widely available for this interesting, though technical, matter. The value of linear programming for decision making can be accomplished without going through the details of simplex. However, interested parties are directed to sources in the reference list. Additional information is available from Hillier and Lieberman (1900), Swanson (1980), or Winston (1900).

REFERENCES

Hillier, F. S., and G. J. Lieberman. 1990. *Introduction to operations research.* 5th ed. New York: McGraw-Hill.

Schrage, L., 1986. *Linear, integer and quadratic programming with LINDO.* 3rd ed. Palo Alto, CA: Scientific Press.

Sullivan, R. S., and S. C., Secrest. 1985. A simple optimization DSS for production planning at Dairyman's Cooperative Creamery Association. *Interfaces* **15** (5): 46–53.

Swanson, L. W. 1980. *Linear programming: Basic theory and applications.* New York: McGraw-Hill.

Winston, W. L. 1991. *Operations research: Applications and algorithms.* 2nd ed. Boston: PWS-Kent.

PROJECT IDEAS

1. A company in Victoria produces bottles of aspirin products as follows:

Product	Sales Price
Super Seltzer	$3.00
Capsules	$3.50
Cheap Seltzer	$2.00
Tablets	$2.50

The company ships these products to two distributors, located at Hearne and Cuero. There is unlimited demand at each distributor. Shipping costs per bottle and contracted minimum quantities for each distributor are as follows:

		Hearne	Cuero
Shipping cost/bottle		.19	.18
Minimum demand/period	Super Seltzer	700	1000
	Capsules	800	1500
	Cheap Seltzer	1000	800
	Tablets	1800	5000

To produce these boons to humanity, raw materials are purchased at the following costs in the given maximum quantities:

	Cost/Ounce	Maximum Ounces
Acetylsalicylic acid	$.60	70,000
Sodium	$.20	25,000

Production costs per bottle and raw materials required per bottle:

	Production Cost/Bottle	Ounces Acetic Acid	Ounces Sodium
Super Seltzer	$.20	2	3
Capsules	.30	4	0
Cheap Seltzer	.15	2	2
Tablets	.10	3	0

Because capsules have become an insurance problem, the total number of bottles of capsules produced is to be no more than 20 percent of the total number of bottles produced. Model this as a linear programming model and solve to maximize profit.

2. (Sensitivity Analysis) A fertilizer company produces three mixes of product and sells them to a wholesaler. The company uses linear programming to plan weekly production. It can produce any amount and can count on being able to sell it all. The three mixes it produces are imaginatively called A, B, and C.

	Profit ($/ton)	Nitrate (ton/ton)	Phosphate (ton/ton)	Potash (ton/ton)
A (tons)	18.50	.05	.05	.10
B	20.00	.05	.10	.05
C	14.50	.05	.05	.05
Available/week		1,100 tons	1,800 tons	2,000 tons

Model: Maximize profit = 18.5A + 20B + 14.5C

s.t.

$$.05A + .05B + .05C \le 1{,}100 \text{ tons nitrate}$$
$$.05A + .10B + .05C \le 1{,}800 \text{ tons phosphate}$$
$$.10A + .05B + .05C \le 2{,}000 \text{ tons potash}$$

Solution: Objective function value = $428,000

Variable	Reduced Cost	Current Coefficient	Allowable Increase	Allowable Decrease
A 8,000 tons	0	18.50	1.50	4.00
B 14,000 tons	0	20.00	17.00	1.50
C 0	4.00	14.50	4.00	∞
Constraint				
Nitrate 0	340.00	1,100	166.67	200.00
Phosphate 0	30.00	1,800	400.00	500.00
Potash 500	0	2,000	∞	500.00

1. What would the price of C have to be before it would be profitable to produce? Why?

2. If the profit of A were to drop to $17.50/ton, what would the impact on the production schedule be? Can you identify what the weekly profit would be? If so, what?

3. Nitrate currently costs $200/ton (the profit calculation includes this cost). If a nitrate salesperson offered you 100 tons of extra nitrate at the cost of $400/ton, how many, if any, extra tons of nitrate would be profitable to purchase? Assume that you cannot store nitrate.

4. Potash currently costs $160/ton, again, included in the profit. A potash dealer is willing to sell up to 1,000 tons of extra potash for $165/ton, or buy any amount you will sell for $155/ton. Again, you cannot store potash from week to week. Should you buy? How much?

3. (Zero–one Programming—requires linear programming code capable of zero–one solution) You have the responsibility of providing analytic support to a company committee in charge of administering new computer projects. This committee has a budget of $3,000,000 to fund projects. There are four company departments (A, B, C, and D) which have submitted project proposals. Each proposal includes estimates of total cost, number of systems analysts required, number of special programmers required, and estimated cash flow for 1995, estimated 1995 after-tax profit, and net present value. There are 12 systems analysts available and 10 special programmers who could be devoted to these projects. The board of directors has given the minimum required limits for 1995 cash flow and after-tax profits. 1995 cash flow from these projects is to be at least $500,000. 1995 after-tax profits from these projects is to be at least $500,000. The board would like to maximize the net present value of the selected projects, subject to the preceding limits.

Project	Estimated Cost ($1,000)	Systems Analysts (People)	Special Programmers (People)	1995 Cash Flow ($1,000)	1995 After-Tax Profit ($1,000)	NPV ($1,000)
A01	230	3	0	50	40	100
A02	370	4	1	75	60	190
A03	180	2	0	40	35	80
A04	90	1	2	10	15	30
A05	570	4	1	160	150	220
B06	750	3	0	240	220	390
B07	370	3	1	100	80	180
B08	250	3	0	55	50	140
B09	190	2	0	30	20	90
B10	200	1	2	0	10	90
C11	310	2	0	50	30	170
C12	430	3	1	125	120	210
C13	680	3	0	205	200	370
C14	550	1	3	0	20	300
C15	560	1	2	0	30	280
D16	290	1	1	100	80	140
D17	200	1	1	50	40	90
D18	150	1	2	0	10	110
D19	250	1	1	50	35	200
D20	350	1	2	60	50	210

The letter in the project name indicates the department that submitted the project. An additional limit, for political purposes, is that each of these four departments receive funding for at least one project.

Report a solution yielding the maximum net present value, identifying the measures for all other features the committee considered important. Then identify the solution if the budget were cut to $2,500,000, as well as increased to $3,500,000. Report the measures of attainment on all scales for each solution.

4. (Integer Programming—requires linear programming code with integer capability) A space technology company has the opportunity to manufacture precision products in orbit. This precision work can be done more efficiently in a weightless environment, but of course there is a high fixed cost in placing the manufacturing facility in orbit. Two alloys (A1 and A2), two crystals (C1 and C2), and one drug (D) are under consideration. Each product uses limited resources of volume, weight, and labor-hours and each has a different profit rate.

	A1	A2	C1	C2	D
Volume (cubic feet)	9	3	10	7	13
Weight (pounds)	59	18	26	26	10
Labor-hours	2.2	0.5	0.7	0.2	1.1
Maximum demand	22	69	90	40	85
Profit	10	1.7	3.5	1.6	2.6

There are 600 cubic feet of space, 2,100 pounds of weight allowance, and 40 labor-hours available per space flight. Each product can be manufactured in multiple units. Model and solve.

5. (Multiple-Objective Programming) A department store chain is planning to open a new store. It needs to decide how to allocate the 100,000 square feet of available floor space among seven departments. Data on expected performance of each department, in terms of square feet (sf) is:

Department	Invest- ment/sf	Risk as a per- centage of Dollars Invested	Minimum sf	Maximum sf	Profit/sf
Electronics	$300	12%	6,000	25,000	$7.00
Furniture	150	6	10,000	30,000	5.00
Menswear	50	3	3,000	5,000	4.00
Women's clothing	400	15	10,000	20,000	20.00
Jewelry	700	18	2,000	10,000	18.00
Books	120	2	3,000	5,000	1.00
Appliances	250	3	12,000	40,000	6.00

The company has $20,000,000 to invest in floor stock. The risk element is a measure of the risk associated with investment in floor stock. The idea is that electronics loses $12/$100 invested per month, based on past records at other places for outdated inventory, pilferage, breakage, and so on. Jewelry is the highest-risk item. Expected profit is *after* covering risk.

Modeling hint: Treat variables as 1,000 square feet of things. In addition, include a constraint to measure total investment, as well as a constraint to measure dollars at risk. Report investment, square footage, and the average risk ratio for each solution.

First, identify the solution that maximizes profit.

1. You may possibly end up with a solution that does not use all available floor space. If you are trying to maximize profit, how can that be?

2. What rate of interest should the chain consider for the opportunity to obtain additional investment capital? Assume the model deals with monthly operations. For how much additional money would that rate apply?

3. If the company obtains another $1,000,000 of investment capital for stock, what would the solution be? (New solution required.) What would

the marginal value of capital be in that case? (Return to the original model, with $20 million investment.)

4. Some planning committee members are concerned about risk. Identify the solutions (to include investment, square footage, and risk ratio) if risk were to be limited to: 12 percent of investment, 11 percent of investment, and 10 percent of investment.

A small but comprehensive automobile manufacturer has to plan this month's production. The company produces eight styles of vehicle, covering the most popular models of cars. Data is available for the expected maximum number of autos that can be sold by style, as well as committed minimum requirements. In addition, production, cost, and profit data is as given. Other costs include such things as painting, advertising, sales expense, and overhead.

Variables		Contracted Minimum	Maximum Demand
MINI	Small car	300	1500
CPE	Coupe	200	3000
HB	Hatchback	500	2000
MID	Midsized car	300	5000
SW	Station wagon	100	1000
VAN	Van	100	2000
LUX	Luxury sedan	50	1200
PIG	Limousine	10	500

Resource Usage	MINI	CPE	HB	MID	SW	VAN	LUX	PIG
Four-cylinder engines	1	1						
Six-cylinder engines			1	1	1			
Eight-cylinder engines						1	1	1
Chrome alloy (ton)	.1	.2	.2	.3	.4	.4	.7	1
Plastic (CF)	4	4	5	6	8	7	10	12
Labor (labor-hours)	30	32	31	35	40	42	45	50
Production cost/car	1660	2084	2272	2820	3480	3604	5140	6600
Other costs	2440	2566	2578	3080	2720	4496	5860	11400
Sales price/car	4600	5200	5400	6500	7000	9000	12000	20000
Profit/car ($)	500	550	550	600	800	900	1000	2000

Resources	Units	Cost/Unit	Units Available
Four-cylinder engines	Each	$500	1000
Six-cylinder engines	Each	$600	2000
Eight-cylinder engines	Each	$800	500
Chrome alloy	Tons	$4000	10000
Plastic	Cubic feet	$100	25000
Labor	Labor-hours	$12	120000

Model

1) maximize profit =
   500 MINI + 550CPE + 550HB + 600MID + 800SW + 900VAN +
   1000LUX + 2000PIG
   subject to:

2)	MINI $\geq$ 300	10) MINI $\leq$ 1500
3)	CPE $\geq$ 200	11) CPE $\leq$ 3000
4)	HB $\geq$ 500	12) HB $\leq$ 2000
5)	MID $\geq$ 300	13) MID $\leq$ 5000
6)	SW $\geq$ 100	14) SW $\leq$ 1000
7)	VAN $\geq$ 100	15) VAN $\leq$ 2000
8)	LUX $\geq$ 50	16) LUX $\leq$ 1200
9)	PIG $\geq$ 10	17) PIG $\leq$ 500

18) .1MINI + 1CPE $\leq$ 1000
19)   1HB + 1MID +   1SW $\leq$ 2000
22)   1VAN + 1LUX + 1PIG $\leq$ 500
21) .1MINI + .2CPE + .2HB + .3MID + .4SW + .4VAN + .7LUX + 1PIG $\leq$ 10000
22) 4MINI + 4CPE + 5HB + 6MID + 8SW + 7VAN + 10LUX + 12PIG $\leq$ 25000
23) 30MINI + 32CPE + 31HB + 35MID + 40SW + 42VAN + 45LUX + 50PIG $\leq$ 120000
24) MINI + CPE + HB + MID + SW + VAN + LUX + PIG = SUM
25) MINI + CPE + HB $\leq$.4 SUM

Model Solution

1) Profit 2607470   (Objective function:)

Decision	Variables: Solution	Reduced Cost	Current c_j	Allowable Increase	Allowable Decrease
MINI	300	0	500	16.279	∞
CPE	445.64	0	550	17.366	17.284
HB	552.62	0	550	966.666	17.160
MID	447.38	0	600	18.75	966.666
SW	1000	0	800	∞	115.698
VAN	100	0	900	965.116	∞
LUX	50	0	1000	915.698	∞
PIG	350	0	2000	∞	915.698
SUM	3245.64	0	0	279.996	150

Constraint Slack/Surplus Variables:

		Solution	Reduced Cost	Current c_j	Allowable Increase	Allowable Decrease
2)	min MINI	0	−16.279	300	260.802	300
3)	min CPE	245.640	0	200	245.640	∞
4)	min HB	52.616	0	500	52.616	∞
5)	min MID	147.384	0	300	147.384	∞
6)	min SW	900	0	100	900	∞
7)	min VAN	0	−965.116	100	340	100
8)	min LUX	0	−915.698	50	340	50
9)	min PIG	340	0	10	340	∞
10)	max MINI	1200	0	1500	∞	1200
11)	max CPE	2554.360	0	3000	∞	2554.360
12)	max HB	1447.384	0	2000	∞	1447.384
13)	max MID	4552.613	0	5000	∞	4552.613
14)	max SW	0	115.698	1000	135.561	603.333
15)	max VAN	1900	0	2000	∞	1900
16)	max LUX	1150	0	1200	∞	1150
17)	max PIG	150	0	500	∞	150
18)	4 cyl eng	254.360	0	1000	∞	254.360
19)	6 cyl eng	0	16.861	2000	252.994	53.550
20)	8 cyl eng	0	1163.954	500	118.458	42.290
21)	chrome	8811.133	0	10000	∞	8811.133
22)	plastic	3170.058	0	25000	∞	3170.058
23)	labor	0	16.860	120000	3016.668	8449.996
24)	SUM	0	−6.977	0	141.406	396.094
25)	40% limit	0	17.442	0	158.437	56.563

LINDO is available in mainframe and PC versions, with most features common to both systems. You should build a data file containing the linear programming model. For large models, typing errors are inevitable.

For the model:	input file (assume name LINEAR DATA)	
Maximize 2 X1 + 4 X2	MAX 2X1 + 4X2	MAX or MIN or spell out to
subject to	ST	break objective from constraints
1 X1 + 3 X2 ≤ 10	X1 + 3 X2 < 10	do not include =
2 X1 + 1 X2 ≥ 5	2 X1 + 1 X2 > 5	spacing does not matter
1 X1 − 1 X2 = 3	X1 − X2 = 3	
X1, X2 ≥ 0	END	it knows you are done

You can specify 0–1 variables (INT) or integer variables (GIN) after the END statement. The best option is to type INT (or GIN) followed by the variable name for each variable so limited. LINDO only reads 60 columns. You can put a constraint or the objective on as many lines as you want. Constants must be to the right of the relationship, and variables to the left of the relationship.

To run:

LINDO	
:	You can enter input on the screen or read from a file: For file,
TAKE	Enter name of the input file (LINEAR DATA)
:	You can obtain output on the screen or place it in a file: For file,
DIVERT	Enter name of output file (LINEAR OUTPUT)
OPTIONS	
HELP	
LOOK	Prints what it understands the model to be. It needs to know which row you want to see
ALL	You want all rows to proof model (you can select row number if you want—the objective is row 1, the first constraint row 2, etc.)
GO	Tells it to solve the LP model
	It tells you the value of the optimal objective function, or else that the model is unbounded or infeasible
?	Then it asks if you want sensitivity analysis

Based upon Schrage (1986).

	YES
ALTER	You can change any single coefficient in the model You must specify row and column (say RHS if right-hand side) and new value, after which you can LOOK or GO
PARA	You can parametrically analyze changes in a right-hand side
QUIT	Leave LINDO back to CM

Simulation

Simulation is a way to model almost any situation. Analytic models (identify the proper formulas with the proper coefficients and solve) are preferred as a means of analysis over simulation. However, analytic models require low degrees of complexity (queuing) or high degrees of certainty (LP). Many business decisions have high degrees of complexity and/or uncertainty (risk). Therefore, simulation has proven to be a valuable technique in many business problems, despite the added work involved and the more nebulous results. Furthermore, with the development of faster and more accessible computer facilities, as well as a number of commercial simulation packages, simulation seems to be the fastest-growing means of analysis.

This chapter will present:

□ The process of simulation

□ How computers can be made to generate probabilistic simulations

□ The importance of statistical distributions in simulation modeling

□ The importance of statistical analysis in interpreting simulation results

□ How the variance of simulation output can be reduced

Complexity

If a decision problem was capable of total description in mathematical form, the best possible decision could be identified by solving the system or formula. EOQ formulas allow precise identification of how much to order at a time, if only ordering and carrying costs are important. If cost of capital is steady and sufficient cash is available, the net present value calculation can identify the long-range benefit from an investment. The critical path method allows identification of an optimal schedule if the time each event will take is known for certain and ample resources are available. All of these methods deal with problems where there is not a great deal of complexity. Decision making is not difficult if these models apply, because the right way to do things would be to identify the formulation of the system and solve it.

Uncertainty

Business decision making is also interesting because not only does complexity often exist, but uncertainty is usually present to some degree as well. In almost all business systems, data can be collected describing past behavior. That is usually done by identifying the average (mean) performance. Sometimes there is enough consistency in results that the mean is highly representative of what will happen. But often, as in the arrivals in a queuing system, there is a great deal of variance. Queuing models have been derived for straightforward situations (uncertain, but not complex). Scheduling models incorporating some elements of uncertainty have been developed (PERT). Decision trees provide a useful means of analyzing quite simple comparative analyses for simple problems. If a problem is well defined, a mathematical solution would be precise in all these examples. Unfortunately, it is not too hard to encounter a real problem where there is a combination of complexity and uncertainty, or a problem too complex to solve. When that happens, simulation may be the only appropriate means of analysis.

Definition of Simulation

Simulation is the process of *designing a model of a real system and conducting experiments with this model* in order to imitate the real system's behavior, usually with the purpose of evaluating alternative decisions. Although it is possible that simulation could be usefully applied in evaluating the feasibility of a system, as well as gaining further understanding of complex systems, its greatest use in supporting decisions is through comparing alternatives. In that respect, it is unlike linear programming and other methods that seek the very best possible decision (optimization). Simulation is not an optimization technique, but rather compares alternative decision models that have been generated.

Simulation could be conducted without a computer. However, that is generally impractical, because of the large number of samples (runs) required and the detail often used in a simulation model. Simulation is very similar to a scientific experiment. However, experimentation on real things can be very time consuming and expensive. In botany, it takes years for some plants to grow, and the value of a proposed treatment may not be apparent until a number of tests are conducted. In a business, trying out an idea without testing it involves risking vast quantities of money, not to mention people's careers. Computer simulation can provide a way to conduct an abstract experiment. In addition, although you should realize that simulation requires great amounts of knowledge of the system being simulated, great amounts of data collection and model building, and great amounts of computer time, it is often far quicker and less costly than experimentation with the real system.

MONTE CARLO SIMULATION

The overall process of simulation analysis relies upon Monte Carlo means of generating hypothesized events from distributions prescribed by the modeler. Monte Carlo is a term taken from the casino—it is assumed that gambling wheels and other games of chance are unbiased. An unbiased generator is used by the computer to draw from the population of possible events, and one run of a simulation is one possible outcome of a complex system. Because many possible outcomes could occur in such a system, many runs (samples) need to be conducted in order to draw inferences. Therefore, the whole concept of Monte Carlo simulation is essentially to conduct tests over and over, until the results form a pattern sufficient to satisfy the analyst. The need for computer time arises from the need for many repetitions.

Simulation Procedure

Problem formulation: The first step in a simulation is defining the problem and generating alternative solutions (decisions). The simulation you design should allow identification of system performances expected from these alternatives.

Model construction: You next need to develop a series of relationships that mathematically describe what happens in the real system. This involves a series of events that may vary in duration according to specified distributions, as well as contingent rules of what happens under what circumstances. Each alternative is modeled differently. Simulation allows you to model any degree of complexity. Simulation has the residual benefit of teaching the analyst a great deal simply by forcing the model to be built. Ideally, a simulation focuses only on the essential features of the real system, which tends to result in simpler models. Often, however, what seem like minor details make a lot of difference in system performance. Although simulation is the most flexible means of analysis (requires the fewest assumptions), each minor detail left out is a source of danger.

Data collection: Once the system of relationships has been developed, the durations of events need to be determined. As mentioned previously, most often mean times are available for just about any activity. However, the distribution of events is usually critical as well. This requires a more detailed data collection operation.

Verification: Whether you write your own code or use a simulation package, you need to verify that the computer program you use runs as it should. The computer component of a simulation model that usually causes the most problem is verifying that the random-number generator acts as you assume it does. It is also important to verify that the computer maintains relationships as you want.

Validation: In addition to verifying the computer system, models need to be validated. This implies ensuring that the models represent the real system being simulated. This can be difficult, because generally you have high degrees of uncertainty and you expect wildly varying results. Validation refers to assuring yourself that the wild results are due to the uncertainty in the system rather than to an error in the model.

Experimentation: Simulation is an excellent tool for conducting experiments. Each model built is a system design. Each run of a model is a sample. You can expect any one run to be quite different from other runs. If the resulting simulations yield very consistent results, you will not need to run very many simulations. On the other hand, if there is a lot of variance in results, you need to make more simulation runs. The same sampling theory that applied to data collection applies to the number of runs to make in a simulation analysis. The number of samples required depends on the variance of the results, as well as the degree of confidence desired. Because you will not know the variance until you obtain some results, this is often a two-phase operation, with phase 1 being a number of samples used to identify model variance.

Evaluation: Once you have statistics from your experiments and you are satisfied with the stability of the results, you need to evaluate the different system performances. If there was any uncertainty involved (usually the case), this is not a clear-cut conclusion, as would be available from analytic techniques. The outcome of a simulation is a matter of hypothesis testing and probability.

Implementation and documentation: Once you complete your series of experiments, you need to report the results and support recommendations by documenting what you did so that the study can be replicated and all assumptions identified.

Simulation can literally be used to model any situation. It is the fastest-growing technique in practice. It can be incorporated in decision support systems. IFPS and Lotus both have random-number capabilities. An example of simulation use in real decision making is presented here to demonstrate one of the beneficial applications of simulation in a DSS context.

OREGON MOTOR VEHICLES DIVISION
Randhawa, Mechling, and Joerger (1989)

The Oregon Motor Vehicles Division (ODMV) continually evaluates ways to improve customer service. At the time of the study, it had 61 field offices. It has developed a computerized resource-planning system to support personnel planning and scheduling decisions with the intent of improving service. The model used was a flexible discrete-event simulation, allowing what-if analysis to estimate the effects of alternative planning strategies.

A typical ODMV field office conducted 35 to 40 different types of transactions, including renewal of licenses, vehicle registration, driver testing, and issuing of titles and special permits. ODMV has a goal of keeping the average customer waiting time to 15 minutes or less.

The system involved three options for customers entering the field office. There was a self-service counter for customers with straightforward administrative requests, such as address changes and applications for replacement titles. They could go straight to the testing area for driver's license testing and photograph. The third option was to take a number to wait for a motor vehicle representative. Driving tests were usually scheduled in advance. Some customers going to the self-service counter found that they had to see a motor vehicle representative. Others took a number for a representative, but found that they could have gone directly to the self-service counter. The number of representatives working at any time varied by office size and time of day.

Problem

In the summer of 1986, customer waiting times grew to exceed the goal of 15 minutes average waiting time per customer. To resolve this problem, receptionists were used to screen customers to ensure that customers had brought all the required information and to direct them to the appropriate station. However, this did not satisfactorily resolve the problem, as customers often would need to return with additional information.

Data Collection

A survey was conducted in September 1986 to determine customer evaluation of the effectiveness of the receptionist plan. The results indicated that 92 percent of the customers felt that the receptionists helped. However, receptionist performance was highly varied.

The problem was clarified by a model evaluating the impact of receptionists by office size on customer waiting. ODMV subsequently asked for a more general model that could be used to evaluate the impact of receptionists. A stipulation was that the system be usable by managers with no computer or simulation experience.

Technical data concerning the volume of activity and trends was available from ODMV. This data did not include service time distributions. Time study was used to develop this additional information.

Alternative Generation

A microcomputer system was developed allowing managers to set specific what-if conditions. This model was capable of varying office size, volume of business, customer arrival rates and testing volumes, representatives, and impact of receptionists on customer preparation. A simulation package was used to develop an event-oriented or process-oriented model capable of reflecting any combination of ODMV system features.

Alternative Evaluation

A menu was developed that would allow the user to control input of a new data file, edit an existing file, or run the simulation. The system made multiple runs to reduce the variance of the estimated mean of the average waiting time. No knowledge of the simulation package was required of the user. An input option allowed the user to enter data from prompts, including a table by hour of the workday, the number of representatives on duty, customer arrival rates, and the number of driving tests scheduled. Data was then entered to indicate the presence of a receptionist and the expected receptionist impact on an average customer.

The model was validated by regular meetings with ODMV personnel, including visits to field offices and meetings with technical staff. The simulation model was thoroughly verified for internal consistency. Test runs were reviewed by ODMV staff, as well as by senior management.

The output of the model included hourly statistical reports including key information, in an understandable format limited to necessary information. The normal package output was manipulated to consolidate results for the user.

Decision

The field office manager had the ability to conduct what-if analysis on the office's system before making the decision to reorganize the office. This what-if analysis included examination of the impact of various system configurations on waiting times, queue length, and worker utilization.

Implementation

The model was adopted. The implementation process in this case blended with the development of the system, as frequent design meetings and thorough testing of the system were used.

Monitoring

The system was found to result in service improvement levels equivalent to a 9 percent increase in staff availability time. The time required for generating and evaluating feasible assignment alternatives was reduced an estimated 50 percent. The decision now could be based on much more information and additional alternatives considered.

The manager of the Systems and Planning Section of ODMV cited this model as a powerful tool for improving customer service. He estimated the reduction of waste in staff time to be as high as 20 percent. He also stated,

"An advantage that is hard to quantify is 'scenario testing' in a what-if mode. The model has enabled us to test and compare a wide range of policy alternatives, which was not possible before its development. Additionally, the insight we have received during the development and validation of this model has had a significant impact in understanding this decision-making environment and the impact of different variables on the system performance."

This example demonstrates some of the advantages of simulation relative to other quantitative approaches. With simulation, humans can be presented with the operation of the entire system, giving them a much more complete picture of the impact of various alternative systems. Although humans are responsible for developing the alternatives to be evaluated, simulation provides the ability to analyze almost any decision-making problem.

RANDOM NUMBERS

The feature that makes Monte Carlo simulation work is random numbers (Figure S3.1). Models are essentially systems of relationships between entities, controlled by event probabilities or durations, determined by generating a random number and transforming that random number through distributions. Random numbers generated by computer systems are meant to be **uniformly distributed** between 0 and 1.

Without a computer, random numbers could be obtained from random-number tables, dice, or other means. But computers cannot roll dice, nor can they throw darts, nor can they come up with anything other than a well-defined, precise procedure. What is done, however, is a formula is encoded, generally quite complex, which generates a stream of numbers, hopefully with the desired characteristics of no **serial correlation** (no regular patterns of digits following other digits) and an equal opportunity for **runs** of subsequent random numbers going up as going down. They should also have a **long cycle,** in fact in the billions.

To demonstrate the workings of random numbers, consider the calculus problem of determining the area under the curve:

$$Y = X^3 \text{ over the region } X = 0 \text{ to } X = 1.$$

This is a standard calculus problem. The analytic approach would be to integrate the function, as follows:

Figure S3.1
Desired random number features.

TECHNICAL

Uniformly Distributed
Each digit has a .1 probability

No Serial Correlation
There is no relationship between digits and following digits

Digit Randomness
Equal probability of increasing or decreasing runs

Long Cycle
The cycle before the sequence repeats should be as long as possible

PRACTICAL

Fast

Minimize Storage Requirements

Reproducible

Should Not Degenerate

This problem could also be simulated. In fact, simulation has proven useful in integrating complex functions (much more complex than this function). Note that it would be preferable and more accurate to use the integration technique. But accuracy through simulation can be gained through many, many runs.

The simulation procedure would begin with a model. We will build a model that will arbitrarily draw an X over the region of interest, in this case between 0 and 1. We want a uniform distribution. This works out very well, because that is precisely what computer systems generate when asked for a random-number function. The next part of the model will be to calculate the functional value, or in this case, cube X. Next, a Y value will be generated through another random number. In this case, Y could vary between 0 and 1 over the functional region. So again, we will not have to transform the random number. We will count the number of times this Y will be below X^3. The area under the curve will be the proportion of cases where $Y < X^3$ times the total area. Here, the total area is 1 (X ranges from 0 to 1, Y ranges from 0 to 1).

Assume that we simulate this model for 30 runs. The values obtained would be as shown in Table S3.1.

Note that the estimated area from simulation after 10 runs is off. The true answer is known to be .25. (Actually, after 10 runs, it would be impossible to obtain .25, as there is no count that would yield .25 for 10 samples.) But the answer is fairly close. So we take more samples. After 20 samples, six of the Y values were less than the X value cubed. This yields an estimated area of .3 (6/20). This is also off. Even after 30 samples, our estimated area is off. For this type of application, thousands of simulation runs should be run, simply to

Table S3.1

n	Random Number X	$f(X)$ X^3	Random Number Y	$Y < f(X)$?
1	.10480	.00115	.81525	No
2	.15011	.00338	.72295	No
3	.01536	.00000	.04859	No
4	.02011	.00081	.96423	No
5	.81647	.54428	.42206	Yes
6	.91646	.76973	.36086	Yes
7	.69179	.33107	.66566	No
8	.14194	.00286	.14778	No
9	.62590	.24520	.76797	No
10	.36207	.04747	.14870	No 2/10 = .2
11	.20969	.00922	.13300	No
12	.99576	.97844	.87074	Yes
13	.71341	.36309	.79666	No
14	.90700	.74614	.95725	No
15	.76393	.44582	.29676	Yes
16	.46573	.10102	.42607	No
17	.25595	.01677	.68066	No
18	.85393	.62268	.26432	Yes
19	.30995	.02978	.46901	No
20	.89198	.70968	.20849	Yes 6/20 = .3
21	.27982	.02191	.33611	No
22	.53402	.15229	.81536	No
23	.74917	.42048	.30883	Yes
24	.34095	.03964	.12659	No
25	.52666	.14608	.92259	No
26	.19174	.00705	.57102	No
27	.39615	.06217	.80428	No
28	.99505	.98522	.25280	Yes
29	.24130	.01405	.00742	Yes
30	.48360	.11310	.57392	No 9/30 = .3

obtain a reasonable degree of accuracy. But the simulation result, barring biased random numbers, will converge to the correct estimate of .25.

We mentioned that simulation models should be verified, to include assuring that the random numbers generated by the computer are not biased. This could be done here by comparing the actual proportion of random numbers that fell within increments. We will count the X and Y random numbers that fell within the increments given in Table S3.2. Note that a number of counts differ from the expected value of 3 for increments of .1, as well as for the expected value of 6 for increments of .2. This is to be expected. The question is, how much difference is significant?

Test for Uniformity

The basic test used to evaluate random-number generators is the χ^2 test. The formula for χ^2 is

$$\chi^2 = \sum_{i=1}^{m} \frac{(O_i - E)^2}{E_i}$$

where O_i is the observed count in cell i, and E_i is the expected count in cell i. Good form calls for each cell to have the same expected count E_i and an expected count E_i of at least 5. In the previous example, there were expected densities of 3 in each of the 10 cells for both X and Y. This is too low to get a very accurate measure. Therefore, we can group cells with equal expected observations by reducing the number of cells to 5, yielding E_i of 6 for each cell.

The χ^2 calculations for X and Y would be as shown in Table S3.3. Now we need a limit to determine if these χ^2 scores are low enough to accept their coming from a uniform distribution. The χ^2 limits are widely published. The cutoff values for the χ^2 limits are a function of the **degrees of freedom,** as well as the **confidence level.** This test is nonparametric, so it should be used to test a hypothesis. The degrees of freedom are determined by

$$\text{Number of cells} - \text{distribution parameters} - 1$$

Table S3.2

Increment	X	Y	Expected	Increment	X	Y	Expected
0–.1	2	2	3				
.1–.2	4	4	3	0–.2	6	6	6
.2–.3	4	4	3				
.3–.4	4	3	3	.2–.4	8	7	6
.4–.5	2	3	3				
.5–.6	2	2	3	.4–.6	4	5	6
.6–.7	2	2	3				
.7–.8	3	3	3	.6–.8	5	5	6
.8–.9	3	4	3				
.9–.1	4	3	3	.8–1.0	7	7	6

Table S3.3

Cell	E_i	$O_i(X)$	$O_i(X) - E_i$	$(O_i(X) - E_i)^2$	$O_i(Y)$	$O_i(Y) - E_i$	$(O_i(Y) - E_i)^2$
0–.2	6	6	0	0	6	0	0
.2–.4	6	8	2	4	7	1	1
.4–.6	6	4	−2	4	5	−1	1
.6–.8	6	5	−1	1	5	−1	1
.8–1.0	6	7	1	1	7	1	1

$$\chi^2(X) = 10/6 = 1.667 \qquad \chi^2(Y) = 4/6 = .667$$

The number of distribution parameters for the uniform distribution by convention is 0. For the negative exponential distribution, which is defined by the parameter mean, there is one parameter. The normal distribution has two parameters, the mean and the variance. Here, we are testing for a uniform distribution, and therefore the degrees of freedom is 5 cells − 0 parameters − 1 = 4. We will use a confidence level of .95, which implies that we are 95 percent confident that *we are not going to misclassify samples drawn from a true uniform distribution*. Note that this is not the same thing as being 95 percent sure that the distribution is truly uniform. The limit for this case, from a χ^2 table, is 9.488. Note that neither sample fails this test. Here, we **fail to reject** the samples coming from a uniform distribution, because 1.667 < 9.488 for X, and .667 < 9.488 for Y. We expect to reject a sample from a valid distribution once out of 20 times.

There are tests that could be conducted to check for serial correlation. One test would count the number of times each digit followed each digit, or a 10 × 10 matrix of cells, tested again by the χ^2 test. There are also tests for runs, counting the number of cases where subsequent random numbers were larger than their predecessors in a sequence, as well as runs of subsequent random numbers smaller than their predecessors. All told, there are a lot of desired features for random numbers. It is therefore not surprising that most random-number generators fail for one or more reasons.

Computer systems vary in their random-number generating streams, and you may find that if you take the same code and call random numbers from one computer system, you will obtain different results on another computer system. This is not bad in itself, but the quality of the random-number generators on computers is not always very good (they may have some biases and may cycle too quickly). You do have the ability to encode your own random-number generator into a FORTRAN code or other language, but you need to have a formula. An example FORTRAN formula is given as the first project idea at the end of this chapter.

Controlling Random Numbers

Simulation results comparing two alternatives will vary for two reasons: (1) pure luck, or chance, because as you can see from the preceding discussion, the random numbers are likely to be anything; and (2) because the systems were different. Through intelligent use of random-number streams, you can control for chance. By applying the same random-number streams to chance events in two models, you can see how each of the systems behave in the same set of circumstances. In order to do this, you need to keep track of the results by run. For instance, assume you are simulating net profit of two systems. System 1 will yield profit = .5 volume − 1,000, whereas system 2 will have profit = .7 volume − 2,050. Assume that volume is drawn from a distribution. By run, you obtain the results given in Table S3.4. Because system 1 has a higher mean, we expect that it has a higher probability of being the better system. However, we can obtain a more complete estimate of system 1's advantage. Two ways to estimate the probability that system 1 is better than system 2 are available.

Normal Probability

Using the pooled variance of any two alternatives, we can use normal distribution theory to estimate the probability of one alternative being better than the other. This approach would *not* require controlling random numbers:

$$Z = \frac{\mu_1 - \mu_2}{\sqrt{\dfrac{Var_1}{n_1} + \dfrac{Var_2}{n_2}}}$$

$$= \frac{1,450 - 1,380}{\sqrt{\dfrac{386,111}{10} + \dfrac{756,778}{10}}} = .207$$

We can calculate a Z score by this formula and go to a normal table to determine the probability of system 1 having a higher profit than system 2. We *are*

Table S3.4

Run	Volume	System 1 Net Profit	System 2 Net Profit	Winner
1	5000	1500	1450	1
2	3000	500	50	1
3	7000	2500	2850	2
4	4000	1000	750	1
5	4500	1250	1100	1
6	6500	2250	2500	2
7	5500	1750	1800	2
8	3500	750	400	1
9	5000	1500	1450	1
10	5000	1500	1450	1
Mean		1450	1380	
Variance		386111	756778	

assuming that the difference in profits is normally distributed, which may not be true.

We can take the Z score .207 to a normal table and find that the implied probability of system 1 having higher profit than system 2 is .58.

Controlled Random Numbers

Given that we control the random numbers by having precisely the same chance events apply in each situation, we can estimate the probability of system 1 being superior to system 2 more accurately (because we do not have to assume any distribution of relative performance) and with greater ease (all we have to do is count cases). Furthermore, this approach can identify the probability of being best for *any number* of alternatives simultaneously. In this case, we had 10 randomly distributed volumes of business. System 1 outperformed system 2 seven of the ten cases. The probability of system 1 being preferred is therefore .7. Note that in both cases, 10 samples are insufficient for accurate estimation of probability (the intent is to demonstrate the method).

Transforming Random Numbers

We have discussed using uniform random numbers. These can be used directly or applied to empirical distributions, where you prescribe the probability of specific conditions occurring. Quite often, however, the systems being simulated are expected to follow other theoretical distributions. For instance, waiting-line models are expected to have negative exponentially distributed arrivals. Waiting-line services are often assumed to follow either negative exponential or normal distributions.

Uniform random numbers can be converted to other distributions by formula in many cases.

Negative Exponential Distribution

To convert a uniform random number R to a negative exponentially distributed random number NE with mean M (where M is the time per event), the formula is

$$NE = -(M) * \ln(1-R)$$

To demonstrate, assume $R = .1$ and $M = 10$:

$$NE = -(10) * \ln(1-.1) = -10*(-.10536) = 1.0536$$

If $R = .8$,

$$NE = -(10) * \ln(1 - .8) = -10*(-1.60944) = 16.0944$$

The Erlang distribution is also often encountered in queuing theory. It consists of a series of n events in sequence (event b starts when event a is completed and so on), where each of the n events is negative exponentially distributed. The formula to convert n uniform random numbers R_i ($i = 1$ to n) to random number Er following an Erlang distribution with parameters M (mean) and n (shape parameter):

$$Er = -(M) * \ln[(1 - R_1) * (1 - R_2) * \cdots * (1 - R_n)]$$

Normal Distribution

Uniform random numbers can be converted to normally distributed random numbers quite easily by using the normal table. You need to know the mean of the normal distribution M, as well as its standard deviation S. Treat the uniform random number R as the cumulative area under the normal curve. Go to the table and identify the Z score associated with this cumulative area. For uniform random numbers (No) below .5, the formula would be

$$No = M - (Z * S)$$

For uniform random numbers above .5, the formula would be

$$No = M + (Z * S)$$

Getting a computer to convert uniform random numbers to normally distributed random numbers is more complex. One of the most efficient ways is to obtain two uniformly distributed random numbers, R_1 and R_2. This method does not work if the uniform random numbers are too high. Therefore, it is difficult to predict how many uniform random numbers need to be obtained. The method works by the sequence given in Table S3.5.

SIMULATION SEQUENCE

Simulation is often very appropriate for waiting-line situations. Here we assume a waiting-line situation involving negative exponentially distributed ar-

Table S3.5

```
        A = 2 * R₁ − 1
        B = 2 * R₂ − 1
        W = A*A + B*B
        IF W > 1 throw away R₁ and R₂ and draw two more random numbers
        IF W ≤ 1
        No₁ = {A*√(− 2*ln (W)/W)} *S + M
        No₂ = {B*√(− 2*ln (W)/W)} *S + M
Assume random numbers R₁ = .1, R₂ = .7, M = 10, S = 2.
A = (2 * .1) − 1 = − .8
B = (2 * .7) − 1 = .4
W = (− .8)*(− .8) + (.4)*(.4) = .80
W ≤ 1, so proceed
No₁ = {− .8*√(− 2*ln (.8)/.8)} *2 + 10 = 8.805
No₂ = {.4*√(− 2*ln(.8)/.8)} *2 + 10 = 15.598
```

rival with a mean of .2 days between arrivals and three service systems, all with mean times of .2 days per service.

System A: negative exponential service	Cost = 20 per day
System B: normal service (std dev = .05)	Cost = 25 per day
System C: constant service	Cost = 30 per day

We assume that no arrivals occur after 1 day, and no services can go on after 1.1 days have elapsed.

Research Question
The research question is which of these systems is expected to provide the greatest profit, given that revenue is 10 times the number of jobs completed in a day.

Model
We can create a simple system where we use random numbers to generate arrivals. We accept no arrivals after 1 day has elapsed, and to be counted as a revenue-generating job completed, service must be completed before 1.1 days have elapsed. Our systems will all involve one server, with a FCFS priority. Services are determined by converting a uniform random number to the appropriate distribution (Figure S3.2) In this *one* run, system A resulted in the most profit. Note that many more possible days need to be simulated before valid conclusions can be drawn.

SUMMARY

Reasons for Simulation
Now that we have some idea of what simulation is and what is involved in accomplishing a simulation, we need a good reason for undertaking such a large amount of work for such a fuzzy conclusion. If an analytical technique is appropriate and the required assumptions of that technique are acceptable, you should not use simulation. However, a realistic assessment of many decision problems often results in the conclusion that simulation is the proper thing to do. Often the complexities of life are too much to analytically describe. In calculus, some curves are too difficult to integrate. Simulation can be used to determine the area under such curves. And often the assumptions required for linear programming, EOQ models, queuing formulations, PERT, and other analytic techniques are unacceptable. Simulation has been found to be very useful in business. If, after you model and run a simulation, you find a gross distortion in the results, you can always correct the model and rerun it. Simulation is useful because you can model any assumptions you want.

Disadvantages
There are a number of pitfalls to worry about, however. First, simulation is expensive, both in analyst time and in computer time. Second, as a scientific

SIMULATE:
Generate arrivals:

Uniform Random Number		Simulated Arrival Time
.7	−.2*(ln[.3]) = .241	.241 days
.3	−.2*(ln[.7]) = .071	.312
.5	−.2*(ln[.5]) = .139	.451
.6	−.2*(ln[.4]) = .183	.634
.1	−.2*(ln[.9]) = .021	.655
.9	−.2*(ln[.1]) = .461	1.116 (exceeds 1 day)

Therefore, we have five arrivals.

Determine services:

Uniform Random Number	A	B		C
.8	−.2*(ln[.2])= .322	.2+.842[.05]	= .242	.2
.2	−.2*(ln[.8])= .045	.2−.842[.05]	= .158	.2
.6	−.2*(ln[.4])= .183	.2+.253[.05]	= .213	.2
.5	−.2*(ln[.5])= .139	.2+0	= .2	.2
.1	−.2*(ln[.9])= .021	.2−1.282[.05]	= .136	.2

Arrival:	A	B	C
.241	.241+.322 = .563	.241+.242 = .483	.241+.2 = .441
.312	.563+.045 = .608	.483+.158 = .641	.441+.2 = .641
.451	.608+.183 = .791	.641+.213 = .854	.641+.2 = .841
.634	.791+.139 = .930	.854+.200 = 1.054	.841+.2 = 1.041
.655	.930+.021 = .951	stop – 4 jobs	stop – 4 jobs
	end – 5 jobs		

Evaluation (profits):

A	B	C
+50−20 = +30	+40−25 = +15	+40−30 = +10

Figure S3.2
Example waiting line simulation.

experiment, sampling error is a problem. Third, the output you get from simulation is descriptive rather than optimal. If you did a bad job of generating alternatives, far better decisions may have been overlooked. Fourth, just about every application requires a new model to be constructed. Although packages (such as SLAM or SIMAN) exist which make modeling easier, complex problems still require significant effort. Finally, thorough understanding of the real problem is necessary. The process of building the simulation model provides a great opportunity for learning about the real problem, but the potential for overlooking crucial elements exists.

Simulation is highly important because of its flexibility. Just about any problem can be analyzed through simulation. However, if there is any alternative technique that is appropriate for a given problem, the alternative technique should be selected.

Other references for simulation include Pegden (1972), Pritsker (1986), and Watson and Blackstone (1989). Forrester (1971) presents an interesting application of simulation.

REFERENCES

Forrester, J. W. 1971. *World Dynamics*. Cambridge, MA: Wright-Allen.

Pegden, C. D. 1982. *Introduction to SIMAN*. State College, PA: Systems Modeling Corp.

Pritsker, A. A. B. 1986. *Introduction to Simulation and SLAM II*. New York: Halsted.

Randhawa, S. U., A. M., Mechling, and R. A., Joerger. 1989. A simulation-based resource-planning system for the Oregon Motor Vehicles Division. *Interfaces* **19** (6):40–51.

Watson, H. J., and J. H. Blackstone, Jr. 1989. *Computer Simulation*. 2nd ed. New York: John Wiley & Sons.

PROJECT IDEAS

1. You are to generate 100 random numbers, using any system you have available. BASIC is the easiest.

BASIC:

```
x = rnd
```

FORTRAN: (you need a function)

```
FUNCTION RND (IXX)
INTEGER A,P,IXX,B15,B16,XHI,XALO,LEFTLO,FHI,K
DATA A/16807/,B15/32768/,B16/65536/,P/2147483647/
XHI = IXX/B16
XALO = (IXX-XHI*B16)*A
LEFTLO = XALO/B16
FHI = XHI*A + LEFTLO
K = FHI/B15
IXX = (((XALO-LEFTLO*B16) -P) + (FHI-K*B15) *B16) +K
IF (IXX.LT.0) IXX = IXX + P
RND = FLOAT (IXX) *4.656612875E-10
RETURN
END
```

Convert these random numbers to the following.

Negative exponential distribution with mean of .5:

BASIC:

```
n = -(.5)*log(x)
```

FORTRAN:

```
en = (-.5)*dlog(x)
```

Normal distribution with mean of .5 and standard deviation of .1:
BASIC:

```
a = 2* x  -1
b = 2*  x  - 1
c = a*a + b*b
if c > 1 then (start over
        —note you do not know how many you get)
rn1 = (a*(- 2*log (c)/c)*std + mean
rn2 = (b*(- 2*log (c)/c)*std + mean
```

Test for fit:
Use the χ^2 test.

2. Snidely Whiplash Enterprises is a printing outfit located to service the need for rapid disk typing near a courthouse with a lot of contract activity. Customers need copies very quickly, and if they do not get rapid service, they will leave. On average, a customer comes in with a job every 40 minutes. Snidely Whiplash has rather poor relations with the owner of the building, and if he opens before 9 a.m. or after 5 p.m., the security guards have instructions to shoot him on sight. Therefore, the working day is exactly 8 hours per day. There are 250 working days per year.

The jobs customers bring in vary in size. The mean number of pages to copy is 42, with a variance of 7 pages. This data is normally distributed. Revenue averages $50/job. The variable cost per job varies by alternative.

The time it takes to do a job is a function of the printer system. Currently, SWE has one letter-quality printer, which is not keeping up with available business. Alternative systems are under consideration, with annualized costs and expected operating times:

	Cost/Year Average	Time/Job	Variance/Job	Variable/Job
1. Laser printer	$10,000	6 minutes	1 minute	$8
2. Inkjet printer	$2,000	45 minutes	7.5 minutes	$6
3. Two letter quality	$1,000	54 minutes	9 minutes	$5
4. Two URN	$2,000	60 minutes	10 minutes	$6

Your job is to conduct a cost analysis of this situation. The four alternatives are given previously. Alternative 3 is to purchase a second letter-quality printer and run both. All other systems involve trading in the current printer. Report expected costs and other factors for each alternative.

Base your analysis on 30 simulation runs without random-number control, as well as another 30 runs controlling random numbers. In your report, first analyze your output with the probability of making the right decision (based on the controlled random-number output). In addition, report on the differences between the uncontrolled and controlled output.

Take the results you get and conduct an analysis of the four alternatives determining the expected profit from each alternative. For each method, estimate the probability of a particular system being best. You should make eight total runs (two for each model).

Glossary

analytic hierarchy process (AHP) A technique capable of converting subjective pairwise comparisons into a scalar value function.

analytic models Mathematical models of decision problems which enable analysis of alternatives.

applications backlog Requests for computer applications that have not yet been completed.

arbitrage Buying low and selling high when a difference in market prices is identified.

artificial intelligence Computer systems seeking to emulate human intelligence.

aspiration levels Target levels, or goals, for particular objectives in multiple-objective analysis.

attribute Characteristic of an entity.

autocorrelation The relationship between error terms and subsequent error terms (when this relationship, which is assumed to be zero in ordinary least squares regression, has an identifiable value in time-series models).

autoregressive moving average (ARIMA) technique A time-series forecasting technique using serial correlation, as well as moving average terms, to forecast cyclical data.

backward chaining In expert systems, selecting the next rule to check on the basis of rules that would lead to identification of the goal variable.

basic variable In linear programming, a variable that is part of the current solution.

binding constraint In linear programming, a constraint that is met at its limit in the current solution.

blackboard A group decision support method using a common screen segmented into areas by group member or by topic.

bounded rationality Decision environment where perfect knowledge is not available.

Box–Jenkins technique An ARIMA forecasting model for time-series data.

branch and bound technique A technique for identifying the optimal solution to integer or zero–one linear programming models.

causal model In regression, a model where independent variables represent a theory of causation of the dependent variable.

CD-ROM Compact disk used to store data in read-only memory.

coefficient The amount that a variable contributes to a function, or a function limit.

coincident indicators Variables that tend to change direction with the same timing as the base variable.

commercial databases Data pertaining to a topic available for purchase, usually electronically.

confidence factor In expert systems, the degree of confidence of a conclusion based on user confidence of input values.

confidence limit In regression models, the range of a coefficient for a given probability level.

constraint In linear programming, a bound on a function.

correlation The degree of relationship between two variables.

cost justification Project adoption decisions made on the basis of validated benefits exceeding estimated costs.

critical success factors   Business elements that have the most bearing on decision-making success.

data   Sets of facts or numbers.

database system   A computerized system storing data with efficient means of data access.

data integrity   Accuracy of data in a database.

data processing   Function within an organization responsible for centralized computing.

decision process   A sequence of activities that could be used to make business decisions, covering problem identification through decision implementation and monitoring of results.

decision rooms   In group DSS, rooms equipped with computer and communication facilities to enhance meetings seeking a group decision.

decision support systems (DSS)   Use of interactive computing to learn about decision problems, often through access to data and models.

Delphi technique   A forecasting method involving iterations anonymously exchanging opinions between experts.

descriptive   Approach to decision making without normative elements—describing how people make decisions rather than seeking to impose decisions based on results of a model.

distribution parameter   Description of the distribution of a variable (mean, variance, shape, and others).

domain   Set of permissible values an attribute can take on; in expert systems, a problem environment.

drill-down   Ability to explore a database to obtain more detailed information about a higher level bit of information.

DSS generator   Computer software easing development of a DSS, generally through fourth-generation languages.

dual price   In linear programming, the marginal change in the objective function per unit increase in a right-hand-side coefficient (shadow price, marginal value).

econometric analysis   Use of statistical measurement in the study of economic problems.

efficient frontier   Characteristic of investment options where added expected return is not available without increase in risk.

electronic mail   Technology harnessing computers to transmit messages or information.

end-user computing   Computer operation by the ultimate user of the results.

entity   An object or thing.

executive information systems (EIS)   Computer systems designed to provide executives with immediate access to status reports, as well as the ability to query available data as expeditiously as possible.

expected value   Evaluation of the mean outcome of all possible events, weighted by their probability of occurrence.

expert systems (ES)   Computer systems seeking to emulate the decision behavior of a human expert.

exponential smoothing   Time-series forecasting technique using changes in trend.

fathom   In integer programming, determining that no better solution is available on a path.

feasibility In linear programming, a model where all constraints can be satisfied simultaneously.

forward chaining In expert systems, a rule selection procedure where rules are checked in order of entry.

fourth-generation languages (4GL) Computer instructions closer to human language than procedural languages, such as FORTRAN or COBOL.

frames Means of representing knowledge through information categories common to all entities.

function A mathematical expression measuring some characteristic in terms of variable values and coefficients.

group decision support systems DSSs developed to support decisions made by a group.

heteroscedasticity Situation where error terms do not have equal variance.

heuristic A procedure to develop an alternative without necessarily optimizing; in expert systems, applying decision rules which are not necessarily the best, but seem to perform well.

hierarchical database A database organized by some hierarchy (as opposed to relational organization).

historical analogy Developing knowledge by comparing the current situation with a similar situation experienced in the past.

hypermedia The use of multiple media in an efficient manner to display information to the user.

hypertext A system allowing the user to access data files in a highly efficient manner.

index of leading indicators A statistic monitored by the Bureau of Commerce seeking to predict changes in gross national product six months into the future.

induction Developing knowledge by inferring conditions based on known facts.

inference engine In expert systems, the means the system uses to conclude facts and develop recommendations.

information Meaningful conclusions drawn from data.

institutionalization Organizational-wide use of a system (such as a DSS).

integer programming Optimization technique where a set of solution values are required to have nonfractional values.

intelligence Processing data into human understanding; wisdom gained from knowledge.

interactive computer use On-line operation of a computer where the user gives new commands dependent on the results of the prior command.

intuitive Dealing with problems in an unstructured manner (as opposed to systematic).

knowledge Human understanding.

knowledge acquisition In expert systems, determining knowledge that is to be included in the system.

knowledge base In expert systems, facts known about a situation.

knowledge representation In expert systems, the means of encoding knowledge that has been acquired.

knowledge validation In expert systems, monitoring the results of expert systems to ensure that proper conclusions are reached.

lags In time-series analysis, shifting a variable back one or more periods, with the intent of examining and using the relationship between one variable which has a phased relationship with another variable.

leading indicator   In time-series analysis, a variable whose trend changes direction a predictable amount of time prior to another variable.

life-cycle analysis   A means of analyzing computer project proposals considering the entire life cycle of the project.

linear programming   A mathematical modeling technique expressing problems in terms of simultaneous linear equations.

links   A term in semantic networks describing the relationship between entities.

local area decision networks   Computer network linking decision support systems.

management information systems (MIS)   Computer systems developed to provide managers throughout the organization with reports and access to data.

management science (MS)   Study of management decisions through mathematical models.

mental model   Personal view of the relationship between actions and expected results.

models   Mental constructs of a decision situation.

Monte Carlo simulation   Simulation using random numbers generated by the computer.

moving average forecast   A time-series forecasting technique using averages (which may be weighted) of prior observations.

muddling through   Concept of human decision making consisting of a series of decisions involving gradual and incremental development of policy change.

multicollinearity   In regression, condition where independent variables are highly correlated with each other (contain high degrees of overlapping information).

multiple objectives   View of decision making consisting of a complex of objectives rather than one single overriding purpose.

multiple optimal solutions   In linear programming, when there are more than one solution providing the optimal objective function value.

network database   A database organized in a network structure where types of data are linked.

nonbasic variable   In linear programming, a variable not included in the current solution.

nonprocedural language   A computer language that is relatively closer to natural human language.

normative   Approach seeking to develop models providing decisions superior to those humans would make.

object oriented   Representation and processing of objects through messages and activation triggered by change in another object.

objective function   In linear programming, the function measuring the value of the solution; linear programming will identify the solution with the best objective function value where all constraints are satisfied.

on-line computing   Interactive computing, where the user can enter new commands based on the results of prior commands.

operations research (OR)   Study of decisions through mathematical models.

optimization   A class of techniques capable of generating the best possible solution to the model.

organization decision support systems   DSSs shared by all (or a significant portion) of an organization.

organizational intelligence   The collective knowledge of an organization, usually integrated into organizational procedures for dealing with standard problems.

preceptive Interpreting new information in light of past theory (as opposed to receptive).

predicate calculus System of formal logic to determine the truth of a proposition.

procedural logic In computer systems, a logic flow that follows the sequence of commands; in expert systems, applying forward chaining.

production rules An expert system means of representing knowledge through if-then types of rules.

program trading Automated trading on financial securities markets; usually trading on futures indexes.

propositional logic See predicate calculus.

protocol analysis A means of knowledge acquisition where the expert is given a scenario, and the expert's responses are recorded and analyzed.

prototyping Approach to computer system development where a small pilot test system is developed, and changes in design are made based on observed performance.

pseudorandom number A number generated by computer with apparent characteristics of a random number.

qualitative forecasting A means of forecasting based on subjective judgmental factors rather than data.

random number A uniformly distributed random number between zero and one with no relationship with random numbers previously generated.

rational decision making View of decision making following formal decision rules.

receptive Interpreting theory in light of new information (as opposed to preceptive).

reduced cost In linear programming, the amount a decision variable is unattractive relative to being included in the optimal solution.

regression analysis A statistical procedure identifying a relationship between a dependent variable and one or more independent variables minimizing some error function.

relational database A database system organized in efficient tables, accessible by keys to relations between tables.

repertory grid Knowledge acquisition technique seeking to develop and test relationships between actions and results; Kelly grids, after an early presenter of the technique.

risk averse Decision-making style where high risk is avoided.

satisficing Decision behavior that settles for less than the apparent optimal solution.

scientific method Approach to knowledge development seeking to identify the cause of events and to develop an overall framework of knowledge about a subject.

semantic networks A means of representing knowledge through entities (nodes) and relationships between entities (arcs, or links).

sensitivity analysis In linear programming, analysis to determine how much an objective function coefficient, constraint limit, or functional coefficient can vary before the current solution would change.

serial correlation In simulation, the relationship between system performance at a point in time and preceding points in time; relationship between pseudorandom numbers and preceding pseudorandom numbers; autocorrelation.

shell A computer package expediting creation of an expert system by providing a system framework and editing features.

simulation Analysis of problems by development of an abstract model of the real problem.

spreadsheet   Computer package with rows and columns that can be used to model many problems involving repetitive computations.

structure—decision or problem   Degree of definition; high structure indicates high definition.

organizational.   Hierarchy of assigned organizational responsibility.

structured query language (SQL)   A standard language to query relational database systems.

supercomputers   Computer systems developed in the 1980s with much larger capacity and speed than was available previously.

surveys   Gathering of data by questioning humans.

systematic   Dealing with problems by applying structured approaches (as opposed to systematic).

systems approach   View of organizations as systems of interrelated elements exchanging information.

systems development life cycle (SDLC)   Approach to computer system implementation involving thorough analysis of requirements and coordination of efforts.

time-series forecast   Forecasting problem where the dependent variable is measured by time.

time study   Gathering of data by observation, to include timing observed events.

unbounded solution   In linear programming, a model where the objective function has no limit in the desired direction of attainment.

utility   A view of decision-making value as a measurable function.

validation   In simulation, checks to ensure that the simulation model reflects real behavior.

value analysis   Means of assessing proposed projects on the basis of unpriced benefits compared to estimated costs.

verification   In simulation, checks to ensure that the computer code (and random-number generator) behaves as expected.

work station   Computer system dedicated to a user with tools to support the specific task. Generally includes a very powerful system with rapid memory retrieval and computing speed.

zero–one programming   Mathematical programming model where a set of the decision variables are required to take on values of one or zero.

Author Index

Subject Index